Maik Kleinschmidt

Venture Capital, Corporate Governance, and Firm Value

GABLER EDITION WISSENSCHAFT

Maik Kleinschmidt

Venture Capital, Corporate Governance, and Firm Value

With a foreword by Prof. Dr. Alexander Bassen

Deutscher Universitäts-Verlag

Bibliografische Information Der Deutschen Nationalbibliothek
Die Deutsche Nationalbibliothek verzeichnet diese Publikation in der
Deutschen Nationalbibliografie; detaillierte bibliografische Daten sind im Internet über
<http://dnb.d-nb.de> abrufbar.

Dissertation Universität Hamburg, 2006

1. Auflage März 2007

Lektorat: Brigitte Siegel / Stefanie Brich

Der Deutsche Universitäts-Verlag ist ein Unternehmen von Springer Science+Business Media.
www.duv.de

Umschlaggestaltung: Regine Zimmer, Dipl.-Designerin, Frankfurt/Main
Gedruckt auf säurefreiem und chlorfrei gebleichtem Papier
Printed in Germany

ISBN 978-3-8350-0718-5

Foreword

Venture capital has become an important driver of economic growth in Europe during the last decades. Corporate governance is a key success factor for the development of private growth companies and thereby for the achievement of the venture capitalists' financial objectives. Despite the high relevance of corporate governance for venture capital-financed companies the topic has so far not been extensively researched. Traditional research on corporate governance focussed almost entirely on public companies.

Maik Kleinschmidt aims in his dissertation at narrowing the knowledge gap by analysing the relationship between venture capital, corporate governance and firm value for the first time in a systematic way. He researches how venture capitalists influence the corporate governance of their portfolio companies. Factors that determine the influence and the impact are analysed in detail. In a second step, the impact of good corporate governance on the firm value of the portfolio companies is researched.

The underlying research design is developed to ensure that the particularities of corporate governance of growth companies are captured. It incorporates both, a theoretical and an empirical analysis. The comprehensive research concept and the corresponding hypotheses are derived from an economic and a managerial theory. Thereby, the control as well as the value-adding role of corporate governance is taken into account. Empirical testing of the theoretical findings is done with qualtiative and quantitative analyses. State-of-the-art methods are used to allow for the characteristic development of growth companies.

With its sophisticated and novel research design, the dissertation contributes extensively to the emerging international theoretical and empirical literature on venture capital and corporate governance. It equally provides significant insight for venture capitalists and managers of portfolio companies. This will, without doubt, become widely accepted by researchers and practitioners and should give impetus to further research on this topic.

Prof. Dr. Alexander Bassen

Acknowledgements

This dissertation has been written during my time as research assistant to the Chair for Business Administration with Concentration in Investments and Finance (Prof. Dr. Alexander Bassen) at the University of Hamburg. Based on my dissertation, I initiated a joint project with researchers from Gent University and the University of Nottingham that was supported by the European Venture Capital Association (EVCA) and the Deutsches Venture Capital Institut (DVCI). I would like to take the opportunity to thank all those who contributed to the dissertation, either directly of indirectly.

First of all, I would like to thank my supervisor Prof. Dr. Alexander Bassen for the interesting time at the chair and the full support of my dissertation project. The discussions with him and his guidance were highly valuable for setting the topic and reach of the dissertation as well as for its realization. I thank Prof. Dr. Michael Zerres for the immediate willingness to take over the role of the second examiner of my dissertation.

Second, the dissertation was significantly advanced by advice and support from Prof. Dr. Sophie Manigart and Prof. Dr. Lutgart van den Berghe from Gent University and Prof. Dr. Mike Wright from the University of Nottingham. Their critical but benevolent comments were very important for the theoretical and empirical parts of the research. Together with their research assistants Tom Baelden and Christophe Spaenjers, they made the international empirical analysis possible. In addition, the discussions with other researchers and Ph.D. students who took part in the Gate2Growth Doctoral Seminar on Entrepreneurship, Finance and Technology 2004/05 as well as in the doctoral consortia of the Babson Kaufmann Entrepreneurship Research Conference 2005 and the Annual Meeting of the Academy of Management 2005 were very valuable for me. Furthermore, the feedback on my presentations of the initial results at the research conferences G-Forum 2005 and the International Entrepreneurship Research Conference 2005 helped to redefine the research concept.

Third, the dissertation would not have been possible without the support from EVCA and DVCI. In particular, EVCA's research director Georges Noël — who initiated the idea to extend the German analysis to Europe — was always available for support of the project.

Fourth, I would like to thank all participants of the empirical analyses. More than 150 managers of venture capital firms and portfolio companies took their time for an interview or for completing a questionnaire. Their answers were the basis for the dissertation and enabled me to gain insight into the relation of corporate governance and venture capital.

Finally, and most importantly, this dissertation was only possible with the encouragement and patience from my family and friends. I am most indebted to my parents for their neverending support during my studies. For his devotion and tolerance I express my deepest gratitude to Leif.

Maik Kleinschmidt

Contents

Figures

Tables

Abbreviations

C	Measurement by criteria
CEO	Chief executive officer
CG	Corporate governance
EBITDA	Earnings before interest, taxes, depreciation and amortisation
IM	Investment manager
IPO	Initial public offering
Max	Maximum value of all cases
MBI	Management buyin
MBO	Management buyout
Mean	Arithmetic mean
Min	Minimum value of all cases
N	Number of cases
OECD	Organisation for Economic Cooperation and Development
REML	Restricted maximum likelihood
ROA	Return on assets
ROE	Return on equity
S	Measurement by self-assessment
Std. Dev.	Standard deviation
VC	Venture capital

1 Introduction

This chapter discusses the relevance of venture capital and corporate governance. The results of the literature review are used to identify the most important aspects of this topic and to reveal existing knowledge gaps. Based on that, the aims of the thesis and the corresponding research approach are defined. This determines the structure of the work, as described in the last paragraph.

1.1 Relevance of the Topic

The relevance of the topic is found in the importance of good corporate governance to the success of venture capital-financed growth companies and in the importance of those companies to the economy.

The particular corporate governance — i.e., the framework of management and control[1] — is considered a key advantage but can also be a severe burden for growth companies. On one hand, the simple structures and processes of founder manager-focussed corporate governance allow for high flexibility in growth companies. Thus, the high velocity of the markets is mirrored by fast decision making in the companies. Small boards get more done, faster. And the high level of managerial ownership seems to prevent conflicts of interest between owners and managers in these companies. On the other hand, the simple form of corporate governance brings about disadvantages, too. Small boards lack diverse viewpoints and relevant experiences in other industries when decisions are made. Moreover, the strong managerial ownership limits the oversight of the companies' managers, which further increases their power.[2] These disadvantages contributed to failures of growth companies — in particular at the height of the New Economy at the turn of the millennium — like EM.TV, Kabel New Media and Lernout & Hauspie Speech Products. The examples indicate that the corporate governance systems of growth companies might not effectively protect shareholders' wealth. Hence, the success of a growth company depends on, among other things, adequate corporate governance that fosters its advantages but limits the related risks. Introducing good corporate governance therefore represents a challenge for growth companies and the venture capitalists that are the first external investors in many of them. Venture capitalists' primary interest is value creation, so they should

1 Grundsatzkommission Corporate Governance (2000), p. 1; Bassen (2002), p. 20.
2 Langberg (2006).

acknowledge the importance of corporate governance and exert adequate influence accordingly.[3]

The importance of venture capital-financed companies to the European economy is significant. In 2005, venture capitalists invested 47 billion Euros in nearly 7.000 private growth companies in Europe. All in all, the venture capital-financed companies employed about 6 million people, and their employment growth between 2001 and 2004 was 5,4% p.a., seven times higher than the average employment growth rate in the European Union.[4] During the coming years, European venture capitalists plan to further increase their activities.[5]

The importance of good corporate governance to the success of growth companies and of those companies to the economy indicates the high relevance of this thesis. It is aimed at shedding light on the relationship between venture capital, corporate governance and the firm value of growth companies. In particular, its aim is to analyse how venture capitalists influence the development of corporate governance in growth companies to foster the associated advantages but reduce the related risks. The specific research questions of the work are derived from a comprehensive literature review.

1.2 Literature Review

In the following paragraph, the most important research about the development of corporate governance in venture capital-financed companies is summarised. The topic brings together two distinct research streams: research on venture capital and research on corporate governance. In relation to this work, the first stream focuses on the influence that venture capitalists exert on the corporate governance of portfolio companies, whereas the latter stream mainly deals with the effectiveness of different corporate governance elements. Hence, the analysis combines two generally separated perspectives. Accordingly, this is mirrored in the review of the most important literature on the development of corporate governance in venture capital-financed growth companies.

---

3 Accordingly, the European Venture Capital Association developed guidelines for venture capitalists' influence on portfolio companies' corporate governance in 2005; refer to EVCA (2005c).

4 EVCA (2005a), p. 4.

5 Investments by European venture capitalists are expected to grow from 0,26% of the European Union gross domestic product in 2004 to about 0,6% in 2007; refer to EVCA (2005b), p. 4.

After presenting the foundations of the research, the literature review is structured along the key aspects of the relationship between venture capital and corporate governance: the reasons, factors and instruments of the venture capitalists' influence, the effects of the influence on corporate governance elements, and the effects of good corporate governance on firm value. Taking into account the different functions of corporate governance, the review distinguishes between the longer established control function and the only recently researched advice function.

1.2.1 Foundations of Research on Venture Capital and Corporate Governance

Firstly, the most influential research on the control function of corporate governance in venture capital finance is introduced before the evolving work on the advice function is presented.

BERLE/MEANS[6] first defined corporate governance in 1932 against the background of conflicts of interest between shareholders and managers of companies. This agency relationship is most dominantly concretised by JENSEN/MECKLING[7], JENSEN[8] and SHLEIFER/VISHNY,[9] who focus only on the control function of good corporate governance that should reduce agency costs. On this basis, SAHLMAN[10] applied the corporate governance mechanisms to venture capital. His research on the structure and governance of venture capital organizations provided the basis for a great part of subsequent work. From an agency-perspective, he describes the structures used to govern the uncertainty and information asymmetries in the two interrelated relationships, the one between the investor and the venture capitalist and the other between the venture capitalist and the portfolio company. For the latter relationship, negotiating comprehensive rights for the venture capitalists in the contracting phase and structuring the financing and active involvement of the venture capitalists in portfolio companies are considered most important. This comprehensive description again laid the basis for more detailed analyses on different aspects of the topic. GOMPERS[11] and LERNER[12] researched how venture capitalists use corporate governance elements to

6 Berle/Means (1932).
7 ensen/Meckling (1976).
8 Jensen (1986).
9 Shleifer/Vishny (1989).
10 Sahlman (1990).
11 Gompers (1995), Gompers/Lerner (1996), Gompers/Lerner (1999).
12 Lerner (1994), Lerner (1995).

reduce investment risk. KAPLAN/STRÖMBERG[13] and SAPIENZA ET AL.[14] consider improvement of the control function of corporate governance as one of the primary value-adding roles of venture capitalists, thus neglecting that it can also have an advice function.

Recently, research appeared that focused on the advice function of corporate governance, which is mainly derived from the resource-based view and the dynamic capabilities approach. A significant contribution comes from EISENHARDT,[15] who describes the conditions for good decision making in high-velocity environments and thereby explains the importance and requirements of good corporate governance. Later, TEECE ET AL.[16] specified the relation between the dynamic capabilities of a company such as corporate governance, its strategic management, and value creation. Their research indicates the value-adding role of the advice function of corporate governance. GABRIELSSON/HUSE[17] apply this understanding to venture capital. They analyse the advantage of advice by qualified non-executive board members to the managers of venture capital-financed companies. As yet, the advice function of corporate governance has been analysed in the context of corporate boards only, which indicates the novelty of this research.

1.2.2 Venture Capitalists' Influence on Corporate Governance

In this section, the most important research on the influence of venture capitalists on the corporate governance of portfolio companies is presented, in particular analyses of their reasons, other influencing factors and the instruments they use for the influence.

1.2.2.1 Reasons

Several authors analysed why venture capitalists influence the corporate governance of portfolio companies. The focus of this research is primarily the relationship between the associated risk in an investment and the influence of venture capitalists. BARNEY ET AL. found that the venture capitalists' level of control depends on the level of business and agency risk of an investment.[18] The subsequent research by FIET analysed this relationship in more detail and compared venture capitalists and business

13 Kaplan/Strömberg (2004).
14 Sapienza et al. (1996).
15 Eisenhardt (1989).
16 Teece et al. (1997).
17 Gabrielsson/Huse (2002).

angels regarding their reactions to market and business risk. According to that research, venture capitalists invest more in the search for information on the associated market risk of a potential investor whereas business angels invest more in information on the associated agency risk. This is explained by the fact that venture capitalists are specialised in reducing agency risk by improving the corporate governance of their portfolio companies. When selecting investments, they focus on market risk, and after the investment is done they utilise safeguards to protect themselves from agency risks.[19] BARNEY ET AL. analysed these contractual safeguards in regard to different types of opportunism. They differentiated between managerial opportunism that occurs if managers make decisions in the company that reduce the investor's wealth, and competitive opportunism that occurs if they harm the company by leaving the current firm and starting a new competing firm. They show that venture capitalists take appropriate measures against a specific type of opportunism only if the risk is great. That means venture capitalists take measures to prevent managerial opportunism if there are obstacles to the monitoring of management's behaviour, and they take measures against competitive opportunism if the returns to starting new firms are large.[20] These findings indicate that venture capitalists adapt their influence on the corporate governance of their portfolio companies according to the associated risk and that, therefore, the influence might well differ for different portfolio companies of the same venture capitalist.

These results indicate that the previous research is primarily based on agency theory and considers risk as the main reason for venture capitalists to influence the corporate governance of their portfolio companies.[21]

1.2.2.2 Factors

Apart from the reasons for the influence, the research also looked at different factors that determine the impact of venture capitalists on corporate governance.

The work of SAPIENZA ET AL. compares venture capitalists' influence on corporate governance in four countries and adds further evidence that the level and nature of this influence differs internationally. The analysis found that the level of involvement of

18 Barney at al. (1989).
19 Fiet (1991); Fiet/Hellriegel (1995); Fiet (1995)
20 Barney et al. (1994).
21 It should be noted that some of the empirical analyses did not find support for this perspective, e.g.: Fredriksen/Klofsten (2001), pp. 214ff.

venture capitalists depends on the origin of the venture capitalist. Thus, venture capitalists in the United States and the United Kingdom are much more active in their portfolio companies than those in France and the Netherlands, which might be exemplary for continental European markets.[22] This finding should be particularly relevant for research in corporate governance as the experience from different national corporate governance systems might impact the venture capitalists' influence.

Apart from that, previous research indicates that the type of venture capitalist might also affect their policy concerning corporate governance. BEUSELINCK ET AL.[23] compared the influence of independent and governmental venture capitalists on the reporting of their portfolio companies. They found that independent venture capitalists have a stronger impact on the reporting, for example the reduction of earnings management, than governmental venture capitalists. Other characteristics that impact corporate governance include the international activity of venture capitalists[24] as well as characteristics of the investment manager, such as his/her experience and commitment.[25] Similarly, characteristics of the investment manager were also found to have a significant impact on the influence of venture capitalists on their portfolio companies. DIMOV/SHEPHERD[26] researched this in more detail and found that different aspects of the human capital of the investment managers have an impact on the assistance they can offer.

1.2.2.3 Instruments

The instruments that venture capitalists use to influence the corporate governance of their portfolio companies can be grouped into contractual safeguards, monitoring, and support and have been intensively researched.

Important work on investment contracts was done by, among others, KAPLAN/STRÖMBERG.[27] One basic finding is that venture capitalists allocate cash-flow and liquidation rights separately from influence rights such board positions, voting, and control rights and that these are contingent on the performance of the

22 Sapienza et al. (1996).
23 Beuselinck et al. (2004).
24 Van den Berghe/Levrau (2002).
25 Ruppen (2001); Rosenstein et al. (1993); Gorman/Sahlman (1989); Van den Berghe/Levrau (2002).
26 Dimov/Shepherd (2005).
27 Kaplan/Strömberg (2003); Kaplan/Strömberg (2004).

portfolio companies. GOMPERS[28] and LERNER[29] analysed financing instruments such as staging and syndication, which are used by venture capitalists in combination with close monitoring to reduce investment risk. They researched under what circumstances which instruments are used. VAN DEN BERGHE/LEVRAU[30] focus in their research on the different types of monitoring: shareholder agreements, differentiated shareholder rights, board membership and relationships with managers. All this work focuses on the control function that should create value by preventing the managers from making mistakes. In contrast to this, HELLMANN/PURI[31] analyse the support venture capitalists can provide to professionalize portfolio companies. They help the companies, for example, improve human resource policies, hire executives, and adopt stock-option plans. Hence, this support includes corporate governance elements that might fulfil an advice function.

All in all, these findings show that different venture capitalists might influence corporate governance in different ways or with different effects based on their characteristics. Consequently, these aspects have to be considered when analysing the impact of venture capitalists on the development of their portfolio companies' corporate governance.

1.2.3 Effects of Venture Capitalists' Influence on Corporate Governance

The research on the effects of venture capitalists' influence on corporate governance has concentrated so far mainly on the replacement of managers, the efficiency of boards, and the quality of reporting information, thus taking into account both the control and the advice functions of corporate governance.

1.2.3.1 Managers

The analyses of POLLOCK ET AL.[32], WASSERMAN[33], MARTENS ET AL.[34] and BOEKER/WILTBANK[35] all indicate that venture capitalists are a main driver of the replacement of founder-chief executive officers (CEOs) in growth companies. They

28 Gompers (1995), Gompers/Lerner (1996), Gompers/Lerner (1999).
29 Lerner (1994), Lerner (1995).
30 Van den Berghe/Levrau (2002).
31 Hellmann/Puri (2002).
32 Pollock et al. (2005).
33 Wasserman (2003).
34 Martens et al. (2005).

found that founder replacement occurs more often in venture capital-backed companies than in non-venture capital-backed companies. Thus, venture capitalists often consider founders incapable of fully developing the portfolio companies' value potential. However, this notion is only partially supported by empirical findings. In the short run, the portfolio companies' ability to raise capital in initial public offering (IPO) processes is increased with a professional CEO. But in the long run, the likelihood of delisting is smaller for companies with a founder-CEO compared to those with a professional CEO.[36] This challenges the practice of venture capitalists replacing founder-CEOs.

1.2.3.2 Boards

A study by FILATOTCHEV ET AL.[37] indicates that venture capitalists increase the independence of the portfolio companies' boards. They analysed the board structure of companies at the time of their IPO and found that the number of independent board members is significantly related to venture capital backing.

ROSENSTEIN38 analysed the effects of venture capitalists on the balance of power in the boards of growth companies and on formal criteria of board efficiency. Boards in venture capital-backed companies are described as standing between the two polar board types of boards in 'conventional small firms' and those in large corporations. Their working style is more formal than in non-venture capital-backed firms, and they have a collaborative relationship with the managers of the firm. Their involvement in strategic decision making is, according to this, higher than for the two other board types. This finding is supported by subsequent research by FRIED ET AL.39 In a later work, ROSENSTEIN ET AL.40 analysed the value added by venture capitalists on boards. They found that CEOs of portfolio companies do not generally rate the value of advice by venture capitalists' representatives on the board as higher than that of other members. Though the value added is significantly higher if the invested venture capitalist is one of the experienced 'top-20' venture capital-firms. This indicates that the ability of venture capitalists is an important factor when analysing the effects of their influence on corporate governance. The effectiveness of venture capitalists as

35 Boeker/Wiltbank (2005).
36 Pollock et al. (2005).
37 Filatotchev et al. (2005).
38 Rosenstein (1988).
39 Fried et al. (1998).
40 Rosenstein et al. (1993).

monitors of companies is underlined by the results of LERNER's41 research. He found that venture capitalists' representation on a board increases around the time of CEO turnover. In contrast to this, the number of other outsiders on the boards remains constant.

1.2.3.3 Reporting Discipline

As yet, there are only a few findings on the effects of venture capitalists' influence on the reporting discipline of portfolio companies. It was shown that venture capital-backed companies have higher discretionary accruals than non-venture capital-backed companies before an investment is done.[42] BEUSELINCK ET AL.[43] provide empirical evidence that the influence of venture capitalists leads to a reduction of these discretional accruals and to a faster reporting of losses than found in non-venture capital-backed companies. This indicates a positive effect of venture capitalists' influence.

These findings indicate that venture capitalists influence portfolio companies to improve corporate governance: On one hand, they strengthen the control function by replacing managers, if required, increasing the independence of boards and improving reporting discipline. On the other hand, they also improve the advice function of corporate governance by increasing the boards' abilities to make strategic decisions.

1.2.4 Effects of Corporate Governance on Firm Value

Venture capitalists' influence should increase firm value, which is the primary goal of the investors. The following presents the findings of previous research on the effects of good corporate governance on firm value. These analyses focus primarily on the control function of corporate governance.

Several studies looked at the relationship between good corporate governance and firm value. The findings of GOMPERS ET AL.[44] indicate that companies with good corporate governance have better performance than companies with bad corporate governance. They analysed the corporate governance of American listed companies and found a significant relationship between corporate governance quality and performance measures such as share price return, Tobin's Q and earnings per share.

41 Lerner (1995).
42 Beuselinck et al. (2004), Hochberg (2002).
43 Beuselinck et al. (2004).
44 Gompers et al. (2003).

BROWN/CAYLOR[45] found a positive relationship between corporate governance and the fundamental performance of listed companies, measured by return on equity (ROE) and return on assets (ROA). Several other studies support these findings. All research in this area has been done exclusively using empirical analyses of listed companies.

In regard to younger companies that are not yet at the point of an IPO, the knowledge on the relationship between good corporate governance and firm value is limited. DAILY/DALTON[46] analysed the relationship between governance structure and the performance of entrepreneurial companies. They looked at the effects of board structures, more particularly at CEO duality and the number and proportion of outsiders on the boards. The study indicates modest positive effects of board independence on firm performance.

This shows that corporate governance research is much more advanced for public companies than it is for young private companies. Furthermore, corporate governance elements relating to the advice function have largely been neglected so far. Nonetheless, a positive value effect of good corporate governance should be expected if the findings for public companies can be applied to growth companies.

1.3 Aims of the Research

The literature review lays a profound basis for this thesis, but it also reveals knowledge gaps in the research on venture capital and corporate governance. This is, on one hand, due to the novelty of the research area and is due, on the other hand, to the fact that the topic brings together two generally separated streams of research. In a nutshell, there are five shortfalls of previous research that should be addressed here. The research on venture capital has in the past focussed mainly on **single corporate governance elements** but neglected to give a comprehensive picture of the corporate governance system of a company and its development. Thereby, the research was built mostly on agency theory and therefore concentrated on the monitoring and bonding functions but **neglected the advice function of corporate governance**. Furthermore, it often falls short of **connecting corporate governance to firm value**, which is actually in the centre of venture capitalists' interest. In contrast to this, traditional corporate governance research analysed this relationship intensively. But it has taken

45 Brown/Caylor (2004).

into account only well-established public companies, which should already have well-developed corporate governance systems. This stream almost entirely **neglected** the development of **corporate governance in young companies**, where greater differences in quality should exist. Moreover, the analyses are almost entirely static because they **neglected developments of corporate governance and firm value**, which leads to a problem of endogeneity.[47] Hence, the primary aim of this work is to combine the perspectives of these two distinct streams of research and to analyse the development of corporate governance in growth companies and its effects on firm value. More precisely, this thesis should contribute to narrowing the knowledge gap and smoothing methodological limitations by answering two research questions.

First, the research will build on previous findings on the influence of venture capitalists on the corporate governance of portfolio companies. Venture capitalists, as the first external shareholders of growth companies, could be a main force behind the development of corporate governance from the foundation of companies to their going public[48] when a sophisticated corporate governance system is mandatory. Thus, corporate governance research at the level of growth companies enables tracking of the professionalisation of the companies' management and control systems. Analysing the influence of venture capitalists on this development requires an understanding of the reasons and the factors of this influence as well as its outcome. Growth companies are characterised by high risks and great potentials but limited resources. And venture capitalists do not only create value by minimising risk but also by adding value in form of support. This requires the research to focus not only on the control function of corporate governance but also on its advice function.[49] Furthermore, the interrelationship of corporate governance elements must be considered when corporate governance is analysed.[50] Accordingly, this research will draw a comprehensive picture including all relevant elements related to the managers, the boards and the reporting of companies. Moreover, the analysis of corporate governance in growth companies and the influence of venture capitalists requires a dynamic research design, which has not often been used in venture capital or in corporate governance research. A longitudinal analysis should deliver valuable knowledge on the development of growth companies.

46 Daily/Dalton (1992), pp. 380 ff.
47 For an explanation refer to 6.2.1.
48 While the strongest development should be noticed for a company that goes public, this holds also for other changes of ownership such as mergers and acquisitions by strategic investors.
49 Hellmann/Puri (2002).
50 Rediker/Seth (1995).

Thus, the first broad research question of this thesis is: **How do venture capitalists influence the corporate governance of portfolio companies throughout their development?** It thereby incorporates several aspects of venture capitalists' influence and the corporate governance of growth companies in a dynamic analysis. Building on the findings from the literature review, three aspects are analysed: The reasons venture capitalists influence portfolio companies' corporate governance are analysed first. Then the impact of their influence on different corporate governance elements is researched. Finally, the abilities of venture capitalists are incorporated in the analysis, too, as the impact on corporate governance might not only be determined by the strength of the influence.

Second, the analysis should also help to narrow the knowledge gap related to the effects of corporate governance on firm value. This is closely connected to the first research question because the primary goal of venture capitalists is generally value creation, which means that the influence of venture capitalists on the corporate governance of portfolio companies should be motivated by expected effects on firm value. This relation has so far been researched only for public companies, but it is equally important for growth companies. In particular, greater effects could be expected because corporate governance should differ more significantly for the latter. In contrast to earlier research, where perceived value creation was analysed, this thesis centres on financial firm value, corresponding to corporate governance research for public companies. It should thereby take into account a comprehensive picture of the corporate governance of growth companies and their fundamental performance as well as investors' valuation. Hence, the second research question of this work is: **What are the effects of good corporate governance on the firm value of growth companies?**

1.4 Research Approach

The research concept was adapted to the research questions and methodological challenges[51]. It was developed with valuable support from Sophie Manigart and Lutgart van den Berghe from Vlerick Leuven Gent Management School as well as Mike Wright from the University of Nottingham. The research concept comprises both theoretical and empirical analyses. Whereas the theoretical analysis is done to build an understanding of the relationships between venture capital, corporate governance and

[51] For a review of methods used in entrepreneurship research, refer to Shane/Venkataraman (2000), pp. 217ff.

firm value and to derive corresponding hypotheses, the empirical analyses verify the hypotheses in practice. In order to ensure a comprehensive framework of the immanent relationships, the analysis is based on economic and managerial theories.[52] They have different foci and might therefore lead to different hypotheses. Because of their particular suitability to mirror the monitoring and bonding function as well as the advice function of corporate governance, the agency theory and the dynamic resource-based view were selected for this research. In a second step, the derived hypotheses are tested for empirical support. It is intended to gain generalisable results on the development of the corporate governance of growth companies and its impact on firm value. The research comprises qualitative and quantitative analyses in order to prevent single-method bias. First, semi-structured interviews were conducted with venture capitalists, managers of portfolio companies and other experts to ensure a profound understanding of the practice. Heterogeneous cases were selected for the interviews to gain a broad perspective from different settings. This should allow comparing the hypotheses derived from theory with common practice in multiple settings. The results of the qualitative analysis were used to design a questionnaire used for the quantitative analysis. A pan-European survey of portfolio companies was carried out to representatively test the hypotheses. CEOs from venture capital-backed companies were surveyed on the corporate governance of their companies, the influence of their venture capitalists and the firm value. In contrast to other studies that collected data from venture capital investment managers, it is expected that this method of data collection will lead to a more objective judgement on the venture capitalists' involvement.[53] A survey allows for a great number of analysed cases and provides generalisable results. In the survey, longitudinal data are collected to track the development of corporate governance. The questionnaire of the survey asks for retrospective information on the companies' situation at different measuring times.

Key factors for the research design are reliability and validity. The design of this work was adapted to fulfil the requirements of both as the following indicates. Reliability means the extent to which a measure yields the same result on repeated trials.[54] For a high reliability, the sample of the quantitative empirical analysis must correspond to the population of the research. In this case, the total population is all the venture capital-financed growth companies in Europe. Several checks were done to ensure the

---

52 Combs/Ketchen (1999), pp. 867ff.
53 For further explanations refer to Shepherd (1997).
54 Carmines/Zeller (1980), pp. 11ff.

most complete sample possible was used. It was found that the Thomson Financial VentureXpert database provides a very good basis as it includes the largest number of companies of this population. Feedback from selected venture capitalists on their current portfolio companies indicated that only very few portfolio companies were not included in the sample. Hence, it can be expected that the sample of the survey corresponds to a great extent to the population of the research.

Validity is the degree to which an analysis accurately assesses the specific concept that should be measured. Internal validity — i.e., the rigour of the analysis — and external validity — i.e., the generalisability of the results — are to be distinguished. The internal validity was ensured in this research by several measures. First, the results were triangulated by qualitative and quantitative research. The findings of the interviews were used to adapt the questionnaire to the practice so that the questions correspond well to the concepts that should be assessed. In a further step, a pre-test of the questionnaire with managers of portfolio companies was done to ensure that the questions are well understood by the respondents. The survey provided very rich data due to a comparatively comprehensive questionnaire that takes into account different forms of measurement (e.g., measurement by self-assessment and criteria) and different measuring times. For most of the constructs, indexes of several variables were built in order to further increase the internal validity.[55] External validity was ensured by taking a European perspective that encompasses different economic regions and different corporate governance systems. Representativeness tests were conducted for the results of the survey to find out whether the group of respondents correspond to the sample of the analysis. The test supports representativeness in regard to the regional distribution but not in regard to the age distribution.[56] This might be explained by the fact that some of the companies in the sample might not have existed anymore at the time of the survey. Nonetheless, this finding limits the representativeness of the analysis only a little because of the presumed explanation.

The design of this research is characterised mainly by four particularities. First, it encompasses integrated theoretical and empirical analyses to build a theory-based understanding of the relationships between venture capital, corporate governance and firm value and to verify them in practice. Second, economic and managerial theories are jointly used as an underlying framework to ensure that the monitoring, bonding

55 Bortz/Döring (1995), pp. 52ff.; Krosnick/Fabrigar (1997), pp. 141ff.

56 For more information refer to 5.3.4.

and advice functions of corporate governance are well captured. Third, the empirical analysis uses a qualitative and a quantitative approach in order to increase the validity of the findings. Fourth, the analyses are dynamic because they track the development of corporate governance over time, which is necessary due to the high rate of change in growth companies and the endogeneity of corporate governance.

1.5 Structure of the Research

The structure of the research results from the research questions with the aspects derived from the literature review on one hand and from the selected research approach on the other hand. The thesis is composed of six chapters whose structure is presented in Figure 1 and detailed in the following.

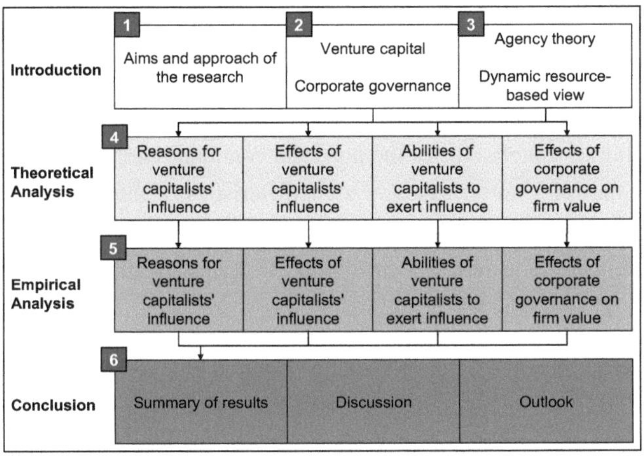

Figure 1: Structure of the thesis

This introductory chapter defines the research concept of the thesis. The research questions are derived from a literature review that reveals the knowledge gaps about the relationship of venture capital, corporate governance and firm value. They determine the aims and the approach of the research that are introduced thereafter.

The second chapter builds the basis for the analyses by defining and introducing the two main concepts of the research. First, the main characteristics of venture capital are described before the venture capital value chain is detailed. As the introduction indicated, the venture capital industry develops cyclically from booms to downturns. This is explained in the historic and recent context. Corporate governance is presented with a comparison of different definitions and a description of its main elements.

Thereafter, the elements are grouped according to their functions: monitoring, bonding and advice. To conclude, the different groups that influence corporate governance and their instruments are briefly described, indicating the relevance of venture capitalists to the development of corporate governance in growth companies.

In chapter three, the two underlying theories are introduced as a basis for the theoretical analysis. The origination and main assumptions of the agency theory and the dynamic resource-based view are illustrated first. Then, the two theories are applied to the topic by explaining the theories' understanding of corporate governance and their perspective on the importance of corporate governance for growth companies.

The next chapter contains the theoretical analysis of the relationship between venture capital, corporate governance and firm value that provides theory-based hypotheses. It starts with the theories' distinct perspectives on the reasons for venture capitalists to influence the corporate governance before the effects of the influence on the different elements are described. Thereafter, the venture capitalists' abilities that are expected to impact the corporate governance of the portfolio companies are analysed, in particular the venture capitalists' control rights, the characteristics of the venture capital firms, and those of the investment managers. In the end, it is analysed what effects corporate governance quality should have on firm value in terms of fundamental performance and valuation.

The structure of the theoretical analysis is mirrored in chapter six, which presents the results of the two empirical analyses. Whereas the results of the interviews are summarised according to the two research questions, the quantitative results are structured according to the four aspects of the theoretic analysis. The sample and methods are detailed before the results of the statistical analyses are presented. Uni- and multivariate analyses are carried out for the venture capitalists' reasons to influence corporate governance, the effects of the influence, the impact of the venture capitalists' abilities and the effects of good corporate governance on firm value.

The last chapter summarises and concludes the thesis. The main results of the theoretical and empirical analyses are recapitulated and then discussed. The limitations are explained, and the results are interpreted against the background of earlier findings and in regard to the different analyses. Finally, the knowledge gaps that the research revealed are detailed in order to propose future analyses.

2 Foundations of Venture Capital and Corporate Governance

This chapter lays the foundations of the work by introducing venture capital and corporate governance. The description of venture capital includes the characteristics of venture capitalists and the actions they take to pursue their goals. It then details the corporate governance elements and their functions as well as how stakeholders can influence those elements. This is the basis for understanding the succeeding chapters.

2.1 Introduction of Venture Capital

This chapter introduces venture capital with a definition and a description of the main characteristics. It then details the different steps of the venture capital value chain before the development of the industry is presented.

2.1.1 Definition

The term "venture capital" is not well defined in the literature, in particular in different regions of the world.[57] There are different definitions but also cognate terms that have partially intersecting meanings. The reason for this is that the term was coined by practice and not the outcome of a theoretical construction.[58]

Generally, venture capital is an equity or equity-related financing form for growth companies.[59] In Europe, financing growth in younger companies is called venture capital, whereas financing buy-outs of established companies is called private equity. In contrast to this, in America both forms of financing are considered either venture capital or private equity.[60] Both definitions have in common that only private companies are financed and that the investment is limited with the goal of realizing financial return. In this work, the broader American perspective is used. Characteristically, venture capital is not only the provision of financing to growth companies but includes also non-financial support for the companies. This is aimed at reducing the investment

57 Bader (1996), p. 4; Schefczyk (2000), p. 15.
58 Bader (1996), pp. 4ff.
59 Bader (1996), p. 10; Schefczyk (2000), p. 18.
60 Kraft (2000), pp. 31ff.; Sahlman (1990), p. 479, EVCA (2004), pp. 2ff.; Bader (1996), pp. 4ff.

risk and fostering the companies' development.[61] The following definition is used in this work:

Venture capital is an equity or equity-related financing form for private growth companies for a limited time, including non-financial support for the company.

2.1.2 Characteristics

The definition introduces four characteristic attributes.

- Equity or equity-related financing
  Venture capital is generally financing with equity character, which give the investors considerable information and control rights.[62] Often, investors prefer mezzanine instruments that are similar to equity, such as convertible debt or dormant participation, to reduce the associated risk.[63]

- Medium-term investments
  Venture capital is provided for a limited investment horizon with the aim of generating financial return.[64] Investors sell their shares in the companies after two to ten years — depending on the development of the portfolio companies — in order to realise their goal.[65] Because of the associated high investment risk, investors expect a relatively high return of 25–45% p.a., depending on the development stage of the investment.[66]

- Concentration on growth companies
  The prospect of such a high return is found only among companies with corresponding growth potential[67]. Therefore, venture capitalists invest only in growth companies. The growth potential of younger companies[68] lies in the market

61 Schefczyk (2000), pp. 41ff.
62 Ruppen (2001), pp. 200ff.
63 Kaplan/Strömberg (2003), S: 286; Sahlman (1990).
64 Ruppen (2001), p. 21; Bader (1996), p. 14.
65 Bader (1996), p. 14.
66 Manigart et al. (2002), p. 302, Schefczyk (2000), p. 18; Bygrave et al. (1989), pp. 98ff.; Zider (1998), pp. 135 ff.
67 Growth in this context means economic growth related to the growth of measures such as sales, earnings, employees, share price and return on investment; to be a growth company the growth rate must be comparatively higher than the average growth of the gross domestic product, but a definite threshold cannot be given, cf. Kock (2002), pp. 660ff.
68 Growth companies can also include management buyins and management buyouts where the financed company is generally also a relatively new entity even if its origins are in an older company. The ownership and management structures are still new in these cases. They are included in the empirical

entry and expansion.[69] In those companies, management often includes the founders of the company who also own the company. This can lead to information asymmetries and conflicts of interest between the old and new shareholders.[70] The managers of these companies possess only limited management experience, and the realization of the companies' growth makes high and changing demands on their management qualities. Furthermore, changes inside the companies, as well as in supply and product markets, also increase the investment risk. This stresses the companies' need for external management support.[71] In order to realise their growth potential, the companies have great capital and support requirements, but because of the associated high risks they have only limited financing possibilities.[72]

- Active investors

  Venture capital investors are active investors, on one hand because of the high support demand of the managers of growth companies and on the over hand because of the high investment risk. The investment risk of venture capital arises for three reasons: the conflicts of interest between the investors and the managers of the companies, the additional conflicts of interest between the outside investors and the founders as inside investors, and the particular risks that result from the high growth of companies.[73] Therefore, the investors influence portfolio companies before (ex-ante) and after (ex-post) the investment is done. Before the investment, investors can negotiate contractual agreements that limit the managers' scope to give them an incentive to foster the companies' development (bonding). Ex-post, the investors can introduce further contractual agreements and use monitoring to supervise the companies and their managers.[74] This influence is in great part related to the corporate governance of portfolio companies.[75] Figure 2 gives an overview of the investors' possibilities for influencing the portfolio companies. Those possibilities are detailed in the following chapters.

---

analyes but have a relatively limited influence due to the small number of later stage companies in the sample and the group of respondents.

69 Kraft (2001), pp. 43ff.; Fenn et al. (1997), pp. 27ff.

70 Schefczyk (2000), p. 18; Roberts (1991), pp. 9ff.

71 Ruppen (2001), p. 28.

72 Ruppen (2001), pp. 27ff.; Berger/Udell (1998), pp. 622ff.; for a theoretical analysis refer to Ueda (2004), pp. 601ff.

73 Lerner (1995), pp. 301ff.; Sapienza et al. (1996), pp. 443ff; Ruppen (2001), p. 28ff.; Gorman/Sahlman (1989), pp. 236ff.; Ruhnka/Young (1991), pp. 116ff.

74 Amit et al. (1998), pp. 441ff.; Coopey (2003), p. 150.; Wang/Zhou (2004), pp. 131ff.; Kaplan/Strömberg (2001), pp. 426ff.

75 For more information of the venture capitalists' influence on the corporate governance refer to Aoki (1999), pp. 1ff.

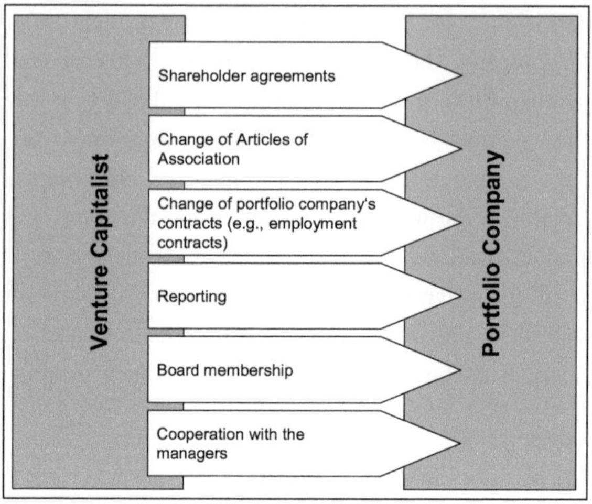

Figure 2: Influence of venture capitalists on portfolio companies

2.1.3 The Venture Capital Value Chain

The value creation of venture capitalism originates from the coactions of three groups: the investors who provide capital for investments, the venture capitalists who collect capital and invest it, and the portfolio companies that use the investments for their development.[76]

Figure 3 shows the value chain with its three layers in a simplified form.[77]

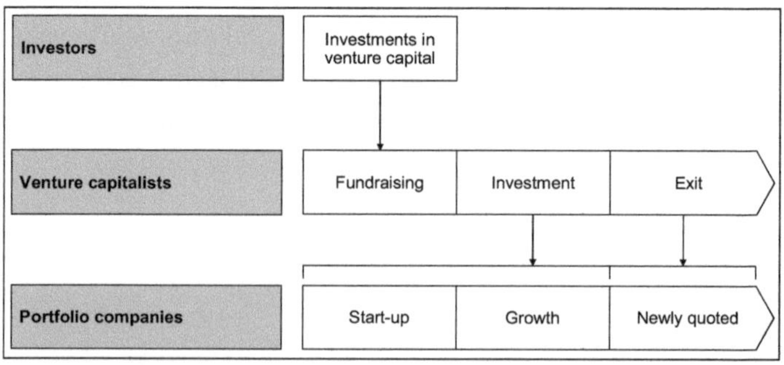

Figure 3: Venture capital value chain[78]

[76] Gifford (1997), pp. 460.

[77] It should be noted that for the level of the investor and the portfolio company only the steps of the value chain that are relevant for the venture capital investment are illustrated. They also have a value chain on a higher level for the realisation of their own business.

2.1.3.1 Fundraising

First, the venture capitalists must raise the capital for investments during a fundraising phase. Normally, the venture capitalists collect capital from several investors to finance a fund that is invested in a portfolio of companies.[79] Conflicts of interest might also occur between the investor and the managers of the venture capital firm, so several instruments are used during the contracting phase to reduce that risk. The investment managers are limited in their decisions by contractual agreements called covenants that, for example, require the managers to diversify the portfolio.[80] Apart from that, the compensation of the investment managers depends on the success of the investments in order to diminish possible conflicts of interest between the investors and the venture capitalist.[81]

There are five groups of investors to distinguish:

- Institutions
  Institutional investors, such as pension funds, insurance companies and banks, supply the greatest part of the funds. They use venture capital investments as a supplement to their portfolios. Apart from the effects of diversification, the high rate of return of venture capital increases the average return of their portfolios. They pursue only financial goals.[82]

- Public authorities
  Public authorities invest in venture capital because of the importance of growth companies for economic development. Apart from public subsidy programmes, several governmental institutions supply funds for investment in growth companies.[83]

---

78 Based on Achleitner (2002), pp. 142ff.

79 Exceptions are listed venture capitalist firms such as TFG AG 3i Group PLC that invest equity that they received through the capital markets. Additionally, corporate venture capitalists and governmental venture capital investors do not have to externally raise funds as they are generally funded internally. For more information on the organisational arrangements of investments in venture capital funds refer to e.g. Schefczyk (2001), pp. 55ff.; Lerner/Gompers (2002), pp. 29ff.; Callison (2000), pp. 97ff.; for more information on the determinants of venture capital funding refer to Jeng/Wells (2000), pp. 241ff.; for more information on the portfolio designs of venture capitalists refer to Kanniainen/Keuschnigg (2003), pp. 521ff.

80 Refer for comprehensive information to e.g. Gompers/Lerner (1996), pp. 463 ff; Feinendegen et al. (2003), pp. 1170ff.; Schmidt/Wahrenburg (2003), pp. 4ff.

81 Refer for comprehensive information to Gompers/Lerner (1999), pp. 3ff.

82 Heim (2001), pp. 487ff.; Fleischhauer./Hoyer (2004), pp. 395ff.

83 Refer for comprehensive information to Leleux/Surlemont (2003), pp. 81ff.

- Companies

  Established companies supply capital generally for investments in growth companies of related industries to pursue strategic goals rather than financial goals. These goals include the revitalisation of the company's culture, access to new technologies and in some cases even ensuring the livelihood of the company. This special type of venture capital is called *corporate venture capital.*[84]

- Private individuals

  There are only few private investors in venture capital.[85] The reasons for this are on one hand the high investment risk and on the other hand the lack of a transparent market for venture capital investments.[86] Normally they pursue only financial goals.[87] A special group of private investors are *business angels* who invest directly in growth companies without the mediation of venture capital companies. In many cases, they are active or past entrepreneurs themselves who invest both their capital and their personal know-how. They sometimes combine financial goals with personal ones.[88]

- Fund-of-Fund

  Apart from the investors that provide capital to venture capitalists, there are also fund-of-fund investors that collect capital from investors to invest it in several venture capital funds.[89] They represent a second intermediary between the capital provider and the growth company.

Figure 4 shows the proportions of the five investor types for the invested capital in Europe in 2005.

---

84 Sykes (1990), pp. 37ff.; Winters/Murfin (1988), pp. 207ff.; Zahra (1991), pp. 259ff.; Sykes/Block (1989), pp. 159ff.; for a theoretical analysis of the advantages and disadvantages of strategic investments by companies, refer to Hellmann (2002), pp. 285ff.

85 Exceptions are labour sponsored venture capital funds in Canada; for more information refer to Cumming/MacIntosh (2002), pp. 1ff.

86 Exceptions are the public venture capital firms.

87 Brinkrolf (2002), pp. 18ff.; Schefczyk (2000), p. 31.

88 Lerner (1998), pp. 773ff.; Landström (1993), pp. 525ff.; Freear et al. (1994),pp. 112ff.; Wetzel (1987), pp. 299ff.

89 Kraft (2001), p. 38, Gompers/Lerner (2002), p. 20.

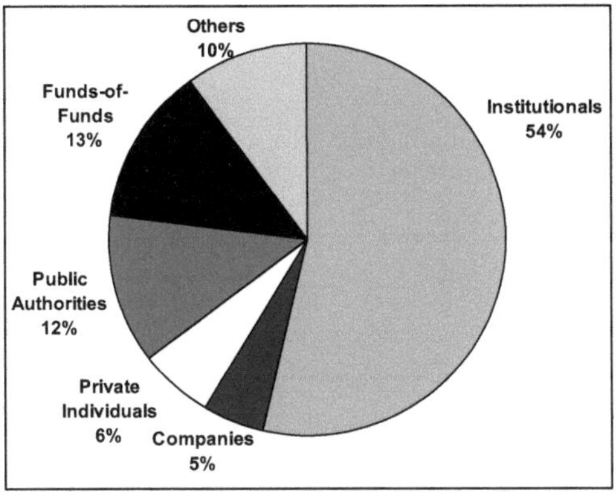

Figure 4: Newly invested capital in Europe 2005 by investor type[90]

2.1.3.2 Deal Sourcing and Screening

Apart from the fundraising, a sufficient deal flow is also of crucial importance for venture capitalists' success, in particular because of the low rate of potential investments among the investment proposals.[91] The acquisition of proposals is done through different channels, for example over the network of the venture capitalists, participation in conferences or membership in industry associations.[92] When selecting potential investments, the focus is first on the fit to the venture capital firm and the specific fund. Often, venture capitalists concentrate their investments on companies in a specific development phase, a specific industry or a specific region.[93] That enables them on one hand to better select and support portfolio companies because of their specialised knowledge and on the other hand to take advantage of synergies between several portfolio companies.[94]

Figure 5 shows the typical development of growth companies and the corresponding financing phases, which are described next.[95]

90 Own illustration based on EVCA (2005).
91 Generally, venture capitalists invest only in one or two out of 100 proposals, Zemke (1995), p. 211.
92 Brinkrolf (2002), p. 28; Schefczyk (2001), p. 34, Fiet (1995), pp. 198ff.
93 Elango et al. (1995), pp. 166ff.; Gupta/Sapienza (1992), pp. 347ff.; Robinson (1987), pp. 63ff.
94 Weber (2002), pp. 107ff.
95 Sahlman (1990), p. 479; Schefczyk (2000), pp. 35ff.

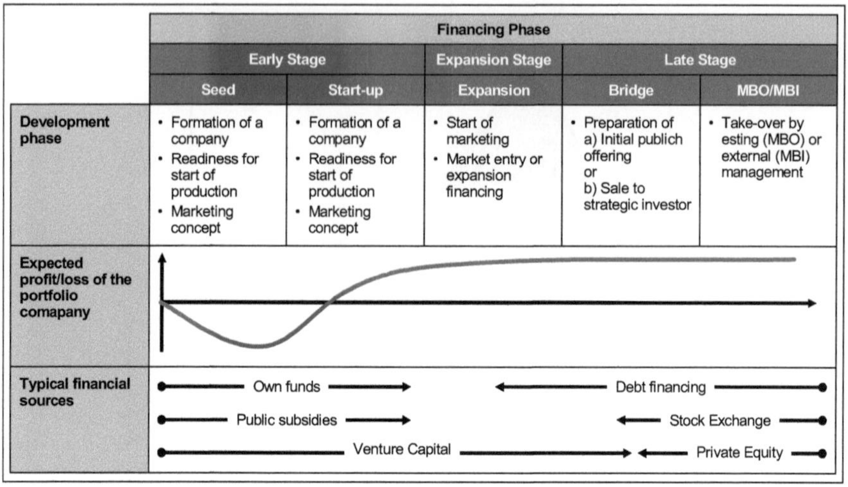

Figure 5: Development phases of growth companies[96]

- Seed

  In this phase, the entrepreneur requires capital to develop a business plan and a prototype before the company is founded.

- Start-up

  The capital need in this phase results from the expenditures that occur because of the founding of the company and product development. Additional costs arise for first marketing measures that prepare for the market launch.

- Expansion

  The market entry of the company generally leads to growing capital needs because the production capacities and the distribution channels must be expanded and because there are greater expenditures for marketing now.

- Bridge-Financing

  Before an IPO of the company or a sale to new investors, companies often need bridge financing because the preparations for such a transaction are costly.

- Management Buyout/Buyin

  Investors enable internal or external managers to take over a company or a business

96 Based on Schefczyk (2000), p. 37.

unit that is then managed independently. Venture capitalists[97] or private equity investors enable the acquisition of the company from its old owners.

After a successful formal screening (if the investment fits the venture capitalist), a detailed and normally multistage screening is done. The investment decision is largely dependent on the expected return.[98] Strategic investors also include expected non-financial utility as a further factor.[99] Several criteria are analysed during the screening, on which all venture capitalists decide themselves. The following categories are generally considered to be the most important:[100]

- Competence and experience of the managers
- Personality of the managers
- Characteristics of the market
- Characteristics of the product
- Financial plans.

2.1.3.3 Contracting

After a successful screening of the proposal, venture capitalists start negotiating a contract with the managers.[101] This phase concentrates on the valuation of the company, the share that the venture capitalist takes over, the financing instrument and its cashflow, and decision rights as well as changes to the company's articles and other contracts.[102] During the structuring of the financing, two instruments are used to reduce risk: In many cases venture capitalists invest together with other venture capitalists in a syndicate to share the invested capital and the associated risk.[103] Moreover,

97 In this case, they are often called *private equity investors* in order to distinguish late stage and early stage investors.

98 Schefzcyk (2001), p. 38; for a study on indicators for the expected return refer to Jain (2001), pp. 223ff.; Brush/Vanderwerf(1992), pp. 157ff.

99 Winters/Murfin (1988), pp. 210ff.; Witt/Brachtendorf (2002), pp. 682ff.

100 Schefczyk (2001), p. 39; Brettel (2002), pp. 309ff.; Macmillan et al. (1987), pp. 125ff.; Eisele et al. (2003), pp. 406ff.; Zacharakis/Shepherd (2005), pp. 674ff.; Baum/Silverman (2004), pp. 411ff.; Franke et al. (2002), pp. 654ff.; Fried/Hisrich (1994), pp. 28 ff.

101 For theoretical analyses of contracting refer to Hellmann (1998), pp. 57ff.; Bowden (1994), Bergemann/Hege (1998), pp. 703ff.

102 Weber (2002), pp. 96ff.; Sahlman (1990), p. 505; Gompers/Lerner (1996), pp. 483ff.; Admati/Pfleider (1994), pp. 394ff.

103 Lerner (1998), pp. 16ff.; Bygrave (1987), pp. 139ff.; Manigart et al. (2002), pp. 3ff.

investments are often not paid out fully in the beginning but in stages as specific milestones are achieved (staging).[104]

Apart from the structuring of the investment, venture capitalists also negotiate covenants that limit the scope of the portfolio companies' management as well as other control and decision rights that give the venture capitalist the ability to reduce its investment risk.[105] During contracting, the companies' articles and other contracts are also screened, and changes might be negotiated in order to align the interests of the venture capitalist, the company and its other shareholders.[106]

2.1.3.4 Venture Management

After closing the investment contract, the first tranche of the committed capital is paid out, and the continuous support of the portfolio company by the venture capitalists begins. The goal of the venture management is reducing the associated risk and increasing the return on the investment.[107] Generally, the support of venture capitalists can be divided into control and support of the portfolio company. The nature of the control and support depends on several factors such as the characteristics of the portfolio company and the profile of the venture capitalist. Among others, the development phase of the portfolio company is an important factor because companies in the seed-phase require different support than companies in a later stage. The emphasis of the required support often changes from more operational questions to strategic, financial and organisational questions over the development of a company from founding to the expansion phase. [108] The control function should reduce the associated risk by bonding the company and monitoring its development and the decisions of the managers and thereby increase the probability of success and the value of the investment.[109] This is done, for example, by membership on the board and the requirement of regular reporting by the portfolio company on its financial and strategic development.[110] Besides this, the support function should further strengthen the portfolio

---

104 Gompers (1995), pp. 1475ff.

105 Weber (2002), pp. 92ff.; Baums/Müller (2002), pp. 401ff.; Sahlman (1990), pp. 489ff.; Hommel et al. (2003), pp. 327ff.; for a theoretical analysis of the distribution of control between venture capitalists and managers of portfolio companies refer to Yerramilli (2004), pp. 1ff.

106 Kaplan/Strömberg (2003), pp. 293ff.; Triantis (2001), pp. 305ff.

107 Sahlman (1990), p. 508.

108 Bader (1996), p. 133; Achleitner/Bassen (2004), p. 162.

109 It should be noticed that control can also lead to disadvantageous effects on performance because of conflicts with managers; for more information refer to Higashide/Birley (2002), pp. 59ff.

110 Schefczyk (2000), p. 301; Schenk (2003), pp. 403ff.; Lerner (1995), pp. 307ff.; Sapienza et al. (1996), p. 454; Fried et al. (1998), pp. 497ff.; Ehrlich et al. (1994), pp. 74ff.

company and thereby increase its value. Therefore, venture capitalists support their portfolio companies in different areas such as strategic development, the acquisition of partners and customers, and negotiations with important stakeholders. This is done, for example, through board membership but also through informal co-operation with company management.[111]

One important element of venture management at portfolio companies is the preparation of the venture capitalists' exit.

2.1.3.5 Exit

The disinvestment of venture capitalists is done by the sale of their shares. This can be done either in one step or in several steps. Partial exits are often required, either because of legal requirements or because of the bad signal that might be associated with a full exit.[112] Because the type of exit the venture capitalist makes has a crucial impact on the future development of the portfolio company, the exit decision is often a matter of difficult negotiations between the different shareholders.[113]

Generally, the following five exit types are possible, but they differ greatly in regard to their fit for a specific investment at a specific time:[114]

- *Buy Back*: Sale of the shares to the old shareholder of the company, generally the entrepreneurs.
- *Trade Sale*: Sale of the shares to a strategic investor, generally an industrial investor that has an interest in the resources of the portfolio company.
- *Secondary Purchase*: Sale of the shares to a financial investor, e.g., another venture capitalist.
- *IPO*: Going public of the portfolio company, which is often linked to a capital increase.

---

111 Brinkrolf (2002), p. 141.
112 For an empirical analysis of full and partial exits refer to Cumming/MacIntosh (2003), pp. 511ff.
113 Bascha/Walz (2001), pp. 286ff.
114 Schefczyk (2000), pp. 44ff.; Cumming/MacIntosh (2003), pp. 520ff.

- *Liquidation*: Withdrawal of the investor by terminating the shareholder agreement or liquidation of the portfolio company, generally connected with total loss of the investment.

The decision on the form and time of an exit depends on external conditions such as the market situation, among other things. In particular, the situation at the stock exchange has a crucial impact on the possibilities of going public and influences not just the return of a specific investment but also the development of the entire venture capital industry.[115] That subject is presented in detail in the next chapter.

2.1.4 Development Status of the Venture Capital Industry

As indicated in the very first paragraph, the venture capital industry underwent both a boom and a decline within the past decade. This shows that the industry's development is relatively cyclical, which increases the risk of investments. The following presents the emergence and recent development of venture capital.

2.1.4.1 Emergence of the Industry

Venture capital is still a young form of financing that first developed over several decades in the USA before investors and companies in Europe used it. The development is affected by cycles, in which fast growth and fast downturns alternate.

The first venture capital firm was founded after the end of the Second World War in Cambridge, Massachusetts. The American Research and Development Corporation was founded with support from Harvard and MIT universities to provide capital for the commercialisation of technological developments of the defence industry. The first fund of this firm was very successful because of the enormous value growth of a few of its investments.[116] In the following decades, the industry grew steadily but slowly. From 1958 on, there were, besides publicly listed funds for private investors, also new funds that operated as small business investment corporations, a new type of enterprise that was created especially for investment firms for small companies. The first strong increase of cash inflows took place at the end of the 1970s and beginning of the 1980s as an effect of a legal amendment in 1979. The law of the Employee Retirement Income Security Act (ERISA) was amended so that pension funds could also invest

115 Gompers (1998), pp. 1089ff.
116 Gompers/Lerner (2002), p. 6; Weber (2002), p. 8.

greater parts of their funds in investments with higher risk. The result was that invested funds of USD 481 millions in 1978 rose to more than USD 5,8 billions in 1986. In the late 1980s, a downturn started because of declining returns on venture capital investments. The reasons for this were over-investments in some industries and a growing number of inexperienced employees in venture capital firms due to the rapid growth of the firms in the years before. Consequently, investments dropped to about USD 1.600 millions in 1991. In the middle of the 1990s, a strong market for IPOs led to increased return expectations and a second strong increase in cash inflow.[117] At the height of the new economy, the industry had its peak in 2000 with investments of USD 103 billions.

In Europe, the venture capital industry began to develop several decades after its beginnings in the USA.[118] Even though the first German venture capitalist, Deutsche Wagnisfinanzierungsgesellschaft, was founded in 1975, the industry developed very slowly. Only after two decades was there strong growth, parallel to the second boom phase in the USA.[119] The gross investments increased between 1995 and 2000 from €542 millions to €4.451 millions, which equals a compounded annual growth rate of 52,4%.[120] The next section details the development of the industry in Germany since 1995, which shows the huge increase and the even more drastic downturn afterwards.

2.1.4.2 Development of Investments

The funds raised by venture capital and private equity investors grew rapidly in the late 1990s to a peak of about €47 billion in 2000. Until 2001, the inflow of funds exceeded the capital in most years. In that year, the new economy had its turning point, and the funds raised started to strongly decrease thereafter. However, the investments decreased more slowly than the fundraising so that between 2002 and 2004 investments exceeded the funds raised. The year 2005 marks a record year: Fundraising more than doubled compared to the previous year and amounted to almost €72 billion. As Figure 6 shows, funds raised and investments developed cyclically in the past decade from growth to decline to growth.

117 Gompers/Lerner (2002), pp. 7ff.; Gompers/Lerner (2001), pp. 146ff.; Kenney (2000), pp. 5ff.
118 For an overview of the development of the European venture capital industry, refer to Ooghe (1991), pp. 381ff.; Manigart (1994), pp. 525ff.
119 Gaida (2002), pp. 191ff.
120 BVK (1995-2000).

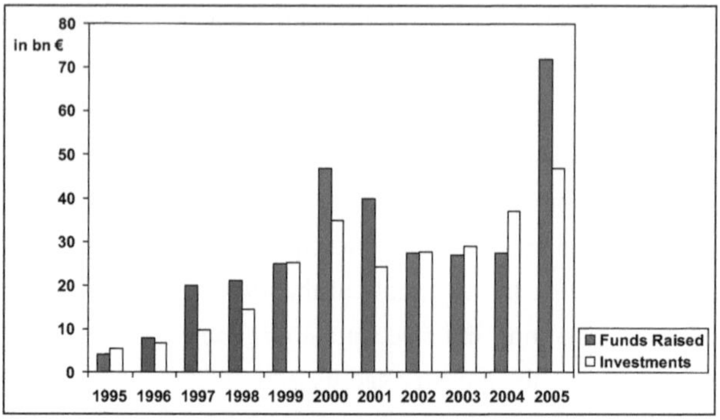

Figure 6: Volume of funds raised and investments in Europe 1995–2005[121]

A look at the origin of the investments shows the strong dependence on institutional investors. Their share varies over the years between 50% and 63%. The second most-important source for venture capital is the funds-of-funds investors with a share between 12% and 16%. The importance of corporate, private and governmental investors differs during the years as Figure 7 shows. Generally, it can be said that the downturn of the industry did not strongly influence the importance of the different investor groups.

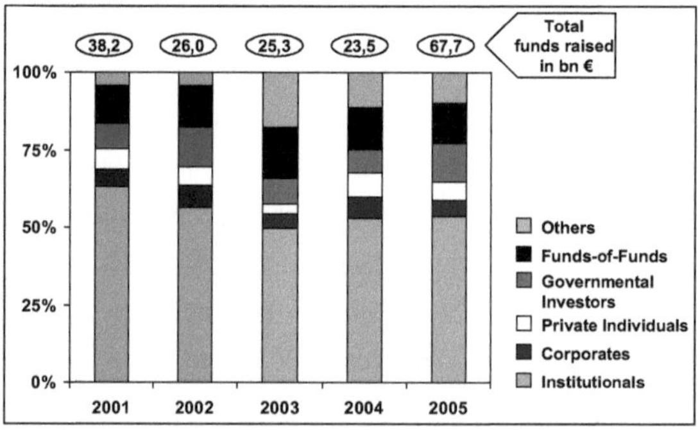

Figure 7: Funds raised by type of venture capitalist in Europe 2001–2005[122]

In contrast to this, the downturn had an impact on the focus of the investments in regard to the development stage of the portfolio companies. Between 2001 and 2005, the share of late stage investments increased from 50% to 73%, which means a strong

121 EVCA (2006).
122 EVCA (2006).

decrease in early stage investments. In particular, investments in start-up and seed phase companies were strongly reduced as Figure 8 shows. Venture capitalists obviously focussed on older, more established companies after the downturn of the new economy.

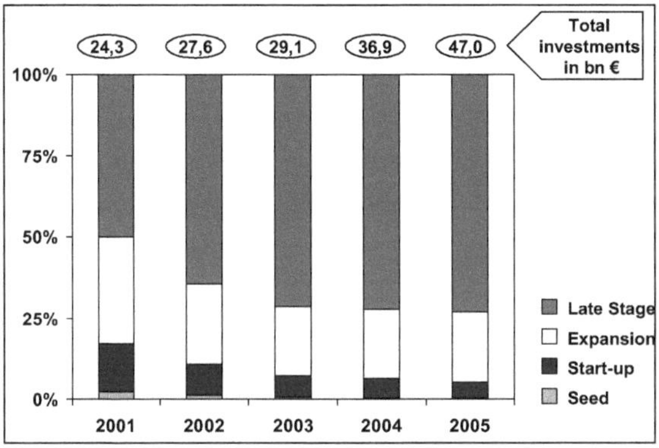

Figure 8: Investments by financing phase in Europe 2001–2005[123]

The development shows the cycle that the European venture capital industry was rotating through during the past ten years. In the USA, two cycles have taken place. The cycles of fast growth and similarly fast decrease in the industry cannot be explained by pure economic factors. It is rather the case that good expectations of return lead to an enormous inflow of capital, which after some time leads to overinvestment. This decreases the generated returns, which in turn leads to a reduction of new capital supplied.[124]

The development also mirrors the high investment risk caused by the characteristics of venture capital, which are detailed in chapter 2.1.2. Good corporate governance can reduce investment risk by effective and efficient management and control, as explained in the next chapter.

123 EVCA (2006).

124 Gompers/Lerner (2002), pp. 4ff.; Gompers (1998), pp. 1089ff.

2.2 Introduction of Corporate Governance

In the following, corporate governance is defined, and then the elements of corporate governance are explained based on several corporate governance codes. These elements can have a bonding, monitoring or advice function. Finally, the different influencing powers of the corporate governance of a company are described.

2.2.1 Definition

Though corporate governance has gained more public attention during the past years because of corporate crises,[125] corresponding concepts have existed for several centuries.[126] Even if today's term was not used, Adam Smith described the concept already in 1776:

> The directors of companies, being managers of other people's money than their own, it cannot well be expected that they should watch over it with the same anxious vigilance with which the partner in a private copartnery frequently watch over their own. [...] Negligence and profusion, therefore, must always prevail, more or less, in the management of the affairs of such a company.127

Today's definitions of corporate governance differ, particularly in regard to the scope of the concept: Narrower and broader definitions exist, depending on the discipline in which they are used.[128] Definitions with a narrow scope focus on the relationship between capital providers and the managers of a company such as, for example, the definition given by SHLEIFER/VISHNY:

> Corporate governance deals with the ways in which suppliers of finance to corporations assure themselves of getting a return on their investment.129

This definition limits corporate governance to the relationship between capital providers and management.

In contrast to this, broader definitions explicitly include other stakeholders apart from capital providers. One corresponding definition is the one by the Organisation for Economic Cooperation and Development (OECD):

---

125 Becht et al. (2002), p. 14.
126 Beiner et al. (2004), p. 2; Worldbank (1999), pp. 1ff.
127 Smith (1776) § V.1.107.
128 Huse/Landström (2002), p. 1; Kozer (2002), p. 4.
129 Shleifer/Vishny (1997), p. 737.

> Corporate governance is only part of the larger economic context in which firms operate that includes, for example, macroeconomic policies and the degree of competition in product and factor markets. The corporate governance framework also depends on the legal, regulatory, and institutional environment. In addition, factors such as business ethics and corporate awareness of the environmental and societal interests of the communities in which a company operates can also have an impact on its reputation and its long-term success.[130]

Apart from the scope, definitions can also differ in regard to their orientation. They can either be task oriented, i.e., focusing on the "what" of corporate governance, or goal oriented, i.e., focusing on the "why" of corporate governance.[131] A task-oriented definition is used for example by HUSE/LANDSTRÖM: "Corporate governance deals with how external stakeholders, internal stakeholders and the board of directors contribute in directing an enterprise."[132] In contrast to this, MELIN/NORDQVIST give a goal-oriented definition: "Corporate Governance can be defined as how the owners' interest is organized and exercised in order to influence in the strategy processes."[133]

This work takes a narrow scope and is task oriented as it focuses on explaining how venture capitalists as shareholders influence corporate governance. Consequently, the following definition is used.

Corporate governance refers to the framework of the management and control of companies.[134]

2.2.2 Elements

This section describes the elements of corporate governance. This is done in relation to corporate governance codes that present the European standards for good corporate governance set by national or international public authorities. A huge number of national and international corporate governance codes exist around the world; they are adapted to different settings and partially differ in their focus.[135] This work summarises the most important corporate governance elements included in European corporate

130 OECD (2004), p. 12.
131 Neubauer/Lank (1998).
132 Huse/Landström (2002), p. 1.
133 Melin/Nordvist (2002), p. 3.
134 German Corporate Governance Code, p. 1; Bassen, (2002a), p. 20.
135 For an up-to-date overview, see ECGI (2006), for a comparison of the corporate governance codes in the European Union, see Weil, Gotshal & Manges (2002).

governance codes such as the German Corporate Governance Code (GCGC) and the Cadbury Report and the most prominent international code, the OECD Principles of Corporate Governance. These codes include principles for good corporate governance that should contribute to the performance of companies.[136] They focus on internal corporate governance elements that can be influenced by stakeholders of the company.[137] The elements of good corporate governance can be divided into four groups, depending on the area of management and control to which they relate:[138]

- Shareholder rights
- Management
- Board
- Reporting and auditing

The elements are shown in an overview in Figure 9.

Main Corporate Governance Elements	
Shareholder rights	Exercise of shareholder rights
Management	Assessment and selection of managers
	Bonding of managers
	Compensation of managers
Board	Composition of board
	Work of board
Reporting and auditing	Reporting discipline

Figure 9: **Elements of good corporate governance**

136 For more information on the development of corporate governance regulations, refer to Demirag et al. (2000), pp. 341ff. or for the case of Germany to Peck/Ruigrok (2000), pp. 420ff. and for the case of the United Kingdom to Short et al. (1999), pp. 337ff.

137 External corporate governance elements include, e.g., ownership structure and corporate law; for more information refer to e.g. Joh (2003), pp. 287 ff.; Walsh/Seward (1990), pp. 421ff.

138 These catagories represent this work's own classification in reference to the German Corporate Governance Code, the Cadbury Report and the OECD Principles of Corporate Governance.

2.2.2.1 Shareholder Rights

Basically, good corporate governance should protect and facilitate the **exercise of shareholders' rights**, which include ownership, information and voting rights.[139] The ownership rights enable shareholders to own and transfer shares and to participate in the return of the company. The information right gives shareholders the right to be sufficiently informed on decisions concerning important corporate changes, such as amendments to the articles of association or extraordinary transactions. Additionally, shareholders should have the opportunity to vote in general shareholder meetings. To effectively ensure that right, they should be provided with sufficient and timely information on the meeting and the agenda and should have the opportunity to ask questions of the board. Shareholders should be able to vote on important decisions such as the compensation schemes for board members, and their voting should also be facilitated if the shareholders are not present at the meeting.[140] All shareholders of the same series of a class should be equally treated.[141]

2.2.2.2 Management

Good corporate governance should ensure that the management is able and willing to lead the company to best fulfil the goals of the shareholders and other stakeholders.[142] This requires the **selection of** capable **managers**, as well as bonding these managers to the company and the goals of the shareholders and adequate remuneration to ensure that the managers will be willing to act in the shareholders' interest.

The selection of new managers requires a formal and transparent process to ensure that capable candidates are selected. The search should be done by a special committee of the board — if the board size requires this — and should be done on the basis of a profile of the required skills and experiences. The composition of management should ensure a multiplicity of qualifications and the ability of the individual members to work together. Apart from an effective selection of new managers, there should also be a continuous **evaluation of the managers**.[143] Additionally, corporate governance should ensure that management acts in the shareholders' interest. This can be done by

139 OECD Principles of Corporate Governance, p. 32; GCGC, pp. 3ff.; Cadbury Report, pp. 48ff.; Weil, Gotshal & Manges (2002), pp. 33ff.; Ringleb et al. (2003), pp. 60ff.; Strieder (2004); pp. 16ff.

140 OECD Principles of Corporate Governance, pp. 32 ff; GCGC, pp. 3ff.; Weil, Gotshal & Manges (2002), pp. 41ff.

141 OECD (2004), pp. 40ff.; GCGC, p. 3; Weil, Gotshal & Manges (2002), pp. 39ff.

142 Weil, Gotshal & Manges (2002), pp. 44ff.

bonding the managers to pursue the goals of the shareholders. The codes focus particularly on providing adequate rules to prevent conflicts of interests.[144] Another element related to this is the managers' remuneration, which should be transparent and linked to the companies' or the managers' performance. Transparency serves as supervision of the managers. Variable compensation parts should give the managers an incentive to realise mid- and long-term performance targets. Therefore, the compensation should be related to relevant and demanding parameters.[145]

2.2.2.3 Board

The board composition and processes should ensure the strategic guidance of the company, the effective monitoring of management and the board's accountability to the company and the shareholders. Board practices vary widely between countries, in particular between countries with a one-tier system (one board for management and supervision) and those with a two-tier system (two separate boards for management and supervision). However, the principles presented are sufficiently general to apply to both systems.

The board composition should ensure that the board is able and willing to effectively supervise management and guide the company. This requires a sufficiently independent and qualified board. Independence is achieved by having members on the board that are not managers of the company and that have no relationships with them or other stakeholders. The board is required to perform supervisory duties. Moreover, the quality and experience of the board members affect their ability to control and guide the company. The **composition of the board** with the individual members is an important element. It should ensure that all required qualifications for an effective board are available. Therefore, the personal characteristics of the individual members should be assessed. Another element is the internal structure of the board, i.e., the division into sub-committees for specific topics.[146] Furthermore, the **work of the board** should ensure that the duties are exercised in an effective and efficient manner. The requirements for its processes range from the frequency of meetings, agenda setting and obtaining the requisite information to the determining which issues the board should

---

143 Weil, Gotshal & Manges (2002), pp. 51ff. and 65; GCGC, pp. 6ff.; Cadbury Report, p. 27.

144 GCGC, p. 7; Weil, Gotshal & Manges (2002), p. 49.

145 OECD Principles of Corporate Governance, p. 61; Cadbury Report, pp. 31ff.; GCGC, pp. 6ff.; Weil, Gotshal & Manges (2002), p. 64.

146 OECD Principles of Corporate Governance, p. 58ff.; Cadbury Report, p. 25, GCGC, pp. 9ff.; Weil, Gotshal & Manges (2002), pp. 51ff.

address. The main responsibilities of the board include both guiding the company on such issues as corporate strategy and major plans of actions and supervising the company and its management.[147]

2.2.2.4 Reporting and Auditing

Good corporate governance in regard to the **reporting discipline** should ensure that all matters concerning the company are disclosed promptly and accurately and that the information reported is reliable. The disclosure should include information on the company's financial situation, performance, ownership, risks and governance. In order to ensure the quality of the disclosed information, the reporting should be done in accordance with standards of accounting and financial and non-financial disclosure. The disclosure should be done through channels that give all stakeholders equal, timely and cost-efficient access to the information.[148] An annual audit of the financial statements should be conducted by an independent auditor to ensure that the financial position and performance of the company is fairly represented.[149]

Having explained the corporate governance elements, the next step is understanding the functions of corporate governance, i.e., what effects the elements should have.

2.2.3 Functions

Good corporate governance provides an effective and efficient framework for the management and control of companies, which, in turn, improves company performance.[150]

The elements should fulfil three functions to achieve performance improvement: monitoring, bonding, and advice. The performance effect can be a result of cost reduction, which is related to control by monitoring and bonding,[151] or of value

---

147 OECD Principles of Corporate Governance p. 60ff.; Cadbury Report, pp. 20ff.; GCGC, pp. 4ff.; Weil, Gotshal & Manges (2002), pp. 61ff.

148 OECD Principles of Corporate Governance, p. 49ff.; Cadbury Report, pp. 32ff.; GCGC, p. 10ff.; Weil, Gotshal & Manges (2002), pp. 46ff.

149 OECD (2004), pp. 54ff.; Ringleb et al. (2003), pp. 244ff.; Strieder (2004); p. 26.

150 Jensen/Meckling (1976), pp. 305ff.; Gompers et al. (2001), p.1.

151 Becht et al. (2002), p. 22; Jensen (1993), p. 850ff.; Goergen et al. (2004), p. 2; Hillmann/Dalziel (2003), pp. 384ff.

creation, which is related to advice to management[152]. The following explains how the elements relate to the three functions.

- **Monitoring** the company's development and management's actions can prevent disregard for the shareholders' interest. Several corporate governance elements fulfil this function. The board should supervise the performance of the company and the management and thereby prevent developments that do not contribute to the overall goal. Reporting and the annual meeting enable shareholders and the public to follow the course the company is taking. Accordingly, the board and the shareholders — and also the public — should be in a position to react to a development and change the company's route, if required. This might lead to reduced costs as unnecessary expenses might be prevented and thereby to reduced risk for the company.

- **Bonding** of the company and the managers can also lead to reduced costs by contractual agreements or incentives. On one hand, the company can be bonded to rules or laws that are in the interest of shareholders. Such rules often relate to the management of a company to, i.e., limit the decision scope of the managers. On the other hand, the remuneration of the managers can lead to a better alignment of the shareholders' and the managers' goals. Bonding should prevent the company from taking actions against the shareholders' interest and should reduce costs and increase performance.

- **Advice** to the company can lead to better results and a higher achievement of the shareholders' objectives. In particular, the board composition can lead to a greater knowledge, skill and experience base that should lead a company to better-informed decision making. Thus, qualified board members can constitute additional management capacity that might positively influence a company's development. Accordingly, corporate governance can lead to value creation by better decision making.[153]

Figure 10 illustrates which corporate governance elements are related with which of the three functions of corporate governance. It shows the main functions of the individual elements.

152 Huse (2005), pp. 43 ff.; Hillmann/Dalziel (2003), pp. 385ff.; Wallman (2005), pp. 1ff.

153 Ingley/Van der Walt (2001), pp. 174ff.; Charan (1998), p 5; Hillman et al. (2000), pp. 235ff.; according to Boeker/Wiltbank (2005), p. 124, this is particularly important in the case of growth companies.

Corporate governance elements	Functions of corporate governance: Bonding	Monitoring	Advice
Exercise of shareholder rights		✓	
Assessment/selection of managers		✓	✓
Bonding of managers	✓		
Compensation of managers	✓		
Composition of board		✓	✓
Work of board		✓	✓
Reporting discipline		✓	

✓ Element tends to fulfil the function

Figure 10: Main functions of corporate governance elements

As explained, good corporate governance should ensure that the shareholders' interest — mainly maximisation of the company's performance — is achieved, either by cost reduction or value creation. There are different influencing powers that affect how the corporate governance in a company is shaped.

2.2.4 Influencing Powers

Institutions as well as markets exert influence on the corporate governance of companies. The different influencing powers are shown at a glance in Figure 11.

- Market for corporate control
  Companies with deficiencies in their corporate governance whose firm value is not maximised run the risk of being taken over. This risk urges companies to improve the processes and structures of corporate governance in order to increase their firm value. Take-overs are advantageous for current shareholders, as the new owners generally have to pay a premium for being able to buy a majority in the company. Accordingly, take-overs might generate the firm value that the management was not able to generate.[154] As the managers risk being replaced in the case of a take-over, the market for corporate control is an incentive for them to implement good corporate governance.

154 Shleifer/Vishny (1997), pp. 756ff.; Gibbs (1993), p. 55; Denis (2001), pp. 206ff.; Franks/Mayer (1998), pp. 641ff.; Franks et al. (2001), pp. 220 ff.; Renneboog (2000), pp. 1966; Gugler (2001), pp. 32ff.

- Factor and product markets

  Companies have to operate successfully in the supply and product markets to maximise firm value. Companies that fail to do so might, in extreme cases, get into financial difficulties. Consequently, the pressure of the factor and product markets can lead to an improvement of corporate governance.[155] The markets give the managers incentives to implement good corporate governance due to the default risk.

- Legislators

  Legislators have the authority to set the principles of management and control of companies and thereby have a crucial influence. In particular, legislation decided the rights of capital providers and their protection.[156] The managers have to implement the laws.

- Owners

  The owners of companies can exert influence on corporate governance in different ways using both internal and external mechanisms.[157] An important internal mechanism is the appointment of board members, either non-executive directors in one-tier-systems or members of supervisory boards in two-tier-systems. Board members should control the management. Additionally, bigger shareholders can also get in direct contact with the managers and demand improvements in the corporate governance. External mechanisms include participation in the general meeting, at which the managers have to render an account. Moreover, institutional investors can increase pressure on the managers to improve corporate governance to maximise the firm value by publishing analyses of companies.[158] This shows that the owners can exert influence both by bonding and by monitoring.

- Employees

  In some countries, such as Germany, employees can influence corporate governance by their representatives in co-determined supervisory boards.[159] This gives them the ability to monitor and bond managers to improve the management and control of companies.

---

155 John et al. (1992), pp. 891ff.; Denis (2001), p. 207.

156 La Porta et al. (2000), pp. 4ff.; Denis (2001), pp. 198ff., Prigge (1998), pp. 953ff.; Shleifer/Vishny (1997), pp. 750ff.; Becht (1999), pp. 1071ff.

157 Bassen (2002a), pp. 118ff.

158 Hermalin/Weisbach (2001), p. 8ff.; Becht et al. (2002), p. 78ff.

159 Gerum/Wagner (1998), p. 352; Roe (1998), p. 361ff.; Hopt (1998), p. 246ff.; Shleifer/Vishny (1986), pp. 461ff.; Holderness/Shehan (1988), pp. 317ff.; Franks et al. (2001), pp. 216ff.

- Debt holders

  Generally, debt financing can increase the incentives for managers to generate high cashflows so the company can service borrowed capital and thereby prevent liquidation.[160] Furthermore, debt holders often negotiate covenants that bond the company to observe certain rules.[161] Finally, in some countries it is common for banks to send representatives to supervisory boards.[162] Accordingly, debt holders bond and monitor managers to improve corporate management and control.

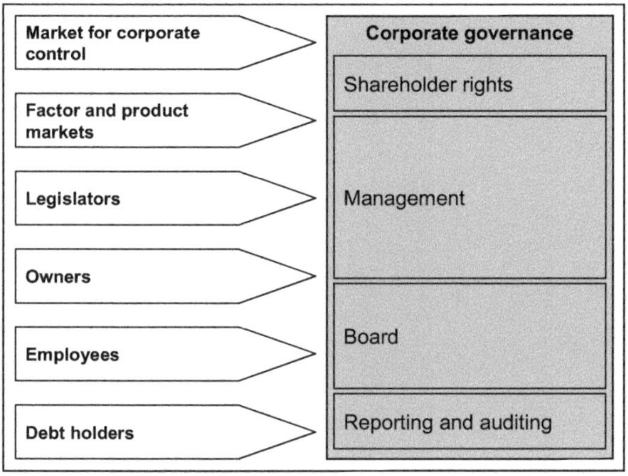

Figure 11: Influencing powers of corporate governance

The explanation of why and how these powers influence corporate governance might differ for different theories.[163] However, the influence of the different powers should lead to an improvement of the management and control of a company. In growth companies, venture capitalists, as the first significant external owners, are expected to be the main influencing powers apart from the factor and product markets. This is because the significance of the other four powers is limited. The markets for corporate control are relatively weak due to the managerial ownership and the fact that the companies are privately held. The corporate governance codes that legislators introduced generally do not apply to private companies. Most growth companies do not have a formal co-determination by employees due to their size. Finally, debt plays a

160 Jensen (1986), p. 324; Denis (2003), p. 205; Shleifer/Vishny (1997), p. 757ff.;

161 Drukarczyk/Schmidt (1998), p. 761 ff; Hertig (1998), p. 809ff.; Renneboog (2000), p. 1967.

162 Kroszner/Strahan (2001), p. 416ff.; Prigge (1998), p. 957.

163 Refer to 3 for explanations of agency theory and the dynamic resource-based view.

small role because growth companies are mainly equity financed.[164] Hence, the influence of venture capitalists is expected to be of great importance for the development of corporate governance and is accordingly analysed in this thesis.

[164] Refer to 2.1.2 for characteristics of venture capital-financed growth companies.

3 Theoretical Foundations

Different theories explain the relation between venture capital and corporate governance from different perspectives. In order to ensure a comprehensive understanding of the relationship, this work combines two disciplines related to the different functions of corporate governance: agency theory as an economic perspective and the dynamic resource-based view as a managerial theory. Whereas agency theory focuses on the control functions of monitoring and bonding, which restrain the managers, the dynamic resource-based view[165] centres on the advice function of corporate governance.[166] Consequently, the importance of corporate governance for the success of venture capitalists is judged differently by the two theories. Nonetheless, as the following introduction of the theoretical foundations shows, both theories consider corporate governance as a key factor for the success of growth companies and thereby for venture capitalists.

3.1 Agency Theory

3.1.1 Introduction

3.1.1.1 Origination

Agency theory is one of the streams of the new institutional economics developed from the 1950s to compensate for the deficits of neoclassic economic theory, which was built on the assumption of perfect markets with perfect information and foresight. The new theories take institutional arrangements into account, try to explain them and try to derive recommendations for an optimal arrangement of institutions. Their key message is that institutions matter for economic performance.[167] Institutions are systems of norms and their guarantees that are targeted at specific utilities and that steer individual behaviour in a specific direction.[168] Apart from agency theory, property

165 For more information on the suitability of the dynamic resource-based view to analyse growth companies, refer to Alvarez/Busenitz (2001), pp. 755ff.

166 Lynall et al. (2003), pp. 417ff.; Hung (1998), pp. 104ff.; Daily et al. (2003), pp. 371ff.; for more information on the value of combining the dynamic resource-based view with organizational economics. refer to Combs/Kechen (1999), pp. 867ff. or Conner (1991), pp. 121ff.

167 Feldman (1995), pp. 1693ff.; Bradley et al. (1984), pp. 857 ff; Furubotn/Richter (2000), pp. 1ff.

168 Richter/Furubotn (2003), p. 513.

rights theory and the transaction cost approach are the most important approaches of the new institutional economics.[169]

Agency theory in particular was developed on the basis of economic literature describing risk sharing among individuals and groups in the 1960s and early 1970s. It broadened this view by including the case that cooperating parties with separate tasks have different goals.[170] Agency theory has developed two streams — positivist agency theory and principal-agent theory — which share assumptions but differ in their mathematical rigor and style. Whereas the positivist agency theory focuses mainly on the relationship between owners and managers of companies, the principal-agent theory is applied also to other relationships such as the employer–employee or buyer–supplier relationships. The positivist stream identifies the governance mechanisms that limit an agent's self-serving behaviour and the latter stream indicates which contract is the most efficient under varying conditions. The principal-agent theory involves careful specification of assumptions that are followed by logical deduction and mathematical proof. In contrast to this, the positivist stream is less mathematical.[171] This work is mainly based on the positivist stream of agency theory.

3.1.1.2 Assumptions

Agency theory deals with incentive and control problems in the event of asymmetrical allocation of information between two parties, the principal and the agent. According to the theory, the two parties have different utilities that they both try to maximise. The aim of the theory is to find an optimal organisation of a principal–agent relationship.[172] It explains performance differences as a result of agency costs that occur because of the separation of ownership and control.

The agent is better informed than the principal and tries to benefit from this information advantage by maximising his own utility, which can have negative effects on the utility of the principal. Three types of possible agency problems must be differentiated:[173]

169 Rau-Bredow (1992), p. 1.
170 Eisenhardt (1989a), p. 58.
171 Eisenhardt (1989a), pp. 59ff.
172 Jensen/Meckling (1976), pp. 309ff.; Ross (1973), p. 134, Grossman/Hart (1983), p. 7.
173 Jensen/Meckling (1976), pp. 305 ff; Amit et al. (1998), pp. 442ff.; Spreemann (1990), pp. 562ff.; Holström (1979), pp. 74ff.; Alchian/Woodward (1988), pp. 67ff.; for an analysis of the venture capitalist–manager of the portfolio company relationship, refer to Amit et al. (1990), pp. 1232ff.

- Adverse Selection

  The principal cannot differentiate between good and bad agents before the closing of a contract because he does not know about certain characteristics of the agents (hidden characteristics).

- Hold-up

  After the closing of a contract, the agent uses gaps in incomplete contracts for his own benefit.[174] Intentions that were not displayed before (hidden intentions) are now revealed and force the principal to renegotiate with the agent.

- Moral Hazard

  The agent benefits from information that the principal does not have (hidden information) or from actions that the principal cannot see (hidden action), which decreases the utility of the principal without his knowledge.[175]

According to agency theory, measures have to be taken to align the interests of the agent and the principal. These measures are costly. Generally, there are two different measures.[176]

- Bonding

  Agency problems can be reduced by binding the interests of the agent to those of the principal. This can be done either by contracts or by incentives. Contracts limit the scope of the agents and should thereby prevent actions that do not maximise the utility of the agent. Incentives should lead to an alignment of the interests of the two parties so that the agent maximises the utility of the principal in his own interest.

- Monitoring

  The monitoring of the agent can also reduce agency problems by reducing the information asymmetries between the two parties. Problems can arise if the principal lacks the ability to monitor the agent.

Agency costs are the difference between the resulting utility of the principal and the utility in the optimal case without agency problems. They consist of two components.

---

174 For a theoretical analysis of incomplete contracts in the venture capitalists–manager of portfolio company relationship, refer to Aghion/Bolton (1992), pp. 473ff.

175 For a theoretical analysis of moral hazard and observability, refer to Holmström (1979), pp. 74ff.

176 Denis (2001), pp. 195ff.; Schoppe et al. (1995), pp. 218ff.

- The principal has expenses for the measures to reduce agency problems, namely bonding and monitoring of the agent.

- There are residual losses that cannot be reduced by these measures due to reasons of efficiency.[177]

In the case of a principal–agent relationship between shareholders and managers of a company, five types of residual losses can be distinguished.[178]

- Shirking: Managers use their work time to follow their private interests instead of pursuing the goals of the shareholders.

- Consumption on the job: High expenses for perquisites such as plush offices and corporate jets reduce a company's financial resources.

- Managers' desire to remain in power: When current managers cannot fully realise firm value, they should be replaced. As managers generally do not like to lose their positions, this might lead to a conflict of interest with the shareholders that can be long lasting and associated with high costs for the company and its owners.

- Managerial risk aversion: Managers and shareholders of a company might bear different levels of risk. Shareholders normally own a well-diversified portfolio so that the holdings in one company represent only a small share of their wealth. Therefore, they might be interested in cashflow-positive investments, even if they are risky. In contrast to this, managers have the majority of their human capital tied to one firm only, which makes them generally more risk averse.[179] Therefore, managers could be unwilling to pursue cashflow-positive but rather risky projects that are worthwhile from the shareholders' perspective. Such a foregone investment is a cost for the owners of the company.

- Free cashflow: Managers might prefer to keep the capital invested in the company within the firm if possible. Whereas it would be in the interest of shareholders to have any capital that cannot be invested in profitable projects in the firm paid out, the managers might invest free cashflows in unprofitable projects or hold onto

177 Jensen/Mecklin (1976), pp. 5ff.; Schoppe et al. (1995), pp. 218ff.
178 Denis (2001), pp. 193ff.; Tirole (2001), pp. 1ff.; for an analysis of agency problems in the venture capitalists–managers of portfolio companies relationship, refer to Duffner (2003), pp. 38ff.

them. This corresponds to costs for the shareholders as they might possibly invest their money more profitably elsewhere.

An optimal organisation of the relationship between principal and agent is reached if the occurring agency costs are minimal.[180] This leads to differences in performance and, in turn, in the valuation of companies.

3.1.2 Venture Capital and Corporate Governance

3.1.2.1 Understanding of Corporate Governance

Agency theory considers corporate governance a way to reduce agency problems. Corporate governance is seen as the framework for the relation between the owners and the managers of a company. It includes the contracts between them, the bonding measures designed to motivate managers to act in the interest of the owners, and the monitoring of the company and the managers. These processes and structures should restrain potentially opportunistic managers and thereby reduce the associated risk. Agency theory focuses on the bonding and monitoring function of corporate governance as explained in the last section. Corporate governance that effectively bonds and monitors managers should minimise agency costs and thereby lead to increased value.[181]

3.1.2.2 Importance of Corporate Governance for Growth Companies

At the time venture capitalists enter a relationship with a portfolio company, the information asymmetries and the level of uncertainty are typically great, and tangible assets that could serve as collateral are scarce.[182]

Generally, venture capitalists face four agency problems when investing in growth companies. First, the managers of the portfolio company might know more about their quality and abilities than the venture capitalists (adverse selection). Second, the investor is concerned that after an investment, circumstances will arise in which the venture capitalist disagrees with the management (moral hazard). Third, the investor is

---

179 For a theoretical analysis of managerial risk taking, refer to Wiseman/Gomez-Mejia (1998), pp. 133ff.; this conflict of interest is particularly severe in research intensive industries where shareholders prefer innovation strategies whereas managers prefer diversification strategies; for more information refer to Hill/Snell (1988), pp. 577ff.

180 Schoppe et al. (1995), p. 214.

181 Huse (2005), p. 43; Jensen/Meckling (1976), pp. 305 ff.

182 Arthurs/Busenutz (2003), pp. 145ff.

concerned that the entrepreneur will not work hard to maximise the company's value after the investment decision (moral hazard). Finally, the entrepreneur can hold up the venture capitalist by threatening to leave the portfolio company, in particular when his or her human capital is very valuable for the company's development (hold-up).[183] These agency problems occur in portfolio companies that are additionally affected by a high degree of inherent uncertainty.[184] This further strengthens the investment risk and thereby the need for managers to be effectively bonded and monitored.

Moreover, venture capitalists are confronted not only with a high degree of risk but also with a weak market for external control and limited oversight by the public, which increases the importance of strong influence by the owners. [185] That is why investors need to implement adequate corporate governance structures to handle the risks associated with investments in young innovative companies.[186]

The importance of good corporate governance depends, according to agency theory, on the level of agency and business risk.[187] The following details why these forms of risk are particularly great in growth companies.

High agency risk: Agency risk concerns the probability that managers will make decisions that do not maximise the wealth of the investors.[188] Growth companies are built on special opportunities. The entrepreneurs or the managers of growth companies must recognise and capitalise on opportunities that others cannot yet see in order to gain high growth.[189] Thus, managers in growth companies have a role of unique importance: being the centre of control and decision making.[190] The very characteristics of growth companies cause their relatively high level of agency risk. More specifically, the following four characteristics of growth companies make it difficult for venture capitalists to effectively bond and monitor portfolio companies.[191]

- The business of growth companies stands out because of its **high specificity**. As innovation increases, complexity also increases. This demands higher information

183 Kaplan/Strömberg (2004), pp. 2177ff.
184 Sapienza/Gupta (1994), p. 1618ff.
185 Sapienza/Gupta (1994), p 1618.
186 Hoffmann (2003), p. 130.
187 Barney et al. (1989).
188 Jensen/Meckling, 1976, pp. 308ff.
189 Shane (2000), p. 448.
190 Begley/Boyd (1987), pp. 79ff.
191 Bassen et al. (2006b), pp. 128ff.

processing capabilities, which increases the agency problems.[192] Owners who lack such high information processing capabilities might not be able to fully understand the business, its associated risks and the information on its development. Additionally, the managers are reluctant to fully disclose specific information in order to prevent others from pursuing opportunities the company is building on.[193] This makes it even more difficult to closely follow and control the development of a growth company, which thereby facilitates opportunistic behaviour by the managers who possess the specific knowledge.

- A comparatively **great part of the companies' assets is intangible or difficult to quantify** such as patents, rights and specific know-how.[194] A high proportion of immaterial assets makes control of the managers even more difficult because the value and development of such assets are difficult to judge. Additionally, traditional accounting measures of firm performance and development may be of limited usefulness in monitoring growth companies because they do not reflect important factors such as the value of intangible assets.[195] This increases the possibility of intentional misinformation of the owners by the managers.[196]

- Due to their **short history**, growth companies lack a track record and a high profile.[197] That means little information is available about the previous development of a business, making it hard for outside owners to evaluate it. Moreover, without historic information, managers can more easily present a false picture of the business.[198]

- The characteristic of **managerial ownership** of growth companies can strengthen or weaken the associated agency risk. There are two different hypotheses — both empirically supported — that predict either positive or negative consequences of a partial ownership of the management.

  According to the convergence of interest hypothesis, managerial ownership should increase a company's value by aligning the interests of owners and managers.[199]

---

192 Markman 2001, p. 289.
193 Shane/Cable (2002), p. 365.
194 Küting (2000b), p. 674; Blair/Wallman (2003), pp. 451ff.
195 Engel et al. (2002), p. 488.
196 Gompers/Lerner (2001), p. 155.
197 Hayn (1998), p. 15.
198 Smith/Smith (2000), p. 399; Achleitner/Bassen (2002), p. 1194.
199 Morck et al. (1988), p. 294.

Because the managers are also owners of the company, they should target value maximisation of the company just as the other owners do. Supporting this hypothesis, the likelihood of opportunistic behaviour, especially consumption on the job, increases with the amount of outside equity.[200] This shows that the managers have incentives to maximise firm value when they own part of the company.

In contrast to this, the entrenchment hypothesis predicts that managers with a substantial share in the company can have negative effects on the value of the firm for the owners. By means of influence and voting rights, they can guarantee their employment at attractive conditions rather than increase the value of the company.[201] According to this hypothesis, managers prefer to increase their living standards by taking advantage of their employment rather than by increasing the value of their shares of the company. BAKER AND GOMPERS (1999) present an overview of different consequences of managerial ownership of the company: The managers might be immune to career concerns,[202] the discipline of the product market,[203] monitoring by large shareholders[204] and value enhancing take-overs[205]. This hypothesis is corroborated by analysing the relationship between firm value and managerial voting power related to their ownership. It can be shown that firm value is positively related to voting power if this is small, but negatively related to voting power if it becomes large.[206] Empirically, it is shown for large firms that management ownership has a positive effect on the firm value if the stake is smaller than 5%; it has a negative effect if the stake is between 5% and 25%, and the effect becomes positive again for stakes over 25%. This supports the entrenchment hypothesis for stakes between 5% and 25% as such an ownership level is associated with, among other things, increased voting power and dominance of inside directors.[207] Such a curve-linear relationship between shareholdings of officers and directors and firm value is also shown empirically by MCCONELL/ SERVAES[208] and, for Switzerland, by BEINER ET AL[209].[210]

---

200 Jensen/Meckling (1976), p. 346.
201 Morck et al. 1988), p. 294; Jensen/Warner (1988), pp. 6 ff.
202 Fama (1980), pp. 288ff.; Holström (1999), pp. 169ff..
203 Hart (1983), pp. 366ff.
204 Shleifer/Vishny (1986), pp. 461ff.
205 Jensen/Ruback (1983), pp. 5ff.; Franks/Mayer (1990), pp. 189ff.
206 Stulz (1987), p. 32ff.
207 Morck et al. (1988), pp. 300ff.
208 McConell/Servates (1990), pp. 601ff.
209 Beiner et al. (2004), p. 29.

High business risk: Business risk is determined by the probability of survival of a business, which is predominantly dependent on its profitability. Therefore, the level of business risk is a function of the uncertainty of profitability.[211] In particular, the following three characteristics of growth companies imply a comparatively high level of business risk.

- Growth companies normally operate in **highly dynamic environments**. To succeed in these industries and to realise high growth, constant change is required, which leads to a high degree of internal dynamic. They are often exploring markets where competitive equilibriums among buyers, suppliers, potential entrants, current competitors, and product or service substitutes have not been established.[212] Growth companies normally cannot take advantage of a high profile in the market, which makes them more vulnerable. Additionally, they typically are built on the challenging assessment and government of innovation, which has become even more difficult during the most recent decades as information technologies and the globalization of industries have blurred industry confines and fragmented competition.[213]

  Because the environment of growth companies is so dynamic and their markets are highly competitive, they are required to respond quickly to changing conditions in order to succeed. This requires great flexibility, which leads to a high degree of internal dynamic.[214] The internal processes undergo constant change rather than being firmly established, which increases the risk.[215] As the internal and external dynamism increase, so does the risk that a company is unprofitable.

Growth companies are **highly dependent on their managers**. Their managers are in many cases the founders who still own parts of the company.[216] They have specific and unique knowledge about the companies' opportunities and assets as well as the capabilities to exploit them.[217] Moreover, they possess information about the day-to-day

---

210 It should be noted that the analysis by Himmelberg et al. (1999) did not find an effect of managerial ownership on firm performance.

211 Barney et al. (1989), p. 64; Porter (2004), pp. 5ff.

212 Porter (2004), pp. 215ff.; Fiet (1995), p. 555; Küting (2000a), p. 597.

213 Prahalad/Hamel (1994), pp. 5ff.

214 McGuire (2000), p. 33.

215 Auge-Dickhut et al. (2000), 4.3.2.1.

216 Bessler et al. (2001), p. 254; He/Conyon (2004), pp. 53ff.

217 Kirzner (1997), pp. 67ff.

business and its future prospects.[218] That means that the success of the business is highly dependent on the entrepreneurs or managers and their personal knowledge and experience, which can have four negative consequences: First, managing growth companies makes great demands on the capabilities of the managers. The team is often small, and its experiences are limited, and there are always more problems than the managers can handle at any given time.[219] Thus, the quality of the managers constitutes an important risk factor for the success of the company. Second, there might be negative consequences if the managers leave the company because they would take key knowledge and experiences with them and leave the company without leadership — the organisation is in many cases centred on them. Third, the possibility of opportunistic behaviour is very high because the managers possess information that the owners lack.[220] They can make use of this information and act against the interest of the outside owners. Finally, the likelihood of opportunism is increased because the managers mainly make the decisions and might be more risk averse than the owners of a company.[221] This is because managers invest most of their non-diversifiable and non-tradable capital in the growth firms, whereas the owners can more easily diversify risk by investing parts of their wealth in different companies.[222] Thus, managers might be reluctant to invest in risky but cashflow-positive projects. Such risk-averse decision making might lead to lower returns for the owners. This is reflected by the findings of RUHNKA/YOUNG that managerial competence is among the greatest concerns of venture capitalists[223] as well as by those of GORMAN/SAHLMAN that investors explain the reason for venture failure to be managerial incompetence.[224] Additionally, KAPLAN/STRÖMBERG found that the managers were the primary internal risk of an investment in the opinion of venture capitalists.[225]

In companies with great growth prospects, managers' efforts can have a relatively large impact on firm performance. This is why risk is comparatively higher in these companies than in more traditional ones.[226]

---

218 Markman et al. (2001), p.275.
219 Fredriksen/Klofsten (2001), p. 203.
220 Shane/Cable (2002), p. 365.
221 Coffee (1987), p. 18; Jensen/Meckling (1976), p. 349.
222 Markman et al. (2001), p. 280.
223 Ruhnka/Young (1987), pp. 167ff.; Sapienza et al. (1996), p. 445.
224 Gorman/Sahlman (1989), pp. 231ff.; Sapienza et al. (1996), p. 445.
225 Kaplan/Strömerb (2004), p. 2190.
226 Smith/Watts (1992), pp. 263ff.

Growth companies generally have a **low level of diversification** as they operate only in a small number of business areas, producing and offering few product lines.[227] In high technology firms, new products, for example, count for more than 50% of their annual sales.[228] This increases the business risk of a company because its survival is dependent on only a few products.[229]

A highly dynamic environment, dependence on the managers, and little diversification are three important factors that cause a high level of business risk. And this business risk reinforces the importance of corporate governance in two ways. First, the consequences of opportunistic behaviour by the managers are more severe in the case of high business risk. Second, such opportunistic behaviour is more likely if the business risk is high because of the different risk structures of owners and managers.

Combining the high level of agency and business risk associated with growth companies, agency theory ascribes high attention to corporate governance for the success of those companies and their investors.

3.2 Dynamic Resource-based View

3.2.1 Introduction

3.2.1.1 Origination

The dynamic resource-based view is a recent adaptation of the resource-based view.[230] The resource-based view has been developed as a counterpart to the market-based view, which was the dominant paradigm to explain competitive advantages in the 1980s.[231] Whereas the latter focuses on the attributes of attractive industries that offer opportunities for companies to succeed, the resource-based view centres on analysing the resource endowment of firms.[232]

The market-based view makes the assumption that firms in one industry possess identical resources and that potential resource heterogeneity in industries lasts only for a short time. Thus, it analyses the impact of a firm's environment on its

227 Küting (2000a), pp. 600ff.
228 Schilling/Hill (1998), pp. 67ff.
229 Küting (2000a), pp. 600ff.
230 Helfat/Peteraf (2002), p. 1.
231 Barney (1990), p. 100; Teece et al. (1997), p. 510; for an analysis of the usefulness of firm analysis from the resource rather than from the product side, refer to Wernerfelt (1984), pp. 171 ff.
232 Barney (1990), p. 100.

performance.[233] In contrast to this, the resource-based view analyses the impact of a firm's internal characteristics on its performance.[234]

The aim of the approach is to explain the relationship between a firm's resources and its performance.[235] Competitive heterogeneity is explained on the premise that competitors differ in their important resources and capabilities in a durable way, which should result in competitive advantages and disadvantages. However, the relationship between resources and performance does not necessarily have to be static.[236] Competitive advantage arises in time and might also shift over time. Therefore, given the external dynamics, the dynamic resource-based view incorporates the evolution of resources that form the basis for competitive advantage.[237] An important contribution to this theory is the recently developed dynamic capabilities approach, which focuses on the importance of capabilities in reconfiguring other resources.[238]

3.2.1.2 Assumptions

The following introduces the well-established assumptions of the resource-based view and then explains the adaptation of the dynamic resource-based view. The resource-based view is built on two assumptions: Firms possess strategic resources that are valuable and rare, and to sustain competitive advantages over time, strategic resources must be imperfectly imitable and substitutable. These assumptions enable a firm to achieve a sustainable competitive advantage "when it is implementing a value creating strategy that is not simultaneously being implemented by any current or potential competitors [...] and these other firms are unable to duplicate the benefits of this strategy."[239]

Firms possess strategic resources that are valuable and rare. Firm resources are assets, capabilities, organizational processes, firm attributes, information and knowledge that are controlled by a firm and enable it to implement strategies to improve efficiency and effectiveness.[240] They could be classified into three categories:[241]

233 Barney (1990), p. 101.
234 Barney (1990), pp. 101ff.; Teece et al. (1997), pp. 513ff.
235 Barney (1990), pp. 100ff.
236 Helfat/Peteraf (2002), p. 1; it should be noted that competitive advantage might not lead to performance because of stakeholder power, for more information refer to Coff (1999), pp. 119ff.
237 Helfat/Peteraf (2002), p. 2.
238 Teece et al. (1997); Eisenhardt/Martin (2000).
239 Barney (1991), p. 102.
240 Barney (1991), p. 101; Daft 1983, pp. 539 ff.
241 Barney (1991), p. 101.

Physical capital resources include assets such as plants, equipment and physical technology but also geographic location and access to raw materials.[242] Human capital resources include experience, talent, judgement, insight, training, and relationships of a firm's employees.[243] Organisational capital resources include a firm's formal and informal planning, coordination systems, and informal relations among groups within a firm or between a firm and its environment.[244] Physical capital resources are also categorised as tangible resources; human and organisational capital resources are intangible.[245]

Strategic resources can be sources of sustained competitive advantage. They must be valuable. That means that the resources enable a firm to implement strategies that improve its effectiveness and efficiency and thereby are the source of a competitive advantage. Furthermore, they must be rare because a firm can gain a competitive advantage only by implementing a strategy that is not simultaneously implemented by many of its competitors.[246] The rareness often comes from the path dependency of strategic resources, which means that strategic resources are not freely acquirable. Thus the potential of a firm is dependent on its current position, which is often shaped by its previous path.[247] Because strategic resources cannot be imitated or substituted they are not tradable. Hence, firms build and accumulate strategic resources over time by choosing appropriate paths over time. For example, a reputation for quality can be achieved by following consistent production and quality control policies for a long time. Consequently, strategic resources cannot be achieved instantaneously but only over time.[248]

Thus, endowment with strategic resources requires the assumption of heterogeneous firms' resources.

To sustain competitive advantages over time, strategic resources must be imperfectly imitable and substitutable. There are three reasons why strategic resources can be difficult to imitate. First, strategic resources could be imperfectly imitable

242 Williamson (1975); Barney (1991), p. 101
243 Becker (1964); Barney (1991), p. 101.
244 Tomer (1987); BARNEY (1991), p. 101.
245 Hall (1992), pp. 136ff.; Hall (1993), pp. 607ff.; Michalisin et al. (1997), pp. 361ff.
246 Barney (1991), p. 106; for a theoretical analysis refer to Peteraf (1993), pp. 179ff.
247 Teece et al. (1997), p. 522, this is a major difference from microeconomic theory, which does not recognise the limitedness of resources; for more information on the path dependency of management in growth companies, refer to Beckman/Burton (2004), pp. 1ff.
248 Dierickx/Cool (1989), p. 1506.

because of the unique history of firms. The resource-based view assumes that a firm's abilities to acquire and exploit resources depend on time and space, namely the unique historical position of that firm. Hence, after a particular time period has passed, firms that did not acquire particular space- and time-dependent resources cannot obtain them anymore. Consequently, these resources are imperfectly imitable.[249] Second, a strategic resource could be difficult to imitate because of causal ambiguity.[250] Causal ambiguity means that the link between a firm's resources and its sustained competitive advantage is not understood at all or only very badly. In that case, success cannot be traced back to specific resources. This makes it difficult for competitors to imitate strategic resources and thereby gain a competitive advantage. This ambiguity must hold for the firm and its competitors in order to prevent the competitors from engaging in activities to reduce the information differences.[251] The incomplete understanding of a source of competitive advantage might be due to the complexity and interdependency of a firm's resources.[252] Third, strategic resources could be difficult to imitate because of social complexity. In this context, a strategic resource could be or could be based on a firm's culture, reputation or customer base or the interpersonal relations between managers in the firm.[253] Here, the relation between a firm's resources and its performance is well understood, but nevertheless competitors fail to imitate the resources. This is because these resources are connected to social activities or attributes of a firm and its employees that might be beyond most firms' abilities to duplicate.[254]

The imperfect substitutability of a strategic resource means that there must be no strategically equivalent valuable resources with which the same strategies could be implemented. If a particular strategy to improve effectiveness and efficiency can be implemented only with the strategic resources of a firm, then those resources can be the source for sustained competitive advantage.[255] The imitability is in large part a function of observability, and the imitability of competitive advantage depends on the imitability of its underlying resources. The more unobservable a competitive advantage is, the more sustaining is it. Intangible resources are more unobservable than

249 Barney (1991), pp. 107ff.; examples for firms that obtained strategic resources because of their historical position can be found e.g. Leaned et al. (1969), Miles/Cameron (1982).

250 Barney 1986b, Lippman/Rumelt (1982), pp. 421ff., Mancke (1974), Rumelt (1984).

251 Lippman/Rumelt (1982), pp. 418ff.; Barney (1991), p. 109.

252 Nelson/Winter (1982); Polanyi (1962); Barney (1991), p. 110.

253 Hambrick (1987); Barney (1986b); Porter (1980); Klein et al. (1978); Klein/Leffler (1981).

254 Barney (1991), p. 110.

255 Barney (1991), pp. 111ff.

tangible resources and are therefore difficult to imitate. That is why strategic resources are often intangible.[256]

Physical, tangible resources are generally not rare because they can be purchased in the open market and are susceptible to imitation.[257] A supplier might provide a particular buyer with exclusive rights to some physical technology by a contract or license. But it is not the technology that is rare in this case but the intangible contract or license. It contains the potentially valuable, nonsubstitutable resource-based advantage that is imperfectly imitable.[258]

Recently, scholars have argued that the assumptions of the traditional resource-based view neglect two aspects. First, the sustainability of a competitive advantage is questionable. This is because changes in the environment may change the value of resources and thereby competitive advantages.[259] A competitive advantage in one time period can lose its value in another period. Apart from this, the resource-based view considers only internally developed resources, but it ignores exchanges, acquisitions or leveraging of resources.[260] This relates in particular to the abilities of firms to also use external resources for building a competitive advantage.[261] To compensate for this, the dynamic resource-based view incorporates the dynamics involved in the environment and focuses on dynamic capabilities as strategic resources that reconfigure other resources.

Dynamic capabilities "are the organizational and strategic routines by which firms achieve new resource configurations as markets emerge, collide, split, evolve and die."[262] These routines have three roles: coordinating and integrating the assets and activities in the firm, learning to improve the resource-base and the activities, and reconfiguring and transforming the resources and activities to reflect changes in the environment. Thus, it is argued that a firm's competitive advantage lies with its managerial and organizational processes.[263] They govern the change of the capabilities of a

256 Godfrey/Hill (1995), p. 523; Michalisin et al. (1997), pp. 364ff.
257 Michalisin et al. (1997), p. 364; Galbreath/Galvin (2004), p. L1.
258 Hall (1992), p. 138; Michalisin (1997), p. 364.
259 Helfat/Peteraf (2002), p. 2; Hillman et al. (2000), p. 242; Peteraf/Bergen (2003), pp. 1038ff.
260 Mathews (2002), p. 31.
261 Knott et al. (2003), pp. 192ff.
262 Eisenhardt/Martin (2000), p. 1107.
263 Teece et al. (1997), pp. 515 ff; according to these authors it was revealed that successful companies demonstrate timely responsiveness and rapid and flexible product innovation, which is coupled with management capability to effectively coordinate and redeploy internal and external competences.

company.[264] Dynamic capabilities consist of identifiable and specific routines. For example, in strategic decision making, managers pool their expertise and knowledge to make choices that shape the strategic moves of their company. Other examples include the research and development process or the processes of transferring and distributing resources.[265]

Even though the dynamic resource-based view is still developing, it seems to ease some of the restrictive assumptions of the traditional resource-based view. In particular, not all four conditions of strategic resources are required for dynamic capabilities. Competitive advantages arise from valuable, somewhat rare, equifinal dynamic capabilities that might be substitutable and fungible. But these competitive advantages are not sustainable. The heterogeneity is not firm specific but rather based on best practice that might incorporate some idiosyncratic details. Apart from that, the path dependency of the evolution of resources is determined by learning mechanisms such as practice or codification, which stress the dynamics of the evolution.[266]

The dynamic resource-based view explains performance differences between firms using differing endowments of strategic resources,[267] in particular dynamic capabilities. Dynamic capabilities reconfigure the resources of a company to match the environment in the best way, which should lead to competitive advantages. They can be developed and managed by a company[268] so that they reflect its competitive environment.[269] The competitive advantage can either be a lower cost base or product differentiation. This, in turn, should result in better company performance.

This shows that the dynamic resource-based view is not a new approach but an adaptation of the resource-based view.

---

264 Winter (2003), p. 992; according to Winter, there are different levels of organisational capabilities; dynamic capabilities govern the change of ordinary — or lower level — capabilities.

265 Eisenhardt/Martin (2000), p. 1107.

266 Eisenhardt/Martin (2000), p. 1111.

267 For an analysis of the performance effects of resource endowments of entrepreneurial companies, refer to Lee et al. (2001), pp. 615ff.

268 Resource management includes the evaluation and expansion of the resource endowment ("resource inventory"), the bundling of the resources and the leveraging of resources. And the effectiveness and efficiency of this coordination might be or might at least lead to a competitive advantage. For further explanations see Sirmon/Hitt (2003), pp. 339ff.; Powell (1992), pp. 120ff.

269 Helfat/Peteraf (2002), pp. 8ff.; Sirmon/Hitt (2003), pp. 344ff.

3.2.2 Venture Capital and Corporate Governance

3.2.2.1 Understanding of Corporate Governance

The dynamic resource-based view considers corporate governance to be either a potential source of competitive advantage[270] or at least a resource that enables a firm to gain a competitive advantage from other strategic resources.[271]

Corporate governance is the framework for management and control of a company;[272] it determines how decisions are made. Decision making is a dynamic capability that coordinates and configures a company's internal and external resources.[273] Good corporate governance means that companies have a good decision making process. This requires that decisions be made based on the best information available, taking into account several alternatives[274] and the company's goals, which are generally related to value creation. Good corporate governance leads to informed decision making. Well-informed decisions might be good decisions and could therefore lead to a competitive advantage.[275] Corporate governance determines a company's ability to make informed decisions. In a nutshell, corporate governance determines the propensity of a company to create competitive advantage.[276]

According to the dynamic resource-based view, good corporate governance enables a firm to effectively and efficiently configure its resources to gain competitive advantage. This is reached by using the best basis for decision making, which is largely determined by the experiences and skills of the people involved. The improvement of corporate governance is focussed on the structures and processes that facilitate making

---

270 This is a perspective often found in research on the corporate governance of family firms, e.g., Carney (2005), pp. 249 ff; indirectly Barney/Hansen (1994), p. 188 also consider corporate governance as a source of competitive advantage.

271 Barney et al. (2001), p. 632; Collis (1994), p. 143 states that organisational capabilities — which are partly determined by corporate governance — are a valuable resource of competitive advantage.

272 German Corporate Governance Code, p. 1; Bassen, (2002a), p. 20.

273 Eisenhardt/Martin (2000), p. 1107; c.f. McGee (1995), pp. 577ff.

274 For more information on the rationalism of comprehensive strategic decision processes, refer to Fredrickson (1984), pp. 445ff.

275 Eisenhardt (1989b), pp. 549ff.; Eisenhardt/Martin (2000), p. 1106; Adner/Helfat (2003), p. 1020; Winter (2003), pp. 993ff. explains why the advantages of dynamic capabilities can be compensated by costs or competition.

276 Carney (2005), p. 249; Castanias/Helfat (1991), pp. 161ff.; Acquaah (2003), p. 64; Lynall et al. (2003), pp. 418.

decisions on the best possible basis. Accordingly, the dynamic resource-based view considers the advice function of corporate governance as particularly important.[277]

Good corporate governance can lead to a company's competitive advantage and is therefore either seen as a strategic resource itself or as a condition for other strategic resource decision making.[278]

The empirical analysis by ACQUAAH provides evidence that the effectiveness of management leads to a sustainable competitive advantage, which shows in sustainable abnormal profitability. Additionally, it was found that managerial capabilities are a particularly strong predictor of sustained over-performance, which reinforces that the effectiveness of management is a valuable, unique and difficult-to-imitate resource.[279]

3.2.2.2 Importance of Corporate Governance in Growth Companies

As introduced before, competitive advantages arise from valuable and somewhat dynamic capabilities.[280] Good corporate governance as the framework for decision making is particularly valuable and rare in growth companies, as the following shows. Besides this, corporate governance has additional characteristics that make it difficult to imitate. Though, due to the equifinality of decision making and changing requirements, the sustainability of competitive advantage resulting from good corporate governance is questionable.

- Valuable: Growth companies often operate in highly dynamic markets.[281] In such markets — also described as 'high-velocity markets' — change is hardly predictable, and successful business models are unclear.[282] Here, dynamic capabilities are particularly valuable as it is constantly necessary to learn how to adapt to the changing market and to quickly build and reconfigure firms' resources and

277 Adner/Helfat (2003), p. 1013; Huse (2005), pp. 43 ff.; c.f. Boyd (1990), pp. 419ff. Makadok (2001), pp. 389ff.; good corporate governance must be adapted to changes in the environment, for more information refer to Hillman et al. (2000), pp. 241ff.; Boeker/Goodstein (1991), pp. 805ff.

278 Barney et al. (2001), p. 632; indirectly Barney/Hansen (1994), p. 188 also considers corporate governance as a source of competitive advantage; Collis (1994), p. 143 states that organisational capabilities — which are partly determined by corporate governance — are a valuable resource of competitive advantage; furthermore this is a perspective often found in research on the corporate governance of family firms, e. g. Carney (2005), pp. 249 ff.

279 Acquaah (2003), p. 76.

280 Eisenhardt/Martin (2000), p. 1111.

281 Porter (2004), pp. 215ff.; Fiet (1995), p. 555; Küting (2000a), p. 597

282 Eisenhardt/Martin, pp. 1106 and 1111.

activities.[283] Accordingly, good decision making is required to gain a competitive advantage, so corporate governance is very important. Empirical evidence demonstrates that knowledge-based resources — and corporate governance quality depends largely on knowledge and abilities — are particularly important for a company's success in dynamic and unpredictable environments.[284]

This shows that corporate governance is very valuable for the successful development of growth companies that very often operate in dynamic markets.

- Rare: To confer a competitive advantage, good corporate governance must be rare among growth companies. Growth companies are generally young[285], and their corporate governance structures are not well established because they were of less importance when the companies were very small, and the ownership and the management were not separated. Moreover, the scarce resources of growth companies might also be an obstacle to implementing good corporate governance. This is, on one hand, due to the limited experiences and skills of the companies' managers and, on the other hand, due to the limited possibilities for investing in further resources.[286]

The limited elaboration of growth companies' corporate governance is clearly shown in regard to the quality of the composition and the work of boards. The members of boards in growth companies might not be selected based on their capabilities but based on their relations to the managers, who often have a say in the selection due to their ownership. The supply of information to board members is also often not optimal as adequate information systems are not in place.[287] In some growth companies, there are not even formal board meetings at all because managers do not see the need for them.[288]

283 Eisenhardt/Martin (2000), p. 1106; Teece et al. (1997), p. 516; Judge/Miller (1991), pp. 449ff.; c.f. Aragon-Correa/Sharma (2003), pp. 71ff.
284 Miller/Shamsie (1996), pp. 538ff.
285 This holds also for later stage growth companies like MBIs and MBOs where the financed company is generally also a relatively new entity even if its origins are in an older company. The ownership and management structures are still new in these cases.
286 Riekert (2004), p. 57; Talaulicar et al. (2001), pp. 511ff.; Boeker/Wiltbank (2005), pp. 123ff.
287 Grundei/Talaulicar (2001), pp. 194ff.; Talaulicar et al. (2003), p. 516ff.
288 Andersson/Gunnarsson (1999) according to Gabrielsson/Huse (2002), pp. 139ff.

These examples show that corporate governance quality is generally considered to be rather poor among growth companies, so such companies with good corporate governance are rare.

- Imperfectly imitable/substitutable: In highly dynamic markets, dynamic capabilities might be causally ambiguous. Because they have to be constantly reconfigured to match market conditions, their effectiveness is difficult to evaluate. This makes it difficult to derive causality. Even successful managers might not know why their dynamic capabilities are successful.[289]

Additionally, corporate governance is also affected by social complexity because its effectiveness is determined by formal and informal structures such as relations between managers and board members.[290] That means that the effectiveness depends, for example, largely on the collaboration of managers and board members, which cannot be easily influenced.

Causal ambiguity and social complexity make corporate governance difficult to imitate. Apart from this, corporate governance cannot be substituted. Although competitors might substitute particular corporate governance elements, it is assumed that there is no substitute for corporate governance because it is the basis of a company. Nonetheless, the sustainability of a competitive advantage built on corporate governance is questionable because its adequacy depends on a company's situation. Therefore, the adequacy of specific corporate governance structures and processes might change rapidly in dynamic markets.

However, it is shown that good corporate governance is both valuable for growth companies and relatively rare. Corporate governance is an important basis for the competitiveness of growth companies if they have structures and processes that enable them to make well-informed decisions. The dynamic resource-based view focuses on the advice function of corporate governance because it largely determines the resources needed for decision making capacity.

---

289 Eisenhardt/Martin (2000), p. 1114.
290 C.f. Hambrick (1987), pp. 88 ff.; Barney (1991), p. 110.

4 Relationship between Venture Capital, Corporate Governance and Firm Value

This chapter builds a theoretical framework for the relationship between venture capital, corporate governance and firm value on the basis of the two perspectives introduced in chapter three. The four aspects that are expected to have the greatest importance in this relationship, based on the literature review, are analysed. First, the reasons for the venture capitalists' influence on the corporate governance of portfolio companies are explained. Thereafter, the expected effects of the influence on corporate governance quality are described. This is followed by a description of the abilities that should determine the venture capitalists' impact. In the end, the effects of good corporate governance on growth companies' firm value are determined.[291] The specific hypotheses are derived in the following.[292]

4.1 Reasons for Venture Capitalists' Influence on Corporate Governance

Venture capitalists' primary reason for influencing corporate governance should be to improve the return on their investment. Because the influence is time and cost consuming, they should expect the benefits to be greater than the costs. The benefits might arise from a reduction of risk or costs on one hand or from value creation on the other hand. Correspondingly, the two underlying theories differ in their explanation of venture capitalists' influence. Whereas agency theory considers costs from agency problems as an impetus, the dynamic resource-based view sees good corporate governance as a basis from which to build a competitive advantage and create value.[293] Besides this, a venture capitalist might also influence the corporate governance of the portfolio companies to attract interest from investors or because of a planned exit from an investment to comply with mandatory corporate governance codes.

---

291 For a literature review on corporate governance in growth companies, refer to Daily et al. (2002), pp. 387ff.

292 An overview of all hypotheses is given in 5.1.

293 Lynall et al. (2003), pp. 417ff.; c.f. for the controversy between the control and collaboration roles of corporate governance, refer to Sundaramaurthy/Lewis (2003), pp. 397ff.

4.1.1 Risk Reduction

According to the agency theory, the reason for implementing efficient corporate governance is the risk of agency problems and consequential value losses.[294] This is because the great information asymmetries that exist in the relationship between a venture capitalist and the managers of a portfolio company increase the risk of opportunistic behaviour by the managers, which in turn could lead to value losses for the venture capitalists.[295] The need for good corporate governance depends, as explained in section 3.1.2.2, on the level of the associated agency and business risk. Agency risk increases the opportunities for managers to act opportunistically, and business risk raises the probability that they would do so and makes the consequences more severe. Consequently, venture capitalists should influence the corporate governance of their portfolio companies if the associated agency and business risks are high. This is proven empirically by BARNEY ET AL., who found that high agency and business risk are associated with venture capitalists' use of more elaborate corporate governance structures and processes to monitor and bond the managers of portfolio companies.[296]

4.1.1.1 Extent of Agency Risk

Agency risk depends on the danger of managerial deviation from value maximisation. The greater it is, the greater is the need for outside oversight of a firm. Therefore, agency risk increases the need for venture capitalist involvement in portfolio companies' corporate governance.[297] Venture capitalists, as particularly important supervisors of the management in growth companies, should be involved more strongly in boards when the agency risk is great.[298]

SAPIENZA/GUPTA prove this empirically by analysing the relationship between agency risk and the extent of interaction between venture capitalists and the managers of portfolio companies. They find support for the hypothesis that the interaction is more frequent in the case of low goal congruence between the venture capitalists and the managers as well as in the case of limited start-up experience for the CEO of a

---

294 Barney et al. (1989), pp. 64ff.
295 Leland/Pyle (1977), p. 371.
296 Barney et al. (1989).
297 Sapienza et al. (1996), p. 445; Fama/Jensen (1983), pp. 301ff.; Sapienza/Gupta (1994), p. 1620; Van den Berghe/Levrau (2002), p. 126.
298 Lerner (1995), p. 302.

portfolio company. Furthermore, their results indicate that the interactions will be more frequent in the case of greater uncertainty due to an early development stage and a high degree of innovativeness in the portfolio company.[299] KAPLAN/STRÖMBERG show that a higher internal risk in a portfolio company leads to a higher level of venture capitalist control.[300] An example for this is the case of executive officer turnover. GOMPERS/LERNER show empirically that venture capitalists increase the number of their board seats significantly more in portfolio companies with CEO succession than in companies without CEO succession. This is also true for other outsides, but to a lesser extent.[301]

BARNEY ET AL. also show empirically a positive relationship between high agency risk and venture capitalists' monitoring activities. They use variables such as the number of years a CEO has been associated with a portfolio company, the percentage of initial financing by the CEO and the percentage of equity held by the company's employees[302] that indicate low agency risk and prove that these are negatively related to the ownership share of the venture capitalists, which as has been shown before, is an indicator for venture capitalists' influence and hence also for their monitoring activities.[303] A similar approach is taken by FREDRISEN/KLOFSTEN who analyse the extent of venture capitalists' influence on the governance of portfolio companies in relation to associated risk. In particular, a board of directors with weak competence — which might increase the agency risk — has a strong effect on the venture capitalists' influence.[304]

Based on the theoretical and empirical evidence, it can be expected that venture capitalists recognise the need for good corporate governance and hence for their influence by assessing the agency risk associated with a particular investment.

---

299 Sapienza/Gupta (1994), pp. 1628ff.

300 Kaplan/Strömberg (2004), p. 2203.

301 Gompers/Lerner (2002), pp. 176ff.

302 Managerial ownership is here seen as an instrument to align the interests of the owners and the managers of a company and is therefore considered as a substitute to monitoring by the owners. Empirical evidence for this comes from SAPIENZA/GUPTA who could not support the hypothesis that the interaction between the VC-investor and the portfolio company is particularly strong in companies with a low level of management ownership; see Sapienza/Gupta (1994), p. 1628.

303 Barney et al. (1989), pp. 66ff.; Barney et al. (1996a), pp. 100ff.

304 Fredriksen/Klofsten (2001), pp. 213ff., their two types of risk "agency risk" and "conformity risk" are here considered to be agency risks becuase they both stand for problems that arise because of information asymmetries between the venture capitalist and the management of the portfolio company.

4.1.1.2 Extent of Business Risk

Business risk is considered to influence the need for good corporate governance.[305] The higher the business risk — indicated by the level of profitability — the greater is the risk for venture capitalists that their investments fail.[306]

Empirical findings from BARNEY ET AL. support this as they indicate that the ownership share and the number of board seats of venture capitalists — which measures venture capitalists' influence — are both negatively correlated with the profitability of a portfolio company.[307] HIGASHIDE/BIRLEY also found that venture capitalists' involvement in portfolio companies increases when they perceive the portfolio companies' performance to be unsatisfactory. In that case, they might feel that they can make an effective contribution to the companies' development.[308]

Further empirical evidence exists for specific elements of business risk. In the following, the findings for three important elements of business risk are presented, more precisely for two internal and one external element.

Business risk arises from the innovations associated with the products and processes of a company. The higher the **degree of innovation** is, the greater are the uncertainties in regard to the technical feasibility of a product, its novelty and its acceptance by the market.[309] This can have a negative impact on the company's profitability and by this increase its business risk. This is reflected in a close interaction between venture capitalists and managers, as SAPIENZA/GUPTA show empirically.[310]

The second element is the **quality of the managers** of a portfolio company. The less experience and fewer capabilities managers of portfolio companies have, the greater is the risk that they make decisions that reduce the company's profitability. Accordingly, the need for venture capitalists to bond and monitor the managers rises. SAPIENZA/GUPTA, for example, prove empirically that in companies in which the CEO has little start-up experience, the interaction between the VC-investor and the portfolio company will be more frequent than in other companies.[311] BAKER/GOMPERS

305 Galbraith (1973); Sapienza/Gupta (1994), p. 1620
306 Barney et al. (1989), p. 65; Barney et al. (1996a), pp. 100ff.
307 Barney et al. (1989), p. 67.
308 Higashide/Birley (2002), p. 78.
309 Sapienza/Gupta (1994), pp. 1622ff.
310 Sapienza/Gupta (1994), p. 1629.
311 Sapienza/Gupta (1994), p. 1628.

similarly found that the number of board seats taken by venture capitalists decreases as the tenure of the CEO of a company increases.[312] In contrast to this, SAPIENZA ET AL. came to a different result in another study. Their results indicate that a greater start-up experience of the managers leads to more interaction between them and the venture capitalists. A possible explanation might be that the managers in that case are more prepared to accept advice from the investors.[313] These mixed results are also supported by the findings of two studies on the relationship between industry risk and venture capitalists' involvement. Analyses from MAC MILLAN ET AL. and from SAPIENZA ET AL. have shown that the industry experience of the managers does not influence the extent of involvement of venture capitalists.[314]

Finally, **external risk** might also increase the business risk of a company because it makes it more difficult for companies to become and stay profitable. Empirical evidence from KAPLAN/STRÖMBERG proves that higher external risk is related to higher control by venture capitalists, for example, in the form of an increase in their liquidation rights and tighter staging, which means that the time between two financing rounds is shorter.[315]

The partially mixed results show that the relationship between business risk and the involvement of venture capitalists in the corporate governance of portfolio companies is not simple. Even though portfolio companies are generally affected with high business risk, it could be expected that venture capitalists should become more involved in those companies that face a relatively strong business risk, at least until a successful outcome is considered probable. Therefore, it is expected that venture capitalists recognise the level of business risk in a company that determines the need for good corporate governance and adapt their influence accordingly.

In his analyses comparing the behaviour of venture capitalists and business angels in relation to their risk assessment, FIET found that venture capitalists consider business risk more important than agency risk. That means that they evaluate a potential investment more on the basis of business risk than of agency risk. A possible explanation might be that venture capitalists are specialists in dealing with agency problems so that

312 Baker/Gompers (2003), p. 587.
313 Sapienza et al. (1996), pp. 439ff.
314 Macmillan et al. (1988), pp. 27ff.; Sapienza et al. (1996), pp. 439ff.; Ruppen (2001), p. 183.
315 Kaplan/Strömberg (2004), p. 2203.

business risk is the greater hazard.[316] This explanation is supported by a later analysis of FIET/HELLRIEGEL who found that venture capitalists control for business risk primarily before an investment is made and control for agency risk primarily after an investment decision.[317] This means that business risk should have a greater impact on contractual arrangements and agency risk should have a bigger impact on mechanisms put into action during the investment.

The theoretical and empirical analyses indicate that the associated agency and business risks explain the strength of venture capitalists' influence on the corporate governance of their portfolio companies.

H1.1: The greater the agency and business risks associated with an investment, the greater is the venture capitalists' influence on the corporate governance.

According to agency theory, bonding and monitoring are the two ways to reduce the risk of opportunistic behaviour by management and value losses for venture capitalists. Consequently, the corporate governance elements that fulfil a bonding or monitoring function should be influenced by agency risk. First, in regard to management are the assessment, selection, compensation and bonding of the managers. Second, in regard to the board (or supervisory board in a two-tier system) are the composition and the work. Third is the reporting discipline.

The requirements for the managers of growth companies are demanding and fast changing. As the companies are generally centred on the managers, they determine the companies' success in a great measure. Therefore, their regular assessment is of high importance. This is particularly true in the case of high agency and business risk as moral hazard is likely to occur, which might have negative effects on the company's development. Hence, it can be expected that venture capitalists strongly influence the assessment of managers if the associated agency and business risks are great.

H1.1.1: The greater the agency and business risks associated with an investment, the greater is the venture capitalists' influence on the assessment of the managers.

The selection of the managers is a hazard to adverse selection because the venture capitalist does not know about all the candidates' characteristics. If the typical high

316 Fiet (1995), pp. 564ff.; Fiet (1991), p. 76.
317 Fiet/Hellriegel (1995), p. 36.

dependency on the management in growth companies is combined with a high risk of opportunistic behaviour and a high risk of severe consequences for opportunistic behaviour, the venture capitalists should closely monitor and even support the selection process of the managers.

H1.1.2: The greater the agency and business risks associated with an investment, the greater is the venture capitalists' influence on the selection of the managers.

According to the agency theory, opportunistic behaviour can be reduced by aligning the interests of venture capitalists and the portfolio companies' managers by giving the managers appropriate incentives. This is particularly important if the managers' abilities and the likelihood of opportunistic behaviour, as well as the potential negative consequences, are great.

H1.1.3: The greater the agency and business risks associated with an investment, the greater is the venture capitalists' influence on the compensation of the managers.

Finally, the risk that managers will hold up the future development of the company by leaving it is also more likely in the case of high agency risk. Moreover, the negative consequences might be very severe if the business risk is high. Hence, it can be expected that the venture capitalists strongly influence the bonding of portfolio companies' managers in the case of high agency and business risks.

H1.1.4: The greater the agency and business risks associated with an investment, the greater is the venture capitalists' influence on the bonding of the portfolio companies' managers.

Agency theory focuses on both, the structure and the work of boards: Independence is, according to agency theory, a prerequisite for the effectiveness of boards as it gives the members an incentive to monitor the managers. Therefore, venture capitalists are expected to influence the composition of the board in cases of strong agency and business risks.

H1.1.5: The greater the agency and business risks associated with an investment, the greater is the venture capitalists' influence on the composition of the board.

Moreover, agency theory also attaches great importance to the work of the board. To monitor and bond the managers of the portfolio companies, the board has to meet regularly and be involved in all important decisions of the company, particularly in cases of high agency and business risk.

H1.1.6: The greater the agency and business risks associated with an investment, the greater is the venture capitalists' influence on the work of the board.

According to agency theory, the venture capitalists also influence the portfolio companies' reporting discipline. Interventions to prevent value losses require that they are well informed about the current development of the portfolio company. Regular reporting provides timely information, which is particularly important in cases of high agency and business risk.

H1.1.7: The greater the agency and business risks associated with an investment, the greater is the venture capitalists' influence on the frequency of reporting.

4.1.2 Value Creation

According to the dynamic resource-based view, the reason for the influence of venture capitalists on the corporate governance of portfolio companies is value creation.[318] Implementing good corporate governance in growth companies can lead to a competitive advantage and thereby create value. Good corporate governance is a valuable resource for growth companies, as was detailed in section 3.2.2.2. Furthermore, due to its rarity among those companies, good corporate governance can lead to a competitive advantage. Hence, venture capitalists might influence their portfolio companies' corporate governance in order to improve the decision making capacity, which should increase the companies' value.

Some studies support the notion that the reason for venture capitalists' influence is not solely the reduction of agency problems. Venture capitalists might exert strong influence in companies despite low agency and business risks where they expect to be able to create value instead. The findings of FREDRIKSEN/KLOFSTEN show that venture capitalists increase their influence on portfolio companies in the absence of agency risk. The analysis showed a positive relation between the venture capitalists' trust in the managers of the portfolio company — a situation with low agency risk — and the frequency of interaction, although this relationship was only weakly

318 This corresponds to the general assumption that venture capitalists' influence is aimed at value creation, refer, e.g., to Manigart et al. (2000).

significant.[319] Thus, venture capitalists might have other motivations than risk- and loss-reduction. Value creation is the reason behind a broad range of support activities that venture capitalists should contribute to the professionalisation of portfolio companies.[320]

Due to the fact that the influence on portfolio companies is time and cost consuming, venture capitalists might have to focus on a limited number of companies to influence. Generally, venture capitalists build portfolios of companies, of which only one or two companies out of ten become really successful whereas most of the other investments fail. So the success of the investment portfolio depends largely on the success of single promising investments.[321] Correspondingly, it might be worthwhile to focus on those companies that are likely to be successful.[322] In regard to their influence on corporate governance, venture capitalists should accordingly concentrate on companies that have the potential to build a competitive advantage from their corporate governance.

The dynamic resource-based view considers resource endowment a condition for the achievement of competitive advantages.[323] As introduced in section 3.2.1, the dynamic resource-based view assumes that resources can be acquired or developed despite the existing path dependency of resources.[324] HELFAT/PETERAF explain capability lifecycles, i.e., the development of capabilities from founding to maturity.[325] Following this view, the resources and capabilities endowments present at founding set the stage for their further development. Thus, the endowment at founding provides initial sources of heterogeneity.[326] Consequently, the initial corporate governance is an important determinant of a company's potential to build a competitive advantage on its corporate governance.

Consequently, venture capitalists might select the companies on which to exert stronger influence according to the companies' initial corporate governance quality. The better the initial corporate governance, the stronger the venture capitalists' influence might be.

---

319 Fredriksen/Klofsten (2001), p. 214; they name this governance supporting concept "coalition risk".
320 Hellmann/Puri (2002).
321 Ellis (2003), p. 54.
322 Dimov/Shepherd (2005) refer to "home-runs".
323 Barney (1991), pp. 101ff.
324 Path dependency of corporate governance is shown by Bebchuk/Roe (1999) at the national level and by Beckman/Burton (2004) for management of growth companies.
325 Helfat/Peteraf (2003), pp. 997ff.
326 Helfat/Peteraf (2003), p. 1001.

H1.2: The better the initial corporate governance quality, the greater is the venture capitalists' influence on the corporate governance.

The dynamic resource-based view puts most emphasis on the corporate governance elements that have an advice function for the company and thereby increase the companies' resource endowment required for management and control. Those elements include management selection and the composition and work of the board.

The crucial role of the managers for the development of a portfolio company makes the managers' selection process highly important and the managers one of the core resources of a growth company. Therefore, the selection of new managers is a very critical task that requires an effective and efficient process. Venture capitalists, with their specific experiences, might be able to add their competence, experiences and capabilities to improve the managers' selection process. Venture capitalists might focus their influence on companies where their contribution can have the greatest impact and might, according to the dynamic resource-based view, influence the managers' selection more strongly in companies that already have high-quality corporate governance. This is because the managers should either be more willing or should be more forced to accept the advice in those companies.

H1.2.1: The better the initial corporate governance quality, the greater is the venture capitalists' influence on the selection process of new managers.

There are also two aspects of the board that emphasise the advising function of corporate governance in portfolio companies: This theoretic perspective places emphasis on the advice role of the board, which is more relevant in companies that have good corporate governance because that might increase the impact of the advice. To carry out the advice role, the board needs qualified members. Hence, it can be expected that venture capitalists influence the composition of the board more strongly if the initial corporate governance quality is high.

H.1.2.2: The better the initial corporate governance quality, the greater is the venture capitalists' influence on the composition of the board.

The advice function of the board can only be fulfilled when the board is involved in the decision making of the portfolio company. Hence, it is necessary that the board address strategic decisions. Venture capitalists might focus their influence on companies where they consider strategic advice particularly helpful, which might be the case of companies with good corporate governance.

H1.2.3: The better the initial corporate governance quality, the greater is the venture capitalists' influence on the work of the board.

4.1.3 Exit Preparation

In the case of a planned exit, venture capitalists might also strengthen their influence on the portfolio companies to ensure the successful sale of the company.[327] This might also influence the companies' corporate governance. Whereas there are no great effects to be expected from a sale-back, a secondary-sale or a trade sale, the preparation for an initial public offering (IPO) might lead to changes in the corporate governance because it greatly influences the success of an IPO.[328] The reasons for this are twofold. On one hand, public companies in many countries have to comply with corporate governance codes that are implemented either by the national legislature or the stock exchange.[329] Therefore, companies that seek approval for a public issuance have to comply with or at least align to those codes. Venture capitalists that want to ensure the success of a public offering might influence their companies in order to fulfil the requirements. However, this does not necessarily strengthen the monitoring, bonding or advice function of corporate governance. On the other hand, the success of an IPO depends largely on interest from investors. Growth companies often lack a high awareness among the public because of their short history and limited size. Connecting well-known names to the company could arouse the public interest. The investors' perception of the board prestige signals organisational legitimacy and could thereby reduce the liability of market newness. This should support a company's chances to realise a successful IPO.[330] Venture capitalists might try to involve reputable people in the boards in order to send a positive signal to the market and thereby contribute to the success of the IPO.

Accordingly, it can be expected that venture capitalists increase their influence on the corporate governance of portfolio companies when a public exit is prepared.

---

327 Certo et al. (2001), pp. 33ff.; Certo (2003), pp. 432ff.; Hochberg (2002), pp. 30 ff.

328 Hartzell et al. (2004), p. 26.

329 Burton et al. (2004), pp. 356ff.; Weimer/Pape (1999); Temorale/Ismann (1999), pp. 263ff.

330 Burton et al. (2004), pp. 356ff.; Certo (2003), p. 439; Deutsche/Ross (2003), pp. 1006ff.; c.f. Welbourne/Cyr (1999), pp. 616ff.

H1.3: Before a potential public exit, venture capitalists increase their influence on the corporate governance of portfolio companies.

They focus particularly on the compliance with corporate governance codes and bring in well-known board members.

H1.3.1: Before a potential public exit, it is more probable that the portfolio companies comply with corporate governance codes.

H1.3.2: Before a potential public exit, it is more probable that the portfolio companies have board members with experience in listed companies.

4.1.4 Development of Reasons for Influence

The three reasons for the influence of venture capitalists on the corporate governance of portfolio companies might all be observed in practice but might change over the development of an investment. Preparation for an exit should obviously be a strong reason only before a potential exit. The explanatory power of the two other reasons for influence might also depend on time. Venture capitalists might base their influence on changing criteria over the life of an investment. Given the maximisation of the return on investment as the main goal of venture capitalists, the focus might change from risk and loss reduction to value creation over time.[331] The two perspectives correspond to two opposing hypotheses, the "trouble-shooting strategy" and the "home-run strategy". Whereas the first hypothesis indicates that the influence of venture capitalists on portfolio companies is increased when the business is performing badly,[332] the latter says that the investors put more effort into companies that are performing well because it is more rewarding.[333] This is supported by an analysis by SAPIENZA ET AL. that found that venture capitalists add more value to companies that are performing well than they do to those that are performing badly.[334]

The agency theory's argument that agency and business risk are important determinants of venture capitalists' influence on the corporate governance of portfolio

331 The value creation aspect also requires the corporate governance to fulfil different functions at different life cycle phases; for more information refer to Lynall et al. (2003), pp. 421ff.

332 Van den Berghe/Levrau (2002), p. 127.

333 Sapienza et al. (1996), pp. 458ff.; Sapienza/Timmons (1989), pp. 245ff.

334 Sapienza et al. (1996), p. 462.

companies might be more relevant in early financing rounds.[335] The real potential of an investment can hardly be predicted at that time, so venture capitalists might try to secure all investments and make efforts to reduce agency problems in all portfolio companies. In some cases, this might not improve the situation so that at a later financing round, the venture capitalists might have given up their goal to reduce the risk. In that case, agency and business risk might not predict venture capitalists' influence anymore. This perspective is supported by the empirical findings that show that the extent of involvement of venture capitalists is higher in early stage companies that in late-stage companies because the degree of uncertainty is higher.[336]

In contrast to this, the explanation of the dynamic resource-based view might be more relevant in later financing rounds as venture capitalists would then be better able to assess the corporate governance of the portfolio companies and decide which portfolio company has the potential to build a competitive advantage on its corporate governance. Consequently, it can be expected that corporate governance quality is a better predictor of venture capitalists' influence in later financing rounds.

Hence, it is expected that the reasons for venture capitalists' influence change from agency and business risk in early financing rounds to the quality of corporate governance at later financing rounds.

H1.4: Agency and business risks have a stronger impact on venture capitalists' influence on the corporate governance of portfolio companies at earlier financing rounds than at later financing rounds.

Finally, it should be remarked that the venture capitalists' influence on corporate governance because of a planned exit should, as a matter of course, occur in the preparation process for an IPO.

According to the underlying theories, there are three different reasons for venture capitalists' influence on corporate governance that might change over time. Hence, the reasons and corresponding hypotheses can either be substitutable or complementary. Figure 12 illustrates the expected relationship between the reasons and the venture

335 It should be noted that there is also the proposition that the dominant corporate governance function depends rather on the CEO tenure than on the investment of a company and that the advice function dominates in the beginning whereas the control function becomes more important in later CEO tenure; for more information refer to Shen (2003), pp. 466ff.

336 Gorman/Sahlman (1989), p. 245; Sapienza et al. (1996), p. 459, Elango et al. (1995), p. 164.

capitalists' influence on the corporate governance of portfolio companies. The impact of this influence is discussed in the next section.

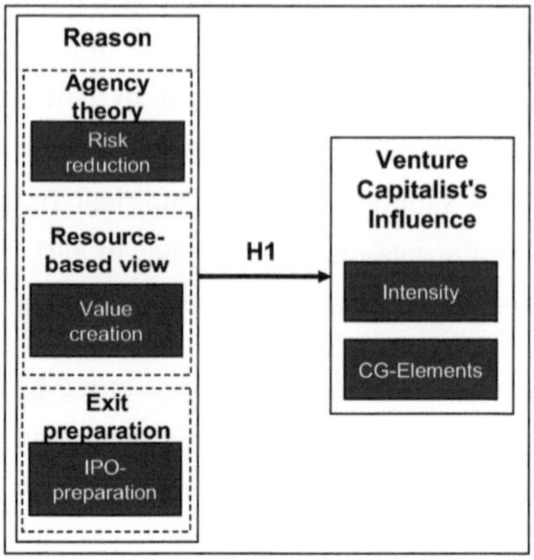

Figure 12: Relationship between reasons and venture capitalists' influence

4.2 Effects of Venture Capitalists' Influence on Corporate Governance

In this section, the expected effects of the venture capitalists influence on the corporate governance of portfolio companies are explained. It is structured along the six corporate governance elements related to the management, the board and the reporting of companies. For every element, the expected effects are first derived from theory before empirical findings are presented. In the end, findings on the effects of venture capitalists' influence on the portfolio companies' performance or value are given, where available.

The basic hypothesis of the following section is:

H2: The venture capitalists' influence has an impact on the portfolio companies' corporate governance.

4.2.1 Management

4.2.1.1 Assessment and Selection of Managers

As explained in section 3.1.2.1, managers are particularly important for the realization of growth companies' value potential. Therefore, the assessment of managers, the potentially required replacement of managers, and the selection of new managers are crucial for the success of venture capitalists' investments.

Agency theory and the dynamic resource-based view both consider these corporate governance elements as important, but they focus on different aspects. According to agency theory, the shareholders have to closely monitor the managers and push for a replacement should the current managers not be effective. This requires frequent assessment of the managers, which can be done by the board or at the shareholder's meeting. If managers are unable to fully generate the value of the business, they should be replaced.[337] When new managers are selected, the shareholders should again closely monitor this process so that no decision is made against their interest. Accordingly, good corporate governance means, in this context, that the shareholders regularly assess the appropriateness of the managers, replace managers if needed and closely monitor the selection process of new managers.[338] Venture capitalists, as blockholders, should have the power to fulfil this monitoring role and the power to push for changes in the current management team, if required. Agency theory asks the shareholders to maintain comprehensive decision rights in the contracting phase in order to reduce the risk of moral hazard, which should give the shareholders the rights they need. So, venture capitalists should be able to improve management assessment and selection.

The dynamic resource-based view focuses more on the advisory role of the venture capitalist in the process of selecting new managers.[339] According to this, the outcome of the managers' selection process depends on the effectiveness of the process. Hence, good corporate governance means that the decisions are made well informed, i.e., a broad range of candidates is taken into account and the decision is made by people with the necessary knowledge. Venture capitalists should be able to improve the selection process because they have, on one hand, the experience of having done this process times before and, on the other hand, a network of specialists for the selection of managers as well as a network of possible candidates.[340] Consequently, they should have knowledge and resources that can contribute to the effectiveness of the managers' selection.

---

[337] Hambrick (1987), pp. 89ff.
[338] C.f. Hillman/Dalziel (2003), p. 385.
[339] C.f. Hillman/Dalziel (2003), p. 386.
[340] Hellmann/Puri (2002), pp. 177ff.

Empirically it is shown that venture capitalists are active in the assessment, replacement and selection of members of the management team. KAPLAN/ STRÖMBERG found that more than half of the investors in their American sample was active either before or after their investment had been made.[341] Another study indicates that this influence on managers is of high importance for venture capitalists. The analysis of FREDERIKSEN ET AL. looked at the perceived influence of the venture capitalists in the view of the CEOs of the portfolio companies. They found that questions concerning the CEO position, and more generally the personnel, were among the areas that are most influenced by venture capitalists.[342] In particular, the replacement of managers has been analysed by several researchers. They show that venture capitalists seem to be particularly focussed in replacing the founder with a professional manager as CEO. Venture capitalists often argue that a professional top management team adds value to the portfolio company and that founders were prone to pursue actions in their own interest rather the company's interest.[343] LERNER found that the representation of venture capitalists at portfolio companies' boards increases around the time of a replacement of the CEO. According to his analysis, venture capitalists added 1,75 board members between financing rounds when the CEO was replaced, compared to an average increase of only 0,24 members between rounds when the CEO was not replaced.[344] The analysis by POLLOCK ET AL. supports this and shows that the number of IPOs with a founder-CEO is significantly higher in companies that are not venture capital-backed than in those that are.[345] Similar results come from CERTO ET AL. who consider this a consequence of weak negotiations between founder-CEOs and investment banks when the issue price of the shares is to be determined.[346] That means a reason for the replacement might be the weak management competence of founder CEOs. These results are a strong indication that venture capitalists are active in the replacement of managers.

Venture capitalists are also actively involved in the selection process of new managers. The analysis of HELLMANN/PURI provides support for this as it shows that the selection process tends to be more professional in venture capital-backed firms than in other growth companies. Venture capital-backed firms make significantly greater use

341 Kaplan/Strömberg (2004), p. 2194.
342 Frederiksen et al. (1990), p. 259.
343 Hellmann (1998), p. 57; Pollock et al. (2005), p. 1; Martens et al. (2005), p. 1.
344 Lerner (1995), p. 310.
345 Pollock et al. (2005), p. 8.
346 Certo et al. (2001), p. 655.

of business and professional contacts when searching for new personnel for functional and managerial positions. This might be related to the venture capitalists' network as well as to other sources of contacts.[347] Similarly, ROSENSTEIN found that the influence on the recruitment of CEOs by venture capitalists' board members is perceived as very valuable by the managers of portfolio companies.[348] This indicates that venture capitalists also positively influence the selection of new managers.

Some of the studies also tried to find a relation between the venture capitalists' influence on these corporate governance elements and the portfolio companies' performance. POLLOCK ET AL. and MARTENS ET AL. found that replacing a founder-CEO has a significant and positive impact on a firm's ability to raise capital in the IPO process.[349] However, one of the two analyses also provides evidence that a founder who stays in the company as a member of the management team or the board also has a positive influence on the company's valuation at the time of the IPO.[350] In contrast to this, the findings of MARTENS ET AL. indicate that the long-term success, measured by the probability of not being delisted, is greater for companies with non-founder-CEOs compared to those with founder-CEOs. Additionally these delistings take place earlier in the case of professional managers as CEOs.[351] But it is questionable here whether low risk of delisting is a good measure for long-term success because delisting as a result of an acquisition by another firm is not necessarily negative for shareholders or the company.

The theoretical and empirical findings indicate that venture capitalists should improve the assessment and selection of the portfolio companies' managers and should, if required, replace managers.

H2.1: The venture capitalists' influence has a positive impact on the assessment and selection of managers.

Consequently, it can be expected that they assess management regularly and effectively.

---

347 Hellmann/Puri (2002), p. 177.

348 Rosenstein et al. (1993), p. 105.

349 Pollock et al. (2005), p. 8; Martens et al. (2005), p. 16.

350 Pollock et al. (2005), p. 8; Martens et al. (2005), pp. 16ff.; they could not support their comparable hypotheses; they found insignificant support for the higher IPO value when the CEO remained a member of the management team and even a negative relationship when the CEO became a board member.

351 Martens et al. (2005), p 18.

H2.1.1: The stronger the venture capitalists' influence, the more likely managers are to be assessed.

H2.1.2: The stronger the venture capitalists' influence, the more efficient is the assessment of the management.

The assessment of the management could disclose deficits in the current management, which should lead to the replacement of managers.

H2.1.3: The stronger the venture capitalists' influence, the more likely managers are to be replaced.

When selecting new managers, the venture capitalists' influence should make the selection process more efficient and effective.

H2.1.4: The stronger the venture capitalists' influence, the better is the managers' selection process.

4.2.1.2 Bonding of Managers

As explained before, the managers of growth companies play a particularly important role because they have specific knowledge and capabilities that are necessary to exploit the growth potential of the company. The high importance of the managers not only requires having appropriate managers but also holding them in the company.

If managers with specific knowledge and capabilities leave a company, it could be a hazard for the company's future success. This can affect a portfolio company in two ways. These managers take with them assets, skills and knowledge that might be crucial for the portfolio company. Additionally, they might increase the competition for the company by using those resources in another company.[352] According to agency theory, shareholders should reduce this risk by effectively bonding the managers to the company. They should be forced or have an incentive to stay in the company.[353] So effective bonding is considered to be in the interest of the investors and therefore seen as good corporate governance. Venture capitalists should, as blockholders, have the power to negotiate adequate bonding measures with the founders during contracting so that it can be expected that they contribute to effective bonding.

352 Shane/Cable (2002), p. 365.
353 Denis (2001), pp. 195ff.

Common bonding instruments are stock option programmes and non-compete clauses. Stock option programmes generally have vesting periods, which means that the managers can take full advantage of the options only after a certain time. Non-compete clauses forbid managers from working for a competitor for some time after they leave the portfolio company.[354]

KAPLAN/STRÖMBERG found in their empirical study that venture capitalists adopt corresponding measures to prevent managers from leaving the company. Many venture capitalists give managers an incentive to stay in the company by introducing shares for the managers that vest over time. Should the management leave the company before a defined date, the shares that are not vested yet can be bought back by the company for a low value. Additionally, they show that most venture capitalists also introduce non-compete clauses that bar managers from working for a competitor after they leave the company.[355] They also found that contracts between venture capitalists and portfolio companies can be contingent on continued employment,[356] which is also a sign of the influence of investors on the bonding of managers.

According to this analysis, venture capitalists obviously realise the necessity of effective bonding of the managers because they use non-compete clauses and stock options as bonding instruments. So, it can be expected that they use their influence to improve the bonding of managers and thereby improve corporate governance.

H2.2: Venture capitalists' influence has a positive impact on the bonding of managers.

4.2.1.3 Compensation of Managers

Apart from the selection of adequate managers and bonding them to the company, it is also crucial for managers' effectiveness that they be compensated adequately. The compensation structure should provide them with incentives to act in the shareholders' interest but should also take the company's resources into account.

The compensation of managers is another corporate governance element that could, according to agency theory, reduce agency problems. Managerial compensation should meet two requirements. On one hand, it is an important instrument to align the goals of the managers and the investors. Adequate incentive structures for the managers could

354 Salop/Salop (1976), pp. 620ff.
355 Kaplan/Strömberg (2003), p. 292.
356 Kaplan/Strömberg (2003), p. 294.

reduce the risk of opportunistic behaviour.[357] The managers should have an incentive to pursue mid- and long-term goals that correspond to the exploitation of the full potential of growth companies. Correspondingly, a great part of the compensation of the managers should depend on the future success of the portfolio companies.[358] Instruments for the alignment of interests are mid- and long-term variable compensation parts such as options and managerial ownership because they allow managers to participate in the long-term development of the company.[359] But it is important to note that the associated managerial ownership can also lead to negative effects as the managers gain control.[360]

On the other hand, the managers' compensation must be seen on the basis of the scarce financial resources of growth companies. Therefore, the compensation, and in particular the cash payments, should not be too high for the resources of the company. This affects both the absolute level of the managers' compensation and the balance between its elements. Stock options and managerial ownership could be used to substitute for cash payments, either fixed or variable payments. They are a comparatively cheap method of payment if the "perceived costs" rather than the economic costs are considered. The economic cost is what an outside investor would be willing to pay for an option whereas the "perceived cost" is what the company sees as a cost. For the grant of options in a fast growth company, the perceived costs might be lower than the economic costs because there is no accounting charge and no outlay of cash.[361]

Finally, the close monitoring that is founded in agency theory could also reduce expenditures for the managers' compensation. This is because control through monitoring could to some extent replace incentives through variable compensation.[362]

Consequently, good corporate governance in this context means that the managerial compensation on one hand reduces the risk of opportunistic behaviour by means of variable elements that are linked to the company's mid- and long-term development and on the other hand should have a relatively low level of cash payments.

---

357 Berle/Means (1932); Aggarwal/Samwick (1999), p. 66; Lippert/Moore (1995), pp. 55.

358 McGuire (2000), p. 34.

359 Markman et al. (2001), pp. 280ff.; for a theoretical analysis of managers' variable compensation refer to Cyert et al. (2002), pp. 453ff.; Bloom/Milkovich (1995), pp. 1ff.

360 Hoffmann, G. (2003), p. 158ff.; for a detailed review on the effects of managerial ownership refer to 3.1.2.2.

361 Murphy (2003), p. 143; Chua/Woodward (1993), pp.52ff.; Beatty/Zajac (1994), pp. 315ff.; c.f. Anderson et al. (2000), pp. 530ff.

362 C.f. Core et al. (1999), pp. 372ff.

It could be expected that venture capitalists realise this lever and influence the managers' compensation accordingly. As blockholders, they should be able to influence the compensation structure either in the contracting phase before the investment is done or during the investment through the board[363] or shareholder meetings.

Empirically, it is shown that venture capitalists as outsiders might align executive compensation to foster long-term value creation of growth companies.[364] Findings suggest that, particularly in high-technology growth companies, stock options play an important role in managers' and board members' compensation.[365] A broader study that looks at high growth companies in general — which are often financed by venture capitalists — supports the strong use of stock options. MURPHY analysed the use of options in so-called new economy firms and found that they are a reason why many of the companies posted positive instead of negative earnings. If, in 1999, all analysed American new economy firms had used only cash for the compensation, 45% of the companies would have had to post negative pre-tax income whereas in reality, with the use of stock options, only 23% did.[366] This underlines how crucial the managers' compensation is for high-growth companies with few financial resources.

Apart from that, venture capitalists might also reduce expenditures for the managers' compensation, but the empirical findings here are mixed. BAKER/GOMPERS show that monitoring replaces financial incentives. The performance elasticity of the managers' compensation is higher in venture capital-backed companies than in non-venture-capital-backed-companies. This is associated with a lower ownership share of the managers.[367] This higher sensitivity indicates that managers' compensation is closely monitored and adjusted to their performance so that the expenditure of the compensation is reduced in the case of weak performance. However, this is in contrast to the results of ENGEL ET AL. who found that companies with venture capital backing have lower overall use of incentive pay. This means that the annual CEO compensation grants are less associated with firm performance than in companies without venture capitalists. This indicates that the compensation, and in particular the variable compensation, could not be reduced by the venture capitalists' close

363 For more information on the relationship between board control and managers' compensation, refer to Boyd (1994), pp. 335 ff.
364 Zahra et al. (2000), p. 955.
365 Van den Berghe/Levrau (2002), p. 131.
366 Murphy (2003), p. 145.
367 Baker/Gompers (2003), p. 585.

monitoring. Their analysis shows that compensation grants of firms with little or no venture capital influence display a significantly stronger association with accounting and stock performance measures than those of firms with more intense monitoring by venture capitalists.[368] This is supported by another empirical study by HE/CONYON indicating that venture capitalists' presence is related to lower incentives for the managers.[369] There are two possible ways of explaining this relationship: First, costly performance pay could be reduced by close monitoring by venture capitalists.[370] That means the overall managers' compensation would be reduced. Second, there could be a problem with measuring the pay–performance relationship. In growth companies, current measures might not be appropriate to assess the performance so that the managers' compensation must also not be associated to current performance but to other information that might only be accessible to well-informed venture capitalists.[371] Venture capitalists might, for example, relate the variable compensation to milestones set in the portfolio companies' business plans that might be not directly related to accounting measures.[372]

According to agency theoretic explanations and the preponderant results of the empirical studies, it could be expected that venture capitalists know the importance of appropriate compensation and balance the use of incentives and expenditures accordingly, which is considered an element of good corporate governance.

H2.3: The venture capitalists' influence has a positive impact on the compensation of managers.

Consequently, it could be expected that venture capitalists' influence on the managers' compensation leads to a stronger use of variable compensation elements.

H2.3.1: The stronger the venture capitalists' influence, the higher is the proportion of the variable compensation.

The variable instruments used should also be influenced by venture capitalist to be linked to mid- and long-term goals.

368 Engel et al. (2001), pp. 502ff.
369 He/Conyon (2004), p. 56.
370 Engel et al. (2001), p. 509; c.f. for the substitutability of corporate governance refer to Rediker/Seth (1995), pp. 85ff.
371 Engel et al. (2001), p. 511 and 514.
372 Engel et al. (2001), p. 514.

H2.3.2: The stronger the venture capitalists' influence, the more likely is the use of variable compensation parts linked to mid- and long-term goals.

Finally, close monitoring by venture capitalists and the scarce resources of the portfolio company should guide the venture capitalist to reduce overall cash compensation.

H3.3.3: The stronger the venture capitalists' influence, the lower is the cash compensation of the managers.

4.2.2 Board

The board constitutes a core corporate governance element for both underlying theories, the agency theory and the dynamic resourced-based view: On one hand, it is a key monitoring instrument that should reduce the opportunistic behaviour of the managers. On the other hand, the board also improves the management of a company because it can contribute to the effectiveness of the decision making by improving the capabilities of the company. Venture capitalists are expected to influence both the composition and the work of boards.[373]

4.2.2.1 Composition

Three aspects of the composition of boards are considered to be particularly important: independence, qualification and size.[374] To fulfil the demanding monitoring and advice functions, members of the board should be independent and qualified. In the case of growth companies, the role as an adviser for the managers is just as important as the role as a controller because they are not only associated with high agency and business risk but also with a lack of competence because of their scarce resources.[375] According to the foundations, it is expected that venture capitalists recognise the importance of the composition of the board and therefore exert influence.

H2.4: The venture capitalists' influence has a positive impact on the composition of the board.

---

373 For a literature review on boards in small and medium-sized companies, refer to Huse (2000) or for a more general review to Johnson et al. (1996); Dalton et al. (1998), pp. 269ff.; for an analysis of factors for the evaluation of boards, refer to Van den Berghe/Levrau (2004), pp. 461ff.

374 Zahra/Pearce (1989), pp. 306ff. refers to composition (independence), characteristics (qualifications) and structure (size, committees); Bassen (2002b), pp. 157ff.

375 Grundei/Talaulicar (2003), p. 194.

First, the appropriateness of **independent boards** is discussed. In this context, independence means that the members of the board are outsiders that "are not members of the top management team, their associates or families; are not employees of the firms or its subsidiaries; and are not members of the immediate past top management group".[376] Whereas, according to agency theory, independence of boards is of great importance, there are also reasons why insiders on boards might be more valuable than outsiders.[377]

Generally, board independence increases, according to agency theory, the ability of boards to exercise control over managers and thereby positively affects a firm's performance.[378] A high proportion of insiders may decrease a board's ability to independently carry out its role because insiders may feel constrained from questioning CEO directives. Board independence enhances the ability of directors to exercise control and thereby to protect shareholders' interest.[379] Furthermore, insiders on boards might be reluctant to pursue long-term goals given the high risk associated with growth companies.[380] In contrast to this, outsiders might be more effective in pursuing long-term value creation by vigorously monitoring executives and ensuring strategic changes when agency conflicts are suspected.[381] Similarly, insiders might be reluctant to propose actions that could conflict with the CEO's plans.[382] Additionally, a particular problem might arise from CEO duality, which means that the CEO is also chairman of the board. This can reduce the board's influence by facilitating the CEO's control.[383]

FAMA/JENSEN explain the higher appropriateness of outside team members by arguing that they tend to be more effective monitors of the managers because they are generally key decision makers at other organisations and are therefore concerned with their reputation in the managerial labour market.[384]

Consequently, a board that includes a great number of independent members is, according to agency theory, considered to be a part of good corporate governance.

376 Zahra/Pearce (1989), pp. 306ff.
377 Zahra/Pearce (1989), pp. 215ff.; Kiel/Nicholson (2005), pp. 623.
378 Baysinger/Hoskisson (1990), pp. 75ff.
379 Sapienza et al.(2000), p. 333.
380 Zahra et al. (2000), p. 954; Wright et al. (1996), pp. 442ff.
381 Zahra et al. (2000), pp. 954ff.; Kroll et al. (1997), pp. 441ff.; Johnson et al (1993), p. 36.
382 Johnson et al. (1993), p. 36.
383 Finkelstei/D'Aveni (1994), pp. 1101ff.
384 Huson et al. (2001), p. 2267; Fama/Jensen (1983); Kaplan/Reishus (1990), p. 409.

Venture capitalists, as blockholders, should have the ability to work towards an independent board because they can appoint own representatives to the board and have a say on the structure of the board in the contracting phase.[385]

Generally, venture capitalists might increase the independence of boards in three ways: by adding their own representatives to boards, by their influence on the selection of outside board members and in a more indirect way by reducing the power of the founders. Empirical studies support that venture capitalists act in accordance with the theory as they try to foster the independence of the boards. They generally expect members to be active and critical. They try to prevent managers from bringing friends or relatives onto the boards.[386] Their own representatives do not enjoy private benefits of control and have strong motivation to exert monitoring.[387] The analysis of BAKER/GOMPERS shows that for the USA, with its one-tier system, that boards in venture capital-backed companies have fewer inside and instrumental directors — such as representatives of banks, lawyers, accountants and consultants — and more independent outside directors.[388] They show that venture capital managers replace inside and instrumental directors in the boards.[389] The study by ROSENSTEIN ET AL. indicates that in the USA, portfolio companies have relatively great shares in boards, particularly the most experienced and successful investors. In more than half of all portfolio companies, they held the majority of seats.[390] This refers to the first way venture capitalists increase boards' independence.

The empirical findings of GABRIELSSON/HUSE refer to the second possibility. They show that the influence of venture capitalists results in more independent boards. The ratio of outsiders on the board is higher and CEO duality is less common, which decreases the power of insiders on the board.[391] This is also backed by the analysis of FILATOTCHEV ET AL. who provide evidence that venture capital-backed companies that go public — and in this case in particular companies with several venture

385 Rosenstein et al, (1993), p. 104; Markman et al. (2001), pp. 281ff.
386 Van den Berghe/Levrau (2002), p. 128.
387 He/Conyon (2004), p. 50.
388 Baker/Gompers (2003), p. 581ff.
389 Baker/Gompers (2003), p. 584.
390 Rosenstein et al. (1990), pp. 240ff.
391 Garbielsson/Huse (2001), pp.134ff.

capitalists in a syndicate — have more independent boards than those without an investment from a venture capitalist.[392]

An indirect way in which venture capitalists impact the structure of the board is by reducing the power of the founders who might have an interest in placing family members, friends or acquaintances on boards. DAILY/DALTON prove empirically that boards in companies where the CEO is not the founder — and this is more likely in the case of venture capital-backed companies as has been shown before — have a significantly higher proportion of outsiders, which indicates a higher independence.[393] BOURESLI ET AL. found in their empirical analysis that the percentage of insiders is significantly smaller in venture capital-backed companies than in non-venture-capital-backed companies, both before and after an IPO.[394]

In the case of small firms, which are typical for venture capital-backed companies, strengthening independence might be of particular importance. This is because small firms typically have small boards made up of the owner manager and family members, sometimes augmented with bankers, attorneys, or friends. The resulting limited influence of outsiders gives the managers of the companies great influence.[395]

Empirical evidence for the value effects of independent boards comes, for example,[396] from HUSON ET AL. who show a positive correlation between the share of independent board members and forced manager turnover.[397] This indicates that independence strengthens the monitoring function of boards. Moreover, it is shown that CEO-duality can reduce board influence by facilitating the CEO's control of both the agenda and the debate in board meetings.[398] JUDGE/ZEITHAML also found a relation between board independence and performance. Their analysis indicates that there is a negative relation between insiders on boards and financial performance.[399] Further empirical support for the particular case of growth companies comes from DAILY/ DALTON who indicate a significant positive relationship between the number and proportion of outsiders on the boards of growth companies and firm performance mea-

---

392 Filototchev et al. (2005), p. 20.

393 Dailey/Dalton (1992), p. 380.

394 Bourseli et al. (2004), pp. 77ff.

395 Rosenstein (1988), p. 161; in the German two-board system, the owner-manager is not member of the supervisory board but as an owner he/she can determine representatives.

396 For further empirical support refer to Rechner/Dalton (1990), pp. 155ff.; Boyd (1995), pp. 301ff.

397 Huson et al. (2001), pp. 2289ff.

398 Sapienza et al. (2000), p. 334; Finkelstein/D'Aveni (1994), pp. 1093ff.

399 Judge/Zeitlhaml (1992), p. 782.

sured by return on equity and return on assets. They explain this as stronger control of the managers.[400] ROSENSTEIN/WYATT use a different approach to support this: they show positive share-price effects of appointments of outside board members.[401]

In contrast to this, some scholars dispute the purported positive effects of outsiders on boards. They suggest that these board members lack the expertise and requisite time to effectively exercise their role.[402] It is argued, for example, that outside members of boards do not have current or past professional or personal associations with the firm, which are necessary to evaluate the firm's situation.[403]

Following agency theory and the greatest part of the empirical studies,[404] it can be expected that the influence of venture capitalists leads to more independent boards, which is considered to have positive effects on the value of growth companies.

H2.4.1: The stronger the venture capitalists' influence, the greater is the proportion of independent members in the board.

Given the different arguments regarding the independence of boards, ZAHRA/PEARCE suggest that the effectiveness of boards is not a question of insiders versus outsiders but is rather a question of the characteristics of the members, in particular their **qualification**.[405] Better-qualified board members can better assess and assist firms and might therefore lead to higher performance for the firm.[406] A board could be ineffective because its members are unable to evaluate the information given to them, to recognise the problems of a firm or to punish the managers. This problem is particularly relevant in growth companies, where good information is often missing and performance is difficult to measure.[407] According to the dynamic resource-based view, the qualification of board members should have a great influence on the effectiveness of the board. The more qualified the members are, the better the decision making process should be. Portfolio companies have typically small management teams with limited experience, which requires involving people who can make up for

---

400 Daily/Dalton (1992), pp. 380ff.
401 Rosenstein/Wyatt (1990), pp. 184ff.
402 Zahra/Pearce (1989), p. 315; Westphal (1999), pp. 7ff.
403 Zahra et al. (2000), p. 954; Johnson et al. (1993), pp. 35ff.
404 Zahra/Pearce (1989), p. 316.
405 Zahra/Pearce, p. 316; for an overview of important qualifications of board members, refer to Nicholson/Kiel (2004), p. 450.
406 Dimov/Shepherd (2005), pp. 2ff.
407 Jensen (1986), pp. 323ff.; Audretsch/Lehman (2002), p. 16.

their deficits. The board members could contribute to this if they complement and strengthen the knowledge, experiences and capabilities of the management team. Consequently, having board members with experiences in different areas to complement the managers is considered good corporate governance because it contributes to informed decision making.[408] Venture capitalists should have gained specific knowledge and experience about the business development of growth companies from their numerous investments, so they should be particularly capable to serve in boards.[409] They are likely to have a comparative advantage over other equity investors in monitoring managers of growth companies. Furthermore, they might know what important functions are missing in the management team of a company and might have access to people who could fill this gap by being a member of the company's board.[410]

AUDRETSCH/LEHMANN provide empirical evidence that the qualification of board members is highly important for the performance of growth companies. They show with a sample from the German Neuer Markt that the level of human capital in the supervisory board dwarfs the role of managerial ownership in influencing firm performance measured by the survival of firms.[411] This supports that high qualification of board members strengthens the corporate governance of a company and enhances the performance of a company.

ROSENSTEIN ET AL. empirically support the particular abilities of venture capitalists as board members. According to their study, the involvement of venture capitalists' representatives on boards is considered by the CEOs of portfolio companies to be more valuable than that of other outside board members, particularly if the venture capitalists belong to the "top 20 investors".[412] Venture capitalists also focus on the overall qualification of the board. They expect boards as a whole to be diversified so that roles are diversified and complement the management team.[413] In order to achieve the required independence and qualification of the board, venture capitalists help find suitable board members within their networks.[414] They pay

---

408 Hillman et al. (2000), pp. 239ff.; social ties of board members are a further important resource, for more information refer to Carpenter/Westphal (2001), pp. 639ff.

409 Berg/Gottschalg (2003), p. 30.

410 Hellmann/Puri (2002), pp. 176ff.

411 Audretsch/Lehmann (2002), pp. 25ff.

412 Rosenstein et al. (1990), p. 244.

413 Van den Berghe/Levrau (2002), p. 131.

414 Ruppen (2001), pp. 171ff.

attention to the diversification of the roles of the board members so that they complement the managers.[415]

According to the theoretical explanation and the empirical findings, it can be assumed that the venture capitalists' influence leads to better-qualified boards in regard to its members' experiences.

H2.4.2: The stronger the venture capitalists' influence, the stronger are the experiences of the board.

The third aspect of the structure of the board is its **size**. Beyond a small number, board size is likely to have a negative relationship with board involvement and effectiveness. As groups get larger, interaction between group members diminishes. Thus when boards get too large effective debate and discussion may be limited and the level of board involvement may decrease.[416] DALTON ET AL. found that this relation between board size and firm performance is stronger for small companies than for larger ones.[417]

Venture capitalists' might increase the size of their boards by introducing additional members. It is shown that boards in venture capital-backed companies are bigger than in non-venture-capital-backed companies.[418] But such an increase must probably be seen in relation to the absolute number because a negative effect of board size on its effectiveness should only be expected beyond a certain size. VAN DEN BERGHE/ LEVRAU suggest six members to be appropriate number of board members for venture capital-backed companies.[419] Empirical studies show that this corresponds to the majority of companies despite the expansion of the boards at the time of the investment by a venture capitalist.[420] Consequently, the size aspect can be considered to be of no particular concern in venture capital-backed companies. Venture capitalists might recognise the advantages of small boards and might therefore not increase their size too much.

---

415 Van den Berghe/Levrau (2002), p. 131.

416 March/Simon (1958); Harrison (1987), pp. 109ff; Sapienza et al. (2000), p.333; Pfeffer (1972), pp. 218ff.; Yermack (1996), pp. 189ff.; Dalton et al. (1999), pp. 674ff.

417 Dalton et al (1999), pp. 674ff.; Daily et al (2002), p. 388.

418 Garbielsson/Huse /2001), pp.134ff.

419 Van den Berghe/Levrau (2002), p. 131.

420 Rosenstein (1993), p. 104; the mean size of venture capital–backed boards in the USA was 5,62, compared to 4,81 for non-venture-capital-backed companies.

4.2.2.2 Work

The analysis of the boards' work refers to two aspects, the formal attributes and the level of involvement. On one hand, the effectiveness of the board's work is determined by attributes such as frequency, preparation and formality of board meetings. On the other hand, the areas that are dealt with and the assigned role of the board are also relevant when the quality of the board's work is assessed, particularly involvement in strategic decision making.[421]

It is expected that the venture capitalists recognise the importance of the boards' work and influence it accordingly.

H2.5: The venture capitalists' influence has a positive impact on the work of the board.

The effectiveness of board meetings is essential to fulfil the demanding role of boards. **Formality** can add to the effectiveness of board meetings. The close monitoring that agency theory considers necessary could be realised through frequent and well-prepared board meetings. Board meetings must take place regularly and promptly so the members can fulfil the monitoring role efficiently. Moreover, the decisions by the board should be based on comprehensive information. This might require having the information before the board meeting in order to prepare.[422] Consequently, good corporate governance in this context requires frequent board meetings that are well prepared. Venture capitalists, as blockholders, should be able to influence the formality of board meetings either at the time of contracting or after the decision through their membership on the board or their decision rights in the shareholder meetings.

ANDERSSON/GUNNARSSON undertook an analysis in Sweden and found that venture capitalists changed the work of the board fundamentally. In one of the two researched cases, there were no formal board meetings before the venture capitalist invested in the company. The founders of the company discussed issues as they emerged. But after the investment of a venture capitalist, this changed as the board then met regularly to discuss operating and strategic issues.[423]

---

421 Ingley/Van der Walt (2005), pp. 632ff.
422 Zahra/Pearce (1989), p. 310.
423 Andersson/Gunnarsson (1999) according to Gabrielsson/Huse (2002), pp. 139ff.

Consequently, it can be expected that the venture capitalists' influence increases the formality of board meetings. Venture capitalists' influence should lead to more frequent and better-prepared board meetings.

H2.5.1: The stronger the venture capitalists' influence, the more frequently board meetings take place.

H2.5.2: The stronger the venture capitalists' influence, the better prepared board meetings are.

Apart from that, the reach of boards is important. The **involvement** of boards in strategic decision making is seen as positive by both agency theory and the dynamic resource-based view. Whereas agency theory stresses its importance in the context of effective monitoring, the dynamic resource-based view focuses on the improvement of managerial resources that might lead to better decisions.[424]

Effective monitoring, which is required by agency theory, is only possible if the board is involved in all important management decisions. Therefore, the board should control the managers in all relevant areas.[425]

According to the dynamic resource-based view, corporate governance could lead to strategic advantages by improving the decision making processes in a company. In growth companies, which often have scarce human resources and limited qualifications in the management team, the involvement of qualified board members in the decision making process could make up for the limitations. Hence, the board should be actively involved in the strategic decision making process and advise the managers in all relevant areas.[426]

Consequently, good corporate governance is assumed to be in place if the board is involved in strategic decision making in all relevant areas of the company. Venture capitalists should understand the necessity for the board to be involved in the decision making process from their investment experience and should also be able to enforce this.

---

424 Hung (1998), pp. 104ff.
425 Sapienza et al. (2000), p. 337.
426 Zahra/Pearce (1989), Hung (1998), pp. 104ff.

Several empirical analyses look at these aspects. Generally, the proportion of outside board members has been found to be positively related to board involvement in strategic decision making.[427] And as was shown before, venture capitalists increase the number of outsiders on boards. JOHNSON ET AL. proved empirically that the hypothesis holds that board involvement grows with outsider members.[428] The findings of ROSENSTEIN ET AL. show the special role of venture capitalists. They found that there is no indication that boards in small firms are generally involved in the strategy formulation of the firm, even if they include outsiders.[429] In contrast to this, boards in venture capital-backed companies are highly involved in strategic decision making. This constructive role of the venture capital-backed board is often appreciated by the managers.[430] Consequently, the venture capitalists' presence, which might generally be linked to a higher proportion of outside board members, should lead to a stronger board involvement in strategic decision making.

Qualitative analyses that might be particularly appropriate to evaluate board involvement support the positive effects of venture capitalists' influence. ANDERSSON/ GUNNARSON also found that the venture capitalists' board members improve the managerial resources of portfolio companies by bringing in managerial competence. This improvement of the resources was achieved by more managerial experience, the new role of the board as a sounding board and its activity to set strategic directions.[431] This is supported by the analysis by GUSTAFSSON that indicates that the representatives of venture capitalists on portfolio companies' boards are involved in both monitoring and support activities. This is achieved by discussing issues in detail during board meetings and by a close working relationship between the venture capitalists' board members and the managers. All the CEOs of the portfolio companies interviewed stated positive effects on their business after venture capitalists had been involved.[432] Another qualitative analysis was done by DEAKINS ET AL. for the United Kingdom. It reveals that venture capitalists change the work of boards. Whereas there is only a small improvement in the boards' involvement in strategic planning, there are greater effects on the outcome: 73% of the CEOs of venture capital-backed

427 Judge/Zeithaml (1992), p. 782; additionally, it was found that non-executive directors are more involved in strategic decision making in non-listed companies than in listed companies; for more information refer to Long et al. (2005), pp. 667ff.
428 Johnson et al. (1993), p. 43.
429 Rosenstein (1988), pp. 161ff.
430 Rosenstein (1988), pp. 165ff.
431 Andersson/Gunnarsson (1999) according to Gabrielsson/Huse (2002), pp. 139ff.
432 Gustafsson (1998) according to Gabrielsson/Huse (2002), p. 138.

companies stated that strategic planning was improved by the board involvement, whereas this was the case in only 50% of non-venture-capital-backed companies.[433]

FRIED ET AL. found comparable results in a quantitative analysis for the USA. Boards in venture capital-backed companies had a higher level of strategic involvement as well as a stronger involvement in the evaluation of the companies' strategy than boards in non-venture-capital-backed companies. They consider board members as consultants for the top management team within as well as between board meetings.[434] Additionally, they also indicate a positive influence on the companies' performance. Using performance in relation to the average performance of companies in an industry as a measure, they found that the sample with the venture capital-backed companies performs better than its counterpart.[435] This is supported by the findings of JUDGE/ZEITHAML that influence by the board in strategic decision making correlates to positive financial performance as measured by accounting indicators.[436]

FREDRIKSEN/KLOFSTEN analyse the performance effect of different types of boards in venture capital-backed companies. Among the three board types in place in companies with rather formal relationships between venture capitalists and the managers of the portfolio companies — in contrast to those companies with more informal relationships characterised by trust and openness — the ones with the highest activity, involvement in decision making and integrity of the members are associated with the highest economic performance.[437]

Given these theoretical and empirical findings, it can be expected that venture capitalists' influence increases the level of involvement of boards. This should be the case in particular for strategic decision making.

H2.5.3: The stronger the venture capitalists' influence, the more involved is the board in strategic decision making.

433 Deakin et al. (2000), p. 121.
434 Fried et al. (1998), p. 498.
435 Fried et al. (1998), p. 499.
436 Judge/Zeitlhaml (1992), pp. 782ff.
437 Fredriksen/Klofsten (1999), p. 6.

4.2.3 Reporting Discipline

Reporting information provides the basis for effective control of companies and is therefore essential for good corporate governance.[438] Agency problems can arise because of asymmetrical information between the managers and the shareholders of a company. To prevent these problems, agency theory proposes closely monitoring the development of the company and the decisions of the managers. But effective monitoring requires comprehensive information as a basis. Hence, the shareholders and the board members have to frequently and promptly receive relevant information in order to be able to intervene if needed.[439] Consequently, the frequent and prompt supply of relevant and accurate information to shareholders and board members is considered good corporate governance. The effectiveness and efficiency of the reporting discipline depends on one hand on formal attributes such as the frequency, timeliness and the content as well as on the accuracy of the reporting on the other hand.

The following hypothesis is based on the foundations laid before:

H2.6: The venture capitalists' influence has a positive impact on reporting discipline.

The **formal attributes** are a basic requirement to keep board members, shareholders and other stakeholders informed about the company's development. The reporting should be frequent and without a big delay so that the different parties can react promptly to the information provided. Furthermore, the information provided should be comprehensive; all important developments should be reported. Given their investment and business development experience, venture capitalists should realise the importance of reporting. As blockholders, they should have the rights to enforce effective reporting in their portfolio companies by means of adequate contractual provisions as well as during the investment phase.[440]

Empirical analyses show that venture capitalists use information from the financial statements at the time a portfolio company is selected[441] and also during the investment phase.[442] They have specific requirements of their portfolio companies' reporting: They generally demand a monthly report by their portfolio companies informing them about

---

438 Bushman/Smith (2001), p. 238; Sloan (2001), pp. 335ff.
439 Bushman/Smith (2001), p. 238; Falconer et al. (1995), pp. 187ff.
440 Falconer et al. (1995).
441 Macmillan et al. (1987), pp. 125ff.; Wright/Robbie (1998), pp. 533ff.
442 Falconer et al. (1995); Huber/Böhler (2003), pp. 1002ff.

the current business development and the achievement of the quantitative and qualitative targets.[443] The findings of FALCONER ET AL. provide evidence that the reporting information provided to venture capitalists is more comprehensive and more frequent than the information in the general shareholder reports. According to their study, the influence of venture capitalists increased the frequency of reporting considerably from a statutory annual or bi-annual report to monthly reports. The reports were additionally more detailed and often also included qualitative information on the performance of the company as well as information specifically required by the venture capitalists. In some cases, the reports had to be provided within a very strict time limit.[444] BEUSELINCK ET AL. found that venture capital-backed companies report losses more promptly than non-venture-capital-backed companies, which also indicates the venture capitalists' influence.[445]

Accordingly, it can be assumed that venture capitalists use their influence to improve the quality of this corporate governance element.

H2.6.1: The stronger the venture capitalists' influence, the more frequent is the portfolio company's reporting.

H2.6.2: The stronger the venture capitalists' influence, the more timely is the portfolio company's reporting.

H2.6.3: The stronger the venture capitalists' influence, the more comprehensive is the portfolio company's reporting.

The second important aspect of reporting is its **accuracy**. If stakeholders base decisions on the information provided, the information must be right. But accounting information can be used at specific dates to mislead potential investors or to influence contract terms.[446] Their close monitoring and control rights should give venture capitalists the ability to recognise problems with the accuracy of the reporting and also the power to enforce changes.[447]

There are two empirical studies that support the idea that venture capitalists' influence results in improved reporting discipline. First, BEUSELINCK carried out an analysis

443 Ruppen (2001), p. 161.
444 Falconer et al. (1995), pp. 190ff.
445 Beuselinck et al. (2004), p. 24.
446 Refer to Healy/Wahlen (1999) for a literature overview.

in Belgium. It indicates that venture capitalists influence the corporate governance of their portfolio companies and thereby reduce their discretional accruals. This is particularly relevant as the same study also found that companies that receive venture capital have higher discretionary accruals in their results than companies that do not.[448] HOCHBERG found similar results in her American research that looked at companies at the time of IPO. She found that venture capital-backed firms have lower earnings management, measured by their discretionary accruals, than similar companies not backed by a venture capitalist.[449]

These findings lead to the next hypothesis:

H2.6.4: The stronger the venture capitalists' influence, the more accurate is the portfolio company's reporting.

The following figure illustrates the expected relationship between the venture capitalists' influence and the impact on corporate governance in an overview.

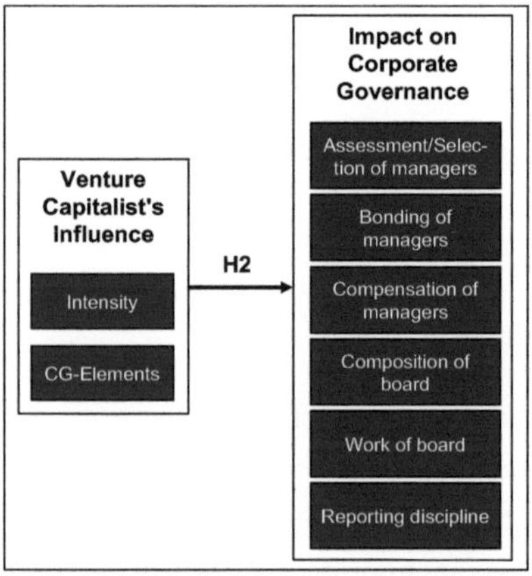

Figure 13: Relationship between venture capitalists' influence and corporate governance

447 Falconer et al. (1995), p. 193.
448 Beuselinck et al. (2004), p. 21.
449 Hochberg (2002), pp. 7ff.

4.3 Abilities of Venture Capitalists To Influence Corporate Governance

According to earlier findings, venture capitalists' impact on the corporate governance of portfolio companies is determined not only by their reasons for the influence but also by their abilities. Following the literature review, the abilities can be distinguished in the control rights and the characteristics of the venture capitalists, i.e., the characteristics of the venture-capital firm on one hand and of the investment manager on the other hand. This section details the relationship between venture capitalists' abilities and their impact on corporate governance.[450]

4.3.1 Control Rights

The venture capitalists' control rights significantly determine their impact on the corporate governance of portfolio companies. If the venture capitalists are willing to influence the corporate governance, they must also have the rights to enforce their points. The control rights enable them to effectively influence portfolio companies.

To begin with, the general hypothesis related to this section is:

H3: The abilities of venture capitalists have an impact on the corporate governance of portfolio companies.

Generally, the level of ownership of a venture capitalist determines the importance of the investor for the portfolio company as well as the importance of that investment for the venture capitalist. But in the case of venture capital, ownership must be differentiated from decision rights because they can differ. Particularly in the influence of venture capitalists on portfolio companies, the decision rights might be more important than the ownership rights. This is because the venture capitalists' decision rights might be greater than their ownership rights. This can be reached by introducing unvested stock options, non-voting stock or explicit covenants that authorise the investor to exercise votes depending on specific targets.[451] These instruments give venture capitalists control rights but grant the managers sufficient ownership in the company to give them incentives to develop the company to increase the value of their shares.

---

450 It should be noted that the impact depends not only on the venture capitalists and their rights but also on characteristics of the management teams of the portfolio companies; for more information refer to Barney et al. (1996b).

451 Van den Berghe/Levrau (2002), p. 127.

Consequently, the control rights of venture capitalists are determined by the levels of ownership and the decision rights. The decision rights include seats in the board as well as veto rights.

The ownership level of the venture capitalists strongly determines the ownership level — and thereby the demand for decision rights — of the managers of the company, who are generally inside investors. BOURSELI ET AL. show empirically that venture capital backing reduces managers' ownership significantly.[452]

In regard to decision rights, the board membership is an important instrument to influence corporate governance that is normally granted only to investors that possess a certain share in a company. According to the empirical analysis of RUPPEN, venture capitalists demand a seat with an ownership share of 17,8%.[453] This supports the finding by BAKER/GOMPERS that a threshold ownership level is more important for venture capitalists than high ownership per se.[454]

According to the empirical analysis for the USA undertaken by KAPLAN/STRÖMBERG, venture capitalists have the majority of board seats in 25% of the analysed cases, whereas the founders dominate the one-tier-system boards in only 14% of the cases. Whereas after the first financing round, control by venture capitalists is less common, it tends to have the majority of votes thereafter. However, in most cases the venture capitalists do not own the majority of the portfolio company's shares.[455] This indicates differences between ownership and decision rights. However, a German analysis by RUPPEN comes to partly different results. In Germany, the venture capitalists dominate the supervisory board only rarely. In about half of all cases they have a voting power of less than 25%, which points to lower control among German venture capitalists than among their US counterparts.[456]

Based on this, it can be expected that the control rights determined by ownership and decision rights are positively related to the venture capitalists' impact on the corporate governance of portfolio companies.

452 Bouresli et al. (2004), p. 80.
453 Ruppen (2001), pp. 52ff.
454 Baker/Gompers (2003), pp. 576ff.
455 Kaplan/Strömberg (2003), pp. 289ff.
456 Ruppen (2001), pp. 64ff.

H3.1: The control rights of venture capitalists have a positive impact on the corporate governance of portfolio companies.

H3.1.1: The stronger the venture capitalists' control right rights, — in terms of ownership rights and board seats — the stronger is their influence on the corporate governance of portfolio companies.

It can be expected that the control rights predominantly determine the corporate governance elements related to the monitoring and bonding functions of corporate governance. This is because these functions are mainly based on decisions made during the contracting phase or in board or shareholder meetings where the control rights are decisive. Venture capitalists can use their control rights, for example, to accomplish their goals in the contracting phase and to introduce requirements for the managers. This can be done by means of the shareholder agreement or by changing the articles of association. Venture capitalists might ask for a number of board seats, for regular reporting or for changes in the board composition. Such negotiations are not limited to the first investment by a venture capitalist but can also be done at later financing rounds. Thus, venture capitalists can enforce their requirements when they have gained further control rights. Additionally, they can use their board seats to exert influence on corporate governance. The board has far-reaching rights related to corporate governance that include, for example, the selection, evaluation and compensation of the managers as well as the reporting of the company. Consequently, it can be expected that venture capitalists' control rights should determine their impact on the elements related to the monitoring and bonding functions of corporate governance.

H3.1.2: The stronger the venture capitalists' control rights, the greater is the impact of their influence on the elements related to the monitoring function of corporate governance.

H3.1.3: The stronger the venture capitalists' control rights, the greater is the impact of their influence on the elements related to the bonding function of corporate governance.

4.3.2 Characteristics of Venture Capitalists

Characteristics of venture capitalists might have an impact on their influence on the corporate governance of portfolio companies. This might be related either to characteristics of the venture capital firms or to those of the specific investment manager. This relationship corresponds to the dynamic resource-based view that traces differences in outcomes back to different resource endowments. Hence, different venture capitalists might have different resources in regard to experience, capabilities and time that might influence the effects of their influence on the corporate governance of portfolio companies.

4.3.2.1 Characteristics of Venture Capital Firms

Venture capital firms differ in various characteristics that might lead to different goals and different patterns of influence on portfolio companies' corporate governance. In particular, four characteristics of venture capital firms are considered to determine their involvement. It is expected that these characteristics influence the impact of the venture capitalists.

H3.2: The characteristics of venture capital firms have a positive impact on the corporate governance of portfolio companies.

First, the **type of venture capital firm** determines its strategy and operations. Following the approach of TYKVOVA, four types of venture capital investors are distinguished according to their own governance structure: independent, bank dependent, corporate and governmental. The results indicate significant differences in their investment behaviour, in the level of syndication, preferred stages, equity positions, time to IPO and retained equity positions after IPO.[457] The differing investment patterns predict differences in the influence of the venture capital firm types on the corporate governance of their portfolio companies.[458] This is supported by BEUSELINCK ET AL. who compare the influence of independent and governmental venture capitalists in regard to their influence on the reporting discipline of their portfolio companies. They find support for the hypothesis that independent venture capital firms have stronger effects on reporting discipline because they reduce earnings management more strongly than public investors.[459] They explain this difference as result of specific characteristics of the investors, in particular the capabilities, goals and investment patterns. Investment managers of governmental venture capital firms are often civil servants who lack experience as well as incentives to effectively influ-

457 Tykvova (2004), pp. 7ff.

458 For differences in the involvement on corporate governance by informal and formal venture capitalists that are not examined here, refer to Whincop (2000), pp. 13ff.; Von Osnabrugge (1999); Sapienza et al. (1996), p. 462.

459 Beuselinck et al. (2004), pp. 10 and 24.

ence the corporate governance of the portfolio companies.[460] They are under less pressure to quickly generate financial returns because they might have different goals and they do not have to raise money from the capital markets. Public venture capital firms might have social rather than financial goals.[461]

Corporate venture capital firms' primary motivation is generally the realization of strategic goals. To achieve this, they foster interaction between portfolio companies and the big corporation. Often, the investment managers are former employees of the corporation and have more knowledge in the specific industry than in the venture capital industry.[462] Hence, corporate venture capital firms are more focussed on strategic issues and less on value generation in the portfolio companies. Additionally, they might lack the experience required to improve corporate governance.

Bank-related venture capital firms also have strategic goals rather than value creation in the portfolio companies. They invest selectively in comparatively small stakes to build relationships with portfolio companies that could become customers of the banks. According to the empirical analysis by HELLMANN ET AL., they lack the required skills and incentives for value creation in portfolio companies.[463] Therefore, their impact on the corporate governance of portfolio companies can be expected to be less strong than the impact of independent venture capital firms.

Consequently, the type of venture capital firms can be expected to influence its strategy and operation and hence also its influence on the portfolio companies' corporate governance. More precisely, it can be expected that independent venture capitalists have a stronger focus on financial issues and value creation, which should lead to a stronger focus on corporate governance compared with corporate, bank-related and governmental venture capital firms.

H3.2.1: Independent venture capital firms' influence has a greater impact on the corporate governance of portfolio companies than that of corporate venture capitalists and bank-related and governmental venture capitalists.

---

460 Leleux/Surlemont (2003), pp.82ff.; Manigart et al. (2002), p. 291 ff.;Beuselinck et al. (2004), p. 10.

461 Lerner (1999), pp. 285ff.; Beuselinck et al. (2004), p. 10.

462 Winters/Murfin (1988); Sykes/Block (1989), pp. 160ff.; Sykes (1990), Sykes (1992); Witt/Brachtendorf (2002).

463 Hellmann/Lindsay/Puri (2004).

Second, **investment experience** might have an influence on the impact of the venture capital firms as well. Abilities can be increased by accumulating experiences over time. The information and skills of a venture capital firm should increase with experience in their industry.[464] Venture capital firms might learn from earlier investments and use that experience to improve future behaviour regarding influence on portfolio companies so that the number of a venture capitalist's investments should have an impact on the effects of its influence.

H3.2.2: The more investment experience a venture capital firm has, the greater are the effects of its influence on the corporate governance of portfolio companies.

Apart from general investment experience, **international experience** might also play a role. International activity can increase a venture capital firm's capabilities in influencing portfolio companies.[465] This might be particularly important in regard to corporate governance because corporate governance systems differ greatly by country[466] so that investing on an international level might provide venture capital firms with insights in best practices from other countries, which might positively impact the effects of the venture capitalists' influence.

H3.2.3: The greater the international experience of the venture capital firms, the greater are the effects of their influence on the corporate governance of portfolio companies.

Another characteristic is the **reputation** of venture capital firms. Venture capital firms with great reputation might be, on one hand, more attractive for portfolio companies because they might send a positive signal to other stakeholders. In order to get the support of reputable venture capitalists, management might have to give their opinion high importance.[467] On the other hand, it might be that those venture capitalists possess a greater assertiveness because their advice is considered more valuable by management.[468] BAKER/GOMPERS show empirically that venture capital firms with better reputations have more board seats in their portfolio companies than those with worse reputations.[469] Hence, it can be expected that the reputation and experience of venture

464 Sapienza et al. (1996), p. 446.
465 Van den Berghe/Levrau (2002), p. 128.
466 Denis/McConell (2003), pp. 1 ff.
467 C.f. Hsu (2004), pp. 1805ff.
468 Baker/Gompers (2003), pp. 589ff.
469 Baker/Gompers (2003), pp. 589ff.

capital firms determine the extent of their influence on portfolio companies' corporate governance.

H3.2.4: The greater the reputation of a venture capital firm, the greater are the effects of its influence on the corporate governance of portfolio companies.

4.3.2.2 Characteristics of Investment Managers

The influence of venture capitalists on portfolio companies' corporate governance is not only determined by the characteristics of the venture capital firms but also by those of the investment managers. This relates, on one hand, to the experiences and capabilities that they possess and, on the other hand, to their commitment.[470]

The influence of investment managers depends on their experiences and capabilities.[471] According to the study by DIMOV/SHEPHERD, there is a relation between the human capital of the investment managers and the performance of their portfolio companies. This is because the assistance of the investment managers influences the success of the portfolio companies.[472] In the case of board members, normally only senior people represent venture capitalists.[473] Nevertheless, their experiences and capabilities might still differ greatly. Consequently, it is expected that the characteristics of investment managers have an impact on the effects of venture capitalists on the corporate governance of portfolio companies.

H3.3: The characteristics of investment managers have a positive impact on the corporate governance of portfolio companies.

Parallel to the explanations for venture capital firms, investment managers can also increase their abilities by accumulating **investment experience**.[474] The specific knowledge and understanding that investment managers acquire over time might guide them to assess the requirements of portfolio companies and to better adjust the influence on corporate governance. However, there might be a specific point at which further gains in experience no longer lead to an increase in performance of the managers.[475] Nonetheless, it is expected that investment managers' experience in the venture capital

---

470 Adner/Helfat (2003), p. 1020.
471 Dotzler (2001), pp. 6ff.
472 Dimov/Shepherd (2005), pp. 3ff.
473 Rosenstein (1993), p. 104; Gorman/Sahlman (1978), p. 234.
474 Carpenter et al. (2003), pp. 812ff.
475 Dimov/Shepherd (2005), p. 5; Shepherd et al. (2003), pp. 383ff.

industry has an impact on their influence on the corporate governance of portfolio companies.

H3.3.1: The greater the investment manager's experience in the venture capital industry, the greater is the impact of his/her influence on the corporate governance of portfolio companies.

Furthermore, the **industry experience** of investment managers might also have an effect on his/her impact on corporate governance. The assertiveness of the propositions by investment managers might be stronger if other shareholders highly value their knowledge and experience. This might be the case — particularly from the perspective of the portfolio companies' managers[476] — if investment managers bring experience in the portfolio companies' industries. Additionally, industry experience might also strengthen the investment managers' abilities to assess portfolio companies' situations and needs, which could have a positive impact on their influence on corporate governance.

H3.3.2: The greater the investment managers' experience in the portfolio company's industry, the greater is the impact of their influence on the corporate governance of portfolio companies.

Similarly, this might be true for the investment managers' **international experience**. The explanation for the expected relationship between international experience and impact on corporate governance given for venture capital firms also holds for investment managers. CARPENTER ET AL. analysed the influence of the experiences of venture capitalists' representatives on the portfolio companies' boards on the companies' willingness to take risk. This was done in the context that investment managers often also serve as board members in portfolio companies. Risk-averse managers might not maximise the companies' value because they do not realise all risky but cashflow-positive project opportunities.[477] The authors take the example of internationalisation of firms — which might be risky but could support value maximisation — and found a significant relationship between the international experience of the venture capitalists' board members and the internationality of portfolio companies.[478] Similarly, their international experience might have an impact on the

476 Van den Berghe/Levrau (2002), p. 131.
477 Jackson/Dutton (1988) describe this as a "threat bias" of managers.
478 Carpenter et al. (2003), p. 812.

investment managers' influence on portfolio companies' corporate governance, in particular because of the great international differences in this field.[479]

H3.3.3: The greater the investment managers' international experience in the venture capital industry, the greater is the impact of their influence on the corporate governance of portfolio companies.

Another factor that might support the acceptance of investment managers' propositions by managers and other shareholders as well as investment managers' capacity to better adapt their influence might be their **start-up experience**. DIMOV/SHEPHERD empirically analysed the effect of investment manager start-up experience on the success of their investments and found marginal support for this.[480] This indicates that previous start-up experience might be a valuable resource for investment managers when supporting and controlling portfolio companies and might also be relevant for influencing corporate governance.

H3.3.4: The greater the investment managers' start-up experience, the greater is the impact of their influence on the corporate governance of portfolio companies.

Apart from the experiences and capabilities of investment managers, their **commitment** might also be of importance for their impact on the corporate governance of portfolio companies. First, the more time they invest, the better they might understand portfolio companies, which should add to their ability to effectively influence portfolio companies. Second, the commitment of the investment managers might also increase the acceptance of his/her proposals among the other shareholders and the portfolio companies' managers.[481] The commitment of the investment managers is determined by their time availability and willingness. The time availability depends mainly on the number of investments a manager has to look after. There are national differences to this, as RUPPEN shows in his empirical analysis. He found that the number of board seats of one investment manager in the USA and in the UK is comparatively higher than in Germany: 5 and 5,5, respectively, compared to 4.[482] This indicates that there might be differences in the time availability of investment managers, which could affect their impact on portfolio companies, also in regard to

479 Weimer/Pape (1999), pp. 152ff.
480 Dimov/Shepherd (2005), p. 14.
481 Ruppen (2001), pp. 54ff.; Sapienza (1992), pp. 15ff.
482 Ruppen (2001), pp. 54ff.

corporate governance. The willingness of investment managers to influence portfolio companies is another factor determined by the relationship between them and the managers of the portfolio companies. An empirical analysis indicates that the time spent monitoring and consulting with a portfolio company depends strongly on the personal fit between the investment managers and the managers of the portfolio company.[483] Based on this, it is expected that the influence of the venture capitalists is also determined by the commitment of the investment managers.

H3.3.5: The greater the commitment of the investment managers, the greater is the impact of their influence on the corporate governance of portfolio companies.

4.3.3 Trust

The extent of the influence on the advice function of corporate governance also depends on mutual trust between the venture capitalists and the managers of the portfolio companies.[484] The advice of the venture capitalists can hardly be enacted against the will of the managers. The interaction between the venture capitalists and the managers in non-routine issues might be much facilitated if a relation of trust and openness exists.[485] The opinion of the venture capitalists might be more relevant for the managers if they trust them. Accordingly, it can be assumed that the impact of venture capitalists' influence increases if the relationship between venture capitalists and managers is trustful.

H3.4: The impact of venture capitalists' influence is greater if their relationship with the managers of portfolio companies is trustful.

The introduced hypotheses on the relation between a venture capitalist's abilities and its expected impact on the corporate governance of portfolio companies are summarised in Figure 14 before considering the impact of the resulting corporate governance quality on firm value, which is analysed next.

483 Van den Berghe/Levrau (2002), p. 131.
484 Sweeting/Wong (1997), pp. 141 ff; c.f. Bassen (2002a), pp. 246ff.
485 Hatherly et al. (1994).

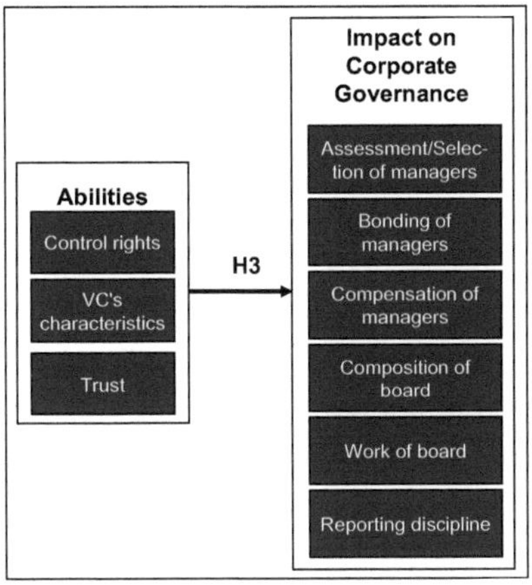

Figure 14: Relationship between venture capitalists' abilities and impact on corporate governance

4.4 Effects of Corporate Governance on Firm Value

Both underlying theoretical perspectives explain the effects of good corporate governance on firm value, although in different ways. In the following, the two explanations are briefly recapitulated.[486]

4.4.1 Theoretical Explanation

According to agency theory, effective and efficient corporate governance should reduce agency costs that arise from diverging interests between investors and managers. The costs, which include expenditures of the investors to bond and monitor the managers as well as some residual losses, should be minimised with optimal corporate governance arrangements.[487] Accordingly, the costs incur at the level of the investor (bonding and monitoring expenditure) as well as at the level of the firm (residual losses). Corporate governance might reduce the residual losses by reducing the costs of consumption on the job and by carrying out cashflow-positive but risky projects that would not have been realised by the managers without monitoring and bonding by the investors.[488] This should result in higher profitability and stronger growth, thus increasing fundamental performance. Additionally, companies with low agency risks due to good corporate governance should also be more attractive for

486 Refer to chapter 3.1.2 and 3.2.2 for more detailed explanations.

487 Jensen/Meckling (1976), pp. 308ff.; Shleifer/Vishny (1997), pp. 740ff.

488 Core (2004), p. 17; Ruppen (2001), p. 17; Schmidt (2001), p. 65.

investors. This is because of the prospects of better future performance but also because of the expectations of lower costs for future measures to reduce agency risk. Therefore, investors should value companies with good corporate governance comparatively highly and should be willing to pay a corresponding premium.[489]

In contrast to this, the dynamic resource-based view does not directly ascribe the effects of corporate governance on value to a reduction in costs but to better competitiveness because of better decision making. Good corporate governance should, according to this view, lead to informed decision making which could be a valuable resource, in particular for growth companies with a high degree of internal and external dynamic.[490] Better management and control of a company due to the involvement of experienced and capable stakeholders such as shareholders and board members should lead to better-informed decisions that could lead to better decisions and a better positioning in the competition. The resulting competitive advantage of a company with good corporate governance should on one hand increase the performance — higher profitability and stronger growth — and on the other hand increase the attractiveness for investors and thereby the valuation of a company.[491]

Consequently, according to both perspectives, good corporate governance should lead to comparatively high firm value.[492] In the following, the empirical findings on the value creation of good corporate governance are presented in detail. The existing research is divided according to the measure for value: The results for the relationship between corporate governance and fundamental performance — in particular profitability and growth — are described first, followed by the results that relate corporate governance and firm valuation.[493]

4.4.2 Fundamental Performance

Before considering the specific findings, it can be expected that corporate governance quality affects the fundamental performance of portfolio companies.

---

489 Dahlquist et al. (2002), pp. 3ff.

490 Eisenhardt/Martin, pp. 1106ff.

491 Barney et al. (2001), pp. 632ff.; Lockett/Thompson (2001), p. 744; Castanias/Helfat (1991), p. 169; Barney (1991), p. 100ff.; Combs/Ketchen (1999), p. 869.

492 Firm value considered in the financial perspective is influenced by the performance of a company and its valuation by investors.

493 For a literature overview of the performance effects of corporate governance refer to Coles et al. (2001), pp. 23ff.

H4.1: The corporate governance quality of a company has positive effects on its fundamental performance.

4.4.2.1 Profitability

Profitability can be measured with different variables depending on the returns and expenditures are taken into account. In the existing studies, the following four measures were used primarily to test a relationship between corporate governance and profitability: return on equity, return on assets, net profit margin and earnings before interest, depreciation and amortisation (EBITDA).

Return on equity: Many studies take return on equity into account because it is a key measure for investors to evaluate the success of an investment. Return on equity is calculated by dividing the earnings available for common stockholders by the average equity of a company.[494] The results are mixed, though.

BROWN/CAYLOR found in their analyses that firms with weak corporate governance have a lower return on equity than those with good corporate governance: On one hand, return on equity of firms in the decile with the worst corporate governance quality — measured by the Corporate Governance Quotient developed by Institutional Shareholder Services — are 4.86% below the industry average. On the other hand, firms in the decile with the best corporate governance generate a mean return on equity that is 18.98% higher than the industry average.[495] An analysis for the United Kingdom done by Deutsche Bank supports these findings: The 20% of the companies in the sample with the highest corporate governance quality generated an average return on equity of 15,9% in 2002, whereas the 20% of companies with the lowest corporate governance quality had only a return on equity of 1,5%.[496] Similar results also come from DROBETZ ET AL.[497] who researched the relationship in Germany. They found a significant positive relationship between corporate governance quality measured with a Corporate Governance Rating and the return on equity of the analysed companies.[498]

494 Brealey/Myers (2000), p. 829.
495 Borwn/Caylor (2004), pp. 5ff.
496 Deutsche Bank (2004), p. 43.
497 Dynamic analysis of 91 German companies listed in the stock exchange segments DAX 30, MDAX, NEMAX and SDAX, January 1998 to March 2002; corporate governance quality measured with Corporate Governance Index with 30 criteria; for more information on the methodology see Drobetz et al. (2003), pp. 8ff.
498 Drobetz et al. (2003), pp. 23ff.; the authors interpret ROE here in the investors' perspective as expected return on investment and therefore hypothesised a negative correlation between corporate governance quality and ROE.

Apart from the results from these developed countries, there is also evidence for a positive relationship in developing countries. The study done by AMAR for 15 emerging markets indicates that the return on equity of companies with good corporate governance is about ten points higher than the average. The positive correlation between corporate governance and return on equity holds for 13 of the 15 markets.[499]

In contrast to these results, the study by GOMPERS ET AL., which received great attention, could not prove a significant relationship between companies with strong shareholder rights — which corresponds to good corporate governance — and return on equity. The analysed correlation was positive but not significantly so.[500] BAUER ET AL., who did the same analysis for Europe, could not find a positive relationship between corporate governance and return on equity either: For both the UK and the European Monetary Union samples, they did not find any significant relationship, positive or negative.[501]

Consequently, at odds with the theory, there is no clear empirical evidence of a positive effect of good corporate governance on the return on equity of companies.

Return on assets: Measuring the performance of companies with return on assets as an independent variable implies the perspective of all capital providers, i.e., investors and creditors. It is calculated by dividing the earnings before interest by the average total assets.[502] It consequently includes the income for both groups.

The worldwide analysis of KLAPPER/LOVE found that firms with weaker corporate governance have lower profits, which indicates that the positive relationship holds for well established as well as for emerging markets, which are generally considered to have more concentrated ownership and weaker legal environments.[503] Further support comes from ROWN/CAYLOR. Their analysis indicates that good corporate governance is related to high return on assets. The firms in the decile with the highest corporate governance quality have a mean return on assets that is 9,78 % higher than the industry average.[504] Similarly, CORE ET AL. found that weak corporate gover-

499 Amar (2001), p. 21.
500 Gompers et al. (2003), p. 129; in the study there is a negative correlation with the governance index but a low level in that index corresponds to great shareholder rights and good corporate governance.
501 Bauer et al. (2003), pp. 13ff.
502 Brealey/Myers (2000), p. 828.
503 Klapper/Love (2002), p. 22.
504 Brown/Caylor (2004), p. 10.

nance results in weak operating performance measured by return on assets.[505] This indicates that weak governance is costly for companies because it decreases operating performance.[506] Consequently, it can be assumed that good corporate governance is positively related to performance measured by return on assets. Additionally, DEUTSCHE BANK showed a positive relationship between corporate governance and return on assets. Here, the average difference between the 20% of companies with the highest and lowest corporate governance quality was 23,1% in 2002.[507]

In contrast to these studies, BEINER ET AL. found a significant but negative relationship between fulfilment of the corporate governance index and return on assets, which they could not explain conclusively.[508]

This overview of the existing studies shows that the greatest part of the analyses found evidence for a positive relationship between corporate governance and return on assets.

Net profit margin: The net profit margin is income divided by sales. It is calculated by dividing earnings before interest by sales.[509]

GOMPERS ET AL. found a significantly positive relationship between the net profit margin and the shareholder rights of companies. They document larger capital expenditure by weak governance firms and suggest that this might be due to over-investments of these companies that lead to poor performance.[510]

In contrast to this, BAUER ET AL. could not find a positive relationship between corporate governance and net profit margin: Their analysis showed no significant relationship for the UK sample and even a significantly negative relationship for the European Monetary Union. They consider the possible bias of accounting numbers to be an explanation for this: It might be that badly governed companies tend to report less conservative earnings statements.[511]

---

505 Core (2004), pp. 11ff.
506 Core (2004), p. 14.
507 Deutsche Bank (2004), p. 44.
508 Beiner et al. (2004), p. 33.
509 Brealey/Myers (2000), p. 828; Gompers et al. (2003), p. 129
510 Gompers et al. (2003), pp. 129ff.; Guay (2004), p. 12.
511 Bauer et al. (2003), pp. 13ff.

The little empirical evidence on the relationship between corporate governance quality and net profit margin is not giving a clear picture yet.

EBITDA margin: The EBITDA margin takes into account only operative expenditures. It is calculated by dividing earnings before interest, taxes, depreciation and amortisation by sales.[512]

Only one study analysed the correlation between corporate governance and this performance measure. DEUTSCHE BANK found for their UK sample a relationship between corporate governance and EBITDA margin. The average spread between the top 20% and the bottom 20% of companies in terms of corporate governance quality is 21%.[513] The study indicates that a positive relationship between corporate governance quality and the EBITDA margin might be proven empirically.

Given the theoretical evidence and the partial empirical evidence, it could be expected that companies with good corporate governance are more profitable than companies with poor corporate governance.

H4.1.1: The better the corporate governance quality of a company, the higher is its profitability.

4.4.2.2 Growth

Growth of a company can be measured with many different variables referring, for example, to sales, assets or employees.[514] However, the empirical findings are rather limited: only two studies took this dimension of firm value into consideration.

In their empirical analysis, GOMPERS ET AL. found a significantly positive relationship between shareholder rights and the sales growth of a company.[515] In contrast to this study, BEINER ET AL found a significant but negative relationship between the fulfilment of the corporate governance index and firm growth, for which they could not provide a conclusive explanation.[516]

---

512 Deutsche Bank (2004), p. 44.
513 Deutsche Bank (2004), p. 44.
514 Kock (2002), pp. 660ff.
515 Gompers et al. (2003), p. 129.
516 Beiner et al. (2004), p. 33.

Consequently, the theoretical indication of a positive relationship between corporate governance and firm growth has not been clearly proven by empirical studies. Nonetheless, it could be expected that the theory holds and that better corporate governance leads to stronger growth, directly by more cashflow-positive projects, and indirectly as a result of a better competitiveness.

H4.1.2: The better the corporate governance quality of a company, the higher is its growth.

4.4.3 Valuation

Several empirical analyses of the relationship between good corporate governance and firm valuation exist. They all use Tobin's Q as the variable measuring the market valuation of the book value of a company. It is calculated by dividing the market value of a company's assets by the estimated replacement cost.[517]

KLAPPER/LOVE analysed the relationship between corporate governance quality and Tobin's Q for 14 countries worldwide. They found an overall positive significant relationship and an even stronger relationship if the analysis was controlled for different countries. This indicates that it is rather the relative than the absolute level of corporate governance quality that is relevant. On average, an increase in the corporate governance index of one standard deviation results in an increase in Tobin's Q of about 23%.[518] This supports the results presented by GOMPERS ET AL. They showed in their analyses that in the 1990s, US firms with strong shareholder rights were valued significantly higher than those with weak shareholder rights.[519] Similar results are also proven for other regions: A positive relationship between corporate governance quality and Tobin's Q for Europe is shown by three studies. BAUER ET AL. showed differences between the correlation for the sample for the European Monetary Union and the UK. In the first, an increase in the Corporate Governance Quality — measured by their index with 300 criteria — led to an average increase in Tobin's Q of 0,14 %, compared to only 0,01 % for the latter sample.[520] These results are supported by the findings of DROBETZ ET AL. BEINER ET AL. show that firms with better corporate governance have a significantly higher firm valuation than those with bad corporate

517 Brealey/Myers (2000), p. 831.
518 Klapper/Love (2002), p. 21.
519 Gompers et al. (2003), p. 128.
520 Bauer et al. (2003), pp. 11ff.

governance. More specifically, an increase in their corporate governance codex — ranging from 1 to 100 — of one point leads to an increase of the company's market capitalization of its book asset value of about 8,52% on average.[521] These results are supported by the findings of DROBETZ ET AL. The study by BLACK ET AL. for Korea indicates that the positive relationship between corporate governance quality and firm valuation also holds for this Asian country: An increase of the corporate governance index — ranging from 0 to 100 — of 10 points leads to an increase in Tobin's of 0,064.[522] However, BASSEN ET AL. who used a sample of German companies and the German Corporate Governance Code as a basis for analysing the corporate governance quality could not find strong support for a positive relationship between good corporate governance and Tobin's Q.[523]

This overview shows that almost all studies proved the theoretically deducted relationship. Consequently, it can be expected that good corporate governance has an impact on firm valuation, and more precisely that it is recognised by investors and therefore leads to a higher firm valuation.

H4.2: The corporate governance quality of a company has positive effects on its fundamental performance.

H4.2.1: The better the corporate governance quality of a portfolio company, the higher is its valuation.

The expected relationship between corporate governance quality and the firm value of growth companies is illustrated in Figure 15. This concludes the theoretical analysis of the four aspects and provides a basis for the empirical analyses that are presented in the next chapter.

---

521 Beiner et al. (2004), pp. 29ff.
522 Black et al. (2003), p. 16.
523 Bassen et al. (2006a), pp. 375ff.

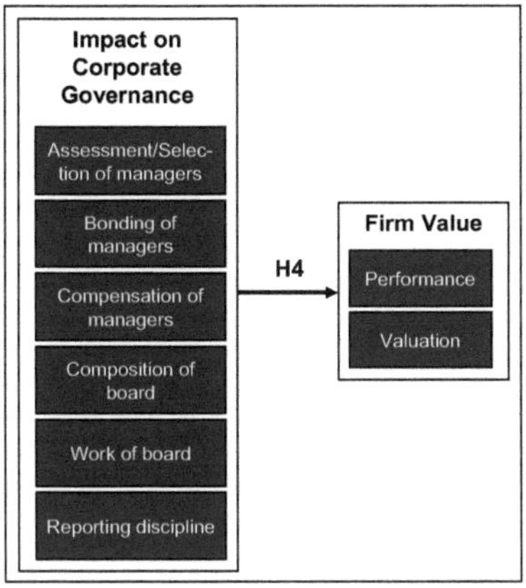

Figure 15: Relationship between impact on corporate governance and firm value

5 Empirical Analyses

This chapter presents the results of the empirical analysis of the theory-based hypotheses. First, the research concept is introduced to summarise the expected relationships between venture capital, corporate governance and firm value before the methods are described in detail. Then, the empirical results are presented, first for the qualitative analysis and then in more detail for the quantitative analysis.

5.1 Research Concept

The four most-important aspects of the relationships between venture capital and corporate governance were derived from the two research questions. With the two underlying theories, agency theory and the dynamic resource-based view, hypotheses were derived for those relationships in the last chapter. Figure 16 shows these relationships at the highest level in an overview.

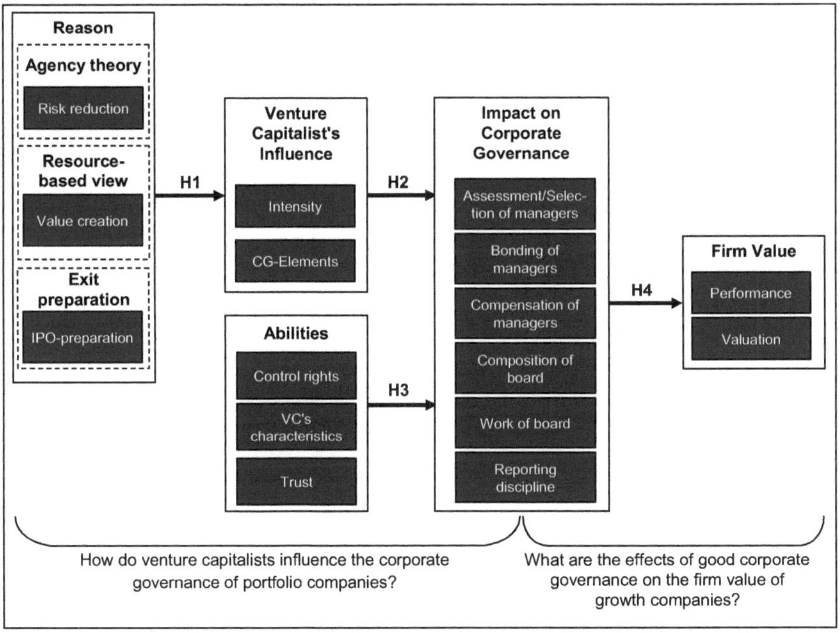

Figure 16: Research concept

In the following, the individual hypotheses are summarised and presented in an overview. The first hypotheses concern the reasons venture capitalists influence the corporate governance of portfolio companies. Agency theory predicts that the main reason for this is the associated business and agency risk of an investment that should be reduced by appropriate corporate governance. By contrast, the dynamic resource-based view regards value creation by good corporate governance as the goal that venture capitalists want to achieve with their influence. A further reason could be the preparation of an exit as a successful sale of a portfolio company could require good corporate governance. Finally, the reasons might change over time so that the different approaches can be substitutive or complimentary. Figure 17 summarises the hypotheses that are tested in the following.

#	Hypothesis
H1.1	The stronger the agency and business risk associated to an investment are the greater is the venture capitalists' influence on the corporate governance.
H1.1.1	The stronger the agency and business risk associated to an investment is the greater is the venture capitalists' influence on the assessment of managers.
H1.1.2	The stronger the agency and business risk associated to an investment is the greater is the venture capitalists' influence on the selection of the managers.
H1.1.3	The stronger the agency and business risk associated to an investment is the greater is the venture capitalists' influence on the compensation of the managers.
H1.1.4	The stronger the agency and business risk associated to an investment is the greater is the venture capitalists' influence on the bonding of the portfolio companies' managers.
H1.1.5	The stronger the agency and business risk associated to an investment is the greater is the venture capitalists' influence on the composition of the board.
H1.1.6	The stronger the agency and business risk associated to an investment is the greater is the venture capitalists' influence on the work of the board
H1.1.7	The stronger the agency and business risk associated to an investment is the greater is the venture capitalists' influence on the frequency of reporting.
H1.2	The better the initial corporate governance quality is the greater is the venture capitalists' influence on the corporate governance.
H1.2.1	The better the initial corporate governance quality is the greater is the venture capitalists' influence on the selection process of new managers.
H1.2.2	The better the initial corporate governance quality is the greater is the venture capitalists' influence on the composition of the board.
H1.2.3	The better the initial corporate governance quality is the greater is the venture capitalists' influence on the work of the board.
H1.3	Before a potential public exit the venture capitalists increase their influence on the corporate governance.
H1.3.1	Before a potential public exit it is more probable that the portfolio company complies with corporate governance codes.
H1.3.2	Before a potential publich exit it is more probable that the portfolio company has board members with experience in listed companies.
H1.4	Agency and business risk has a stronger impact on the venture capitalist's influence on the corporate governance of portfolio companies at earlier financing rounds than at later financing rounds.

Figure 17: Overview of hypotheses about the relationship between venture capitalists' reasons and influence on corporate governance

The second expected relationship is that venture capitalists' influence leads to better corporate governance of the portfolio companies. Although both theories agree on this, they focus on different corporate governance elements. Whereas agency theory centres on the monitoring and bonding function of corporate governance, the dynamic resource-based view concentrates on the advice function. This is mirrored in the following hypotheses.

#	Hypothesis
H2	The venture capitalists' influence has an impact on the portfolio companies' corporate governance
H2.1	The venture capitalists' influence has a positive impact on the assessment and selection of managers.
H2.1.1	The stronger the venture capitalists' influence is the more likely is the assessment of the managers.
H2.1.2	The stronger the venture capitalists' influence, the more efficient is the assessment of the management.
H2.1.3	The stronger the venture capitalists' influence, the more likely managers are to be replaced.
H2.1.4	The stronger the venture capitalists' influence, the better is the managers' selection process.
H2.2	Venture capitalists' influence has a positive impact on the bonding of managers.
H2.3	The venture capitalists' influence has a positive impact on the compensation of managers.
H2.3.1	The stronger the venture capitalists' influence, the higher is the proportion of the variable compensation.
H2.3.2	The stronger the venture capitalists' influence, the more likely is the use of variable compensation parts linked to mid- and long-term goals.
H2.3.3	The stronger the venture capitalists' influence is the lower is the cash compensation of the managers.
H2.4	The venture capitalists' influence has an impact on the composition of the board.
H2.4.1	The stronger the venture capitalists' influence is the greater is the proportion of independent members in the board.
H2.4.2	The stronger the venture capitalists' influence, the stronger are the experiences of the board.
H2.5	The venture capitalists' influence has a positive impact on the work of the board.
H2.5.1	The stronger the venture capitalists' influence, the more frequently board meetings take place.
H2.5.2	The stronger the venture capitalists' influence, the better prepared board meetings are.
H2.5.3	The stronger the venture capitalists' influence is the more involved is the board in strategic decision making.

#	Hypothesis
H2.6	The venture capitalists' influence has a positive impact on reporting discipline.
H2.6.1	The stronger the venture capitalists' influence, the more frequent is the portfolio company's reporting.
H2.6.2	The stronger the venture capitalists' influence, the more timely is the portfolio company's reporting.
H2.6.3	The stronger the venture capitalists' influence, the more comprehensive is the portfolio company's reporting.
H2.6.4	The stronger the venture capitalists' influence, the more accurate is the portfolio company's reporting.

Figure 18: Overview of hypotheses about the relationship between venture capitalists' influence and the quality of corporate governance

The third group of hypotheses addresses the abilities required of venture capitalists to affect corporate governance. Agency theory considers the ownership rights as crucial for the venture capitalists to push through their goals. The dynamic resource-based view focuses instead on the characteristics of venture capital firms and investment managers that could cause changes in corporate governance. Moreover, the second perspective also regards the trustfulness of the relationship between managers of portfolio companies and venture capitalists as important for the effectiveness of the venture capitalist's influence. The corresponding hypotheses are presented in Figure 19.

#	Hypothesis
H3	The abilities of venture capitalists have an impact on the corporate governance of portfolio companies.
H3.1	The control rights of venture capital firms have a positive impact on the corporate governance of portfolio companies.
H3.1.1	The stronger the venture capitalists' control right rights, — in terms of ownership rights and board seats — the stronger is their influence on the corporate governance of portfolio companies.
H3.1.2	The stronger the venture capitalists' control rights, the greater is the impact of their influence on the elements related to the monitoring function of corporate governance.
H3.1.3	The stronger the venture capitalists' control rights, the greater is the impact of their influence on the elements related to the bonding function of corporate governance.

#	Hypothesis
H3.2	The characteristics of venture capital firms have positive impact on the corporate governance of portfolio companies.
H3.2.1	Independent venture capital firms' influence has a greater impact on the corporate governance of portfolio companies than that of corporate venture capitalists and bank-related and governmental venture capitalists.
H3.2.2	The more investment experience a venture capital firm has, the greater are the effects of its influence on the corporate governance of portfolio companies.
H3.2.3	The greater the international experience of the venture capital firms, the greater are the effects of their influence on the corporate governance of portfolio companies.
H3.2.4	The greater the reputation of a venture capital firm, the greater are the effects of its influence on the corporate governance of portfolio companies.
H3.3	The characteristics of investment managers have positive impact on the corporate governance of portfolio companies.
H3.3.1	The greater the investment managers' experience in the portfolio company's industry, the greater is the impact of their influence on the corporate governance of portfolio companies.
H3.3.2	The greater the investment manager's experience in the portfolio company's industry is the greater is the impact of his/her influence on the corporate governance of portfolio companies.
H3.3.3	The greater the investment managers' international experience in the venture capital industry, the greater is the impact of their influence on the corporate governance of portfolio companies.
H3.3.4	The greater the investment managers' start-up experience, the greater is the impact of their influence on the corporate governance of portfolio companies.
H3.3.5	The greater the commitment of the investment managers, the greater is the impact of their influence on the corporate governance of portfolio companies.
H3.4	The impact of the venture capitalists influence is greater if their relationship with the managers of portfolio companies is trustful.

Figure 19: Overview of hypotheses about the relationship between venture capitalists' abilities and the quality of corporate governance

Finally, the fourth group of hypotheses relates the corporate governance of the portfolio companies to their firm value, measured by fundamental performance and valuation of the companies. Both agency theory and the dynamic resource-based view predict positive effects of corporate governance on firm value, as detailed in the last chapter. The following table presents the relevant hypotheses.

#	Hypothesis
H4.1	The corporate governance quality of company has effects on its fundamental performance.
H4.1.1	The better the corporate governance quality of a company is, the higher is its profitability.
H4.1.2	The better the corporate governance quality of a company is, the higher is its growth.
H4.2	The corporate governance quality of company has effects on firm valuation.
H4.2.1	The better the corporate governance quality of a portfolio company is, the higher is its valuation.

Figure 20: Overview of hypotheses about the relationship between the quality of corporate governance and firm value

The research comprises a qualitative as well as a quantitative analysis to ensure both an in-depth understanding of the research topic and generalisable results. This approach also prevents single method bias.[524] In the next section, the results of expert interviews are presented before the results of the survey are introduced in more detail.

5.2 Qualitative Analysis

After laying the theoretical foundations, a qualitative analysis in the form of in-depth interviews was conducted. This was done for three reasons. First, the interviews were used to compare the findings from the theoretical analysis with the common practice. Second, they ensured that a comprehensive picture of the relationship between venture capital and corporate governance was gained comprising all important factors. Third, they helped to operationalise the theory-based hypotheses in order to ensure that the quantitative analysis well captures the ideas of the research concept.

For the analysis, 19 semi-structured interviews were conducted with venture capitalists, CEOs of portfolio companies and other experts. In order to ensure a comprehensive picture, interviews were done in Germany, Belgium, the United Kingdom and Luxembourg as well as with different types of venture capitalists and portfolio companies at different development stages. The interviews were done between July and October 2005 either personally or by telephone. They all addressed the two research questions with the four aspects of the research: the reasons for the venture capitalists' influence, its impact on corporate governance, the abilities of the venture capitalists to influence the portfolio companies' corporate governance, and the effects

524 Blaikie (1991), pp. 115 ff.; Johnson/Onwuegbuzie (2004), pp. 14ff.; Fielding/Schreier (2001).

of good corporate governance on firm value. Figure 21 shows the conducted interviews in an overview.

Venture Capitalists	Portfolio Companies	Other Experts
4 in Germany • 2 independent VCs • 1 CVC • 1 governmental VC 3 in Belgium • 2 independent VCs • 1 financial Institution-related VC 2 in UK • 2 independent VCs	3 in Germany • 1 small successful early stage company • 2 formerly fast growing companies, now after restructuring 2 in Belgium • 1 startup • 1 buyout 2 in UK • 2 startups	1 lawyer in Germany 1 consultant in UK 1 funds-of-funds investor in Luxembourg

Figure 21: Overview of interviews

To begin with, the findings related to the research question about **how venture capitalists influence the corporate governance of portfolio companies** are presented. In regard to the reasons, the interviews with the **venture capitalists** largely support that agency risks are a main concern for them and that they influence the corporate governance of their portfolio companies accordingly. Indicators for this risk are the perceived bad information basis and a conflict of interest with the managers. Furthermore, before a potential exit of a portfolio company, the influence on corporate governance is increased. However, corporate governance as a source of value creation is only recognised by some of the interviewees. The interviewees supported the hypothesis that their influence changes over time during an investment, but the specific factors of this change could not be revealed in the interviews. In contrast to this, the venture capitalists stated that their approaches regarding the corporate governance of portfolio companies are rather similar. Regardless of the origination and type of the venture capitalists, they all seem to influence the six corporate governance elements introduced before: assessment, selection, bonding, and compensation of managers; composition and work of boards; and reporting discipline. Interviews with a specialised lawyer and a consultant supported this notion. According to them, the venture capitalists' influence is mainly determined in the contracting phase, and the contracts are largely standardised so that the resulting influence on corporate governance by the investors is rather similar. The focus of the influence might change over time during an investment: Whereas reporting is more important in the early phase of an investment, management assessment and selection gets more important in later stages when the demands on managers increase. Generally, a positive impact on corporate governance quality is expected. In regard to the required abilities, venture capitalists consider control rights important to accomplish changes in corporate governance. Moreover, several interviewees also pointed to the relevance of a trustful relationship with the managers of the portfolio companies because they might be able to effectively affect the portfolio companies only if the managers trust them. This argument contradicts the notion that corporate governance is enforced when venture capitalists perceive a bad information basis.

Similarly, the findings from the interviews with the **portfolio companies** support that the venture capitalists are important drivers of corporate governance development. In contrast to the interviewed venture capitalists, the managers of the portfolio companies recognised differences between the influence of different venture capitalists, in terms of both extent and direction. However, the hypothesised factors for such differences could not be well tested during the interviews. In most of the cases, the interviewees perceived that the venture capitalists' influence improved corporate governance. The managers of the portfolio companies distinguished between the support they received from different venture capitalists, which was traced back to different approaches and experiences of the investors. Correspondingly, the results from the interview with a consultant revealed different profiles of venture capitalists that should lead to differences in their impact on the corporate governance of portfolio companies. In particular, the most professional investors are said to have a comparatively strong influence. This is supported by an interview with a fund-of-fund investor in which factors such as number of funds, size of funds and reputation were named as indicators of the professionalism of a venture capitalist. Apart from that, the interviewed managers of portfolio companies stressed the importance of the venture capitalists' control rights for the extent of their influence on corporate governance. The control rights determine the negotiation power of the venture capitalists and the managers of the portfolio companies and might prevent the investors from pushing through strict burdens. All interviewees realised an improvement of corporate governance because of the venture capitalists' influence, though the extent differed between the investors and the companies.

The second research question is related to the **influence of corporate governance on firm value**. Referring to this relationship, the majority of the interviewed **venture capitalists** reported positive effects because of cost reductions. By their influence, corporate governance costs at the portfolio companies could be prevented, which they documented with examples. The impact on the growth of portfolio companies was recognised only indirectly through better decision making. However, specific examples were not given. By contrast, only a few investors supported a relationship between good corporate governance and the valuation of portfolio companies. These venture capitalists considered that new investors would value better historic information on the portfolio companies' development while they would calculate a discount on the firm value should the provided information be of poor quality. Generally, the interviewees supported the notion that good corporate governance increases firm value. But they also stressed that bad corporate governance does not inevitably lead to bad performance. These findings correspond to the results of the interviews with the managers of **portfolio companies**. Generally, they also supported a positive relationship between corporate governance and firm value, but they argued that this relationship is indirect, for example by providing a better information basis and by advice from board members and better decision making. Furthermore, the interviewees stressed that good corporate governance in the case of growth companies might not be well assessed by the criteria of corporate governance codes because they neglect the particular and changing requirements of these companies. The majority of both venture capitalists and the managers of portfolio companies doubted that the effects of good corporate governance on firm value could be shown empirically.

The results from the interviews, by and large, support the theory-based hypotheses. However, the hypotheses on the differences of venture capitalists' influence at different times in the development of portfolio companies or due to the abilities of the venture capitalists could not be supported because the number of interviews was too limited.

The qualitative analysis also indicated that two elements that are less relevant in the theoretical analysis are relatively important in practice: exit preparation as a reason to influence corporate governance and the trustfulness of the relationship between venture capitalists and the managers of portfolio companies. Venture capitalists' actions are generally targeted at a successful exit from their investment. They realise the importance of good corporate governance for the success of an exit because potential investors fear risks that might arise from bad governance. Particularly in the case of an IPO, there are high requirements for the professionalism of corporate governance from the legislature, the stock exchange and potential investors. Furthermore, venture capitalists realise that the success of their investment is largely dependent on the co-operation of the portfolio companies' managers. First, changes to the development of the portfolio company can only be effective if the managers support them because they make most of the decisions in the company and implement the actions accordingly. That means that the managers might only be willing to take decisions and actions proposed by the venture capitalists if they trust them. Additionally, the venture capitalists cannot monitor all decisions and actions by the managers, so they must also be able to trust the managers of the portfolio companies. All in all, with the reinforcement of the two aspects, the hypotheses derived from theory seem to be comprehensive.

The interviews were used to **align the theoretical analysis with the needs of a quantitative analysis**. In order to test the theory-based hypotheses, it is required to operationalise all concepts to variables that can be queried in a survey. This was facilitated by the interviews that provided deeper knowledge on the practice of the relationship between venture capitalists and portfolio companies in different European countries. In particular, there are three important aspects that were derived from the findings of the qualitative analysis. First, the venture capitalists and portfolio companies agreed that the necessity of elaborate corporate governance structures and processes depends largely on the specific characteristics of a portfolio company. Therefore, the effectiveness of corporate governance cannot always be definitively measured by the compliance with general corporate governance elements. This is in contrast to general corporate governance research, which generally uses standardised corporate governance ratings to survey corporate governance quality. But it should be noted that that research is almost entirely focussed on large and established companies, whereas this analysis is looking at growth companies in the process of development. Accordingly, the quantitative analysis uses a second measure for the quality of corporate governance that is based on a self-assessment of the managers of the portfolio companies as it can be expected that they can best evaluate whether the corporate governance of a company is adequate for its specific development stage. Secondly, it was found that the analysis of the development of corporate governance in the portfolio companies can best be pursued by analysing its development between the financing rounds of the venture capitalists. At these times, greater changes are to be expected for two reasons: The venture capitalists negotiate or renegotiate their rights and changes to the portfolio companies' structures and processes before an investment is done. In the case of a second or third financing round, the earlier development of the company is taken into account during the renegotiations so that venture capitalists' position can be enforced or stay stable. Consequently, the questionnaire for the quantitative analysis measures corporate governance quality and the influence of the venture capitalists at the points of time of a financing round. Thirdly, the effects on firm value for the analysed growth companies cannot be measured in the same way as it is done in traditional corporate governance research. This is due to the fact that those companies often do not yet generate positive results, especially if they are still in an early development phase. Furthermore, the most common measure for firm value, Tobin's Q, cannot be used for these companies because a market value is unavailable. Hence, the analysis must use measures specific for the venture capital business. Apart from measures for growth and profitability, the survey therefore takes into account measures for valuation multiples that are often used by venture capitalists to calculate the firm value of portfolio companies. Numerical measures might not always be suitable due to strong development in growth companies. Negative results might be inevitable when pursuing growth potentials and therefore expected in the companies' business plans. Accordingly, negative results cannot always be interpreted as bad performance. Because of this, relative measures are used in this thesis as well those that compare the companies' performance to their competitors' and their own business plans.

Hence, the findings of the qualitative analysis basically support the theoretically derived hypotheses. The results of the interviews were used to verify the research concept and to align the questionnaire for testing the hypotheses to practice. In the following section, the details of the survey are introduced.

5.3 Methods of the Quantitative Analysis

After ensuring an in-depth understanding of the research topic with the theoretic and qualitative analysis, a quantitative analysis was done to achieve generalisable results. In the following, the data sources and the variables for testing the hypotheses are introduced.

5.3.1 Data Sources

The information for the quantitative analysis was collected from two sources: a survey and a database. The combination provided a unique and relatively comprehensive data set.

5.3.1.1 Survey

The quantitative analysis was conducted by means of a pan-European survey of venture capital-financed portfolio companies. This section describes the details of the survey: the questionnaire, the sample, and the execution.

Given the national differences in corporate governance, the questionnaire had to be adapted to suit portfolio companies with one-tier and two-tier board systems. This relates in particular to questions on board structure. Consequently, there were two versions of the questionnaire that differed in the number of questions and to the wording of some questions. The latter difference relates to the term used for the boards: The questionnaire for companies with a one-tier system used the term board whereas the version for companies with a two-tier system used supervisory board. Because the questions about board members were targeted at members who are not managers of the company, the two versions used the terms non-executive members of the board and members of the supervisory board, respectively.

The questionnaire included questions in five areas: information about the portfolio company, information about the corporate governance of the portfolio company (including information about the six corporate governance elements), information about the portfolio company's firm value, and information about the venture capitalists. Table 1 shows the number of questions for each area. It indicates that the questionnaire for portfolio companies with a one-tier systems included 104 questions, which is two more than the one for companies with a two-tier system. This is because questions about the number of independent non-executive board members and dual leadership were asked only in the first version.

Area		Number of questions
Information about portfolio companies		17
Information about venture capitalists		11
Information about corporate governance	Assessment and selection of managers	9
	Bonding of managers	5
	Compensation of managers	6
	Composition of board	14/16
	Work of board	10
	Reporting discipline	11
	Other	5
Firm Value		14
Total		**102/104**

Table 1: Questions by areas

In order to track the development of the analysed portfolio companies, a great number of questions in the questionnaire asked for several answers for different points in time. Altogether, five measuring times correspond to the findings of the qualitative study: the time before the first financing round (t=0), the time after the 1st financing round (t=1), the time after the 2nd financing round (t=2), the time after the 3rd financing round (t=3) and today (t=4). In particular, the questions referring to corporate governance and firm value as well as those about the venture capitalists were asked for the first four measuring times, if possible. The questionnaire was adapted because the analysed companies are at different points in their development and had different numbers of financing rounds. Hence, there were three versions of the questionnaire available depending on the number of financing rounds of the portfolio companies: Companies with only one financing round were asked to answer the questions for two measuring times (before the first financing round and after the first financing round); companies with two financing rounds answered the questions for three measuring times (additionally after the second financing round), and companies with three or more financing rounds answered the questions for four measuring times (additionally after the third financing round). This enabled tracking of changes to the corporate governance from founding until after the third financing round. The questions about the portfolio companies generally asked for information at two times: before the first financing round and today. All companies were to provide this information. The last measuring time was used as a substitute for the situation after the last financing round to simplify answering the questionnaire.

Another distinctiveness of the questionnaire was the fact that some information was requested in two ways. The questionnaire takes into account that the analysed portfolio companies are generally in the process of development, which might make it difficult to assess the appropriateness of corporate governance for the company in its current situation, on one hand, and the success of its general and financing development, on the other hand. Therefore, information about the companies' corporate governance and firm value was gathered using criteria and self-assessment. In these cases, some questions asked how well relevant criteria were fulfilled at a measuring time, and additional questions asked for a self-assessment by the respondent of how appropriate the corporate governance element was at the same measuring time, i.e., how well the companies performed at a measuring time. This allowed the use of different measures to assess the quality of corporate governance and the success of the companies' development. Figure 22 shows for which measuring times the information on the different areas was requested and what form of assessment was used.

Information collected with questionnaire	Type of answer		Measuring times				
	Assesment with criteria	Self-assessment by respondent	t=0	t=1	t=2	t=3	t=4
Basic information about portfolio companies	X		X				X
Performance data of portfolio comapnies	X	X	X	X	X	X	X
Characteristics of VC investment manager	X		X	X	X	X	X
Corporate governance quality	X	X	X	X	X	X	X
VC's influence on corporate governance		X		X	X	X	X

Figure 22: Overview of information collected with questionnaire

Depending on the questions, there were different answer possibilities. The questionnaire included open-ended and close-ended questions. The open-ended questions primarily had numeric answers. The close-ended questions had different formants: Some of the questions were dichotomous (e.g., Yes/No/NA), whereas others had ranked answer possibilities (e.g., ++, +, o, –, – – or a continuum from very strong to no influence where not every answer possibility was labelled). A few questions had a set of specific answers from which the respondents could chose (e.g., greater importance of fixed compensation, greater importance of variable compensation, equal importance). The mixture of question formats delivered precise information where necessary and less-detailed information in other areas. This facilitates responding to the questionnaire but ensures a high degree of detail for specific areas. To ensure the adequacy of the questions, a pre-test with five CEOs of portfolio companies and investment managers of venture capitalists from Germany, Belgium and the United Kingdom was conducted between 10 November and 24 November 2005. The respondents tested whether all questions were well comprehensible and that the answer possibilities were clear and complete. According to the feedback of the test persons, the wording and answer possibilities of some of the questions was adapted. The questionnaire was prepared as an online questionnaire to facilitate answering for the respondents as well as to allow the invitation of a great number of participants. The final questionnaire with all answer possibilities is attached as Annex 1.

In order to ensure a broad basis for the analysis, the most comprehensive sample of European venture capital-financed companies was collected. Extensive investigations revealed that the VentureXpert database from Thomson Financial offers the most complete set of European portfolio companies, so this database was used for the sample of the survey. It was verified whether the portfolios of several venture capitalists are completely included in the sample, and it was found that only a very few portfolio companies were missing. All portfolio companies that met the following four criteria were included in the sample:

- Locations in Europe
- Still active at the cut-off date (to prevent including companies that do not exist anymore[525])
- Received at least one financing round between 1 January 2001 and the cut-off date (this period ensures that all companies had at least one financing round after the new economy bubble burst in 2000)
- In one of the following development stages at the time of at least one financing round: seed, start-up, early stage, first stage, other early stage, expansion, second stage, other expansion, third stage, other later stage, bridge, leveraged buyout (i.e., growth companies of early and late stages were included in the sample[526]).

At the cut-off date, 30 November 2005, the initial sample included 6.062 companies, of which 65 were double entries. Additionally, for 1.386 of these companies, no contact details were available. The sample was completed by 14 portfolio companies for which company details were provided by venture capitalists.[527] Hence, the original sample comprised 4.496 venture capital-financed portfolio companies that were

525 It should be noted that this might lead to a survival bias of the analysis because unsuccessful portfolio companies that ceased to exist before the cut-off date are not included in the sample; this limitation is discussed in section 6.2.1.

526 This follows the American definition of venture capital. However, the importance of late stage companies in the empirical analysis is limited due to the small number of cases.

527 59 professional venture capitalists were asked to provide company details on their current portfolio companies. These venture capitalists were selected according to criteria for investment success and reputation. Four of the contacted venture capitalists provided information on their portfolio companies.

contacted. The invitation to the survey was sent to the CEO of the portfolio companies by email if the personal email address was available. This was only possible in 135 cases. The other 4.503 CEOs of the portfolio companies were invited by fax. Due to problems with wrong addresses,[528] only 3.505 invitations could have been delivered to the portfolio companies, which is the basis for the calculation of the response rate. This sample includes portfolio companies from 35 countries, with the biggest number of contacted companies in the United Kingdom, France and Germany. The following table shows the distribution of contacted portfolio companies by country. The invitations were sent out between 1 and 7 December 2005, a reminder was sent to the companies that had not started the survey after ten days. Another reminder was sent to the companies that had started but not completed the survey after another ten days. The invitation and the reminders included the Internet address of the online questionnaire and an individual access code that ensured that only the contacted portfolio companies were able to answer the questionnaire. Furthermore, it meant the answers from the questionnaire could be combined with other information on the portfolio companies from the VentureXpert database.

---

528 Data quality was checked, and in many cases the addresses were corrected manually. Accordingly, it can be expected that a relatively large proportion of the companies that could not be reached might not exist anymore. This is also confirmed by my answers from addressees that received the invitation incorrectly.

Company nation	Contacted companies by fax	Contacted companies by e-mail	Contacted companies total	Invitations that reached respondents
France	853	35	888	779
Netherlands	208	2	210	184
Belgium	139	3	142	126
Luxembourg	6	1	7	4
France/BeNeLux total	***1.206***	***41***	***1.247***	***1.093***
United Kingdom	1.032	21	1.053	859
Ireland	128	4	132	106
United Kingdom/Ireland total	***1.160***	***25***	***1.185***	***965***
Finland	312	14	326	257
Sweden	267	7	274	218
Denmark	178	18	196	171
Norway	112	9	121	99
Iceland	2	0	2	1
Faroe Islands	1	0	1	0
Northern Europe total	***872***	***48***	***920***	***746***
Germany	556	7	563	445
Switzerland	106	2	108	85
Austria	89	1	90	80
Germany/Austria/ Switzerland total	***751***	***10***	***761***	***610***
Spain	173	0	173	141
Italy	98	1	99	54
Portugal	47	1	48	42
Greece	11	0	11	8
Croatia	8	0	8	2
Cyprus	4	0	4	1
Slovenia	3	0	3	2
Turkey	3	0	3	2
Macedonia	1	0	1	1
Southern Europe total	***348***	***2***	***350***	***253***
Poland	56	2	58	51
Hungary	39	0	39	29
Russia	22	0	22	11
Czech Republic	12	0	12	7
Bulgaria	7	0	7	5
Slovakia	5	1	6	5
Latvia	5	0	5	3
Lithuania	5	0	5	4
Romania	4	0	4	2
Estonia	3	0	3	3
Serbia and Montenegro	1	0	1	0
Eastern Europe total	***159***	***3***	***162***	***120***
Grand total	***4.496***	***129***	***4.625***	***3.787***

Table 2: Original sample of survey by nation

By 24 February 2006, the cut-off date of the survey, 283 of the contacted portfolio companies had started to complete the online questionnaire and 139 of those companies completed the survey. That equals a response rate of 3,7%, which is comparable to other similar analyses in the field of venture capital research.[529] Figure 23 shows the calculation of the response rate in an overview.

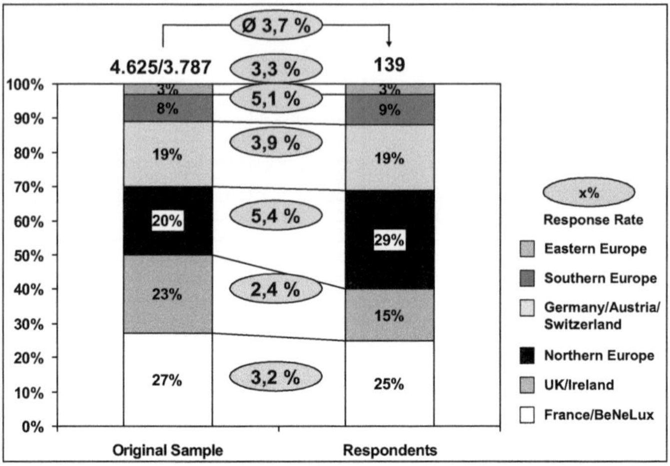

Figure 23: Comparison of original sample and respondents

5.3.1.2 Database

The identification of the respondents by means of an individual access code meant information collected through the questionnaire could be complemented with information from the VentureXpert database. In particular, the database includes information on the portfolio companies' business and investment history as well as information on the venture capital firms and their investments. Apart from that, an online route planner[530] was used to calculate the distance between the venture capitalists and the portfolio companies. As introduced before, it is expected that the lead venture capitalist exerts the greatest influence among the invested venture capitalists.[531] Hence, the information about the venture capitalist related to the lead-venture capitalists in a specific financing round. The respondents had to indicate for every financing round which venture capitalist was the lead-investor. In the tables of the next section, it is noted when the data were not collected from the questionnaire but from the database.

529 For an overview refer to Dennis (2003), pp. 279ff.

530 Web address of the routeplanner: http://routing.msn.de

531 Wright/Lockett (2003), pp. 2092ff.

5.3.2 Variables

The following briefly introduces the response, explanatory and control variables used for the quantitative analysis of the four aspects. In the tables in the annex, the variables are described and their scale, possible values and sources are specified.

5.3.2.1 Reasons

- Response variables

  The response variable for the hypotheses on the reasons is the venture capitalists' influence on the corporate governance of the portfolio company (interval scale). Measures are available for the six corporate governance elements and are aggregated to indexes for the overall influence as well as for the influence on the elements that have a monitoring, bonding and advice function, according to the explanations in section 2.2.3. The respondents were asked to rate the strength of the venture capitalists' influence after they answered the questions on the corresponding corporate governance elements on a four step continuum between "no influence" and "very strong" influence.

- Explanatory variables

  There are three explanatory variables for these hypotheses. First, the index for agency and business risk includes measures for these risk types. The items for agency risk include measures for managerial ownership (ratio scale), portfolio company age (nominal scale), specificity of the business (interval scale), importance of intangible assets (interval scale), degree of technology of the product (interval scale), and number of years CEO worked for the portfolio company (nominal scale). The items for business risk include measures for the degree of dynamics of the environment (interval scale), attractiveness of the market (interval scale), number of products of the company (ratio scale), start-up experience of the top-management team (interval scale), and functional experience of the top-management team (interval scale). These measures were used in several studies before so it can be expected that they are reliable.[532]

  The second independent variable is the quality of corporate governance in the previous period. Following the dynamic resource-based view that a good resource

[532] E. g. Barney et al. (1989); Barney et al. (1994); Sapienza/Gupta (1994); Fredriksen/Klofsten (2001); Fiert (1995).

endowment should cause venture capitalists to influence corporate governance, the corporate governance quality indexes are used here.

The third variable is a dummy variable that indicates whether, at a specific measuring time, an IPO was planned. In that case, the venture capitalist should, according to the hypotheses, influence corporate governance in order to prepare the exit.

- Control variables

  In order to account for other effects that might influence the response variables but that are not related to the theory-based hypotheses, control variables are introduced. They include the size of the company (measured by the number of employees), the location (in terms of European regions) and the distance between the venture capitalist and the portfolio companies (measured in kilometres).

In the table in Annex 2 the variables for testing the hypotheses on the reasons for the venture capitalists to influence the corporate governance of portfolio companies are described.

5.3.2.2 Effects on Corporate Governance Quality

- Response variables

  The response variable corporate governance is collected in the survey in two ways. First, there is a self-assessment of the corporate governance quality by the respondent for each corporate governance element (interval scale). These assessments are summed up in indexes for the three corporate governance functions[533] as well as for all elements (ratio scale). Besides this, the corporate governance quality is measured by means of criteria for all elements. They are included in the indexes for the corporate governance elements, the corporate governance functions and the overall corporate governance quality (all ratio scale). Corresponding to the results from the theoretic and qualitative analyses, the analysed criteria are those that are generally influenced by the venture capitalist.

  Figure 24 shows the correlation of the two corporate governance measures. The means of the overall corporate governance quality measured by self-assessment and measured by criteria are not strongly correlated, although the values for the four measuring times are at similar levels.

[533] For more information refer to 2.2.3.

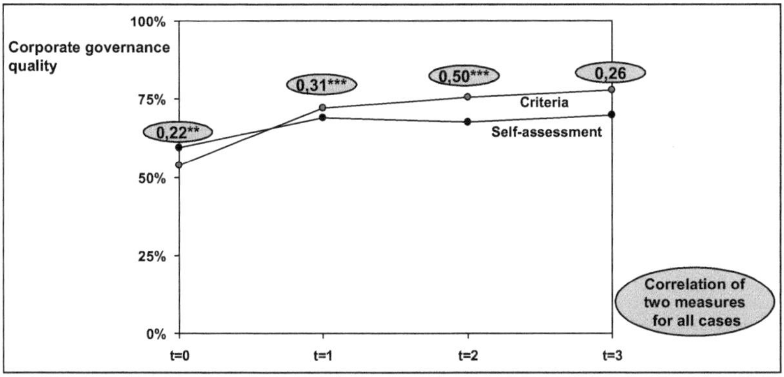

Figure 24: Comparison of two measures for corporate governance quality

- Explanatory variables

  The explanatory variables related to these hypotheses concern the strength of the venture capitalist's influence. As explained in section 5.3.2.1, there are variables for each corporate governance element but also indexes that combine them.

- Control variables

  The corporate governance quality might be influenced strongly by the development stage, the location and the size of the portfolio company. Apart from that, the venture capitalists' abilities can have a significant impact on the corporate governance quality, as the hypotheses predict. Hence, these four variables are taken into account when testing the hypotheses.

An overview of the individual variables is presented in Annex 3.

5.3.2.3 Abilities

- Response variables

  The response variable for these hypotheses is the portfolio company's corporate governance quality. In particular, the corporate governance indexes that are determined by both the self-assessment of the respondents and the assessment by means of criteria for the fulfilment of corporate governance elements. These variables are explained in detail in section 5.3.2.2.

- Explanatory variables

  The explanatory variables linked to the hypotheses on the impact of the venture capitalist's abilities are associated with three factors. The control rights of the venture capitalist are measured by its ownership share in the portfolio company (ratio scale) and by its board seats (dichotomous: yes or no). The abilities of the venture capitalist depend on the lead venture capital firm's characteristics and on the abilities of its investment manager in a specific portfolio company. Factors for the abilities of the venture capital firm include the type of investor (dichotomous: independent or not), its investment and international experience (both interval scale) and its reputation (derived from its presence in industry news and events; dichotomous: strong or weak presence). Similarly, the abilities of the investment manager include experience and his/her commitment, which is measured by the number of contacts with the managers of the portfolio company (ratio scale). Third, the trust between the venture capitalist and the portfolio company's managers is operationalised in the survey by the respondent's assessment of how trustful the relationship was at the measuring times (interval scale).

- Control variables

  The control variables for the impact of the venture capitalist's abilities include, apart from the development stage, the size and location of the portfolio company and the strength of the influence of the venture capitalist. This is done because the influence by the venture capitalist is considered the main other factor affecting corporate governance quality. The operationalisation of this variable was detailed in section 5.3.2.2.

Annex 4 includes a table with the information on all variables for this part.

5.3.2.4 Effects on Firm Value

- Response variables

  In this research, firm value as the response variable must be operationalised differently from the corporate governance research on public companies because of the very limited data available. It is therefore traced back to basic factors of firm value. On one hand, the firm performance is measured by variables for the fundamental performance of the firm, in particular profitability and growth. The growth rates are collected for employees, sales and cashflows allowing for companies at different development stages that might or might not generate sales already (ratio scale). Profitability as the second influence factor for firm performance is similarly measured at different levels (ratio scale). The ratios EBITDA margin, net profit margin, return on equity and return on assets are collected in the survey (ratio scale). On the other hand, the valuation of a portfolio company also influences its firm value. Corresponding to the practice in the venture capital industry, the questionnaire asked for changes in the multiples used for valuation by investors between two financing rounds. To make allowance for differences that might result from different development stages, the changes of three multiples are collected: the changes of the sales, the cashflow[534] and the EBITDA multiple (ratio scale). Apart from this specific information, the questionnaire also asked for respondent assessments. They were asked to evaluate the impact of good corporate governance on the performance and valuation of their companies (interval scale). Moreover, they were asked to provide relative measures of firm value: the competitiveness of their companies and the change in valuation between two financing rounds (interval scale).

- Explanatory variables
  The explanatory variables associated with the hypotheses about the influence of corporate governance quality on firm value are the variables for corporate governance that have been introduced before. Again they are used at different levels and in two forms: self-assessment and assessment by criteria.

- Control variables
  Further variables with an expected influence on firm value are size, development stage and location. Moreover, the industry of the portfolio company can determine firm performance and valuation, so this was taken into account as well.

All variables that have been used in the analysis are described in Annex 5.

5.3.3 Statistical Methods

The data collected during the survey were analysed with uni- and multivariate statistical methods. Descriptive analyses were carried out on the explanatory and response variables before the hypotheses derived in chapter 4 were tested using sophisticated statistical techniques. The following paragraphs introduce the methods that were used in this research.

[534] The cashflow multiples could not be used for statistical analyses because too few respondents provided this information.

5.3.3.1 Descriptive Analyses

In a first step, basic information on the collected data was gained by descriptive analyses. For all variables of the research, the following general information was determined: the number of observations ("N"), the minimum value of all observations ("Min"), the maximum value of all observations ("Max"), the arithmetic mean of all observations ("Mean"), and the standard deviation of all observations ("Std. Dev."). This information was gained for all measuring times, i.e., for up to four points in time depending on the variable. As the observations represent a time series, the development of the variables was analysed. In the expectation that the observation of a measuring time depends on the observation of the preceding measuring time, t-tests of paired samples were carried out using SPSS 13.

A paired t-test compares the means of two variables by computing the difference between the two variables for each case. It is tested if the average difference is significantly different from zero (null hypothesis). The equation of the t-test is:

$$t = \frac{\overline{D}}{\frac{s_D}{\sqrt{n}}}$$

$$where:$$

$$D = x_1 - x_2$$

and x_n are the observations at a measuring time and sD is the standard deviation of the differences between x_1 and x_2. D is normally distributed with a mean of 0. t tests the null hypothesis that the mean difference $\overline{D}$ between the two observations is 0. Consequently, the difference of the observations at the two measuring times is significant if the null hypothesis is refuted.[535]

The results of the descriptive analyses are presented in figures for the most important variables and in tables that include information on the observations of all variables.

5.3.3.2 Multivariate Analyses

To test the hypotheses, multivariate analyses were carried out. As the descriptive information indicates, the data gained from the survey are characterised by time-dependent explanatory and response variables. This means that the observations from the

535 Janssen/Laatz (2002), pp. 316ff.

different measuring times are not independent; observation at a later measuring time can be dependent on the observation at an earlier measuring time.

A particularity of this research is that the number of measuring times is not equal for the portfolio companies (unbalanced design). The measuring times represent the events of venture capital financing rounds, and the portfolio companies had had one, two or three financing rounds when the questionnaires were completed. That means if a company had not yet reached the second or third financing round, the data for that and the following measuring times could not be collected. This required a statistical technique that takes into account repeated measurements as well as unbalanced designs.

For this research, the technique of mixed models from SPSS 13 was used because it meets the demands of the research design. It offers a flexible modelling tool that can adequately reproduce the given dependency structures. Therefore, that technique is preferred over general linear models. In this case, it is not the typical mixed models technique that is used because fixed and random effects are not used simultaneously. All explanatory variables are assumed to be fixed effects.

Corresponding to the variables of the specific hypotheses, the explanatory elements can be differentiated in covariates and factors. The factors include, for example, the development stage and the region of the portfolio company. For the factors, it was tested whether the response variable differed for categories of the factors and whether differences between the reference category and the factor categories were significant. For the covariates, such as size of the company, distance between the venture capitalist and the portfolio company and corporate governance quality, it was tested whether there was a linear relationship between the covariate and the response variable. For example, the greater the venture capitalists' influence, the better is the corporate governance quality. Time was included in all models as a covariate in the form of the financing round. This tested whether the response variable followed a linear trend over time. Auto-correlations of the 1st order and heterogeneous variances were taken into account. The model parameters were estimated with the REML (restricted maximum likelihood) method.

The general equation of the mixed model is (as random effects were not taken into account):

$$y = X\beta + \varepsilon$$

or:

$$\begin{bmatrix} y_1 \\ y_2 \\ \cdot \\ \cdot \\ \cdot \\ y_n \end{bmatrix} = \begin{bmatrix} x_{11} & x_{12} & \cdot & \cdot & \cdot & x_{1p} \\ x_{21} & x_{22} & \cdot & \cdot & \cdot & x_{2p} \\ \cdot & \cdot & & & & \cdot \\ \cdot & \cdot & & & & \cdot \\ \cdot & \cdot & & & & \cdot \\ x_{n1} & x_{n2} & \cdot & \cdot & \cdot & x_{np} \end{bmatrix} \begin{bmatrix} \beta_1 \\ \beta_2 \\ \cdot \\ \cdot \\ \cdot \\ \beta n \end{bmatrix} + \begin{bmatrix} \varepsilon_1 \\ \varepsilon_2 \\ \cdot \\ \cdot \\ \cdot \\ \varepsilon_n \end{bmatrix}$$

where y denotes the vector of observed y_i's, X is the known matrix of x_{ij}'s, β is the unknown fixed-effects parameter vector and ε is the unobserved vector of independent and identically distributed Gaussian random errors.

The structure of variances is auto regressive (1st order) with heterogeneous variances. The correlation between two elements is:

ρ for adjacent elements,
ρ^2 for elements with a distance of 2,
ρ^3 for elements with a distance of 3,
ρ^4 for elements with a distance of 4,
and ρ is between –1 and 1.

An example of the structure of variance for the case of 4 measuring times is:

$$\begin{matrix} \sigma_{12} & \sigma_2\sigma_1\rho & \sigma_3\sigma_1\rho_2 & \sigma_4\sigma_1\rho_3 \\ \sigma_2\sigma_1\rho & \sigma_{22} & \sigma_3\sigma_2\rho & \sigma_4\sigma_2\rho_2 \\ \sigma_3\sigma_1\rho_2 & \sigma_3\sigma_2\rho & \sigma_{32} & \sigma_4\sigma_3\rho \\ \sigma_4\sigma_1\rho_3 & \sigma_4\sigma_2\rho_2 & \sigma_4\sigma_3\rho & \sigma_{42} \end{matrix}$$

The results of the mixed models analyses include the coefficients and the confidence levels for all explanatory variables as well as the lower and the upper level of the coefficient. (The following discussion differentiates between the explanatory variable that relates to the explanatory variable of the analysis and the control variables that are explanatory variables for which the analysis is controlled.) Furthermore, the log likelihood value and the R^2 that indicate the quality of the model are given. In the next sections, only the coefficient and confidence level for the explanatory variable that relates to the hypothesis and R^2 of the model are presented. The significance is indicated by the following signs: "*" for the 90% confidence level, "**" for the 95% confidence level and "***" for the 99% confidence level. In the case of covariates, the coefficient x can be interpreted as follows: The value of the response variable increases/decreases by x units if the explanatory variable increases by 1 unit. Similarly, for the case of a factor as coefficient, the interpretation is: The value of the response variable increases/decreases by x units in comparison to the reference category of the factor variable.[536]

Four of the hypotheses included dichotomous response variables ("Yes" — 1 /"No" — 0 or "Variable Compensation or Equal" — 1/"Fix" — 0). These hypotheses could not be tested with the mixed models technique because dichotomous response variables cannot be used with this method. Therefore these hypotheses were tested using the logistic regression technique. However, this technique does not take repeated measurement into account, so it must be assumed that the observations at different measuring times are independent.

The goal of the logistic regression is to predict the probability for which the response variable has the value 1 under consideration of several influencing factors. Correspondingly, influencing factors can increase or reduce this probability. The strength of this influence is described by the odds ratio.

$$\log it[\theta(x)] = \log\left[\frac{\theta(x)}{1-\theta(x)}\right] = \alpha + \beta_1 x_1 + \beta_2 x_2 + \ldots + \beta_2 x_2 + \beta_i x_i$$

The odds ratio indicates the effects of the explanatory variable on the response variable. The odds ratio is the factor for which the probability of occurrence of the response variable increases per unit of the explanatory variable.

For the odds ratio, 95% confidence intervals were used. A significant effect of the influencing factor is only proven if the significance is equal to or less than 0,05. The Nagelkerke's R^2 can be compared to the R^2 of the linear regression and is between 0 and 1.

The results of the tests include the coefficients, values of significance, lower and upper limits of the 95% confidence interval, and odds ratios of the explanatory variables, as

536 McCulloch/Searle (2000); Verbeke/Molenberghs (2000); Norusis (2006).

well as the log likelihood values and R^2 of the models. In the tables of the next sections, only the coefficients with indication of significance, odds ratios and the R^2 values are given.[537]

For example, an odds ratio (one odd divided by second odd) of 1,5 can be interpreted as follows: If the value of the influencing factors increases by one unit, then the relationship between the probability of occurrence and the probability of non-occurrence (odd) increases by the factor 1,5. If the influencing factor is an index between 1 and 100 and the odd for an index value of 4 is 3,5, then the odd increases for an index value of 4 to 5,25 (3,5*1,5). For factors, the increase is also related to the reference category.

5.3.4 Representativeness

A test for goodness of fit was carried out to verify whether the results of the analysis are representative for European venture capital-financed companies. This was done by means of a chi-square test that tests whether the respondents correspond to the original sample of the survey. If the null-hypothesis that the two groups are not significantly different is supported, then it can be assumed that the group of respondents corresponds to the sample.

Chi-square is calculated with the following formula

$$x^2 = \sum \frac{(O-E)^2}{E}$$

where O is an observed frequency and E is an expected frequency asserted by the null-hypothesis. The value of this equation can be compared to the chi-square distribution to determine the goodness of fit.

For this research, the test was carried out for the regional and age distributions of the portfolio companies. The required information was collected from the VentureXpert database. Whereas the null-hypothesis was supported for the regional distribution,[538] which means that the respondents correspond to the original sample, it was not supported for the age distribution. It was found that there are relatively more respondents in the younger age groups (up to five years and six to ten years) than in the

537 Kraft (1997), pp. 636 ff.; Hosmer/Lemeshow (1989); Norusis (2006).

original sample. This might be due to aged data in the VentureXpert database from which the sample was derived, i.e., some of the older portfolio companies in the sample might not be active at the time of the survey. This is confirmed by the high number of invitations that could not be delivered to the addressees.[539] Thus, mortality of companies might lead to relatively few older companies in the group of respondents. Nonetheless, this finding limits the representativeness of the results, and it must be observed when interpreting them.

5.3.5 Basic Information on Respondents

In the following, basic information about the 139 respondents that completed the questionnaire is presented. This allows better classification of the analysis with regard to the characteristics of the portfolio companies that were included.

- Number of financing rounds

  The largest part of the portfolio companies had received only one financing round from a venture capitalist (65 companies; 47%). Apart from that, 44 companies (32%) had two financing rounds, and 30 companies (21%) had already completed 3 or more financing rounds when the questionnaire was completed. This is presented in Figure 25.

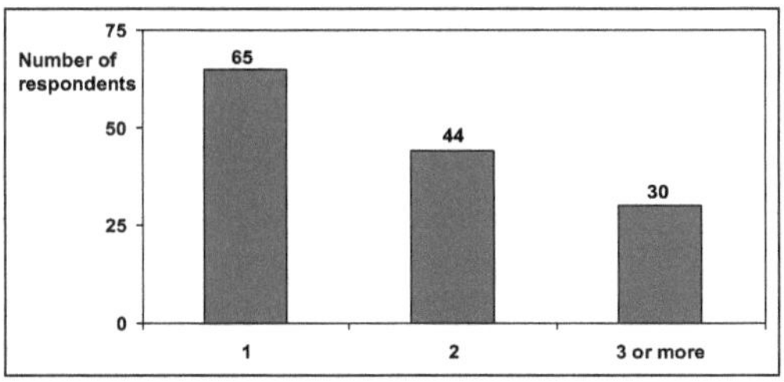

Figure 25: Respondents by number of financing rounds

This has consequences for the availability of data for the analysis because the number of measuring times for a portfolio company depends on the number of completed financing rounds. Information on the situation before and after the first financing round could be collected for all 139 companies, whereas the information for the situation after the second and third financing rounds could be collected for

538 Refer to Figure 23 for an overview of the regional distribution of the original sample and the group of respondents.

539 For more information refer to 5.3.1.1.

only 74 and 30 companies, respectively. These numbers represent the maximum number of cases that could be analysed for the four measuring times.

- Development stage

  The portfolio companies can be divided into five groups according to their development stage. Figure 26 presents the development stages of the 139 portfolio companies at the time of their first financing by a venture capitalist. Almost one third of all companies were still in the seed phase; fewer companies were in the start-up phase. With 50 companies, the biggest group was at that time in the expansion phase. Altogether, 113 companies or 81% of all analysed portfolio companies were early-stage investments whereas the other 26 companies or 19% were late stage companies, primarily buyouts.

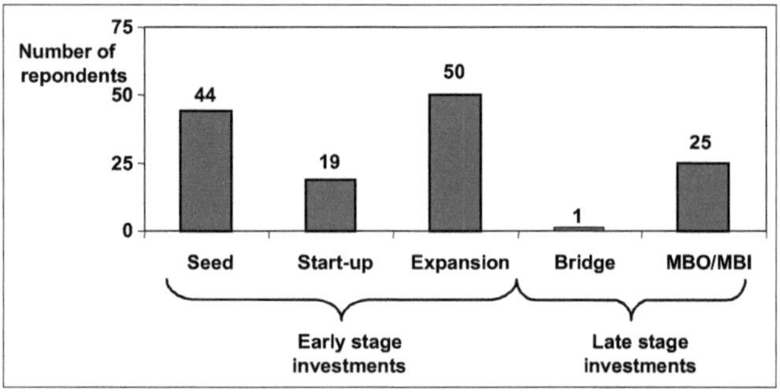

Figure 26: Respondents by development stage[540]

[540] For more information refer to 2.1.3.

- Age

  As noted before, there are more younger companies among the 139 respondents than in the original sample. Still, the mean age is comparatively high with 15 years, which is mainly due to some outliers (late stage investments). For the analysis, three age-groups were created: portfolio companies that were at the time of the survey up to five years old, between six and ten years or eleven years or older. The largest group with 50 companies (36%) is the first one, followed by the second one with 47 companies (34%) and the third one with 42 companies (30%). Figure 27 shows the distribution of ages in an overview.

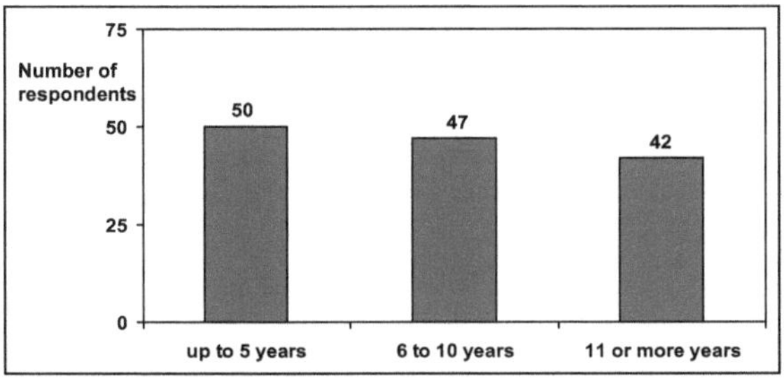

Figure 27: Respondents by age group

- Company size

  Following the company classification from the European Union, the 139 portfolio companies were grouped according to number of employees. Micro businesses have up to nine employees; in the study 29 of these companies (21%) are analysed. The largest group among the respondents is small companies with 10–49 employees (56 companies; 40%). Additionally, there are 34 medium companies (25%), which have 50–249 employees, included in the survey. Finally, 20 large companies (14%) with more than 250 employees completed the questionnaire. On average, the companies have 208 employees. For a graphical presentation see Figure 28.

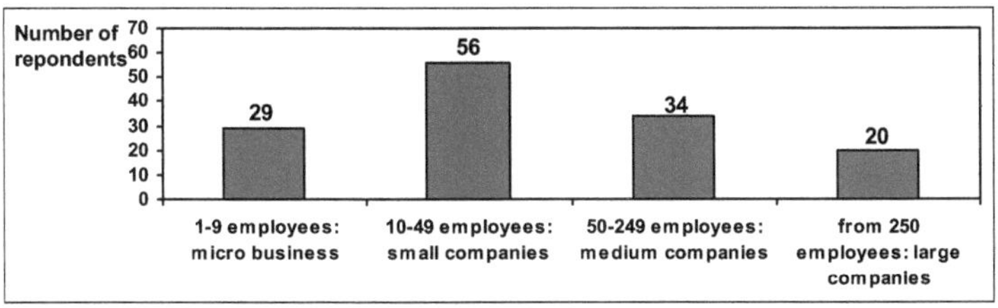

Figure 28: Respondents by number of employees

- Industries

  Taking industry factors into account in the analysis requires the creation of groups of industries with a sufficient number of portfolio companies. All respondents were therefore grouped into eight industrial sectors as follows: hard- and software (23; 17%), medical and health (27; 19%), biotechnology (16; 12%), communication and Internet (16; 12%), other business or consumer services (18; 13%), industrials/energy (20; 14%), electronics and semiconductors (10; 7%) and other industries (8; 6%). This distribution is shown in Figure 29.

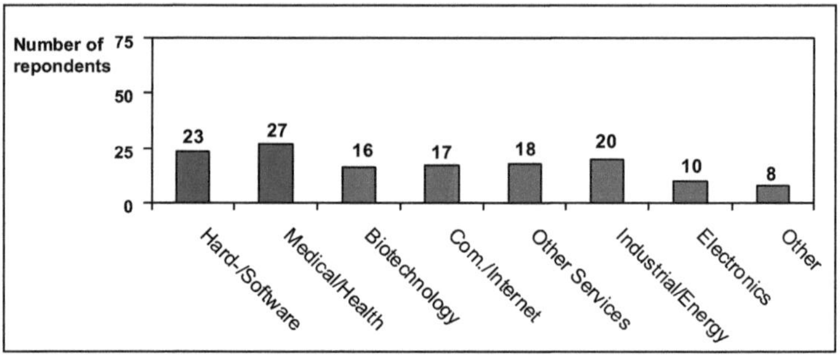

Figure 29: Respondents by industry

5.3.6 Basic Information on Invested Venture Capitalists

This paragraph describes the main characteristics of the lead venture capitalists that are invested in the 139 analysed portfolio companies. These characteristics are used, among others, to test the hypothesised relationships between the venture capitalists, their influence and their impact on corporate governance.

- Type of lead venture capital firm

  The respondents were asked to provide information about their lead venture capitalists for each financing round because it is expected that this is the most influential investor. In the following figure, the lead venture capitalists are grouped according to their type. The vast majority of lead investors are independent venture capital firms (100 or 72% in the first financing round, 39 or 81% in the second financing round and 24 or 86% in the third financing round). Venture capitalists associated with a financial institution are the second most important group (23, 11 and 3 venture capitalists in the first, second and third financing round, respectively). Corporate venture capitalists and governmental investors play a relatively unimportant role as lead venture capitalists, as Figure 30 indicates.

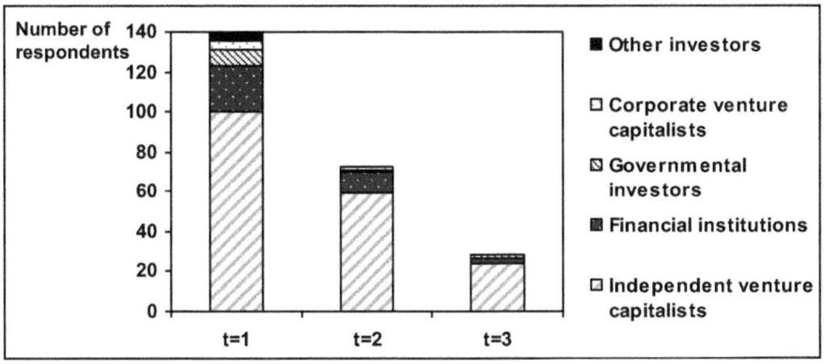

Figure 30: Venture capitalists by type

- International scope of lead venture capital firm

  The lead venture capitalists were also analysed in regard to the scope of their international activity, i.e., in which geographic regions they invest. It was distinguished between regional investments (i.e., in one region within a country), investments with a national scope, investments in several European countries and investments in Europe and beyond (global). Figure 31 shows that the largest group of lead venture capitalists invests on a global level (in most cases in Europe and North America, sometimes also additionally in Asia; 76, 43, 15 in the first, second and third financing rounds, respectively). The second most-important group is national investors, followed by venture capitalists that have a European scope. Regional investors are of limited importance for the analysis, particularly in the second and third financing rounds.

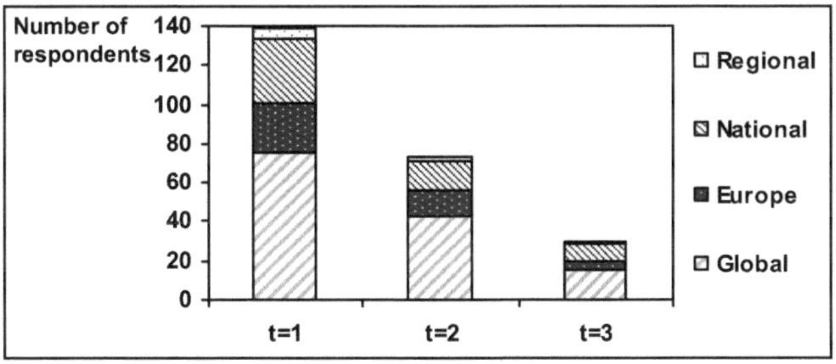

Figure 31: Venture capitalists by international scope

- Size of lead venture capital firm

  The size of the invested venture capital firms was measured in terms of the number of portfolio companies, which also indicates the investment experience of the firms. The invested firms were divided in four groups: Firms with less than 20 portfolio companies are dominant with 53, 27 and 11 lead venture capitalists in the first, second and third financing rounds, respectively. Investors with 20–99 portfolio companies and those with 100–499 portfolio companies come thereafter. The group of the biggest investors, those with more than 500 portfolio companies, are still well represented with 16, 9 and 3 lead venture capital firms in the three financing rounds. An overview of the distribution is given in Figure 32.

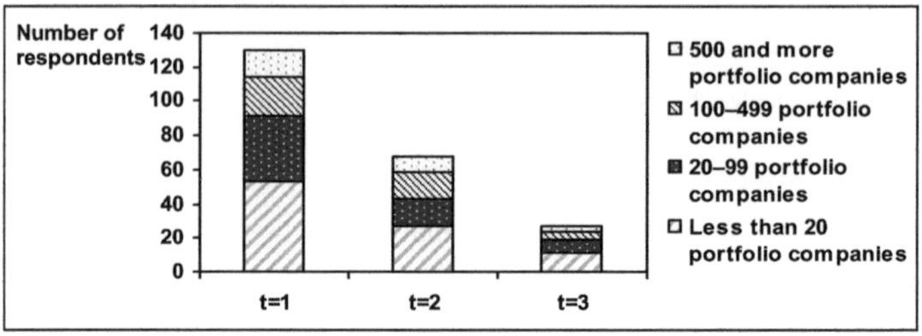

Figure 32: Venture capitalists by number of portfolio companies

- Contacts

The following figure shows the number of contacts per quarter between the investment managers of the lead venture capitalists and the managers of the portfolio companies. It indicates that they are regularly in contact, particularly after the first and second financing rounds. In 58 (44%) and 29 (46%) of the portfolio companies (after the first and second financing rounds, respectively), the managers had ten or more contacts with the investment managers per quarter. In only one exception in the second financing round did the investment manager have no contact at all with the portfolio company.

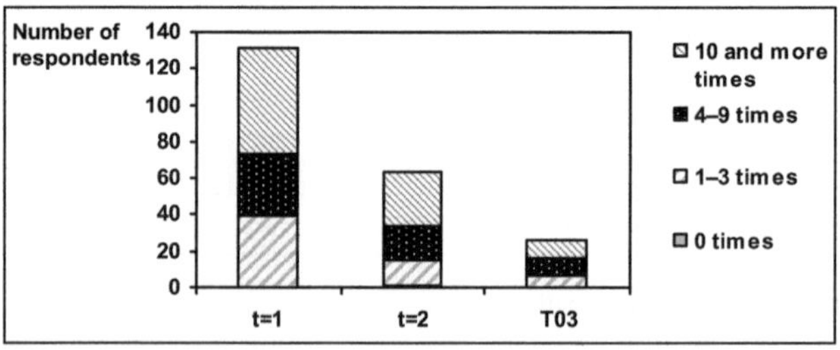

Figure 33: Number of contacts between venture capitalists and portfolio companies

5.3.7 Perceived Relationship Between Venture Capital, Corporate Governance and Firm Value

Before the detailed results of the analysis are presented in the next sections, the results of three basic questions are described corresponding to the two research questions. They refer to the respondents' assessment of the impact of venture capitalists on corporate governance quality and of the latter on firm value.

With the first question, respondents assessed whether the impact of the venture capitalist on the portfolio company's corporate governance was positive or negative. 59% of the respondents evaluated the impact as positive or very positive, whereas only 6% of the respondents assessed the impact as negative or very negative. The remaining 35% did not perceive a significantly positive or negative influence. The average perceived impact was 3,7 on a scale from 1 ("– –") to 5 ("++").

The second and third questions dealt with the impact of good corporate governance on firm value as measured by the company's performance as well as by its valuation. Referring to the first relationship, 43% of the respondents perceived a positive or very positive impact on performance, whereas 47% did not perceive any impact, and 10% perceived the impact as negative or very negative. The average on the 5-step scale was 3,4, thus still positive. A similar impact was perceived in regard to the portfolio company's valuation. 43% of the assessments were positive and only 8% of the assessments were negative. Again, the group of respondents that perceives neither a positive nor a negative influence of good corporate governance is the greatest with 49%. The average perceived impact is positive at 3,4. Figure 34 shows the results of the three questions on the relationships between venture capital, corporate governance and firm value in an overview.

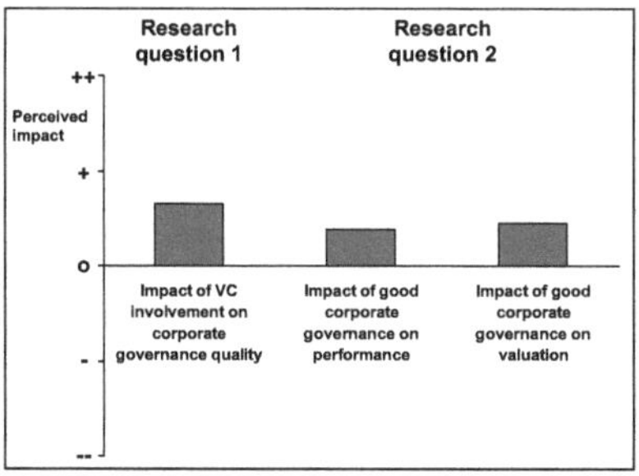

Figure 34: Mean respondents' perception of the impact of venture capitalists and good corporate governance

These findings indicate the respondents' general perceptions. They can be compared with the results from the detailed statistical analyses conducted to test the hypotheses derived from theory. The corresponding results are presented in the next sections.

5.4 Reasons for Venture Capitalists' Influence on Corporate Governance

5.4.1 Descriptive Results for Development of Reasons and Influence

5.4.1.1 Risk Reduction

The first reason for the venture capitalists' influence that is analysed is the portfolio companies' agency and business risk. The explanatory variables were collected for two measuring times: for the time before the first financing round and for the current situation at the time the respondent completed the questionnaire. The agency risk index includes variables for the managerial ownership, the age of the portfolio companies, the specificity of the businesses, the importance of intangible assets, and the degree of technology of the products. The mean of this index is 73% at both measuring times. By contrast, the mean business risk grows over time from 64% to 69%. It relates to variables for founder-CEOs, the start-up and functional experience of the top management-teams, the number of products, the degree of the dynamics of industries, and the attractiveness of markets. These two indexes are combined in the agency and business risk index that increases from 68% before the first financing round to 71% today. Figure 35 shows the development of the three indexes in an overview.

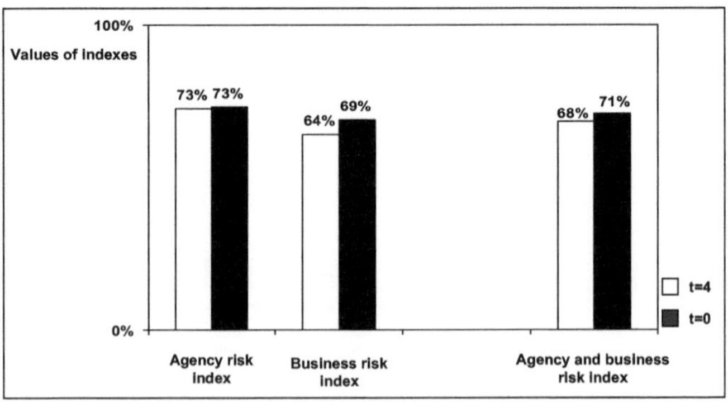

Figure 35: Development of agency and business risk over time

5.4.1.2 Value Creation

Value creation is the second reason derived from the theoretical analysis for venture capitalists to influence corporate governance. The precedent corporate governance quality is thereby expected to have a positive impact on the strength of the venture capitalists' influence. Accordingly, corporate governance quality is used as an explanatory variable for testing the hypotheses. Corporate governance quality measured by self-assessment of the respondents as well as by criteria increases over time. The mean of the overall corporate governance quality index increases from 59% to 70% as measured by self-assessment whereas the index derived from the criteria increases from 54% to 78% in the same time. Detailed information on the development is introduced in paragraph 5.5.1.

5.4.1.3 Exit Preparation

The third reason for increased influence of the venture capitalists on corporate governance is the preparation of an exit, in particular an IPO. Therefore, the respondents were asked to indicate whether the portfolio companies planned to go public at the measuring times. The proportion of companies that prepared a public exit remained similar over the three measuring times. After the first financing round, 23 of 139 companies (17%) planned an IPO; after the second financing round, 11 of 73 companies (15%), and after the third financing round, five of 30 companies (17%). This indicates that the number of cases for these tests of the associated hypotheses is relatively small.

The descriptive analysis of the variables related to venture capitalists' reasons for influencing the corporate governance of portfolio companies is presented in an overview in Annex 6. The table includes the number of analysed cases ("N"), the minimum and maximum observed values ("Min."/"Max"), the mean value ("Mean") and the standard deviation ("Std. Dev.").

5.4.1.4 Strength of Influence

After the introduction of the explanatory variables of the hypotheses, the development of the response variables is described. The venture capitalists' influence was assessed by respondents on a scale ranging from "no influence" (1) to "very strong" influence (4) for the different corporate governance elements. All elements were included in an index of the strength of the overall venture capitalists' influence. Over the three measuring times, the index fluctuates around 2,7 on the four-step scale. T-tests were carried out to analyse whether significant changes occurred between the time before and after the first financing round as well as between the first and second financing rounds. However, the differences of those means are not significant. Figure 36 shows this development.

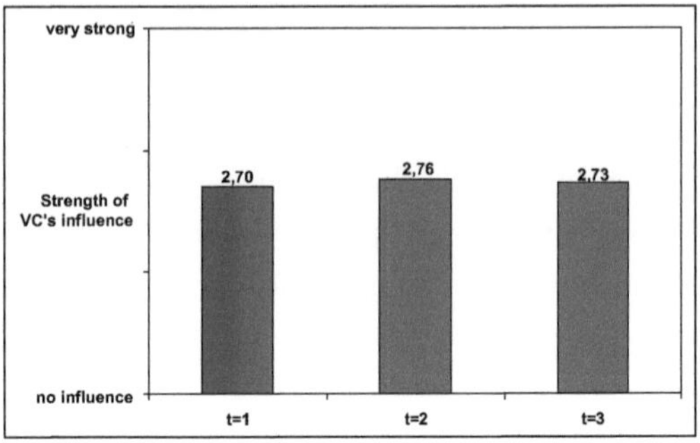

Figure 36: Development of overall venture capitalists' influence on corporate governance

This index can be broken down into the influence on the different corporate governance elements as Figure 37 shows, there are differences among these elements as well as between measuring times. The strongest influence is exerted on the work of the boards and the bonding and compensation of managers. For these elements, significant increases were found by means of t-test analyses. Whereas the influence on the work of the boards and the managers' compensation increases, particularly between the first and the second financing rounds, the influence on the bonding of managers increases in importance between the second and the third financing rounds. The weakest influence is exerted on the selection of managers.

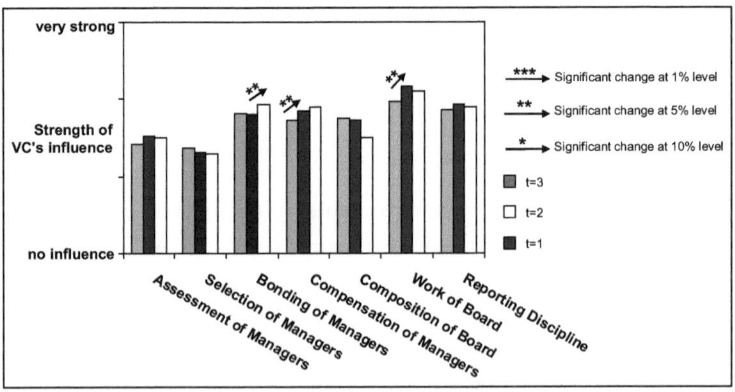

Figure 37: Development of venture capitalists' influence on corporate governance elements

More detailed information on the variables related to the venture capitalists' influence is introduced in a table in Annex 7.

5.4.2 Results for Hypotheses' Tests

5.4.2.1 Risk Reduction

According to the first hypothesis, the portfolio companies' business and agency risk determines the strength of the venture capitalists' influence: the higher the risk, the stronger is the influence (H1.1). Because this hypothesis is derived from agency theory, it relates in particular to the monitoring and bonding function of corporate governance. Consequently, the influence on all corporate governance elements was used as a response variable as well as the influence on only those elements that relate to the monitoring or bonding function. The explanatory variable is the agency and business risk index. In order to take into account other explanatory effects, the analyses were controlled for the distance between the locations of the venture capitalists and the portfolio companies, the size and national location of the portfolio company and the time (financing round). However, the R^2 of these three analyses are very low ranging from 0,012 to 0,035, which indicates that the model does not very well explain the response variables. The coefficients for all three explanatory variables are negative but not significantly so. That means that the findings rather contradict the hypothesis but that no conclusion can be drawn because there is no significant result.

In a second step, the relationship between the agency and business risk and the influence on individual corporate governance elements was analysed. The hypotheses relate to the assessment (H1.1.1), selection (H1.1.2), compensation (H1.1.3) and bonding (H1.1.4) of managers, the composition (H1.1.5) and work (H1.1.6) of the board and the reporting discipline (H1.1.7). Again, the R^2 of these analyses are very low, and all the coefficients of the explanatory variables are negative against the expectation. Only one of the tests delivered a significant result. It was found that agency and business risk had a weakly negative impact on the venture capitalists' influence on the composition of the board. The coefficient is low with 0,012 at the 90% confidence level, as Table 3 shows. This table, as well as the following tables, includes the most important results from the statistical analyses that use the mixed models technique. Every row represents one analysis for the testing of one hypothesis. The given information includes the response, explanatory and control variables and the coefficient for the impact of the explanatory variable and the R^2 of the test. Moreover, it is denoted whether the result for the explanatory variable is significant: "*" marks a significant result at the 90% confidence level, "**" at the 95% confidence level and "***" at the 99% confidence level. The presented findings indicate that the hypotheses on the relationship between agency and business risk and the venture capitalists' influence on corporate governance cannot be supported.

#	Hypothesis	Response variable	Explanatory variable	Coefficient	Control variables	R-square
H1.1	The greater the agency and business risks associated with an investment, the greater is the venture capitalists' influence on the corporate governance.	Index of VC's influence on all CG elements	Agency and business risk index	-0,088	lvcdist, cempngr, finrou, landgr	0,012
H1.1	The greater the agency and business risks associated with an investment, the greater is the venture capitalists' influence on the corporate governance.	Index of VC's influence on CG elements with monitoring function	Agency and business risk index	-0,122	lvcdist, cempngr, finrou, landgr	0,013
H1.1	The greater the agency and business risks associated with an investment, the greater is the venture capitalists' influence on the corporate governance.	Index of VC's influence on CG elements with bonding function	Agency and business risk index	-0,160	lvcdist, cempngr, finrou, landgr	0,035
H1.1.1	The greater the agency and business risks associated with an investment, the greater is the venture capitalists' influence on the assessment of the managers.	VC's influence on assessment of managers	Agency and business risk index	-0,001	lvcdist, cempngr, finrou, landgr	0,054
H1.1.2	The greater the agency and business risks associated with an investment, the greater is the venture capitalists' influence on the selection of the managers.	VC's influence on compensation of managers	Agency and business risk index	0,004	lvcdist, cempngr, finrou, landgr	0,017
H1.1.3	The greater the agency and business risks associated with an investment, the greater is the venture capitalists' influence on the compensation of the managers.	VC's influence on compensation of managers	Agency and business risk index	-0,004	lvcdist, cempngr, finrou, landgr	0,031
H1.1.4	The greater the agency and business risks associated with an investment, the greater is the venture capitalists' influence on the bonding of the portfolio companies' managers.	VC's influence on bonding of managers	Agency and business risk index	-0,008	lvcdist, cempngr, finrou, landgr	0,055
H1.1.5	The greater the agency and business risks associated with an investment, the greater is the venture capitalists' influence on the composition of the board.	VC's influence on composition of board	Agency and business risk index	**-0,012***	lvcdist, cempngr, finrou, landgr	0,030
H1.1.6	The greater the agency and business risks associated with an investment, the greater is the venture capitalists' influence on the work of the board.	VC's influence on work of board	Agency and business risk index	-0,004	lvcdist, cempngr, finrou, landgr	0,052
H1.1.7	The greater the agency and business risks associated with an investment, the greater is the venture capitalists' influence on the frequency of reporting.	VC's influence on reporting discipline	Agency and business risk index	0,002	lvcdist, cempngr, finrou, landgr	0,042

Table 3: Statistical results for the hypotheses H1.1–H1.1.7

5.4.2.2 Value Creation

The hypothesis that the precedent corporate governance quality affects the venture capitalists' impact on corporate governance (H1.2) is derived from the dynamic resource-based view. Accordingly, the hypothesis was tested with venture capitalists' influence on all elements as well as with their influence on the elements with an advice function. Furthermore, the corporate governance quality used as an explanatory variable was measured by self-assessment (denoted in the table with "S") and criteria ("C"). In the mixed models analysis, several control variables were taken into account: the distance between venture capitalists and portfolio companies, the size, development stage and location of the portfolio companies and time. Nonetheless, the four analyses did not deliver a significant result, and the R^2 were again very low as Table 4 shows. That means this basic hypothesis cannot be supported.

#	Hypothesis	Version	Response variable	Explanatory variable	Coefficient	Control variables	R-square
H1.2	The better the initial corporate governance quality, the greater is the venture capitalists' influence on the corporate governance.	S	Index of VC's influence on all CG elements	CG quality index (self-assessment)	0,091	lvcdist, cempngr, finrou, cdev, landgr	0,018
H1.2	The better the initial corporate governance quality, the greater is the venture capitalists' influence on the corporate governance.	C	Index of VC's influence on all CG elements	CG quality index (criteria)	0,010	lvcdist, cempngr, finrou, cdev, landgr	0,012
H1.2	The better the initial corporate governance quality, the greater is the venture capitalists' influence on the corporate governance.	S	Index of VC's influence on CG elements with advice function	CG advice index (self-assessment)	0,080	lvcdist, cempngr, finrou, cdev, landgr	0,015
H1.2	The better the initial corporate governance quality, the greater is the venture capitalists' influence on the corporate governance.	C	Index of VC's influence on CG elements with advice function	CG advice index (criteria)	-0,043	lvcdist, cempngr, finrou, cdev, landgr	0,018
H1.2.1	The better the initial corporate governance quality, the greater is the venture capitalists' influence on the selection process of new managers.	S	VC's influence on selection of new managers	CG quality index (self-assessment)	0,000	lvcdist, cempngr, finrou, cdev, landgr	0,025
H1.2.1	The better the initial corporate governance quality, the greater is the venture capitalists' influence on the selection process of new managers.	C	VC's influence on selection of new managers	CG quality index (criteria)	0,000	lvcdist, cempngr, finrou, cdev, landgr	0,032
H1.2.1	The better the initial corporate governance quality, the greater is the venture capitalists' influence on the selection process of new managers.	S	VC's influence on selection of new managers	CG advice index (self-assessment)	-0,005	lvcdist, cempngr, finrou, cdev, landgr	0,039
H1.2.1	The better the initial corporate governance quality, the greater is the venture capitalists' influence on the selection process of new managers.	C	VC's influence on selection of new managers	CG advice index (criteria)	0,000	lvcdist, cempngr, finrou, cdev, landgr	0,041
H1.2.1	The better the initial corporate governance quality, the greater is the venture capitalists' influence on the selection process of new managers.	S	VC's influence on selection of new managers	Efficiency of selection of new managers	-0,081	lvcdist, cempngr, finrou, cdev, landgr	0,046
H1.2.1	The better the initial corporate governance quality, the greater is the venture capitalists' influence on the selection process of new managers.	C	VC's influence on selection of new managers	Index of quality of selection of managers	**-0,005**	lvcdist, cempngr, finrou, cdev, landgr	0,142

Table 4: Statistical results for the hypotheses H1.2–H1.2.1

For a more detailed analysis, the hypotheses that relate to the individual corporate governance elements with an advice function were tested. In particular, it was analysed whether corporate governance quality — measured by both self-assessment and criteria — affects the subsequent venture capitalist influence on the selection of managers (1.2.1), the composition of the board (1.2.2) and the work of the board (1.2.3). The resulting R^2 of these analyses are slightly higher than in the first tests but still comparatively low. All coefficients are also very low and fluctuate around zero. Three of the analyses have significant results. The quality of the advice function and of the board's composition — both measured by criteria — have a very weak negative impact on the influence on this element. By contrast, the corporate governance advice index measured by self-assessment has a weakly positive effect on the venture capitalists' influence on the work of the board. However, because of the very low coefficients, the explanatory power of these results is very limited. So these tests can also shed no light on the venture capitalists' reasons for influencing portfolio companies' corporate governance.

#	Hypothesis	Version	Response variable	Explanatory variable	Coefficient	Control variables	R-square
H.1.2.2	The better the initial corporate governance quality, the greater is the venture capitalists' influence on the composition of the board.	S	VC's influence on composition of board	CG quality index (self-assessment)	0,000	lvcdist, cempngr, finrou, cdev, landgr	0,005
H.1.2.2	The better the initial corporate governance quality, the greater is the venture capitalists' influence on the composition of the board.	C	VC's influence on composition of board	CG quality index (criteria)	-0,002	lvcdist, cempngr, finrou, cdev, landgr	0,000
H.1.2.2	The better the initial corporate governance quality, the greater is the venture capitalists' influence on the composition of the board.	S	VC's influence on composition of board	CG advice index (self-assessment)	0,001	lvcdist, cempngr, finrou, cdev, landgr	0,005
H.1.2.2	The better the initial corporate governance quality, the greater is the venture capitalists' influence on the composition of the board.	C	VC's influence on composition of board	CG advice index (criteria)	**-0,003***	lvcdist, cempngr, finrou, cdev, landgr	0,019
H.1.2.2	The better the initial corporate governance quality, the greater is the venture capitalists' influence on the composition of the board.	S	VC's influence on composition of board	Efficiency of composition of board: advice	0,035	lvcdist, cempngr, finrou, cdev, landgr	0,007
H.1.2.2	The better the initial corporate governance quality, the greater is the venture capitalists' influence on the composition of the board.	C	VC's influence on composition of board	Index of quality of board composition	**-0,003***	lvcdist, cempngr, finrou, cdev, landgr	0,002
H1.2.3	The better the initial corporate governance quality, the greater is the venture capitalists' influence on the work of the board.	S	VC's influence on work of board	CG quality index (self-assessment)	0,003	lvcdist, cempngr, finrou, cdev, landgr	0,052
H1.2.3	The better the initial corporate governance quality, the greater is the venture capitalists' influence on the work of the board.	C	VC's influence on work of board	CG quality index (criteria)	0,002	lvcdist, cempngr, finrou, cdev, landgr	0,045
H1.2.3	The better the initial corporate governance quality, the greater is the venture capitalists' influence on the work of the board.	S	VC's influence on work of board	CG advice index (self-assessment)	**0,004***	lvcdist, cempngr, finrou, cdev, landgr	0,064
H1.2.3	The better the initial corporate governance quality, the greater is the venture capitalists' influence on the work of the board.	C	VC's influence on work of board	CG advice index (criteria)	0,000	lvcdist, cempngr, finrou, cdev, landgr	0,059

Table 5: Statistical results for the hypotheses H1.2.2–H1.2.3

5.4.2.3 Exit preparation

Hypothesis H1.3 says that venture capitalists' increase their influence before a potential public exit of portfolio companies. A mixed models analysis was carried out that took the distance between the venture capitalists and the portfolio companies, the size, development stage and location of the portfolio companies and the time into account as control variables. The resulting coefficient of the impact was comparatively high but not significant. Correspondingly, the R^2 of the test is only 0,015. A more detailed hypothesis predicts that more members are brought to the board that already have experience as board members in listed companies (H1.3.2). In this case the R^2 is higher with 0,139 and the hypothesis is significantly supported. The coefficient of the explanatory variable is 0,660 at the 99% confidence level as Table 6 indicates.

#	Hypothesis	Version	Response variable	Explanatory variable	Coefficient	Control variables	R-square
H1.3	Before a potential public exit, venture capitalists increase their influence on the corporate governance of portfolio companies.	C	Index of VC's influence on all CG elements	Planned IPO	2,657	lvcdist, cempngr, finrou, cdev, landgr	0,015
H1.3.2	Before a potential public exit, it is more probable that the portfolio companies have board members with experience in listed companies.	C	Experience as managers or board member in listed companies of independent board members	Planned IPO	0,660***	lvcdist, cempngr, finrou, cdev, landgr	0,139

Table 6: Statistical results for the hypotheses H1.3–1.3.2 (mixed models technique)

Similarly, support was found for hypothesis H1.3.1, which says that portfolio companies before a potential IPO more often comply with corporate governance codes than do other portfolio companies. The analysis had a very high R^2 of 0,570 and a very high odds ratio of 160,567. That means that the probability that portfolio companies comply with the corporate governance code is 160 times greater if an IPO is planned than if one is not. Table 7 shows the result of the logistic regression used for this test because the response variable is dummy coded.

#	Hypothesis	Version	Response variable	Explanatory variable	Coefficient	Control variables	R-square
H1.3.1	Before a potential publich exit it is more probable that the portfolio company complies with corporate governance codes.	C	Compliance with CG code	Planned IPO	5,078***	lvcdist, cempngr, finrou, cdev, landgr	0,570

Table 7: Statistical results for the hypothesis H1.3.1 (logistic regression technique)

5.4.2.4 Development of Reasons

According to the last hypothesis that relates to the reasons venture capitalists' influence the corporate governance of portfolio companies, the importance of the reasons changes over time (H1.4). Whereas business and agency risks are expected to be more important in the beginning, corporate governance quality is expected to become more important later on. Correspondingly, the first test used only observations from the first financing round into account, whereas the second test was done only with observations from the second and third financing rounds. There was no change in the findings on the impact of agency and business risks because this analysis did not deliver a significant result. By contrast, the analysis on the influence of the precedent corporate governance quality on venture capitalists' influence delivers support for the hypothesis. The coefficient of the explanatory variable is 0,429 at the 99% confidence level. Table 8 indicates that value creation as a reason is supported by the analysis for later financing rounds, which partly supports the hypothesis that the reasons of venture capitalists change over time.

#	Hypothesis	Version	Response variable	Explanatory variable	Coefficient	Odds-Ratio	Control variables	R-square
H1.4	Agency and business risks have a stronger impact on venture capitalists' influence on the corporate governance of portfolio companies at earlier financing rounds than at later financing rounds.	S	Index of VC's influence on all CG elements	Agency and business risk index	-0,104	160,567	lvcdist, cempngr, finrou, landgr	0,020
H1.4	Agency and business risks have a stronger impact on venture capitalists' influence on the corporate governance of portfolio companies at earlier financing rounds than at later financing rounds.	S	Index of VC's influence on all CG elements	CG quality index (self-assessment)	0,429***	160,567	lvcdist, cempngr, finrou, cdev, landgr	0,155

Table 8: Statistical results for the hypothesis H1.4

#	Hypothesis	Support
H1.1	The greater the agency and business risks associated with an investment, the greater is the venture capitalists' influence on the corporate governance.	?
H1.1.1	The greater the agency and business risks associated with an investment, the greater is the venture capitalists' influence on the assessment of the managers.	?
H1.1.2	The greater the agency and business risks associated with an investment, the greater is the venture capitalists' influence on the selection of the managers.	?
H1.1.3	The greater the agency and business risks associated with an investment, the greater is the venture capitalists' influence on the compensation of the managers.	?
H1.1.4	The greater the agency and business risks associated with an investment, the greater is the venture capitalists' influence on the bonding of the portfolio companies' managers.	?
H1.1.5	The greater the agency and business risks associated with an investment, the greater is the venture capitalists' influence on the composition of the board.	?
H1.1.6	The greater the agency and business risks associated with an investment, the greater is the venture capitalists' influence on the work of the board.	?
H1.1.7	The greater the agency and business risks associated with an investment, the greater is the venture capitalists' influence on the frequency of reporting.	?
H1.2	The better the initial corporate governance quality, the greater is the venture capitalists' influence on the corporate governance.	?
H1.2.1	The better the initial corporate governance quality, the greater is the venture capitalists' influence on the selection process of new managers.	?
H1.2.2	The better the initial corporate governance quality, the greater is the venture capitalists' influence on the composition of the board.	?
H1.2.3	The better the initial corporate governance quality, the greater is the venture capitalists' influence on the work of the board.	~
H1.3	Before a potential public exit, venture capitalists increase their influence on the corporate governance of portfolio companies.	?
H1.3.1	Before a potential public exit it is more probable that the portfolio company complies with corporate governance codes.	✓
H1.3.2	Before a potential public exit, it is more probable that the portfolio companies have board members with experience in listed companies.	✓
H1.4	Agency and business risks have a stronger impact on venture capitalists' influence on the corporate governance of portfolio companies at earlier financing rounds than at later financing rounds.	~

Figure 38: Overview of the results for hypotheses about the relationship between venture capitalists' reasons and influence on corporate governance

In the above figure, the results of the tests that analysed the relationship between the venture capitalists' reasons and their influence on the corporate governance of portfolio companies are summarised. It indicates whether the hypotheses are largely supported (✓), the findings are mixed (~) or the test did not deliver a significant result (?). The overview shows that the findings are unsatisfactory. Reasons for this outcome will be discussed in section 6.2.

5.5 Effects of Venture Capitalists' Influence on Corporate Governance

5.5.1 Descriptive Results for the Development of Corporate Governance Quality

The corporate governance quality of the analysed portfolio companies significantly increases over time, which is shown by both corporate governance measures.

Figure 39 shows that the mean of corporate governance quality measured by self-assessment increased from 59% at the time before the first financing round to 70% at the time after the third financing round. A particularly great increase takes place with the first financing by a venture capitalist when the perceived corporate governance quality increases by ten basis points. A t-test for paired samples delivered significant differences between the means for t=0 and t=1 as well as between t=2 and t=3. However, the small decline between t=1 and t=2 is not significant because the null-hypothesis of the t-test could not be rejected.

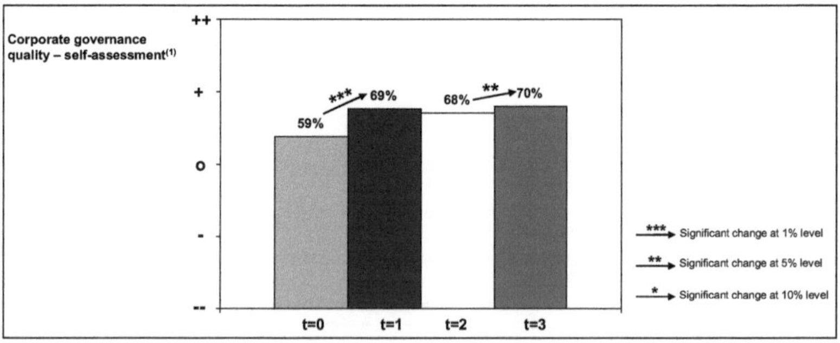

Figure 39: Development of corporate governance quality — self-assessment

For corporate governance quality measured by criteria, an even stronger increase was found. Over the three financing rounds, the mean index increased from 54% to 78%, with a significant increase of 18 basis points at the time of the first venture capital financing round.

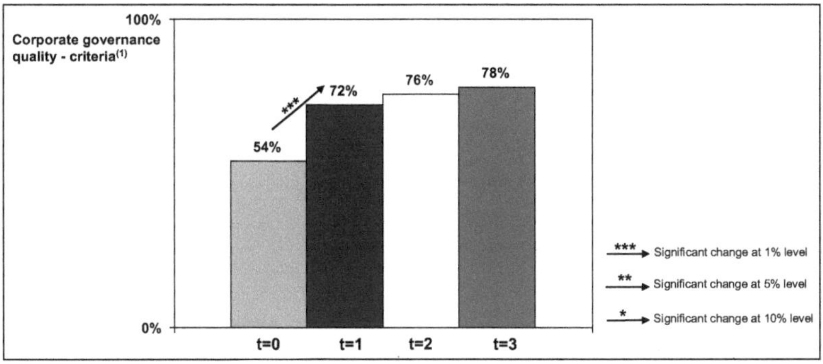

Figure 40: Development of corporate governance quality — criteria

The comparison of the two measures reveals a difference in the development. Although both indexes increase over time, the basis at the time before the first financing round is relatively higher when the quality is measured by self-assessment than when measured by criteria. However, at the following measuring times, the quality measured by criteria is higher than that measured by self-assessment.

In the following, the development of the three corporate governance functions is described. The monitoring function increases significantly after all three financing rounds when the quality is measured by self-assessment of the respondents, but it increases only after the first financing round when it is measured by criteria. The level of quality was consistently assessed higher by the respondents than it was measured by means of criteria. Figure 41 shows this comparison in an overview.

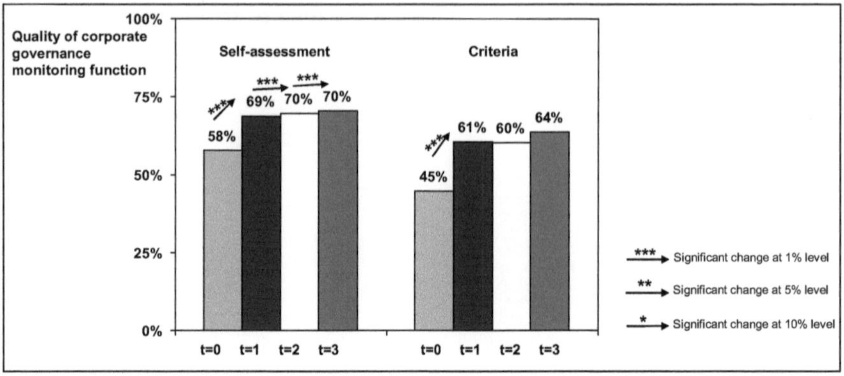

Figure 41: Development of the quality of the corporate governance monitoring function

In regard to the bonding function, the quality of corporate governance of the analysed companies also increased. However, the increase as assessed by the respondents is relatively limited (from 65% before the first financing round to 70% after the third financing round). This is in contrast to a stronger increase of 14 basis points when the quality is measured by criteria. For an overview, see Figure 42.

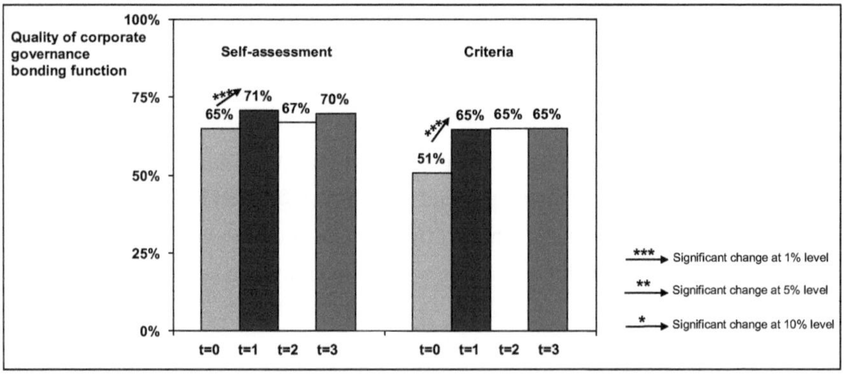

Figure 42: Development of the quality of the corporate governance bonding function

The quality of the advice function increases over the three financing rounds from 56% to 68% when measured by self-assessment and from 44% to 79% when measured by criteria. The second measurement is, with 35 basis points, the greatest increase of all corporate governance functions. Particularly at the first financing round, there is a significant improvement in the quality, as

Figure 43 shows.

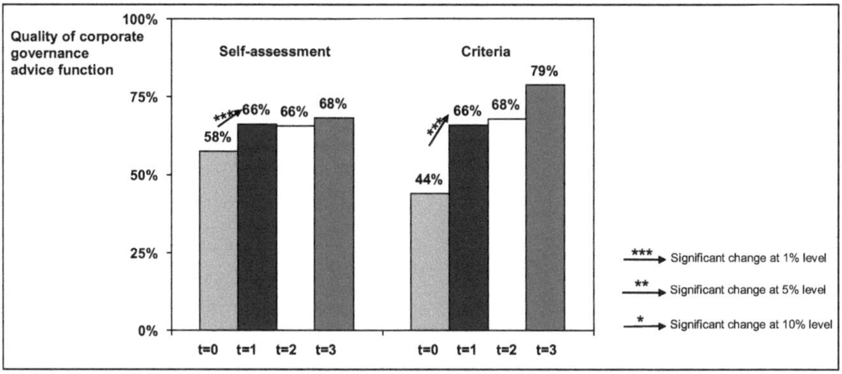

Figure 43: Development of the quality of the corporate governance advice function

In the following, the development of the individual elements is presented and compared. Generally, for all corporate governance elements, a significant increase with the first venture capital financing was found, but the level of the increase differs for the elements and the two measures.

According to the perception of the respondents, the composition and work of the board were the least efficient corporate governance elements before the first investment by a venture capitalist. Correspondingly, these elements saw also the greatest increase over time. The bonding of the managers was consistently assessed as the most adequate of the corporate governance elements. Figure 44 shows all corporate governance elements in an overview.

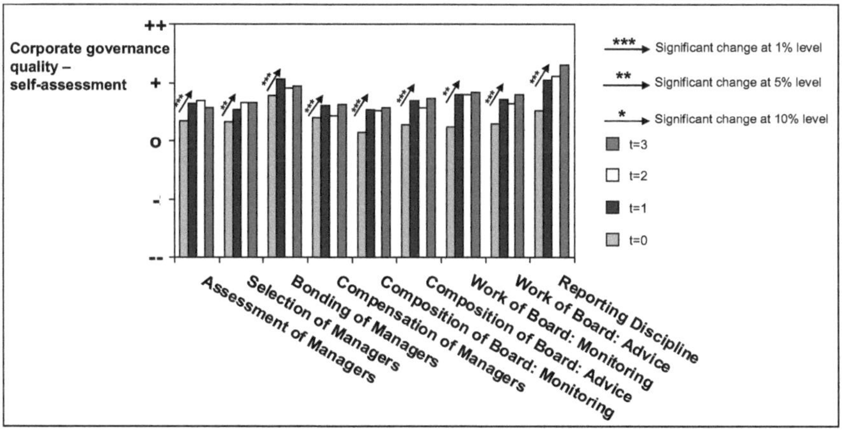

Figure 44: Development of the quality of corporate governance elements — self-assessment

Similarly, the composition and work of the board had the lowest level of fulfilment when measured using the criteria. In addition to that, the criteria related to the compensation of the managers were on average less fulfilled than those related to the other corporate governance elements. The biggest increase was found for the composition of the board, with 24 basis points. The development of all corporate governance elements is presented in Figure 45.

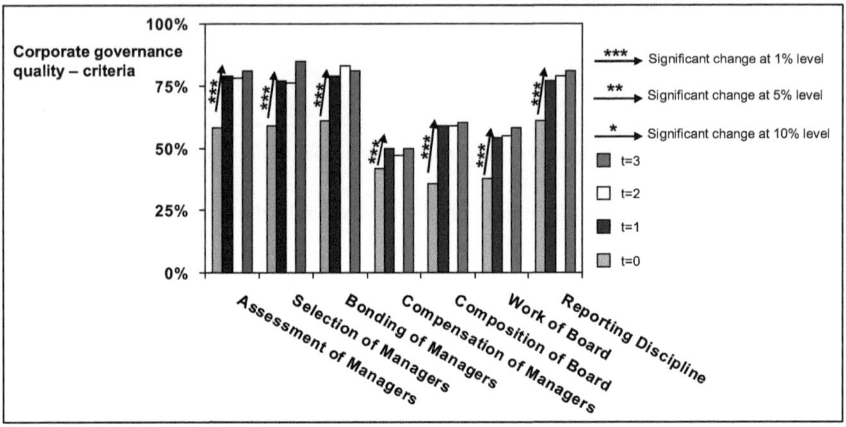

Figure 45: Development of the quality of corporate governance elements — criteria

The development of the individual variables of corporate governance at the different levels (overall corporate governance, corporate governance functions, corporate governance elements, and corporate governance criteria) over the four measuring imes is presented in the table in Annex 8. It includes the number of portfolio companies that were taken into account for the calculation of the value ("N"), the minimum and maximum values ("Min"/"Max") and the arithmetic mean ("Mean") and standard deviation ("Std. Dev.") of the variables. These variables are used as response variables in the analyses to test the hypotheses on the relationship between the influence of venture capitalists and the corporate governance of portfolio companies.

5.5.2 Results for Hypotheses' Tests

After describing the development of corporate governance quality over the time of the first three financing rounds, the results of the hypotheses' tests related to the relationship between the venture capitalists' influence and the corporate governance quality of portfolio companies are presented here. It should prove whether the increase in corporate governance quality after the financing by venture capitalists found in the descriptive analyses can be traced back to the venture capitalists' influence. The analyses were primarily done using the mixed models technique, but for some hypotheses the logistic regression technique had to be used because of dichotomous response variables.[541]

The basic hypothesis H2 predicts that the venture capitalists' influence has an impact on the portfolio companies' corporate governance. It was tested with the two measurements for corporate governance quality: self-assessment ("S") and criteria ("C"). Mixed models analyses were conducted that controlled for influences from the venture capitalists' abilities, the size of the portfolio company, the measuring time, the development stage and country of the portfolio company and the corporate governance quality before the first financing round (t=0). Both hypotheses were supported at a confidence level of 99% with coefficients of 0,129 for the analysis taking into account the self-assessment measure and 0,194 for the measurement by criteria. The coefficients of determination, R^2, for the two tests are relatively high at 0,350 and 0,369. Table 9 shows the results in detail.

#	Hypothesis	Version	Response variable	Explanatory variable	Coefficient	Control variables	R-square
H2	The venture capitalists' influence has an impact on the portfolio companies' corporate governance	S	CG quality index (self-assessment)	Index of VC's influence on all CG elements	**0,129*** **	lvcabi, cempngr, finrou, cdev, landgr, cgqind(t=0)	0,350
H2	The venture capitalists' influence has an impact on the portfolio companies' corporate governance	C	CG quality index (criteria)	Index of VC's influence on all CG elements	**0,194*** **	lvcabi, cempngr, finrou, cdev, landgr, cgqinc(t=0)	0,369

Table 9: Results for hypothesis H.2

After this general finding that venture capitalists' influence leads to an improvement of the portfolio companies' corporate governance, it was determined which corporate governance elements are affected by this influence. The results are presented for the three elements related to the managers, the board and the reporting discipline, in that order.

The following two tables present the results for the hypotheses on the relationship between the venture capitalists' influence and the quality of the assessment and selection of the managers. The tests indicate that the hypotheses are largely supported. The venture capitalists' influence has a significantly positive effect on the assessment and selection of the managers in the portfolio companies (H2.1). Similarly, the influence on the two underlying elements of the assessment of the managers (H2.1.2) and

541 For more information on the techniques, see 5.3.3.2.

the selection of the managers (H2.1.4) is also supported. The effect of the venture capitalists' influence on the first element is, with a coefficient of 0,228, comparatively stronger than the coefficient of the second element at 0,184. The R^2 of the analysis of H2.1.4 using the index of the quality of selection of managers as a response variable is comparatively low at 0,150, but the coefficient for the explanatory variable is still highly significant. In contrast to these findings, the hypothesis that tested the effect of the venture capitalists' influence on the replacement of managers could not be significantly supported. All analyses were controlled for the six variables introduced above. Table 10 gives the details of these analyses, which used the mixed models technique.

#	Hypothesis	Version	Response variable	Explanatory variable	Coefficient	Control variables	R-square
H2.1	The venture capitalists' influence has an impact on the assessment and selection of managers.	S	Efficiency of Assessment and Selection of Managers	VC's influence on assessment and selection of managers	**0,171*** **	lvcabi, cempngr, finrou, cdev, landgr, maas(t=0)	0,281
H2.1.2	The stronger the venture capitalists' influence, the more efficient is the assessment of the management.	S	Efficiency of assessment of managers	VC's influence on assessment of managers	**0,228*** **	lvcabi, cempngr, finrou, cdev, landgr, masse(t=0)	0,379
H2.1.3	The stronger the venture capitalists' influence, the more likely managers are to be replaced.	C	Replacements of managers per financing round	VC's influence on assessment of managers	0,107	lvcabi, cempngr, finrou, cdev, landgr, mrepn(t=0)	0,232
H2.1.4	The stronger the venture capitalists' influence, the better is the managers' selection process.	S	Efficiency of selection of new managers	VC's influence on selection of new managers	**0,184*** **	lvcabi, cempngr, finrou, cdev, landgr, msele(t=0)	0,232
H2.1.4	The stronger the venture capitalists' influence, the better is the managers' selection process.	C	Index of quality of selection of managers	VC's influence on selection of new managers	**0,184*** **	lvcabi, cempngr, finrou, cdev, landgr, mseind(t=0)	0,150

Table 10: Statistical results for hypotheses H2.1–H2.1.4 (mixed models)

One of the response variables was dichotomous, so a logistic regression analysis had to be conducted. However, the analysis that tested whether assessment of the managers becomes more likely with a stronger influence by the lead venture capitalist was significantly supported as well (Table 11). The probability that the managers are assessed is 18 times higher for every unit that the venture capitalists' influence increases.

#	Hypothesis	Version	Response variable	Explanatory variable	Coefficient	Control variables	R-square
H2.1.1	The stronger the venture capitalists' influence is, the more likely is the assessment of the managers.	C	Conduct of assessment of managers	VC's influence on assessment of managers	**1,085*** **	lvcabi, cempngr, finrou, cdev, landgr, massn(t=0)	0,454

Table 11: Statistical results for hypotheses H2.1.1 (logistic regression)

Next, it was analysed whether the venture capitalists' influence affected the quality of the portfolio companies' bonding measures for the managers (H2.2). The results were mixed; the two different measures of corporate governance quality used as response variables led to different results. Whereas the use of the self-assessment measure delivered a highly significant coefficient of 0,198, the analysis using the measurement by criteria delivered a high but not significant coefficient of 1,825. This is reflected in an R^2 of 0,347 for the first analysis and 0,261 for the second.

#	Hypothesis	Version	Response variable	Explanatory variable	Coefficient	Control variables	R-square
H2.2	Venture capitalists' influence has a positive impact on the bonding of managers.	S	Efficiency of bonding of managers	VC's influence on bonding of managers	**0,198*** **	lvcabi, cempngr, finrou, cdev, landgr, mbone(t=0)	0,374
H2.2	Venture capitalists' influence has a positive impact on the bonding of managers.	Q	Index of quality of bonding of managers	VC's influence on bonding of managers	1,825	lvcabi, cempngr, finrou, cdev, landgr, mboind(t=0)	0,261

Table 12: Statistical results for the hypothesis H2.2

The impact of the venture capitalists' influence on the third corporate governance element was tested in a next step. The results indicate that the influence has a significantly positive impact on the adequacy of the managers' compensation (H2.3). The coefficient that relates to the measurement by criteria is very high at 2,935 (R^2=0,565) and compares to 0,162 (R^2=0,596) when the corporate governance quality is measured by self-assessment. In contrast to this, no significant support was found for hypothesis H2.3.3, which expected an impact on the level of cash compensation of the managers. Table 13 presents the detailed results.

#	Hypothesis	Version	Response variable	Explanatory variable	Coefficient	Control variables	R-square
H2.3	The venture capitalists' influence has an impact on the compensation of managers.	S	Efficiency of compensation of managers	VC's influence on compensation of managers	**0,162*** **	lvcabi, cempngr, finrou, cdev, landgr, mcome(t=0)	0,596
H2.3	The venture capitalists' influence has an impact on the compensation of managers.	C	Index of quality of compensation of managers	VC's influence on compensation of managers	**2,935** **	lvcabi, cempngr, finrou, cdev, landgr, mbvin(t=0)	0,565
H2.3.3	The stronger the venture capitalists' influence is the lower is the cash compensation of the managers.	C	Level of compensation compared to industry	VC's influence on compensation of managers	-0,021	lvcabi, cempngr, finrou, cdev, landgr, mcomco(t=0)	0,507

Table 13: Statistical results for hypotheses H2.3–H2.3.3 (mixed models)

Two analyses with dichotomous explanatory variables were tested using a logistic regression. Corresponding to the finding on cash compensation, the venture capitalists' influence seems not to have a significant impact on the level of variable compensation. However, the odds ratio is relatively high at 169,647. On the other hand, a relatively high and significant coefficient was found for the use of variable compensation linked to mid- and long-term goals (H2.3.2), as Table 14 shows. For this analysis, the odds ratio is even higher. The use of these compensation elements is 2.414 times more probable for every unit (on a four unit scale) that venture capitalist influence increases.

#	Hypothesis	Version	Response variable	Explanatory variable	Coefficient	Control variables	R-square
H2.3.1	The stronger the venture capitalists' influence, the higher is the proportion of the variable compensation.	C	Importance of annual bonus versus variable compensation linked to mid-/long-term development	VC's influence on compensation of managers	-0,01	lvcabi, cempngr, finrou, cdev, landgr, mcomim(t=0)	0,691
H2.3.2	The stronger the venture capitalists influence the more likely is the use of variable compensation parts that are linked to mid- and long-term goals.	C	Managers with variable compensation linked to mid-/long-term development	VC's influence on compensation of managers	**1,395*** **	lvcabi, cempngr, finrou, cdev, landgr, mcomve(t=0)	0,708

Table 14: Statistical results for hypotheses H2.3.1–H2.3.2 (logistic regression)

The descriptive results indicated that the quality of the composition and work of the board increased strongly at the time of venture capital investments. Table 15 includes the results for the statistical analyses related to the composition of the board. First, the basic hypothesis of whether venture capitalists' influence has a positive impact on the composition was tested, again using the different measures for corporate governance quality (H2.4). Although there was no significant relationship found for the strength of the influence and the efficiency of board composition as perceived by the respondents, a highly significant and strongly positive impact was found for the quality index measured by criteria. These differences resulted although both analyses were equally controlled for the lead-venture capitalists' abilities, the portfolio companies' size, development stage, location and previous corporate governance quality as well as for time effects (financing round). The venture capitalists' influence as an explanatory variable for the index of the quality of board composition has a coefficient of 5,868 at a confidence level of 99%. The R^2 of this analysis is 0,223. Corresponding to the detailed hypotheses, this relationship was broken down into criteria for the independence and the qualification of the board members. Against the expectations, the analysis did not support an increase in the independence of boards with venture capitalists' influence (H2.4.1). By contrast, the qualifications of the board members measured in the form of experiences in different areas improved with a stronger venture capitalist influence (H2.4.2). This was found for four out of the six analysed kinds of experiences. Using similar control variables as before, the hypotheses related to the industry experience, international experience, functional experience and experience as a board member in listed companies were supported. The strongest impact was found for functional experience with a coefficient of 0,431. In regard to the board members' executive and start-up experience, the analysis delivered positive but not significant results.

#	Hypothesis	Version	Response variable	Explanatory variable	Coefficient	Control variables	R-square
H2.4	The venture capitalists' influence has an impact on the composition of the board.	S	Efficiency of composition of board: monitoring	VC's influence on composition of board	0,043	lvcabi, cempngr, finrou, cdev, landgr, bsome(t=0)	0,444
H2.4	The venture capitalists' influence has an impact on the composition of the board.	S	Efficiency of composition of board: advice	VC's influence on composition of board	0,084	lvcabi, cempngr, finrou, cdev, landgr, bsoae(t=0)	0,239
H2.4	The venture capitalists' influence has an impact on the composition of the board.	C	Index of quality of board composition	VC's influence on composition of board	**5,868*** **	lvcabi, cempngr, finrou, cdev, landgr, bsiind(t=0)	0,223
H2.4.1	The stronger the venture capitalists' influence is, the greater is the proportion of independent members in the board.	C	Proportion of independent board members	VC's influence on composition of board	0,014	lvcabi, cempngr, finrou, cdev, landgr, bspin(t=0)	0,038
H2.4.2	The stronger the venture capitalists' influence, the stronger are the experiences of the board.	C	Industry experience of independent board members	VC's influence on composition of board	**0,235** **	lvcabi, cempngr, finrou, cdev, landgr, bsoiex(t=0)	0,409
H2.4.2	The stronger the venture capitalists' influence, the stronger are the experiences of the board.	C	Executive experience of independent board members	VC's influence on composition of board	0,172	lvcabi, cempngr, finrou, cdev, landgr, bsoeex(t=0)	0,284
H2.4.2	The stronger the venture capitalists' influence, the stronger are the experiences of the board.	C	International experience of independent board members	VC's influence on composition of board	**0,299** **	lvcabi, cempngr, finrou, cdev, landgr, bsotex(t=0)	0,399
H2.4.2	The stronger the venture capitalists' influence, the stronger are the experiences of the board.	C	Functional experience of independent board members	VC's influence on composition of board	**0,431*** **	lvcabi, cempngr, finrou, cdev, landgr, bsofex(t=0)	0,160
H2.4.2	The stronger the venture capitalists' influence, the stronger are the experiences of the board.	C	Startup experience of independent board members	VC's influence on composition of board	0,135	lvcabi, cempngr, finrou, cdev, landgr, bsosex(t=0)	0,221
H2.4.2	The stronger the venture capitalists' influence, the stronger are the experiences of the board.	C	Experience as managers or board member in listed companies of independent board members	VC's influence on composition of board	**0,183* **	lvcabi, cempngr, finrou, cdev, landgr, bsolex(t=0)	0,173

Table 15: Statistical results for hypotheses H2.4–H2.4.2

After the analyses related to the composition of the board, the impact of the venture capitalists on the work of the board was analysed (H2.5). First, the self-assessment measures are described. The impact of the venture capitalists' influence on the self-assessed efficiency of the work of the board is significantly positive in regard to the monitoring function of the board but not in regard to the advice function. For the impact on the response variable efficiency of the work of the board, the coefficient for monitoring is 0,203 at a confidence level of 99% controlling for the introduced control variables above. Then the measurement by criteria was used for the analyses. The result was relatively high and positive but not significant, despite an R^2 of 0,279. But more detailed tests delivered significant relationships for specific criteria. The venture capitalists' influence leads to significantly more frequent (H2.5.1) and better prepared (H2.5.2) board meetings. The third expected relationship was not supported: There is a negative but not significant result for the impact on the involvement of boards in strategic decision making (H2.5.3). These findings are summarised in Table 16.

#	Hypothesis	Version	Response variable	Explanatory variable	Coefficient	Control variables	R-square
H2.5	The venture capitalists' influence has an impact on the work of the board.	S	Efficiency of work of board: monitoring	VC's influence on work of board	**0,203***	lvcabi, cempngr, finrou, cdev, landgr, bwome(t=0)	0,251
H2.5	The venture capitalists' influence has an impact on the work of the board.	S	Efficiency of work of board: advice	VC's influence on work of board	0,045	lvcabi, cempngr, finrou, cdev, landgr, bwoae(t=0)	0,219
H2.5	The venture capitalists' influence has an impact on the work of the board.	C	Index of quality of work of board	VC's influence on work of board	1,273	lvcabi, cempngr, finrou, cdev, landgr, bwoind(t=0)	0,279
H2.5.1	The stronger the venture capitalists' influence, the more frequently board meetings take place.	C	Number of board meetings per year	VC's influence on work of board	**0,610**	lvcabi, cempngr, finrou, cdev, landgr, bwomn(t=0)	0,203
H2.5.2	The stronger the venture capitalists' influence, the better prepared board meetings are.	C	Distribution of agenda and relevant information	VC's influence on work of board	**0,117**	lvcabi, cempngr, finrou, cdev, landgr, bwoin(t=0)	0,403
H2.5.3	The stronger the venture capitalists' influence, the better prepared board meetings are.	C	Proportion of time devoted to strategic issues	VC's influence on work of board	-0,91	lvcabi, cempngr, finrou, cdev, landgr, bwost(t=0)	0,198

Table 16: Statistical results for hypotheses H2.5–2.5.3

The last group of hypotheses is related to the relationship between the venture capitalists' influence and the reporting discipline of the portfolio companies. The two corporate governance measures consistently support a positive impact (H2.6). The coefficient of the explanatory variables is, at 2,269, much stronger for the index of the corresponding criteria than for the self-assessment by the respondents (0,108). The more detailed analyses found that the venture capitalists' influence significantly increases the frequency (H2.6.1) and the timeliness (2.6.2) of the portfolio companies' reporting. By contrast, it does not have a significant influence on the comprehensiveness of the information provided (H2.6.3) or on the extent of target-actual differences (2.6.4). As Table 17 shows, all tests have been controlled for the lead venture capitalists' abilities, the portfolio companies' size, development stage, and location, as well as the financing round and the original quality of the corporate governance element.

#	Hypothesis	Version	Response variable	Explanatory variable	Coefficient	Control variables	R-square
H2.6	The venture capitalists' influence has a positive impact on reporting discipline.	S	Efficiency of reporting discipline	VC's influence on reporting discipline	**0,108**	lvcabi, cempngr, finrou, cdev, landgr, rmone(t=0)	0,247
H2.6	The venture capitalists' influence has a positive impact on reporting discipline.	C	Index of quality of reporting discipline	VC's influence on reporting discipline	**2,269**	lvcabi, cempngr, finrou, cdev, landgr, rind(t=0)	0,398
H2.6.1	The stronger the venture capitalists' influence, the more frequent is the portfolio company's reporting.	C	Number of reports per year	VC's influence on reporting discipline	**0,783***	lvcabi, cempngr, finrou, cdev, landgr, rrn(t=0)	0,436
H2.6.2	The stronger the venture capitalists' influence, the more timely is the portfolio company's reporting.	C	Timeliness of reporting	VC's influence on reporting discipline	**0,154***	lvcabi, cempngr, finrou, cdev, landgr, ront(t=0)	0,458
H2.6.3	The stronger the venture capitalists' influence, the more comprehensive is the portfolio company's reporting.	C	Completeness of reporting	VC's influence on reporting discipline	**1,668**	lvcabi, cempngr, finrou, cdev, landgr, rcompr(t=0)	0,281
H2.6.4	The stronger the venture capitalists' influence, the more accurate is the portfolio company's reporting.	C	Extent of target-actual differences	VC's influence on reporting discipline	0,064	lvcabi, cempngr, finrou, cdev, landgr, rdiff(t=0)	0,298

Table 17: Statistical results for hypotheses H2.6–2.6.4

The presentation of these results indicates that the basic hypothesis that venture capitalists' influence leads to better corporate governance is supported. Although this holds also for a large part of the more detailed hypotheses related to individual corporate governance elements, there are also some expected relationships that could not be significantly supported. For an overview, Figure 46 indicates whether the hypotheses are largely supported (✓),the findings are mixed (~) or the test did not deliver a significant result (?).

#	Hypothesis	Support
H2	The venture capitalists' influence has an impact on the portfolio companies' corporate governance	✓
H2.1	The venture capitalists' influence has a positive impact on the assessment and selection of managers.	✓
H2.1.1	The stronger the venture capitalists' influence is the more likely is the assessment of the managers.	✓
H2.1.2	The stronger the venture capitalists' influence, the more efficient is the assessment of the management.	✓
H2.1.3	The stronger the venture capitalists' influence, the more likely managers are to be replaced.	?
H2.1.4	The stronger the venture capitalists' influence, the better is the managers' selection process.	✓
H2.2	Venture capitalists' influence has a positive impact on the bonding of managers.	~
H2.3	The venture capitalists' influence has a positive impact on the compensation of managers.	✓
H2.3.1	The stronger the venture capitalists' influence, the higher is the proportion of the variable compensation.	?
H2.3.2	The stronger the venture capitalists' influence, the more likely is the use of variable compensation parts linked to mid- and long-term goals.	✓
H2.3.3	The stronger the venture capitalists' influence is the lower is the cash compensation of the managers.	?
H2.4	The venture capitalists' influence has an impact on the composition of the board.	~
H2.4.1	The stronger the venture capitalists' influence is the greater is the proportion of independent members in the board.	?
H2.4.2	The stronger the venture capitalists' influence, the stronger are the experiences of the board.	~
H2.5	The venture capitalists' influence has a positive impact on the work of the board.	~
H2.5.1	The stronger the venture capitalists' influence, the more frequently board meetings take place.	✓
H2.5.2	The stronger the venture capitalists' influence, the better prepared board meetings are.	✓
H2.5.3	The stronger the venture capitalists' influence is the more involved is the board in strategic decision making.	?
H2.6	The venture capitalists' influence has a positive impact on reporting discipline.	✓
H2.6.1	The stronger the venture capitalists' influence, the more frequent is the portfolio company's reporting.	✓
H2.6.2	The stronger the venture capitalists' influence, the more timely is the portfolio company's reporting.	✓
H2.6.3	The stronger the venture capitalists' influence, the more comprehensive is the portfolio company's reporting.	?
H2.6.4	The stronger the venture capitalists' influence, the more accurate is the portfolio company's reporting.	?

Figure 46: Overview of the results for hypotheses about the relationship between the venture capitalists' influence and corporate governance quality

5.6 Abilities of Venture Capitalists' to Influence Corporate Governance

5.6.1 Descriptive Results for Venture Capitalists' Abilities

The lead venture capitalists' abilities to influence corporate governance considered in the research are their control rights, the characteristics of venture capital firms and the characteristics of the investment managers associated with an individual portfolio company. Moreover, the trustfulness of the relationship between the lead venture capitalists' investment managers and the managers of the portfolio company is also taken into account. The lead venture capitalists in many portfolio companies changed over time so the variables measuring the abilities cannot be seen as a development but rather as three snapshots. Furthermore, it must be taken into consideration that the group of portfolio companies whose answers are included declines over the three measuring times, so that the number of companies that provided information for the time after the third financing round is small.

On the highest level, the mean index of the lead venture capitalists' abilities includes the level of control rights and the characteristics of the venture capital firms and the investment managers. The average of this index fluctuates between 58% and 62%, as Figure 47 shows. T-tests did not deliver any significant differences between these values.

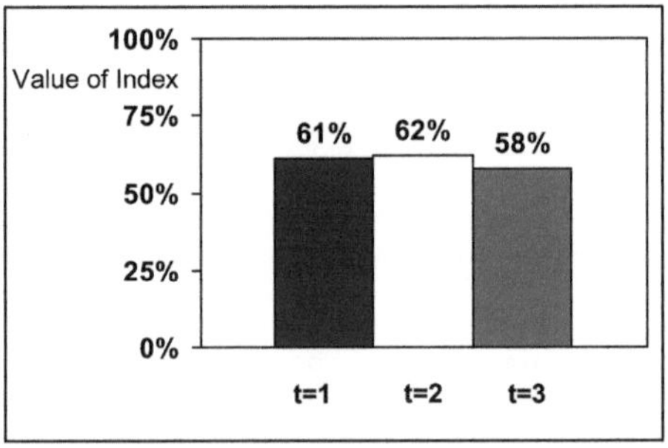

Figure 47: Index of venture capitalists abilities' over time

The fulfilment of the three underlying subindexes is presented in Figure 48. The average control rights index that relates to the ownership and board membership rights of the lead venture capitalists decreases from 62% to 45%, though there were no significant changes found for the values at the three measuring times. The average of the index of characteristics of the lead venture capital firms remains equal around 54%. It takes the reputation and the experience of the venture capitalists into account. The mean of the characteristics of the investment managers grows insignificantly from 69% to 73% and concerns the experiences and commitment of the investment managers.

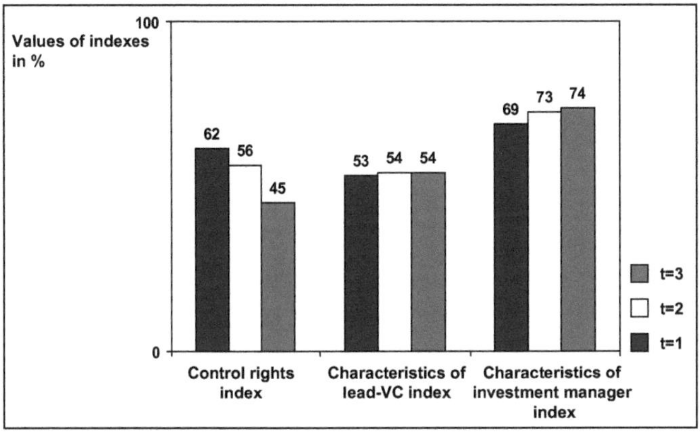

Figure 48: Subindexes of venture capitalists' abilities over time

Apart from these abilities, trust between the venture capitalists and the portfolio companies is expected to influence corporate governance quality. In the analysed portfolio companies, the level of trust is relatively high with an average between 4,4 and 4,8 on a scale of 1 to 5. The increase after the third financing round might be due to the fact that only in successful investments are venture capitalists willing to provide capital for a third time. The means for the three measuring times are presented in Figure 49.

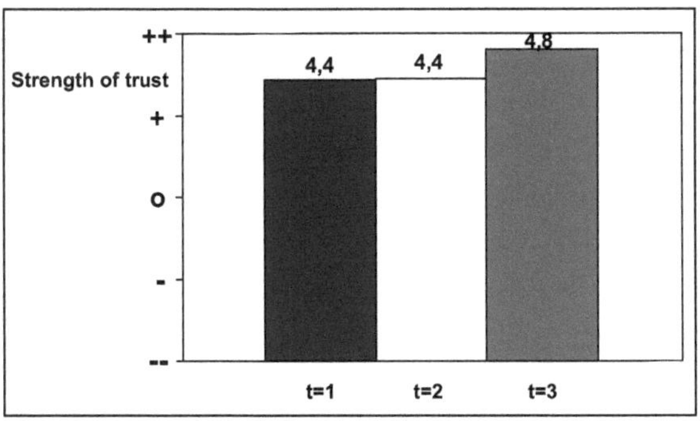

Figure 49: Trust between investment managers and portfolio companies' managers over time

Information on all variables related to the venture capitalists' abilities is introduced in the table in Annex 9.

5.6.2 Results for Hypotheses' Tests

After the description of the abilities of the lead venture capitalists, multivariate tests were done to find out whether the abilities have a significant influence on the corporate governance quality of the portfolio companies. This basic hypothesis was analysed again for the two measures of corporate governance quality: the indexes for self-assessment and corporate governance criteria (H3). Both tests were controlled for the strength of the venture capitalists' influence, the trust between the venture capitalists and the portfolio companies, the size, development stage and location of the portfolio companies, the financing round, and the corporate governance quality before the first financing round. The resulting R^2 are relatively high at 0,424 and 0,369. The coefficients of the explanatory variables are 0,067 for the self-assessment measure and 0,219 for the measurement by criteria, as Table 18 shows. That means that the basic hypothesis related to the abilities is supported. In the following, the impact of the individual elements of this index are analysed using the more detailed hypotheses, in particular the control rights of the lead venture capitalists and the characteristics of the venture capital firms and the investment managers.

#	Hypothesis	Version	Response variable	Explanatory variable	Coefficient	Control variables	R-square
H3	The abilities of venture capital firms have impact on the corporate governance of portfolio compaies	S	CG quality index (self-assessment)	Index of abilities	**0,067***	vciind, imtrus, cempngr, finrou, cdev, landgr, cgqind(t=0)	0,424
H3	The abilities of venture capital firms have impact on the corporate governance of portfolio compaies	C	CG quality index (criteria)	Index of abilities	**0,219*****	vciind, imtrus, cempngr, finrou, cdev, landgr, cgqinc(t=0)	0,369

Table 18: Statistical results for hypothesis H3

First, it was analysed whether there is a significant relationship between the lead venture capitalists' control rights and corporate governance quality (H3.1) at different levels: for the overall corporate governance index, the index for the monitoring function and the index for the bonding function. Furthermore, these response variables were analysed again for the two measures. As an explanatory variable, the control rights index was used along with the variables that relate to the lead venture capitalists' ownership rights and board seats. All tests were controlled for the variables introduced before. Although the R^2 of the models was relatively high, ranging from 0,269 to 0,506, only one of the tests delivered a significant result. The control rights were found to have a significantly positive impact on corporate governance quality measured by criteria, with a coefficient of 0,101. This indicates that there is only weak support for the hypothesis that the venture capitalists' control rights significantly affect the corporate governance quality of portfolio companies.

#	Hypothesis	Version	Response variable	Explanatory variable	Coefficient	Control variables	R-square
H3.1	The control rights of venture capital firms have effects on their impact on the corporate governance of portfolio companies.	S	CG quality index (self-assessment)	Control rights of lead-VC-F index	-0,003	vciind, imtrus, cempngr, finrou, cdev, landgr, cgqind(t=0)	0,433
H3.1	The control rights of venture capital firms have effects on their impact on the corporate governance of portfolio companies.	C	CG quality index (criteria)	Control rights of lead-VC-F index	**0,101****	vciind, imtrus, cempngr, finrou, cdev, landgr, cgqinc(t=0)	0,357
H3.1	The control rights of venture capital firms have effects on their impact on the corporate governance of portfolio companies.	S	CG monitoring index (self-assessment)	Control rights of lead-VC-F index	0,028	vciind, imtrus, cempngr, finrou, cdev, landgr, cgmind(t=0)	0,389
H3.1	The control rights of venture capital firms have effects on their impact on the corporate governance of portfolio companies.	C	CG monitoring index (criteria)	Control rights of lead-VC-F index	0,037	vciind, imtrus, cempngr, finrou, cdev, landgr, cgmcin(t=0)	0,269
H3.1	The control rights of venture capital firms have effects on their impact on the corporate governance of portfolio companies.	S	CG bonding index (self-assessment)	Control rights of lead-VC-F index	-0,044	vciind, imtrus, cempngr, finrou, cdev, landgr, cgbind(t=0)	0,506
H3.1	The control rights of venture capital firms have effects on their impact on the corporate governance of portfolio companies.	C	CG bonding index (criteria)	Control rights of lead-VC-F index	-0,012	vciind, imtrus, cempngr, finrou, cdev, landgr, cgbcin(t=0)	0,436
H3.1.1	The stronger the venture capitalist's control rights are, the stronger is the impact of its influence on the corporate governance of portfolio companies.	S	CG quality index (self-assessment)	Ownership rights of lead-VC	-0,016	vciind, imtrus, cempngr, finrou, cdev, landgr, cgqind(t=0)	0,486
H3.1.1	The stronger the venture capitalists' control right rights, — in terms of ownership rights and board seats — the stronger is their influence on the corporate governance of portfolio companies.	C	CG quality index (criteria)	Ownership rights of lead-VC	0,023	vciind, imtrus, cempngr, finrou, cdev, landgr, cgqinc(t=0)	0,333
H3.1.1	The stronger the venture capitalists' control right rights, — in terms of ownership rights and board seats — the stronger is their influence on the corporate governance of portfolio companies.	S	CG quality index (self-assessment)	Board seat lead-VC	-0,528	vciind, imtrus, cempngr, finrou, cdev, landgr, cgqind(t=0)	0,432
H3.1.1	The stronger the venture capitalists' control right rights, — in terms of ownership rights and board seats — the stronger is their influence on the corporate governance of portfolio companies.	C	CG quality index (criteria)	Board seat lead-VC	**6,673***	vciind, imtrus, cempngr, finrou, cdev, landgr, cgqinc(t=0)	0,352
H3.1.2	The stronger the venture capitalists' control rights, the greater is the impact of their influence on the elements related to the monitoring function of corporate governance.	S	CG monitoring index (self-assessment)	Ownership rights of lead-VC	0,010	vciind, imtrus, cempngr, finrou, cdev, landgr, cgmind(t=0)	0,464
H3.1.2	The stronger the venture capitalists' control rights, the greater is the impact of their influence on the elements related to the monitoring function of corporate governance.	C	CG monitoring index (criteria)	Ownership rights of lead-VC	0,008	vciind, imtrus, cempngr, finrou, cdev, landgr, cgmcin(t=0)	0,315
H3.1.2	The stronger the venture capitalists' control rights, the greater is the impact of their influence on the elements related to the monitoring function of corporate governance.	S	CG monitoring index (self-assessment)	Board seat lead-VC	0,974	vciind, imtrus, cempngr, finrou, cdev, landgr, cgmind(t=0)	0,381
H3.1.2	The stronger the venture capitalists' control rights, the greater is the impact of their influence on the elements related to the monitoring function of corporate governance.	C	CG monitoring index (criteria)	Board seat lead-VC	2,604	vciind, imtrus, cempngr, finrou, cdev, landgr, cgmcin(t=0)	0,266

#	Hypothesis	Version	Response variable	Explanatory variable	Coefficient	Control variables	R-square
H3.1.3	The stronger the venture capitalists' control rights, the greater is the impact of their influence on the elements related to the bonding function of corporate governance.	S	CG bonding index (self-assessment)	Ownership rights of lead-VC	-0,026	vciind, imtrus, cempngr, finrou, cdev, landgr, cgbind(t=0)	0,609
H3.1.3	The stronger the venture capitalists' control rights, the greater is the impact of their influence on the elements related to the bonding function of corporate governance.	C	CG bonding index (criteria)	Ownership rights of lead-VC	-0,04	vciind, imtrus, cempngr, finrou, cdev, landgr, cgbcin(t=0)	0,500
H3.1.3	The stronger the venture capitalists' control rights, the greater is the impact of their influence on the elements related to the bonding function of corporate governance.	S	CG bonding index (self-assessment)	Board seat lead-VC	-3,455	vciind, imtrus, cempngr, finrou, cdev, landgr, cgbind(t=0)	0,528
H3.1.3	The stronger the venture capitalists' control rights, the greater is the impact of their influence on the elements related to the bonding function of corporate governance.	C	CG bonding index (criteria)	Board seat lead-VC	-0,027	vciind, imtrus, cempngr, finrou, cdev, landgr, cgbcin(t=0)	0,428

Table 19: Statistical results for hypotheses H3.1–H3.1.3

Next, it is analysed whether the characteristics of the lead venture capital firms influence the corporate governance of portfolio companies. The basic hypothesis (H3.2) was tested for overall corporate governance quality as well as for the index of the corporate governance advice function. Although no significant relationship was found for the corporate governance index, there was support for the latter response variable. Controlling for the different above mentioned variables, the corresponding coefficients are 0,089 for the self-assessment measurement and 0,115 for the measurement by criteria. The R^2 of the two models are 0,355 and 0,209, respectively. Hypothesis H2.2.1 relates to the expectation that independent venture capitalists have a greater impact on the corporate governance of portfolio companies than other types of venture capitalists. Similarly, it was supported only for the advice function of corporate governance. Although the coefficients are very high, 4,362 for the advice index measured by self-assessment and 5,442 for the advice index measured by criteria, only the first result was significant. This corresponds to a much higher R^2 of the first analysis, 0,344, compared with 0,191 for the latter. These findings are presented in Table 20.

#	Hypothesis	Version	Response variable	Explanatory variable	Coefficient	Control variables	R-square
H3.2	The characteristics of venture capital firms have effects on their impact on the corporate governance of portfolio companies.	S	CG quality index (self-assessment)	Characteristics of lead-VC-F index	0,033	vciind, imtrus, cempngr, finrou, cdev, landgr, cgqind(t=0)	0,430
H3.2	The characteristics of venture capital firms have effects on their impact on the corporate governance of portfolio companies.	C	CG quality index (criteria)	Characteristics of lead-VC-F index	0,011	vciind, imtrus, cempngr, finrou, cdev, landgr, cgqinc(t=0)	0,349
H3.2	The characteristics of venture capital firms have effects on their impact on the corporate governance of portfolio companies.	S	CG advice index (self-assessment)	Characteristics of lead-VC-F index	0,089**	vciind, imtrus, cempngr, finrou, cdev, landgr, cgaind(t=0)	0,355
H3.2	The characteristics of venture capital firms have effects on their impact on the corporate governance of portfolio companies.	C	CG advice index (criteria)	Characteristics of lead-VC-F index	0,115*	vciind, imtrus, cempngr, finrou, cdev, landgr, cgacin(t=0)	0,209
H3.2.1	Independent venture capital firms' influence has a greater impact on the corporate governance of portfolio companies than that of corporate venture capitalists and bank-related and governmental venture capitalists.	S	CG quality index (self-assessment)	Independent lead-VC-F	1,275	vciind, imtrus, cempngr, finrou, cdev, landgr, cgqind(t=0)	0,423
H3.2.1	Independent venture capital firms' influence has a greater impact on the corporate governance of portfolio companies than that of corporate venture capitalists and bank-related and governmental venture capitalists.	C	CG quality index (criteria)	Independent lead-VC-F	-5,643	vciind, imtrus, cempngr, finrou, cdev, landgr, cgqinc(t=0)	0,372
H3.2.1	Independent venture capital firms' influence has a greater impact on the corporate governance of portfolio companies than that of corporate venture capitalists and bank-related and governmental venture capitalists.	S	CG advice index (self-assessment)	Independent lead-VC-F	4,362*	vciind, imtrus, cempngr, finrou, cdev, landgr, cgaind(t=0)	0,344
H3.2.1	Independent venture capital firms' influence has a greater impact on the corporate governance of portfolio companies than that of corporate venture capitalists and bank-related and governmental venture capitalists.	C	CG advice index (criteria)	Independent lead-VC-F	5,332	vciind, imtrus, cempngr, finrou, cdev, landgr, cgacin(t=0)	0,191

Table 20: Statistical results for hypotheses H3.2–H3.2.1

The following table describes the results for the analyses related to the hypothesis that stronger investment experience of the lead venture capital firm has a positive impact on the corporate governance quality of portfolio companies. For the explanatory variable, three measures were used: the number of portfolio companies, the invested capital and the age of the venture capitalists. Nevertheless, there is no significant result, although all coefficients of the explanatory variables are positive and the R^2 of the models are relatively high, ranging between 0,188 and 0,448.

#	Hypothesis	Version	Response variable	Explanatory variable	Coefficient	Control variables	R-square
H3.2.2	The more investment experience a venture capital firm has, the greater are the effects of its influence on the corporate governance of portfolio companies.	S	CG quality index (self-assessment)	Number of portfolio companies lead-VC-F	0,002	vciind, imtrus, cempngr, finrou, cdev, landgr, cgqind(t=0)	0,453
H3.2.2	The more investment experience a venture capital firm has, the greater are the effects of its influence on the corporate governance of portfolio companies.	C	CG quality index (criteria)	Number of portfolio companies lead-VC-F	0,002	vciind, imtrus, cempngr, finrou, cdev, landgr, cgqinc(t=0)	0,353
H3.2.2	The more investment experience a venture capital firm has, the greater are the effects of its influence on the corporate governance of portfolio companies.	S	CG advice index (self-assessment)	Number of portfolio companies lead-VC-F	0,003	vciind, imtrus, cempngr, finrou, cdev, landgr, cgaind(t=0)	0,371
H3.2.2	The more investment experience a venture capital firm has, the greater are the effects of its influence on the corporate governance of portfolio companies.	C	CG advice index (criteria)	Number of portfolio companies lead-VC-F	0,004	vciind, imtrus, cempngr, finrou, cdev, landgr, cgacin(t=0)	0,185
H3.2.2	The more investment experience a venture capital firm has, the greater are the effects of its influence on the corporate governance of portfolio companies.	S	CG quality index (self-assessment)	Invested capital VC-F	0,000	vciind, imtrus, cempngr, finrou, cdev, landgr, cgqind(t=0)	0,448
H3.2.2	The more investment experience a venture capital firm has, the greater are the effects of its influence on the corporate governance of portfolio companies.	C	CG quality index (criteria)	Invested capital VC-F	0,001	vciind, imtrus, cempngr, finrou, cdev, landgr, cgqinc(t=0)	0,352
H3.2.2	The more investment experience a venture capital firm has, the greater are the effects of its influence on the corporate governance of portfolio companies.	S	CG advice index (self-assessment)	Invested capital VC-F	0,001	vciind, imtrus, cempngr, finrou, cdev, landgr, cgaind(t=0)	0,367
H3.2.2	The more investment experience a venture capital firm has, the greater are the effects of its influence on the corporate governance of portfolio companies.	C	CG advice index (criteria)	Invested capital VC-F	0,001	vciind, imtrus, cempngr, finrou, cdev, landgr, cgacin(t=0)	0,188
H3.2.2	The more investment experience a venture capital firm has, the greater are the effects of its influence on the corporate governance of portfolio companies.	S	CG quality index (self-assessment)	Age of VC-F	0,423	vciind, imtrus, cempngr, finrou, cdev, landgr, cgqind(t=0)	0,439
H3.2.2	The more investment experience a venture capital firm has, the greater are the effects of its influence on the corporate governance of portfolio companies.	C	CG quality index (criteria)	Age of VC-F	3,452	vciind, imtrus, cempngr, finrou, cdev, landgr, cgqinc(t=0)	0,360
H3.2.2	The more investment experience a venture capital firm has, the greater are the effects of its influence on the corporate governance of portfolio companies.	S	CG advice index (self-assessment)	Age of VC-F	2,438	vciind, imtrus, cempngr, finrou, cdev, landgr, cgaind(t=0)	0,351
H3.2.2	The more investment experience a venture capital firm has, the greater are the effects of its influence on the corporate governance of portfolio companies.	C	CG advice index (criteria)	Age of VC-F	2,582	vciind, imtrus, cempngr, finrou, cdev, landgr, cgacin(t=0)	0,190

Table 21: Statistical results for hypothesis H3.2.2

Two other characteristics analysed are the international experience (H3.2.3; values given for the impact of global investors: lvcint=3) and the reputation (H3.2.4) of the venture capitalists. Despite relatively high R^2 values and the use of four response variables for each explanatory variable, there were no significant results. Reputation led to comparatively high coefficients, particularly in regard to the corporate governance's advice function, but none of these coefficients is significant. Hence, the analysis did not support these hypotheses. Table 22 shows the results in an overview.

#	Hypothesis	Version	Response variable	Explanatory variable	Coefficient	Control variables	R-square
H3.2.3	The greater the international experience of the venture capital firms, the greater are the effects of their influence on the corporate governance of portfolio companies.	S	CG quality index (self-assessment)	International activity of VC-F: region	-1,09	vciind, imtrus, cempngr, finrou, cdev, landgr, cgqind(t=0)	0,429
H3.2.3	The greater the international experience of the venture capital firms, the greater are the effects of their influence on the corporate governance of portfolio companies.	C	CG quality index (criteria)	International activity of VC-F: region	-6,18	vciind, imtrus, cempngr, finrou, cdev, landgr, cgqinc(t=0)	0,356
H3.2.3	The greater the international experience of the venture capital firms, the greater are the effects of their influence on the corporate governance of portfolio companies.	S	CG advice index (self-assessment)	International activity of VC-F: region	-2,29	vciind, imtrus, cempngr, finrou, cdev, landgr, cgaind(t=0)	0,347
H3.2.3	The greater the international experience of the venture capital firms, the greater are the effects of their influence on the corporate governance of portfolio companies.	C	CG advice index (criteria)	International activity of VC-F: region	4,001	vciind, imtrus, cempngr, finrou, cdev, landgr, cgacin(t=0)	0,198
H3.2.4	The greater the reputation of a venture capital firm, the greater are the effects of its influence on the corporate governance of portfolio companies.	S	CG quality index (self-assessment)	Reputation of VC-F	2,101	vciind, imtrus, cempngr, finrou, cdev, landgr, cgqind(t=0)	0,437
H3.2.4	The greater the reputation of a venture capital firm, the greater are the effects of its influence on the corporate governance of portfolio companies.	C	CG quality index (criteria)	Reputation of VC-F	1,831	vciind, imtrus, cempngr, finrou, cdev, landgr, cgqinc(t=0)	0,352
H3.2.4	The greater the reputation of a venture capital firm, the greater are the effects of its influence on the corporate governance of portfolio companies.	S	CG advice index (self-assessment)	Reputation of VC-F	3,429	vciind, imtrus, cempngr, finrou, cdev, landgr, cgaind(t=0)	0,351
H3.2.4	The greater the reputation of a venture capital firm, the greater are the effects of its influence on the corporate governance of portfolio companies.	C	CG advice index (criteria)	Reputation of VC-F	2,074	vciind, imtrus, cempngr, finrou, cdev, landgr, cgacin(t=0)	0,188

Table 22: Statistical results for hypotheses H3.2.3–H3.2.4

The third element of the analysed abilities refers to the characteristics of the investment managers of the lead venture capitalists. Corresponding to hypothesis H3.3, it is predicted that these characteristics have an impact on the corporate governance of the portfolio companies. The analyses were done using the mixed models technique and were controlled for the lead venture capitalists' influence, the trust between them and the managers of the portfolio companies, as well as the size, development stage, and location of the portfolio companies; the time; and the original corporate governance quality at t=0. Corresponding to the above hypotheses' tests, four response variables were used: the overall corporate governance quality as well as the quality of the advice function, measured by self-assessment and by criteria. The hypothesis is supported by all four analyses, but the strength of the impact differs. The impact on the self-assessed corporate governance measures is much lower than for the measure related to criteria. Moreover, the impact is greater on the advice function than on the overall corporate governance quality.

#	Hypothesis	Version	Response variable	Explanatory variable	Coefficient	Control variables	R-square
H3.3	The characteristics of investment managers have effects on their impact on the corporate governance of portfolio companies.	S	CG quality index (self-assessment)	Abilities of VC-IM index	**0,054****	vciind, imtrus, cempngr, finrou, cdev, landgr, cgqind(t=0)	0,432
H3.3	The characteristics of investment managers have effects on their impact on the corporate governance of portfolio companies.	C	CG quality index (criteria)	Abilities of VC-IM index	**0,197*****	vciind, imtrus, cempngr, finrou, cdev, landgr, cgqinc(t=0)	0,373
H3.3	The characteristics of investment managers have effects on their impact on the corporate governance of portfolio companies.	S	CG advice index (self-assessment)	Abilities of VC-IM index	**0,075***	vciind, imtrus, cempngr, finrou, cdev, landgr, cgaind(t=0)	0,358
H3.3	The characteristics of investment managers have effects on their impact on the corporate governance of portfolio companies.	C	CG advice index (criteria)	Abilities of VC-IM index	**0,258*****	vciind, imtrus, cempngr, finrou, cdev, landgr, cgacin(t=0)	0,229

Table 23: Statistical results for hypothesis H3.3

In the following, the impact of the individual characteristics of the investment managers is analysed in detail. To begin with, their experience in the venture capital industry is taken as an explanatory variable for the response variables of overall corporate governance quality and quality of the advice function, measured by self-assessment and by criteria (H3.3.1). The four tests deliver very positive results, of which three are also significant. Venture capital experience has a coefficient of 6,581 at the 90% confidence level when explaining the overall corporate governance quality index measured by criteria and 9,217 at the 95% confidence level when explaining the quality of the advice function. The R^2 are 0,379 and 0,206, respectively. Using the self-assessment measure, only the test with the advice index as a response variable was significant, with a coefficient of 3,600 at the 90% confidence level and an R^2 of 0,352. There is less significant support for the hypothesis that more experience in the portfolio companies' industries has a positive impact on corporate governance quality (H3.3.2). On the other hand, the mixed models analysis delivered a highly significant and very positive impact for the investment managers' industry experience on the overall corporate governance quality, with a coefficient of 8,151. By contrast, the other three results were not significant despite relatively high R^2 values between 0,192 and 0,418, as Table 24 indicates.

#	Hypothesis	Version	Response variable	Explanatory variable	Coefficient	Control variables	R-square
H3.3.1	The greater the investment manager's experience in the venture capital industry, the greater is the impact of his/her influence on the corporate governance of portfolio companies.	S	CG quality index (self-assessment)	Experience in VC industry VC-IM	2,119	vciind, imtrus, cempngr, finrou, cdev, landgr, cgqind(t=0)	0,400
H3.3.1	The greater the investment manager's experience in the venture capital industry, the greater is the impact of his/her influence on the corporate governance of portfolio companies.	C	CG quality index (criteria)	Experience in VC industry VC-IM	**6,561***	vciind, imtrus, cempngr, finrou, cdev, landgr, cgqinc(t=0)	0,379
H3.3.1	The greater the investment manager's experience in the venture capital industry, the greater is the impact of his/her influence on the corporate governance of portfolio companies.	S	CG advice index (self-assessment)	Experience in VC industry VC-IM	**3,600***	vciind, imtrus, cempngr, finrou, cdev, landgr, cgaind(t=0)	0,352
H3.3.1	The greater the investment manager's experience in the venture capital industry, the greater is the impact of his/her influence on the corporate governance of portfolio companies.	C	CG advice index (criteria)	Experience in VC industry VC-IM	**9,217****	vciind, imtrus, cempngr, finrou, cdev, landgr, cgacin(t=0)	0,206
H3.3.2	The greater the investment managers' experience in the portfolio company's industry, the greater is the impact of their influence on the corporate governance of portfolio companies.	S	CG quality index (self-assessment)	Industry experience VC-IM	0,227	vciind, imtrus, cempngr, finrou, cdev, landgr, cgqind(t=0)	0,418
H3.3.2	The greater the investment managers' experience in the portfolio company's industry, the greater is the impact of their influence on the corporate governance of portfolio companies.	C	CG quality index (criteria)	Industry experience VC-IM	**8,151*****	vciind, imtrus, cempngr, finrou, cdev, landgr, cgqinc(t=0)	0,362
H3.3.2	The greater the investment managers' experience in the portfolio company's industry, the greater is the impact of their influence on the corporate governance of portfolio companies.	S	CG advice index (self-assessment)	Industry experience VC-IM	1,272	vciind, imtrus, cempngr, finrou, cdev, landgr, cgaind(t=0)	0,341
H3.3.2	The greater the investment managers' experience in the portfolio company's industry, the greater is the impact of their influence on the corporate governance of portfolio companies.	C	CG advice index (criteria)	Industry experience VC-IM	3,916	vciind, imtrus, cempngr, finrou, cdev, landgr, cgacin(t=0)	0,192

Table 24: Statistical results for hypotheses H3.3.1–H3.3.2

Similarly, significant support for a positive impact of the investment managers' international experience was found in only one of the four analyses (H3.3.3). Although all analyses resulted in high coefficients between 2,159 and 4,985, only the impact on corporate governance quality measured by self-assessment was significant. For the confidence level of 95%, the coefficient of the explanatory variable is 3,296 when the above introduced control variables are taken into account. The R^2 is relatively high at 0,401. Apart from that, the start-up experience of the investment managers was also in one case a significant explanatory variable of corporate governance quality. If the quality of the advice function measured by criteria is used as a response variable, then the coefficient is 9,269 at the confidence level of 95%. The R^2 of this model is 0,187.

#	Hypothesis	Version	Response variable	Explanatory variable	Coefficient	Control variables	R-square
H3.3.3	The greater the investment managers' international experience in the venture capital industry, the greater is the impact of their influence on the corporate governance of portfolio companies.	S	CG quality index (self-assessment)	International experience VC-IM	**3,296****	vciind, imtrus, cempngr, finrou, cdev, landgr, cgqind(t=0)	0,401
H3.3.3	The greater the investment managers' international experience in the venture capital industry, the greater is the impact of their influence on the corporate governance of portfolio companies.	C	CG quality index (criteria)	International experience VC-IM	3,365	vciind, imtrus, cempngr, finrou, cdev, landgr, cgqinc(t=0)	0,372
H3.3.3	The greater the investment managers' international experience in the venture capital industry, the greater is the impact of their influence on the corporate governance of portfolio companies.	S	CG advice index (self-assessment)	International experience VC-IM	2,159	vciind, imtrus, cempngr, finrou, cdev, landgr, cgaind(t=0)	0,302
H3.3.3	The greater the investment managers' international experience in the venture capital industry, the greater is the impact of their influence on the corporate governance of portfolio companies.	C	CG advice index (criteria)	International experience VC-IM	4,985	vciind, imtrus, cempngr, finrou, cdev, landgr, cgacin(t=0)	0,167
H3.3.4	The greater the investment manager's start-up experience is, the greater is the impact of his/her influence on the corporate governance of portfolio companies	S	CG quality index (self-assessment)	Startup experience VC-IM	1,457	vciind, imtrus, cempngr, finrou, cdev, landgr, cgqind(t=0)	0,392
H3.3.4	The greater the investment manager's start-up experience is, the greater is the impact of his/her influence on the corporate governance of portfolio companies	C	CG quality index (criteria)	Startup experience VC-IM	2,699	vciind, imtrus, cempngr, finrou, cdev, landgr, cgqinc(t=0)	0,384
H3.3.4	The greater the investment managers' start-up experience, the greater is the impact of their influence on the corporate governance of portfolio companies.	S	CG advice index (self-assessment)	Startup experience VC-IM	2,673	vciind, imtrus, cempngr, finrou, cdev, landgr, cgaind(t=0)	0,319
H3.3.4	The greater the investment managers' start-up experience, the greater is the impact of their influence on the corporate governance of portfolio companies.	C	CG advice index (criteria)	Startup experience VC-IM	**9,269****	vciind, imtrus, cempngr, finrou, cdev, landgr, cgacin(t=0)	0,187

Table 25: Statistical results for hypotheses H3.3.3–H3.3.4

The last trait of the investment managers analysed is their commitment to the portfolio companies. Again, tests were carried out for the two corporate governance measures at the highest level as well as for the advice function. In contrast to the expectations, hypothesis H3.3.5 is not supported by the tests. The coefficients for all explanatory variables are relatively low and not significant even though the R^2 values are relatively high for three of the analyses. Table 26 shows the results in an overview.

#	Hypothesis	Version	Response variable	Explanatory variable	Coefficient	Control variables	R-square
H3.3.5	The greater the commitment of the investment managers, the greater is the impact of their influence on the corporate governance of portfolio companies.	S	CG quality index (self-assessment)	Number of contacts per quarter VC-IM	0,009	vciind, imtrus, cempngr, finrou, cdev, landgr, cgqind(t=0)	0,433
H3.3.5	The greater the commitment of the investment managers, the greater is the impact of their influence on the corporate governance of portfolio companies.	C	CG quality index (criteria)	Number of contacts per quarter VC-IM	0,015	vciind, imtrus, cempngr, finrou, cdev, landgr, cgqinc(t=0)	0,343
H3.3.5	The greater the commitment of the investment managers, the greater is the impact of their influence on the corporate governance of portfolio companies.	S	CG advice index (self-assessment)	Number of contacts per quarter VC-IM	0,045	vciind, imtrus, cempngr, finrou, cdev, landgr, cgaind(t=0)	0,344
H3.3.5	The greater the commitment of the investment managers, the greater is the impact of their influence on the corporate governance of portfolio companies.	C	CG advice index (criteria)	Number of contacts per quarter VC-IM	0,131	vciind, imtrus, cempngr, finrou, cdev, landgr, cgacin(t=0)	0,187

Table 26: Statistical results for hypothesis H3.3.5

Finally, the trust between the lead venture capitalists' investment managers and the portfolio companies' managers is also expected to affect corporate governance quality (H3.4). Corresponding to the analysis above, it was tested with four different response variables: the two measures for overall corporate governance quality and the quality of the corporate governance's advice function. The tests were controlled for the strength of the venture capitalists' influence and the portfolio companies' size, development stage, location, and financing round as well as the original corporate governance quality before the first financing round. Significant results were found only for the two tests using self-assessment measures. The coefficient of the impact of the trustfulness of the relationship is relatively high at 4,405 for the overall corporate governance quality and at 6,883 for the advice function. The R^2 values are also comparatively high at 0,428 and 0,340. The two analyses using measures by criteria also delivered positive coefficients, but they were not significant. There might be a relationship between the perception of the respondents and the trust of the investment managers. Table 27 presents the results for this hypothesis.

This concludes the detailed results for the hypotheses related to the venture capitalists' abilities to influence the corporate governance of their portfolio companies. Figure 50 indicates whether the hypotheses are supported or not.

#	Hypothesis	Version	Response variable	Explanatory variable	Coefficient	Control variables	R-square
H3.4	The impact of the venture capitalists influence is greater if their relationship with the managers of portfolio companies is trustful.	S	CG quality index (self-assessment)	Trustfullness of relationship VC-M	**4,405*** **	vciind, cempngr, finrou, cdev, landgr, cgqind(t=0)	0,428
H3.4	The impact of the venture capitalists influence is greater if their relationship with the managers of portfolio companies is trustful.	C	CG quality index (criteria)	Trustfullness of relationship VC-M	0,830	vciind, cempngr, finrou, cdev, landgr, cgqinc(t=0)	0,348
H3.4	The impact of the venture capitalists influence is greater if their relationship with the managers of portfolio companies is trustful.	S	CG advice index (self-assessment)	Trustfullness of relationship VC-M	**6,883*** **	vciind, cempngr, finrou, cdev, landgr, cgaind(t=0)	0,340
H3.4	The impact of the venture capitalists influence is greater if their relationship with the managers of portfolio companies is trustful.	C	CG advice index (criteria)	Trustfullness of relationship VC-M	1,672	vciind, cempngr, finrou, cdev, landgr, cgacin(t=0)	0,181

Table 27: Statistical results for hypothesis H3.4

#	Hypothesis	Support
H3	The abilities of venture capitalists have an impact on the corporate governance of portfolio compaies	✓
H3.1	The control rights of venture capital firms have a positive impact on the corporate governance of portfolio companies.	~
H3.1.1	The stronger the venture capitalists' control right rights, — in terms of ownership rights and board seats — the stronger is their influence on the corporate governance of portfolio companies.	~
H3.1.2	The stronger the venture capitalists' control rights, the greater is the impact of their influence on the elements related to the monitoring function of corporate governance.	?
H3.1.3	The stronger the venture capitalists' control rights, the greater is the impact of their influence on the elements related to the bonding function of corporate governance.	~
H3.2	The characteristics of venture capital firms have positive impact on the corporate governance of portfolio companies.	~
H3.2.1	Independent venture capital firms' influence has a greater impact on the corporate governance of portfolio companies than that of corporate venture capitalists and bank-related and governmental venture capitalists.	~
H3.2.2	The more investment experience a venture capital firm has, the greater are the effects of its influence on the corporate governance of portfolio companies.	?
H3.2.3	The greater the international experience of the venture capital firms, the greater are the effects of their influence on the corporate governance of portfolio companies.	?
H3.2.4	The greater the reputation of a venture capital firm, the greater are the effects of its influence on the corporate governance of portfolio companies.	?
H3.3	The characteristics of investment managers have positive impact on the corporate governance of portfolio companies.	✓
H3.3.1	The greater the investment managers' experience in the portfolio company's industry, the greater is the impact of their influence on the corporate governance of portfolio companies.	~
H3.3.2	The greater the investment manager's experience in the portfolio company's industry is the greater is the impact of his/her influence on the corporate governance of portfolio companies.	~
H3.3.3	The greater the investment managers' international experience in the venture capital industry, the greater is the impact of their influence on the corporate governance of portfolio companies.	~
H3.3.4	The greater the investment managers' start-up experience, the greater is the impact of their influence on the corporate governance of portfolio companies.	~
H3.3.5	The greater the commitment of the investment managers, the greater is the impact of their influence on the corporate governance of portfolio companies.	?
H3.4	The impact of the venture capitalists influence is greater if their relationship with the managers of portfolio companies is trustful.	~

Figure 50: Overview of the results for hypotheses about the relationship between venture capitalists' abilities and corporate governance quality

5.7 Effects of Corporate Governance on Firm Value

5.7.1 Descriptive Results for Development of Firm Value

In this section, the development of the portfolio companies' firm value is described. The firm value was analysed with two general perspectives: firm performance and firm valuation. Besides this, the variables for firm value include self-assessment measures and measures in the form of criteria.

To start with, the relative performance of the companies was assessed by the respondents. They evaluated how competitive their companies were and how well they performed compared to their own business plans. Although the means of both measures were on the positive side of the scale, an increase was found only for competitiveness. It significantly grew at the time of the first and second financing rounds, as Figure 51 shows.

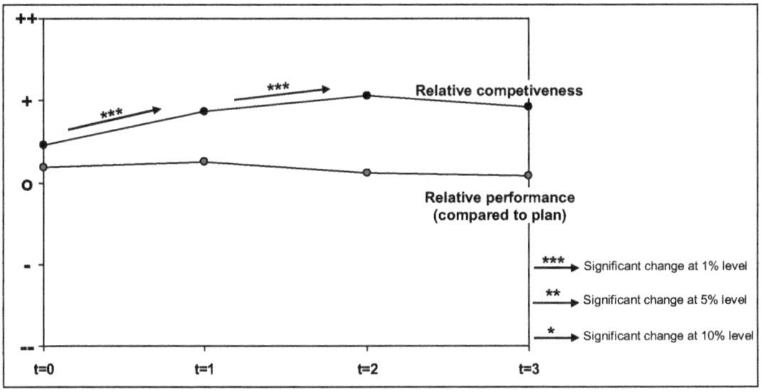

Figure 51: Development of portfolio companies' competitiveness

Next, the performance was measured by criteria for profitability and the growth of the companies. The collected performance measures are EBITDA margin, net profit margin, return on equity and return on assets. The means of the first three measures develop similarly over the course of the four measuring times: they decline over time and become negative for the last measuring time. A particularly strong decline was found for the return on equity with a reduction from 15% to –4,6%. As this development might not have been expected, it should be noted that the mean for the time after the second and third financing rounds could possibly be biased by the small number of respondents. In contrast to the three other measures, return on assets does not steadily decline. The mean fluctuates between 5,5% and 10,3%. The reasons for the different development of this measure are unclear. Either the companies are highly financed by debt, which is improbable, or the differences are caused by the fact that the companies that responded to the relevant questions differ. Figure 52 shows the developments in an overview.

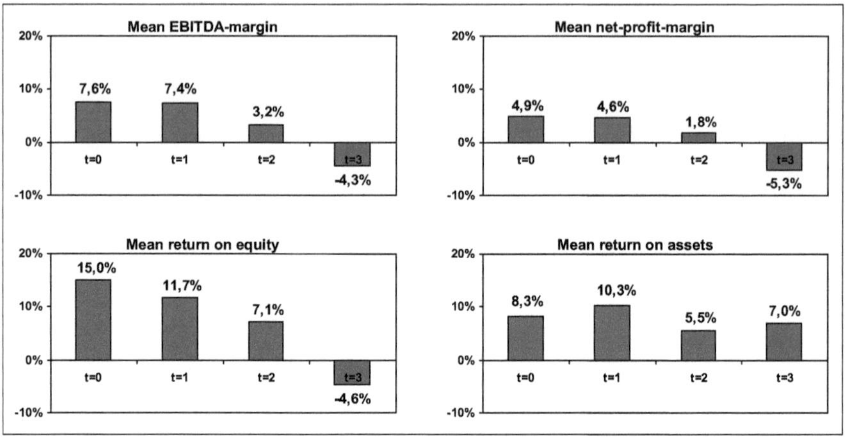

Figure 52: Development of portfolio companies' profitability measures

The growth rates of the analysed portfolio companies increase with venture capital financing but decline afterwards, as expected. The growth rate in terms of employees precedes the growth of sales and cashflows. The means of the growth rates are relatively high, ranging from 17% for the cashflows before the first financing round to 94% for employees after the first financing round. The high values can be explained by basis effects because growth companies before the first financing round are comparatively small. A significant development was found for the changes in the growth rate of employees between the first three measuring times and for the change in the growth rate of cashflows between the first two measuring times, as Figure 53 indicates.

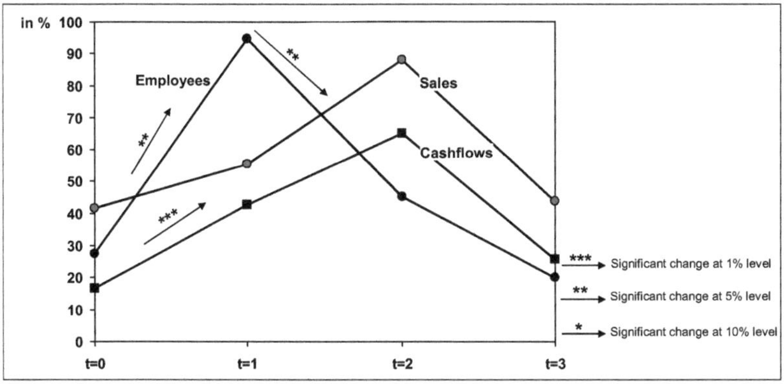

Figure 53: Development of portfolio companies' growth rates

The second perspective of the firm value is the valuation of the portfolio companies. First, the respondents provided a self-assessment of the development of their companies' valuations. Between the first and the second financing rounds, the mean valuation improved whereas between the second and the third financing rounds, the valuation remained almost constant. A t-test demonstrated that this development is significant at the 99% level, as Figure 54 shows.

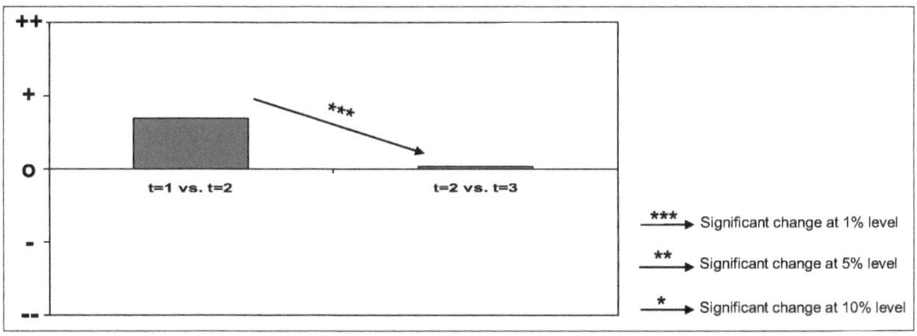

Figure 54: Development of portfolio companies' valuation

The more detailed analyses using changes of sales and EBITDA multiples as measures provide a similar picture. Between the first and second financing rounds, both measures increase, by 89,3% and 18,8% respectively, whereas between the second and third financing rounds the growth declines to 28,8% for the mean sales multiple and even turns to a reduction of 4,3% for the mean EBITDA multiple. However, t-tests did not deliver a significant change between the two measuring times. The changes of the two variables are presented in Figure 55.

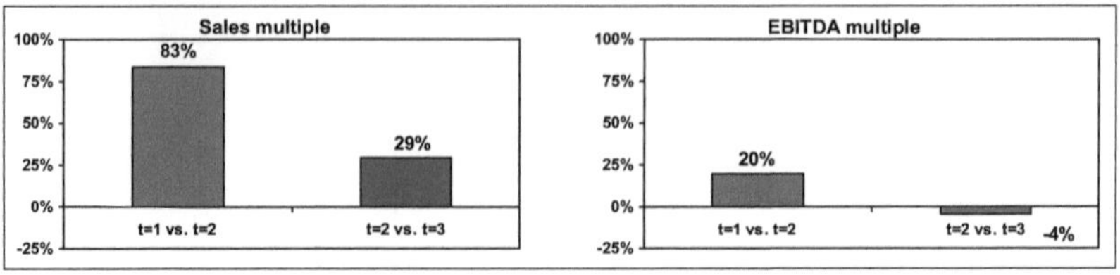

Figure 55: Development of portfolio companies' multiples

Annex 10 gives detailed information related to all measures of firm value. It includes the minimum and maximum values, the mean and standard deviation as well as the number of observations.

5.7.2 Results for Hypotheses' Tests

After describing the development of firm value, this section presents the results of the tests of the hypotheses that relate to the relationship between the corporate governance quality and firm value. Corresponding to the structure of the last section, the hypotheses that refer to the portfolio companies' performance will be analysed first, and the hypotheses that refer to their valuation will be described second. Because the effects of good corporate governance might be observable only after a lag, the relationship is tested not only with the explanatory and response variables from the same period (labelled "same period" in the table) but also with the explanatory variable from one period and the response variable from the subsequent period ("next period").

The self-assessed relative performance measures were used first to the test the impact of good corporate governance on the performance of the portfolio companies (H4.1). All analyses that relate competitiveness with the corporate governance quality of the same period delivered positive results. Both analyses that use the competitiveness of the portfolio companies as a response variable and the corporate governance quality with the two different measures (self-assessment and criteria) support the hypothesis. However, the two resulting coefficients are relatively low, with 0,012 for the self-assessment measure and 0,003 for the measurement by criteria. This is supported by the results of the tests that use performance relative to the companies' business plans as a response variable; again the strength of the impact is very low (0,023 and 0,004). Furthermore, the resulting R^2 values are relatively low for three of the four tests using the mixed models technique. The results for the impact of corporate governance on the performance of the subsequent period contrast those findings. Although only two tests were significant, they predict a weak but negative impact of good corporate governance on performance. Again, the R^2 values of the analyses were relatively low. Thus the results show that the hypothesis is weakly supported if the immediate impact of good corporate governance is analysed, but it is contradicted if the impact on future performance is analysed. Table 28 shows these findings.

#	Hypothesis	Version	Response variable	Explanatory variable	Coefficient	Control variables	R-square
H4.1	The corporate governance quality of company has effects on its fundamental performance.	S - same period	Competitiveness relative to direct and indirect competitors	CG quality index (self-assessment)	**0,012*** **	pcindust, cempngr, finrou, cdev, landgr	0,150
H4.1	The corporate governance quality of company has effects on its fundamental performance.	S - same period	Competitiveness relative to direct and indirect competitors	CG quality index (criteria)	**0,003** **	pcindust, cempngr, finrou, cdev, landgr	0,114
H4.1	The corporate governance quality of company has effects on its fundamental performance.	S - next period	Competitiveness relative to direct and indirect competitors	CG quality index (self-assessment)	**-0,011*** **	pcindust, cempngr, finrou, cdev, landgr	0,109
H4.1	The corporate governance quality of company has effects on its fundamental performance.	S - next period	Competitiveness relative to direct and indirect competitors	CG quality index (criteria)	-0,003	pcindust, cempngr, finrou, cdev, landgr	0,091
H4.1	The corporate governance quality of company has effects on its fundamental performance.	S - same period	Performance according to plan	CG quality index (self-assessment)	**0,023*** **	pcindust, cempngr, finrou, cdev, landgr	0,212
H4.1	The corporate governance quality of company has effects on its fundamental performance.	S - same period	Performance according to plan	CG quality index (criteria)	**0,004* **	pcindust, cempngr, finrou, cdev, landgr	0,115
H4.1	The corporate governance quality of company has effects on its fundamental performance.	S - next period	Performance according to plan	CG quality index (self-assessment)	**-0,024*** **	pcindust, cempngr, finrou, cdev, landgr	0,207
H4.1	The corporate governance quality of company has effects on its fundamental performance.	S - next period	Performance according to plan	CG quality index (criteria)	-0,001	pcindust, cempngr, finrou, cdev, landgr	0,119

Table 28: Statistical results for hypothesis 4.1

These findings can be compared to the more detailed analyses using measures for the profitability and growth of the portfolio companies. In regard to the profitability measures, significant results were found for the net profit margin and the return on equity as well as the return on assets but not for the EBITDA margin. The test relating self-assessed corporate governance quality to the net profit margin of the same period delivers support for the hypothesis with a coefficient for the explanatory variable of 0,155 at the 95% confidence level. However, it must be noted that the R^2 of this analysis is only 0,017. Besides this, the two corporate governance quality measures significantly affect the return on equity of the subsequent period. Here, the influence is much stronger with coefficients of 0,264 and 0,218, and the R^2 values for these analyses are also comparably high at 0,376 and 0,439. This can, therefore, be seen as stronger support for the hypothesis. By contrast, the results of the tests relating to return on assets are mixed. Although there is support for a positive relationship between corporate governance measured by self-assessment and return on assets of the same period, the other three tests deliver negative but not significant coefficients.

Although the coefficient of the first analysis is comparably strong at 0,233, the explanatory value is limited by a low R^2 of only 0,013. As Table 29 indicates, the relationship between good corporate governance and profitability can only be supported for some measures. Additionally, differences in the impact might occur at different measuring times.

#	Hypothesis	Version	Response variable	Explanatory variable	Coefficient	Control variables	R-square
H4.1.1	The better the corporate governance quality of a company is, the higher is its profitability.	S - same period	EBITDA-margin	CG quality index (self-assessment)	0,136	pcindust, cempngr, finrou, cdev, landgr	0,028
H4.1.1	The better the corporate governance quality of a company is, the higher is its profitability.	C - same period	EBITDA-margin	CG quality index (criteria)	0,020	pcindust, cempngr, finrou, cdev, landgr	0,028
H4.1.1	The better the corporate governance quality of a company is, the higher is its profitability.	S - next period	EBITDA-margin	CG quality index (self-assessment)	0,224	pcindust, cempngr, finrou, cdev, landgr	0,090
H4.1.1	The better the corporate governance quality of a company is, the higher is its profitability.	C - next period	EBITDA-margin	CG quality index (criteria)	0,036	pcindust, cempngr, finrou, cdev, landgr	0,091
H4.1.1	The better the corporate governance quality of a company is, the higher is its profitability.	S - same period	Net-profit-margin	CG quality index (self-assessment)	**0,155****	pcindust, cempngr, finrou, cdev, landgr	0,017
H4.1.1	The better the corporate governance quality of a company is, the higher is its profitability.	C - same period	Net-profit-margin	CG quality index (criteria)	0,029	pcindust, cempngr, finrou, cdev, landgr	0,028
H4.1.1	The better the corporate governance quality of a company is, the higher is its profitability.	S - next period	Net-profit-margin	CG quality index (self-assessment)	0,057	pcindust, cempngr, finrou, cdev, landgr	0,089
H4.1.1	The better the corporate governance quality of a company is, the higher is its profitability.	C - next period	Net-profit-margin	CG quality index (criteria)	-0,04	pcindust, cempngr, finrou, cdev, landgr	0,097
H4.1.1	The better the corporate governance quality of a company is, the higher is its profitability.	S - same period	Return-on-equity	CG quality index (self-assessment)	0,221	pcindust, cempngr, finrou, cdev, landgr	0,035
H4.1.1	The better the corporate governance quality of a company is, the higher is its profitability.	C - same period	Net-profit-margin	CG quality index (criteria)	0,083	pcindust, cempngr, finrou, cdev, landgr	0,043
H4.1.1	The better the corporate governance quality of a company is, the higher is its profitability.	S - next period	Return-on-equity	CG quality index (self-assessment)	**0,264***	pcindust, cempngr, finrou, cdev, landgr	0,376
H4.1.1	The better the corporate governance quality of a company is, the higher is its profitability.	C - next period	Return-on-equity	CG quality index (criteria)	**0,218****	pcindust, cempngr, finrou, cdev, landgr	0,439
H4.1.1	The better the corporate governance quality of a company is, the higher is its profitability.	S - same period	Return-on-assets	CG quality index (self-assessment)	**0,233****	pcindust, cempngr, finrou, cdev, landgr	0,013
H4.1.1	The better the corporate governance quality of a company is, the higher is its profitability.	C - same period	Return-on-assets	CG quality index (criteria)	-0,004	pcindust, cempngr, finrou, cdev, landgr	0,009
H4.1.1	The better the corporate governance quality of a company is, the higher is its profitability.	S - next period	Return-on-assets	CG quality index (self-assessment)	-0,020	pcindust, cempngr, finrou, cdev, landgr	0,113
H4.1.1	The better the corporate governance quality of a company is, the higher is its profitability.	C - next period	Return-on-assets	CG quality index (criteria)	-0,024	pcindust, cempngr, finrou, cdev, landgr	0,107

Table 29: Statistical results for hypothesis 4.1.1

In Table 30, the results for the tests of the relationship between corporate governance quality and the growth of portfolio companies are presented. It was derived from theory that better corporate governance should contribute to a stronger growth of the portfolio companies. This was tested as before with the two corporate governance measures, different measures for growth (employees, sales, cashflows), and taking into account that the impact might be observable in the same or the next period. Nevertheless, the analyses did not deliver a significant result. All tests had a comparatively low R^2, and none of the coefficients related to the explanatory variables was significant at the minimum confidence level of 90%. Although most of these coefficients were positive, i.e., generally corresponded to the hypothesis, some of them were negative. On the basis of these results, the hypothesis can be neither supported nor rejected.

#	Hypothesis	Version	Response variable	Explanatory variable	Coefficient	Control variables	R-square
H4.1.2	The better the corporate governance quality of a company is, the higher is its growth.	S - same period	Growth in employees	CG quality index (self-assessment)	-0,366	pcindust, cempngr, finrou, cdev, landgr	0,017
H4.1.2	The better the corporate governance quality of a company is, the higher is its growth.	C - same period	Growth in employees	CG quality index (criteria)	-0,083	pcindust, cempngr, finrou, cdev, landgr	0,012
H4.1.2	The better the corporate governance quality of a company is, the higher is its growth.	S - next period	Growth in employees	CG quality index (self-assessment)	0,139	pcindust, cempngr, finrou, cdev, landgr	0,031
H4.1.2	The better the corporate governance quality of a company is, the higher is its growth.	C - next period	Growth in employees	CG quality index (criteria)	0,195	pcindust, cempngr, finrou, cdev, landgr	0,026
H4.1.2	The better the corporate governance quality of a company is, the higher is its growth.	S - same period	Growth in sales	CG quality index (self-assessment)	-0,182	pcindust, cempngr, finrou, cdev, landgr	0,057
H4.1.2	The better the corporate governance quality of a company is, the higher is its growth.	C - same period	Growth in sales	CG quality index (criteria)	0,303	pcindust, cempngr, finrou, cdev, landgr	0,061
H4.1.2	The better the corporate governance quality of a company is, the higher is its growth.	S - next period	Growth in sales	CG quality index (self-assessment)	-0,122	pcindust, cempngr, finrou, cdev, landgr	0,061
H4.1.2	The better the corporate governance quality of a company is, the higher is its growth.	C - next period	Growth in sales	CG quality index (criteria)	0,525	pcindust, cempngr, finrou, cdev, landgr	0,068
H4.1.2	The better the corporate governance quality of a company is, the higher is its growth.	S - same period	Growth in cashflows	CG quality index (self-assessment)	0,028	pcindust, cempngr, finrou, cdev, landgr	0,012
H4.1.2	The better the corporate governance quality of a company is, the higher is its growth.	C - same period	Growth in cashflows	CG quality index (criteria)	-0,03	pcindust, cempngr, finrou, cdev, landgr	0,010
H4.1.2	The better the corporate governance quality of a company is, the higher is its growth.	S - next period	Growth in cashflows	CG quality index (self-assessment)	0,457	pcindust, cempngr, finrou, cdev, landgr	0,035
H4.1.2	The better the corporate governance quality of a company is, the higher is its growth.	C - next period	Growth in cashflows	CG quality index (criteria)	-0,056	pcindust, cempngr, finrou, cdev, landgr	0,033

Table 30: Statistical results for hypothesis 4.1.2

Next, whether corporate governance quality has a positive impact on the valuation of portfolio companies is analysed (H4.2). This is done first with a self-assessment by the respondents as a response variable. They were asked to assess how the valuation changed between the financing rounds on a scale from "– –" to "++". Although the R^2 is 0,298 for the test with the corporate governance quality measured by self-assessment and 0,305 for the test with the corporate governance quality measured by criteria, there were no significant results. The coefficients for the explanatory variables are very low and fluctuate around zero (Table 31), so this hypothesis cannot be supported.

#	Hypothesis	Version	Response variable	Explanatory variable	Coefficient	Control variables	R-square
H4.2	The corporate governance quality of a company has positive effects on its fundamental performance.	S	Change of valuation between financing rounds	CG quality index (self-assessment)	0,008	pcindust, cempngr, finrou, cdev, landgr	0,298
H4.2	The corporate governance quality of a company has positive effects on its fundamental performance.	C	Change of valuation between financing rounds	CG quality index (criteria)	-0,004	pcindust, cempngr, finrou, cdev, landgr	0,305

Table 31: Statistical results for hypothesis 4.2

Finally, the hypothesis was also tested with criteria, namely the percentage change of the sales and EBITDA multiples used in the different financing rounds, i.e., the change between the first and second financing rounds and the change between the second and third financing rounds. The R^2 of these four analyses (taking into account the two measures of corporate governance) are relatively high, ranging between 0,271 and 0,626. Similarly, the coefficients of corporate governance quality as an explanatory variable are comparatively high, but they are positive for the self-assessment measures and negative for the measures by criteria. However, only one of the tests using the mixed models technique delivered a significant result at the 95% level. Corporate governance quality measured by self-assessment has a strong positive effect on the EBITDA multiples used for the valuation of portfolio companies. The coefficient is in this case 2,301, as Table 32 shows. These findings indicate that the hypothesis is partly supported. Self-assessed corporate governance quality seems to have a positive impact on the valuation of the portfolio companies, but a significant impact was found only for the EBITDA multiple.

#	Hypothesis	Version	Response variable	Explanatory variable	Coefficient	Control variables	R-square
H4.2.1	The better the corporate governance quality of a portfolio company, the higher is its valuation.	S	Change of sales multiple	CG quality index (self-assessment)	1,898	pcindust, cempngr, finrou, cdev, landgr	0,626
H4.2.1	The better the corporate governance quality of a portfolio company, the higher is its valuation.	C	Change of sales multiple	CG quality index (criteria)	-1,051	pcindust, cempngr, finrou, cdev, landgr	0,550
H4.2.1	The better the corporate governance quality of a portfolio company, the higher is its valuation.	S	Change of EBITDA multiple	CG quality index (self-assessment)	**2,301****	pcindust, cempngr, finrou, cdev, landgr	0,271
H4.2.1	The better the corporate governance quality of a portfolio company, the higher is its valuation.	C	Change of EBITDA multiple	CG quality index (criteria)	-2,015	pcindust, cempngr, finrou, cdev, landgr	0,336

Table 32: Statistical results for hypothesis 4.2.1

To summarise the findings of these analyses, Figure 56 indicates whether the five hypotheses are supported or not. In this case, three of them are partly supported ("~") and for two hypotheses, there was no significant finding ("?").

#	Hypothesis	Support
H4.1	The corporate governance quality of company has effects on its fundamental performance.	~
H4.1.1	The better the corporate governance quality of a company is, the higher is its profitability.	~
H4.1.2	The better the corporate governance quality of a company, the higher is its growth.	?
H4.2	The corporate governance quality of a company has positive effects on its fundamental performance.	?
H4.2.1	The better the corporate governance quality of a portfolio company, the higher is its valuation.	~

Figure 56: Overview of the results for hypotheses about the relationship between corporate governance quality and firm value

6 Conclusion

This chapter summarises the key results of the research and answers the research questions. In a second step, these findings are discussed taking into account limitations and relations with the results of earlier research. Finally, an outlook is given that directs the need for further research on the basis of this analysis.

6.1 Summary of Results

The analysis is intended to answer two key research questions derived from the literature in the fields of venture capital and corporate governance:

How do venture capitalists influence the corporate governance of portfolio companies throughout their development?

What are the effects of good corporate governance on the firm value of growth companies?

The research questions comprise the following four aspects, which focus on the relationship between venture capital, corporate governance and firm value:

- the venture capitalists' reasons for influencing corporate governance
- the effects of their influence on corporate governance
- the impact of the venture capitalists' abilities
- the effects of good corporate governance on firm value.

To answer these two research questions, three distinct analyses were undertaken. First, a theoretical analysis on the basis of agency theory and the dynamic resource-based view were done. The combination of an economic and a managerial theory ensured a comprehensive picture. The results of this theoretical analysis were hypotheses that were tested in an empirical analysis. Second, a qualitative empirical analysis was carried out with expert interviews in several European countries that delivered first findings on the verification of the hypotheses and helped to prepare the questionnaire. Finally, a large-scale quantitative analysis of portfolio companies across Europe was done to collect data to test the hypotheses. For the tests, uni- and multivariate statistical techniques were used. According to the three-step approach of the research, the main findings for the two research questions are presented in the following.

6.1.1 Influence of Venture Capital on Corporate Governance

The first research question analyses how venture capitalists influence the corporate governance of their portfolio companies and thereby encompasses three aspects. The reasons venture capitalists influence corporate governance are analysed first. In a second step, it is researched what impact the influence has and whether the impact is determined by the venture capitalists' abilities. According to **agency theory**, the venture capitalists influence corporate governance to reduce the risk of their investments. The strength of their influence should thereafter be determined by the agency and business risk of the portfolio company. Consequently, they should focus on the elements associated with the control and bonding functions of corporate governance, such as the assessment and bonding of managers, the independence of the board, and the reporting discipline. The key condition for the venture capitalists' impact on these elements is that they possess sufficient control rights to enforce their goals, in particular voting rights and board seats. By contrast, the **dynamic resource-based view** considers good corporate governance as a valuable resource to achieve a competitive advantage. Hence, venture capitalists should improve the corporate governance of their portfolio companies in order to increase their value by creating a better competitive position. However, a competitive advantage can only be built on a good basis, so venture capitalists are expected to focus their influence on companies that already have comparatively good corporate governance. Value creation through good corporate governance is particularly associated with the advice function. To improve these elements, such as the selection of managers, the qualification of board members and the involvement of board members in the strategic decision making process, venture capitalists need relevant experience and capabilities. These required abilities refer to characteristics of the venture capital firms and the investment managers who work for them and include, for example, the type of the venture capital firm and experience in the venture capital industry and the portfolio companies' industries. A third reason for venture capitalists to influence the corporate governance of their portfolio companies, apart from risk reduction and value creation, is the optimal preparation of a portfolio company about to issue its shares publicly. In this case, it is also expected that venture capitalists increase their influence, in particular to ensure that the portfolio company complies with required corporate governance rules and to send a quality signal to the market by bringing reputable board members into the company. The reasons for the venture capitalists' influence could change over time, as they have to decide where their investment of resources is most promising. Accordingly, it is expected that the focus changes from risk reduction in the early phase of an investment when it is difficult to differentiate between more- and less-promising portfolio companies to value creation at later phases where it might be possible to make this differentiation. While the reasons, the focus and the required abilities of the venture capitalists differ for the explanations of the two theories, both theories predict that venture capitalist influence improves the corporate governance of the portfolio companies. This theoretic analysis resulted in hypotheses that were tested empirically.

During the **interviews** with venture capitalists and managers of portfolio companies, it was attempted to translate the relationships that were derived from theory into practice. It was found that the venture capitalists take standard measures to influence corporate governance, mostly during the contracting phase. However, the extent of these measures depends on their negotiating power. For example, in the case of bad performance, these measures might be adapted. In particular, the interviewees from portfolio companies revealed that venture capitalists are not always in a position to push through strict burdens for the managers. They also recognised differences in the approaches and effectiveness of venture capitalists. Several venture capitalists stressed that trust plays an important role because their influence might only be effective if the managers of the portfolio companies trust them. This emphasises that venture capitalists might not always be able to enforce their measures on the corporate governance of portfolio companies. The reason for their influence is mainly explained by risk reduction and exit preparation. In contrast, corporate governance is generally not seen as a key to improve portfolio companies' competitive positions.

The results from the **quantitative analysis** are mixed. For the hypothesis on the reasons, only very weak support was found. The agency and business risk that were expected to increase venture capitalists' influence were not in a significant relationship with the strength of the influence, and the findings rather indicated a negative than a positive influence. Corporate governance quality — referring to the value creation hypotheses derived from the dynamic resource-based view — was also significantly related to the venture capitalists' influence in only a very few cases, and the impact was very low. However, the impact of corporate governance quality on the venture capitalists' influence on the corporate governance is significant when the analysis is done for the second and third financing rounds. This indicates that value creation might be a reason only at a later point when the potential of a portfolio company and the adequacy of its corporate governance can be assessed.

In contrast to these limited findings, the effects of a potential IPO were more significant. According to the results, a portfolio company will more probably comply with a corporate governance code and have board members with experience from listed companies when it plans a public offering than when it does not. The venture capitalists' influence is, in the beginning, focussed on the corporate governance bonding and monitoring function whereas in the later financing rounds, the advice function becomes comparatively more important.

There are relatively strong differences in the assessment of the portfolio companies' corporate governance quality between the measurement by self-assessment of the respondents and the measurement by criteria. Although the quality of all individual elements is rather similar in the perception of the respondents, there are strong differences when the fulfilment of criteria is analysed. In particular, the criteria related to the compensation of the managers as well as the composition and work of the board are less often fulfilled than those of the other elements. However, the quality of all corporate governance elements increases significantly with venture capitalist financing.

Similarly, the majority of the hypotheses that predict a positive relationship between venture capitalists' influence and the portfolio companies' corporate governance are supported. Particularly strong is the impact of venture capitalists on the adequacy of managers' compensation, the composition of the board and the reporting discipline. In some cases, there are differences between the assessments by self-assessment and those by criteria; mostly the significance is stronger for the self-assessment measures.

In regard to abilities, it was distinguished between the control rights of the venture capitalists, the characteristics of the lead venture capital firms and the characteristics of the investment managers. Although the general hypothesis that stronger abilities of the venture capitalists lead to better corporate governance in the portfolio companies is supported, the significance of the positive impact of the control rights is weak. In contrast, the findings on the abilities of venture capital firms and particularly of the investment managers are more significant. Independent venture capital firms, for example, might have a stronger impact than other types of venture capital firms.

Moreover, the investment managers' experience in the venture capital industry, in the industry of the portfolio companies, and internationally also positively affect corporate governance. Apart from that, a strong impact on the corporate governance quality measured by self-assessment derives from the trust between the venture capitalists and the managers of portfolio companies. Hence, although the reasons of the venture capitalists might be not very clear, their influence has a strongly positive effect on most corporate governance elements in the portfolio companies. This is supported not only by the statistical analyses but also by the respondents' perceptions. The majority of them perceived a positive or very positive impact on corporate governance as a result of the venture capitalists' influence. Additionally, the abilities of the venture capitalists determine how strong the improvement of the corporate governance is.

6.1.2 Influence of Corporate Governance on Firm Value

The second research question deals with the effects of good corporate governance on the firm value of portfolio companies. As the increase of the companies' value is the primary motivation for venture capitalists, this relationship is also expected to support their influence on corporate governance. The two underlying theories of this research both support the hypothesis that better corporate governance results in a higher firm value. According to **agency theory**, good corporate governance should reduce agency costs that arise from the diverging interests of the venture capitalists and the managers of the portfolio companies. Agency problems such as consumption on the job and not carrying out cashflow-positive but risky projects that incur costs for the venture capitalists might be prevented by effective oversight of the portfolio companies. The resulting lower costs should lead to improved performance and a better valuation of the companies. By contrast, the **dynamic resource-based view** considers the better competitiveness that could be reached through good corporate governance as the reason for a higher firm value. In particular, good corporate governance should lead to better-informed decision making that could lead to better decisions and ultimately to a better competitive position. Good corporate governance should thereafter be related to high firm value in terms of both performance and valuation. This shows that agency theory explains the relationship between corporate governance and firm value as reduced costs whereas the dynamic resource-based view explains it as higher competitiveness.

During the qualitative analysis, the **interviewees** brought up some examples that support the hypothesis that corporate governance and firm value are positively related.

Venture capitalists delivered examples of situations in which their oversight of portfolio companies prevented unnecessary costs. One portfolio company manager cited an example of the positive effect of good corporate governance on the decision making process. Generally, the interviewees supported the notion that good corporate governance increases firm value, though they also stated that bad corporate governance does not inevitably lead to bad performance. Furthermore, venture capitalists denied that they pay a premium for companies with good corporate governance, but they said would consider a deduction in the case of bad corporate governance — for example for the lack of complete reports about the historic development of a company. Furthermore, the interviewees stressed that good corporate governance in the case of growth companies might not be well assessed by the criteria of corporate governance codes because they neglect the particular and changing requirements of these companies. Therefore, the majority of the respondents doubted that an analysis of the relationship between the fulfilment of corporate governance criteria and the portfolio companies' firm value would lead to significant results, although they supported the general notion.

In the **survey**, data on the portfolio companies' performance and valuation were collected in order to analyse their relationship with corporate governance quality. The results of the statistical tests delivered only weak support for the hypothesis of a positive relationship. In most cases the impact was not significant or only very weak. In regard to the companies' performance, support was found for the tests that related corporate governance quality to the return on equity and, to a lesser extent, to the net profit margin and the return on assets. Although the impact was observed after a time lag for the first measure, the effects on the other two measures were observed without delay. There was no significant relationship found for any of the growth measures. The results for the valuation measures are also mixed. The only significant and relatively strong positive impact of good corporate governance was found on the EBITDA multiple. That means that better-perceived corporate governance led to a higher EBITDA multiple used for the portfolio companies' valuation in the next financing round. The limited significant findings for these hypotheses might be due to a reduced number of responses from the portfolio companies. The perception of the respondents regarding the effects of good corporate governance on firm value is similar. Although there is a tendency to support a positive impact, the biggest group of respondents did not perceive any effect. Consequently, on the basis of the findings, the hypotheses can be weakly supported because all significant tests deliver results that correspond to the expectations.

In a nutshell, the findings narrowed the knowledge gap in regard to the two research questions in a significant way, which was made possible by an adequate research approach. Venture capitalists influence all six analysed corporate governance elements. Their motivations are the preparation of an IPO and, at later financing rounds, the improvement of corporate governance to build a competitive advantage on good decision making. With their influence, venture capitalists strongly improve all the analysed corporate governance elements of their portfolio companies. This is shown by both measures, the self-assessments by the managers of the portfolio companies and the fulfilment of criteria for good corporate governance. The abilities of the venture capitalists play an important role on their impact on corporate governance. In particular, the venture capital firms' and the investment managers' characteristics can lead to a reinforced positive impact. Finally, the positive impact on corporate governance also has a positive impact on the portfolio companies' firm value. For some of the measures of profitability and valuation, a significant impact was found. In one sentence: Venture capitalists increase the value of their portfolio companies by improving their corporate governance.

6.2 Discussion

6.2.1 Limitations of the Analyses

When the results of these analyses are discussed, the limitations of the research have to be taken into account. The limitations are related to the original sample of the empirical analyses, the respondents whose answers were considered, the quality of the information that was collected, and the explanatory power of the results of the analyses.

The sample of the qualitative and quantitative analysis might be affected by **survival and selection bias**. First, only surviving companies are included in the research. That means that relatively unsuccessful companies that do not exist anymore were not analysed, although retrospective questions ask about times at which such companies might still have been active. As a result, the results might be relevant only for successful growth companies. Second, there is a selection bias because venture capitalists are expected to invest only in relatively promising companies. This selection might have an impact on the sample because it includes only companies that have better prospects than other companies. The bias that comes from the selection may affect the companies' development as much as the venture capitalists' influence. However, because the statistical analyses were controlled for the original status of all response variables, this bias should be attenuated.

As has been shown before, the respondents geographically correspond to the original sample. However, in terms of company age, the 139 **respondents are comparatively younger than the companies included in the sample**. This might be due to aged data in the database from which the sample was collected, i.e., it is supposable that not all companies in the original sample are still active and venture capital-financed. Nevertheless, because there are relatively few older companies among the respondents, the findings might underestimate information from older venture capital-financed companies.

Further limitations are related to the **data quality**. The questionnaire collected retrospective information, which can biased because the respondents might not be able to give objective information on an earlier situation. However, the responses demonstrate that the respondents significantly differentiated between their answers for different measuring times, in particular for the time before and after the first financing round. Apart from that, the explanatory value of the results from the third and fourth measuring times (after the second/third financing round) is limited because of a relatively small number of responses. A relatively low number of the respondents had had two or three financing rounds at the time they completed the questionnaire, so those results might be more susceptible to the influence of outliers. Hence, the explanatory value of the results decreases with the number of financing rounds. However, in the analyses for the first two measuring times, all companies were taken into account so that for these results the representativeness is ensured. Moreover, the corporate governance quality was measured in two ways: by the self-assessment of the respondents and by criteria for good corporate governance. The correlation of the two measures is not very high, which means that the managers of the portfolio companies do not always consider the criteria as adequate for their company in its particular situation. This leads to partly differing results when the two measures are used to analyse the impact on or the impact of corporate governance quality. The research cannot deliver an answer as to which measure is better suited for the analysis of corporate governance. Moreover, the analysis of the portfolio companies' performance is done for the time before the first financing round by a venture capitalist and after every financing round. This is done to collect performance data that correspond to the measuring times of the other information. But it is not assumed that performance per se has a relationship to venture capitalist financing of portfolio companies. To prevent influences from performance differences before the venture capitalists' investments, the analyses were controlled for the company performance before the first financing round.

Finally, research on corporate governance is affected by **endogeneity** or reverse causality.[542] This general problem relates to the relationship of corporate governance and firm value because these two variables are interrelated. Although corporate governance is expected to influence firm value, it might also be the case that firm value influences corporate governance. An example of this problem is research on the relationship between ownership and performance:[543] not only can the ownership have an impact on the performance, but managerial ownership, for example, could depend on the previous performance of the company. The direction of the influence can in most cases not be clearly observed because the analyses use cross-sectional data that do not allow correcting for unobserved firm heterogeneity. Nonetheless, the use of panel data can help identify the causality. Therefore, this quantitative analysis takes into account time series data that track the development of growth companies to reduce the problem of endogeneity.

These limitations are taken into account in the interpretation of the results presented in the next section.

6.2.2 Interpretation of Results

The interpretation of the results is structured along the four aspects of the research questions. It thereby brings together the results of the three undertaken analyses summarised before. The particularities of these findings in regard to the different analyses as well as to earlier research are discussed in the following.

6.2.2.1 Influence of Venture Capitalists on Corporate Governance

In regard to the first aspect of the analyses, the **reasons** venture capitalists influence corporate governance, the findings partly contradict the expectations and differ

542 Börsch-Supan/Köke (2002), pp. 295ff.
543 Demsetz/Lehn (1985); Morck et al. (1988).

between the analyses. Against several earlier analyses[544] that predicted that agency problems, and thereby agency and business risks, are the main reasons for venture capitalists to influence the corporate governance of their portfolio companies, this quantitative analysis did not deliver significant results in this respect. As the measures for the agency and business risks were derived from those analyses,[545] it is unlikely that this is due to a bad measurement. These results could, however, be traced back to two explanations.

First, agency and business risks could be generally behind the venture capitalists' influence on corporate governance, but the venture capitalists might not adapt their influence according to the level of risk. The interviewed venture capitalists agreed that risk reduction is their main motivation for influencing portfolio companies' corporate governance. This was confirmed by a specialist lawyer who deals with the contracts of several venture capitalists. He saw a similar approach of all venture capitalists regarding the corporate governance elements related to the monitoring and bonding function. He described the majority of the elements that were looked at in this analysis as standard measures included in all contracts. Hence, the elements on which agency and business risks are expected to have an influence are not dependent on the characteristics of a particular portfolio company but are enforced in all cases. This might be the reason why a significant relationship between the level of agency and business risks and the influence on corporate governance could not be found in the quantitative analysis.

Second, these results might be due to the venture capitalists' notion that they cannot always push their goals through, which might make them unlikely to increase their influence on the corporate governance even in the case of portfolio companies with great risks. The interviews revealed that the level of influence depends on the venture capitalists' power, i.e., if the founder managers have much power because of a good negotiating position, venture capitalists will not invest much effort to influence the company because they know that their impact might be limited. But in these cases in which the managers have great power, the agency risks are expected to be particularly strong. Thus, there might be cases with high agency and business risks in which venture capitalists do not invest resources to exert influence on corporate governance.

---

544 E.g. Fiet (1991), Fiert (1995), Sapienza/Gupta (1994), Sapienza et al. (1996), Gompers/Lerner (2004)

545 E. g. Barney et al. (1989); Barney et al. (1994); Sapienza/Gupta (1994); Fredriksen/Klofsten (2001); Fiert (1995).

Accordingly, it could be difficult to find empirical support for the hypothesis that the strength of the venture capitalists' influence depends on the agency and business risks associated with the portfolio companies. Nevertheless, the general notion that venture capitalists' introduce measures for risk reduction might still hold, as the interviews showed.

There was also only weak empirical support for the hypotheses related to value creation as a reason for venture capitalists' influence. However, the attempt to test these analyses at later measuring times was more promising. Due to the limited data availability for the third and fourth measuring times, the possibility of receiving significant results is relatively low. Nevertheless, the analysis of the basic hypothesis delivered significant support for the idea that corporate governance quality has an impact on the influence of venture capitalists in subsequent financing rounds. This can be explained by the fact that they can differ between companies with better and worse corporate governance only after they have invested in the company for some time. It would need further research to derive stronger support for this notion. All in all, even if the reasons of venture capitalists for influencing corporate governance have been intensively researched in the past, these results reveal that the associated relations are still not fully understood.

The **effects of venture capitalists' influence on corporate governance quality** are the second aspect that was analysed. Here the focus of the discussion is the differing findings for corporate governance quality measured by self-assessment and by criteria. In particular, for the first measuring time, the quality of the corporate governance elements was perceived relatively better by the respondents than measured by the criteria. Even in cases where several criteria were not fulfilled, the respondents assessed corporate was as relatively adequate. This is in accordance with the statements of several interviewees that some of the corporate governance elements might not be adequate for growth companies at an early point of the lifecycle. Although the differences between the two measures decrease at later measuring times, they remain relatively strong for three of the corporate governance elements: the compensation of managers and the composition and work of the board. This indicates that, from the respondents' point of view, the criteria associated with these elements are of relatively little importance. This also influences the tests on the impact of the venture capitalists' influence on corporate governance. Although both measures delivered significant support for most of the hypotheses, the strength of the impact often differed. In the majority of cases in which a particularly strong influence was found, the quality was measured by criteria. This concerns, for example, the assessment and compensation of managers, the qualification of board members and the reporting discipline. It shows that the venture capitalists obviously influence portfolio companies to fulfil many of the corporate governance criteria that the respondents perceive as less important. Given the consistent results on the hypotheses related to the relationship of venture capitalists' influence and corporate governance quality, it seems that investors are an important driver of the development of corporate governance.

The results for the third aspect of the first research question concern the **impact of the venture capitalists' abilities on the corporate governance quality** of portfolio companies. The interviewed managers of portfolio companies stressed the importance of control rights and trust on the impact of venture capitalists. Corresponding to earlier research,[546] the quantitative analysis also delivered support for the importance of control rights when measurement by criteria was used. However, when the respondents' point of view is taken into account with the measurement by self-assessment, then no significant results are found. This reveals differences between the results of analyses using the corporate governance measures by criteria and those using self-assessment. Although most tests delivered stronger support for the hypotheses when the measures by criteria were used, the impact of the characteristics of venture capital-firms and investment managers is also strong when self-assessment measures are used. Furthermore, the strong impact of trust between the venture capitalists' investment managers and the managers of the portfolio companies could significantly only be shown using self-assessment measures. This indicates that the differences in the findings might have to do with a biased view of the respondents. They might overrate the positive impact of the venture capitalists' influence and of corporate governance quality as well as the qualification of the investment managers, if they have good co-operation. Because the research on the impact of venture capitalists' abilities apart from the control rights is still very limited, further analyses will be required to better understand these relationships.

546 E.g. Kaplan/Strömberg (2003), pp. 289ff.; Baker/Gompers (2003), pp. 576ff.; Bouresli et a. (2004), p. 80.

6.2.2.2 Influence of Corporate Governance on Firm Value

The second research question deals with the **impact of good corporate governance on firm value**. The theory-based hypothesis that corporate governance has a positive impact on the performance and valuation of companies was tested empirically for the first time for venture capital-financed growth companies. Earlier empirical research always concentrated on established public companies, and the results did not always deliver support for the hypothesis.[547] Similar to the mixed results in previous studies, these analyses also did not deliver consistent results. Although the interviewees of the qualitative analysis supported the general notion that good corporate governance should lead to improved firm value, the majority doubted that this could be shown in a quantitative analysis. When the impact on fundamental performance was analysed, statistically significant but relatively weak support was found when relative measures were used. The tests that included criteria for profitability corresponded partly to the hypothesis. Generally, the support was stronger when self-assessed corporate governance quality was used as an explanatory variable. Whereas corporate governance's impact on the net profit margin and the return on assets was observed without a time lag, an effect on the return on equity could be observed only with a time lag of one period. In particular, the difference between the tests of the last two measures could only be explained by effects from the capital structure of the companies. Against expectations, the companies must be heavily financed by debt.[548] Although there was some support for a positive impact on the companies' profitability, the quantitative analysis on the impact on the companies' growth did not deliver any significant results. Just as the interviewees did not back this hypothesis, the research did not deliver support for a relationship between good corporate governance and firm growth.

The last hypothesis of this research deals with the expected positive impact of corporate governance on the portfolio companies' valuation. Some of the interviewed venture capitalists stated that they would consider reducing the valuation of a company if it could not provide complete reports about its previous development, which would be an example of bad corporate governance. None of the interviewees would, in contrast, be prepared to pay a premium for a company with good corporate governance. Nonetheless, the statistical tests of the results from the survey delivered positive

547 E.g., Gompers et al. (2003), p. 129; Bauer et al. (2993), pp. 13ff.; Beiner et al. (2004), pp. 33.

548 This is only expected for later stage companies, but their proportion in the analysis is not too strong. There is no information on the portfolio companies' capital structure available.

and relatively strong support for the hypothesis when the EBITDA multiple is used. However, it is remarkable that the two measures of corporate governance differ strongly in their impact. Whereas the impact of corporate governance measured by criteria on the sales and EBITDA multiples are strongly negative but insignificant, the impact of corporate governance measured by self-assessment is strongly positive and partly significant. The other valuation measures did not significantly support or contradict the hypothesis. Hence, further research is required here to clarify the relationship between corporate governance quality and the valuation of growth companies.

The results related to the impact of corporate governance quality on portfolio companies' performance and valuation reveal differences in the value effects of the two corporate governance measures. Apart from one exception, all analyses with significant results included the self-assessed corporate governance quality as the explanatory variable. If good corporate governance should, according to its definition and the theory, result in a high firm value, then this would indicate that for growth companies, self-assessment of the adequacy of corporate governance elements would be a better measure than measurement by criteria. However, this finding could also be due to the fact that the respondents defined the adequacy of the corporate governance according to the companies' performance. This relates to the problem of endogeneity of corporate governance and firm value because both variables influence each other, so it is difficult to explain causality.

As this interpretation of the results shows, this research has advanced knowledge about the relationship of venture capital and the corporate governance and firm value of portfolio companies considerably, but it also poses new questions. The following outlook therefore introduces the need for further research.

6.3 Outlook

The theoretical and empirical analyses included a novel approach with distinct improvements over earlier research,[549] particularly in regard to four aspects. To begin with, this research is among the first on corporate governance that focuses on private growth companies instead of established public companies. Thus, it enables a view on the development of corporate governance from founding to the public or private sale of the company, where there is greater firm heterogeneity in regard to corporate governance. Second, the research is not only based on agency theory but introduces a new theoretical perspective to corporate governance: the dynamic resource-based view. These two theories explain the demand and the effects of good corporate governance from different angles. The combination of an economic and a managerial theory ensures a more comprehensive picture than either could provide alone. Whereas agency theory focuses on the problems that the managers of the portfolio companies' can create for venture capitalists, the dynamic resource-based view considers them an asset with upside potential. As the findings on the relationship between venture capital and corporate governance indicate, the dynamic resource-based view is well suited to complement agency theory. Third, the empirical research of the theoretical findings is done with both qualitative and quantitative analyses. Triangulation of the results increases their explanatory power by preventing single-method bias. The expert interviews increased the understanding of the relationships between venture capital, corporate governance and firm value. That understanding was used to complement the hypotheses derived from theory and to prepare the survey. Thus the interviews ensured reliable results from the quantitative analysis. The pan-European survey was done to gather generalisable information for testing the hypotheses of the research using uni- and multivariate analyses. The findings of both studies were jointly interpreted. Fourth, during the empirical analyses, longitudinal data were collected to research the development of corporate governance. This provides a unique data set covering up to five measuring times in the development of growth companies. It enables tracking of the development of corporate governance and thereby reduces the problem of endogeneity.

These innovative aspects of the research enabled the collection of significant results about the relationship between venture capitalists' influence, the quality of corporate governance and the firm value of portfolio companies. In particular, it was found that venture capitalists improve the corporate governance quality of their portfolio companies significantly. Their abilities, and in particular the characteristics of the investment managers and the trust they develop with the managers of portfolio companies, have an additional positive impact on corporate governance quality. This

[549] For an overview of the methods used in earlier research on entrepreneurship and the associated problems, refer to Shane/Venkataraman (2000), pp. 217ff.

improvement leads to a increased profitability of portfolio companies and partly to an increased valuation at a future financing round.

Nonetheless, the analyses revealed the need for further research in this area because most of the aspects are still not fully understood. There are in particular three areas that should be analysed in the future based on these results. First, the venture capitalists' reasons for influencing corporate governance are expected to change over time. This has not been taken into account by other studies that focus primarily on agency theory. Thus, they neglect that venture capitalists might not invest resources in companies with agency problems after some time. Because only a few investments are expected to be successful, venture capitalists might instead focus on investments with relatively more potential and improve their corporate governance. This notion is not supported by agency theory. Therefore, future research should be based on a second theoretic perspective, such as a resource-based view or stewardship theory, that has a more positivist perspective. The research requires longitudinal data to track development. A qualitative approach to this topic might be useful because it captures a more comprehensive picture. Moreover, the new findings on the importance of the abilities of investment managers suggest further research of venture capitalist value creation on this level. As the comparison of the impact of the characteristics of venture capital firms and investment managers indicates, stronger differences are found there. Accordingly, the analysis of the impact of the experience and capabilities of investment managers should be a rich area for research that advances the knowledge on the value creation of venture capitalists. It could also be used to develop a profile for ideal candidates for venture capitalists. For that, a more detailed analysis on the characteristics of investment managers and their impact is required. Such an analysis should combine the research in the areas of venture capital and human resources and would thereby open a new stream of research. Finally, a striking finding of this research is the different results of the two measures of corporate governance, which is emphasised by the statements of the interviewees. The criteria for good corporate governance derived from theory, venture capital practice and corporate governance codes seem to be not equally adequate during the development of growth companies. Therefore, further research should focus on the question of which elements are important at specific development stages. The adequacy of the elements could thereby be defined by the analysis of their value effect, i.e., those elements that increase firm value should be considered adequate. A longitudinal analysis could advance the knowledge of this area, which would be valuable for researchers and practitioners alike.

However, high importance must be paid to the problem of endogeneity to ensure reliable results. This outlook shows that there is a great demand for future research on the relationship between venture capital, corporate governance and firm value. This thesis is an early step on the way to closing the existing knowledge gaps.

Annex

Universität Hamburg
Maik Kleinschmidt
Prof. Dr. Alexander Bassen

Universiteit Gent
Prof. Dr. Sophie Manigart
Prof. Dr. Lutgart Van den Berghe

The University of Nottingham
Prof. Dr. Mike Wright

Survey on Venture Capital and Corporate Governance

Thank you for supporting our international research project that is aimed at analysing the influence of venture capitalists on the corporate governance of portfolio companies.

Please provide us with information on your company, its corporate governance, and your venture capital and private equity investors on the following pages. Most of the questions require answers for different points of time, namely the situation after the different financing rounds, in order to show developments of your company. The average time for completion is approximately 20 minutes. All information will be treated with highest confidentiality.

The results of the study should provide valuable insight about the corporate governance of growth companies, the support of venture capitalists and the contribution of corporate governance to the value of companies. You will receive the results after completion of the study in the first half of 2006.

In case of any question please do not hesitate to contact us:

Email: Maik.Kleinschmidt@wiso.uni-hamburg.de
Phone: +49 (0) 40 - 428 38 40 63
Fax: +49 (0) 40 - 428 38 27 80

This project is supported by the European Venture Capital Association (EVCA) and the Deutsches Venture Capital Institut

What development stage is the company currently in? ▪ Seed: before founding of the company ▪ Start-up: after founding of the company ▪ Expansion: after market entry ▪ Bridge: preparation of change in ownership, e.g. IPO, trade-sale ▪ MBO/MBI: after separation from parent company/change in ownership	☐Seed ☐Start-up ☐Expansion ☐Bridge ☐MBO/MBI
How many different products/product lines does the company currently offer?	__________
How many employees does the company currently have?	__________
How many years has the CEO/managing director worked in the company by now?	__________years
Is the current CEO one of the founders of the company?	☐Yes ☐No ☐NA
Which legal form has the company? (e.g. Ltd., SA, AG)	
How many financing rounds with participation of venture capitalists have taken place so far?	☐1 ☐2 ☐3 or more
Does the company currently have only one single board or two separate boards for management and control (apart from additional advisory boards)? ▪ One board: e.g. board of directors ▪ Two boards: e.g. management and supervisory board	☐One Board ☐Two Boards

	Name of venture capitalist/private equity firm	Member of Syndicate	After the1st financing by VC		After the 2nd financing by VC		After the 3rd financing by VC	
			Owner-ship	Seat on Board	Ownership	Seat on Board	Ownership	Seat on Board
VC 1:	____________	☐	____%	☐	____%	☐	____%	☐
VC 2:	____________	☐	____%	☐	____%	☐	____%	☐
VC 3:	____________	☐	____%	☐	____%	☐	____%	☐
VC 4:	____________	☐	____%	☐	____%	☐	____%	☐
VC 5:	____________	☐	____%	☐	____%	☐	____%	☐

	After the 1st financing by VC	**After the 2nd financing by VC**	**After the 3rd financing by VC**
Please indicate the lead investor for every financing round, i.e. the investor with the strongest influence on your company.	Name ____________	Name ____________	Name ____________
Has the investment manager of the lead-investor substantial experience in the following areas: ▪ Work experience in the venture capital industry (> 5 years)?	☐Yes ☐No ☐NA	☐Yes ☐No ☐NA	☐Yes ☐No ☐NA
▪ Work experience in your or a elated industry?	☐Yes ☐No ☐NA	☐Yes ☐No ☐NA	☐Yes ☐No ☐NA
▪ International work experience?	☐Yes ☐No ☐NA	☐Yes ☐No ☐NA	☐Yes ☐No ☐NA
▪ Start-up experience?	☐Yes ☐No ☐NA	☐Yes ☐No ☐NA	☐Yes ☐No ☐NA
How trustful was the relationship with the investment manager of the lead-investor?	☐ ++ ☐ + ☐ O ☐ - ☐ --	☐ ++ ☐ + ☐ O ☐ - ☐ --	☐ ++ ☐ + ☐ O ☐ - ☐ --
How many times per quarter did you have contact with the investment manager on average (personally and by phone)?	______Times	______Times	______Times

	Before the 1st financing by VC	After the 1st financing by VC	After the 2nd financing by VC	After the 3rd financing by VC
Were the managers assessed at least once a year in an effective manner by the shareholders and/or the supervisory board?	☐Yes ☐No ☐NA	☐Yes ☐No ☐NA	☐Yes ☐No ☐NA	☐Yes ☐No ☐NA
How effective was the assessment of the managers by the shareholders/supervisory board?	☐ ++ ☐ + ☐ O ☐ - ☐ --	☐ ++ ☐ + ☐ O ☐ - ☐ --	☐ ++ ☐ + ☐ O ☐ - ☐ --	☐ ++ ☐ + ☐ O ☐ - ☐ --
If members of the top-management-team left the company/were replaced: how many left/were replaced?	______	______	______	______
How strong was the influence of the VCs on the company's way to assess its managers?		very strong ☐ ☐ ☐ ☐ no infl.	very strong ☐ ☐ ☐ ☐ no infl.	very strong ☐☐☐☐ no infl.
When searching for new managers: ▪ Was a profile of the preferred candidate developed?	☐Yes ☐No ☐NA	☐Yes ☐No ☐NA	☐Yes ☐No ☐NA	☐Yes ☐No ☐NA
▪ Was the network of the VC used?		☐Yes ☐No ☐NA	☐Yes ☐No ☐NA	☐Yes ☐No ☐NA
▪ Was a head-hunter used?	☐Yes ☐No ☐NA	☐Yes ☐No ☐NA	☐Yes ☐No ☐NA	☐Yes ☐No ☐NA

	Before the 1st financing by VC	After the 1st financing by VC	After the 2nd financing by VC	After the 3rd financing by VC
How effective was the selection of new managers?	☐ ++ ☐ + ☐ O ☐ - ☐ --	☐ ++ ☐ + ☐ O ☐ - ☐ --	☐ ++ ☐ + ☐ O ☐ - ☐ --	☐ ++ ☐ + ☐ O ☐ - ☐ --
How strong was the influence of the VCs on the company's way of selecting new managers?		very strong ☐ ☐ ☐ ☐ no infl.	very strong ☐ ☐ ☐ ☐ no infl.	very strong ☐ ☐ ☐ ☐ no infl.

	Before the 1st financing by VC	After the 1st financing by VC	After the 2nd financing by VC	After the 3rd financing by VC
How many percent of the company's shares were owned by the top-management team (accumulated ownership)?	____%	____%	____%	____%
Did the managers have stock options programmes with vesting periods?	☐Yes ☐No ☐NA	☐Yes ☐No ☐NA	☐Yes ☐No ☐NA	☐Yes ☐No ☐NA
Were there non-compete clauses for the managers?	☐Yes ☐No ☐NA	☐Yes ☐No ☐NA	☐Yes ☐No ☐NA	☐Yes ☐No ☐NA
How effectively were the managers bonded to stay in the company and foster its long-term development?	☐ ++ ☐ + ☐ O ☐ - ☐ --	☐ ++ ☐ + ☐ O ☐ - ☐ --	☐ ++ ☐ + ☐ O ☐ - ☐ --	☐ ++ ☐ + ☐ O ☐ - ☐ --
How strong was the influence of the VCs on the company's way to bond its managers?	very strong ☐ ☐ ☐ ☐ no infl.	very strong ☐ ☐ ☐ ☐ no infl.	very strong ☐ ☐ ☐ ☐ no infl.	very strong ☐ ☐ ☐ ☐ no infl.
Did the manager's compensation include an annual bonus?	☐Yes ☐No ☐NA	☐Yes ☐No ☐NA	☐Yes ☐No ☐NA	☐Yes ☐No ☐NA

	Before the 1st financing by VC	After the 1st financing by VC	After the 2 nd financing by VC	After the 3rd financing by VC
Did the manager's compensation include a variable element that was linked to the company's mid- and long-term development (> 2 years)?	☐Yes ☐No ☐NA	☐Yes ☐No ☐NA	☐Yes ☐No ☐NA	☐Yes ☐No ☐NA
Was the fixed or the variable compensation (bonus and mid-/long-term variable parts) more important?	☐Fix ☐Variable ☐Equal	☐Fix ☐Variable ☐Equal	☐Fix ☐Variable ☐Equal	☐Fix ☐Variable ☐Equal
How did the overall manager's compensation compare to their potential salary in other positions outside the firm?	☐ ++ ☐ + ☐ O ☐ - ☐ --	☐ ++ ☐ + ☐ O ☐ - ☐ --	☐ ++ ☐ + ☐ O ☐ - ☐ --	☐ ++ ☐ + ☐ O ☐ - ☐ --
How strong were the manager's financial incentives to foster the long-term development of the company?	☐ ++ ☐ + ☐ O ☐ - ☐ --	☐ ++ ☐ + ☐ O ☐ - ☐ --	☐ ++ ☐ + ☐ O ☐ - ☐ --	☐ ++ ☐ + ☐ O ☐ - ☐ --
How strong was the influence of the VCs on the company's way to compensate its managers?		very strong ☐ ☐ ☐ ☐ no infl.	very strong ☐ ☐ ☐ ☐ no infl.	very strong ☐ ☐ ☐ ☐ no infl.
How many members did the board have?	_____	_____	_____	_____
How many non-executive members did the board have?	_____	_____	_____	_____

	Before the 1st financing by VC	After the 1st financing by VC	After the 2nd financing by VC	After the 3rd financing by VC
How many independent non-executive members, i.e. not related to any of the company's managers, employees, shareholders, suppliers or clients did the supervisory board have?	☐ ++ ☐ + ☐ O ☐ - ☐ --	☐ ++ ☐ + ☐ O ☐ - ☐ --	☐ ++ ☐ + ☐ O ☐ - ☐ --	☐ ++ ☐ + ☐ O ☐ - ☐ --
Who had the strongest influence on the selection of the independent non-executive members?		☐Management ☐VC ☐Equal	☐Management ☐VC ☐Equal	☐Management ☐VC ☐Equal
Had the management influence on the selection of the VC's representative on the board?		☐Yes ☐No ☐NA	☐Yes ☐No ☐NA	☐Yes ☐No ☐NA
How many of the non-executive board members had the following experiences: ▪ Experience in your or related industry	____	____	____	____
▪ Executive experience	____	____	____	____
▪ International experience	____	____	____	____
▪ Functional experience in finance/ marketing/sales	____	____	____	____
▪ Start-up experience	____	____	____	____
▪ Experience as manager or board member in listed companies	____	____	____	____

	Before the 1st financing by VC	After the 1st financing by VC	After the 2nd financing by VC	After the 3rd financing by VC
Was the chairman of the board also the CEO?	☐Yes ☐No ☐NA	☐Yes ☐No ☐NA	☐Yes ☐No ☐NA	☐Yes ☐No ☐NA
Was the board supported by specialised experts as consultants or members of an advisory board?	☐Yes ☐No ☐NA	☐Yes ☐No ☐NA	☐Yes ☐No ☐NA	☐Yes ☐No ☐NA
How well did the non-executive supervisory board members meet the requirements to effectively monitor the management?	☐ ++ ☐ + ☐ O ☐ - ☐ --	☐ ++ ☐ + ☐ O ☐ - ☐ --	☐ ++ ☐ + ☐ O ☐ - ☐ --	☐ ++ ☐ + ☐ O ☐ - ☐ --
How well did the non-executive board members meet the requirements to effectively advice the management?		☐ ++ ☐ + ☐ O ☐ - ☐ --	☐ ++ ☐ + ☐ O ☐ - ☐ --	☐ ++ ☐ + ☐ O ☐ - ☐ --
How strong was the influence of the VCs on the structure of the non-executive board members?		very strong ☐ ☐ ☐ ☐ no infl.	very strong ☐ ☐ ☐ ☐ no infl.	very strong ☐ ☐ ☐ ☐ no infl.
How often did the board meet per year?	______times	______times	______times	______times
Did you provide all board members with the agenda and all relevant information well ahead of the board meeting (>1 week)?	always ☐ ☐ ☐ ☐ never	always ☐ ☐ ☐ ☐ never	always ☐ ☐ ☐ ☐ never	always ☐ ☐ ☐ ☐ never
How many hours did the board meetings take on average?	______hours	______hours	______hours	______hours

	Before the 1st financing by VC	After the 1st financing by VC	After the 2nd financing by VC	After the 3rd financing by VC
Did the company have documentation of the roles and responsibilities of the board?	☐Yes ☐No ☐NA	☐Yes ☐No ☐NA	☐Yes ☐No ☐NA	☐Yes ☐No ☐NA
What proportion of the time of board meetings was spent on average for topics related to the following areas? Please distribute 100 % to the three areas)	100 % thereof:	100 % thereof:	100 % thereof:	100 % thereof:
▪ Operational matters	____%	____%	____%	____%
▪ Monitoring matters	____%	____%	____%	____%
▪ Strategic matters	____%	____%	____%	____%
How effectively and efficiently did the board's work fulfil its monitoring function?	☐ ++ ☐ + ☐ O ☐ - ☐ --	☐ ++ ☐ + ☐ O ☐ - ☐ --	☐ ++ ☐ + ☐ O ☐ - ☐ --	☐ ++ ☐ + ☐ O ☐ - ☐ --
How effectively and efficiently did the board's work fulfil its advice function?	☐ ++ ☐ + ☐ O ☐ - ☐ --	☐ ++ ☐ + ☐ O ☐ - ☐ --	☐ ++ ☐ + ☐ O ☐ - ☐ --	☐ ++ ☐ + ☐ O ☐ - ☐ --
How strong was the influence of the VCs on the way the board worked?		very strong ☐ ☐ ☐ ☐ no infl.	very strong ☐ ☐ ☐ ☐ no infl.	very strong ☐ ☐ ☐ ☐ no infl.
How many reports did your company prepare for the shareholders per year?	____	____	____	____

	Before the 1st financing by VC	After the 1st financing by VC	After the 2nd financing by VC	After the 3rd financing by VC
What information was regularly provided in the reports to shareholders and supervisory board members: ▪ Cash-flow-statement	☐Yes ☐No ☐NA	☐Yes ☐No ☐NA	☐Yes ☐No ☐NA	☐Yes ☐No ☐NA
▪ Profit-and-loss-account	☐Yes ☐No ☐NA	☐Yes ☐No ☐NA	☐Yes ☐No ☐NA	☐Yes ☐No ☐NA
▪ Balance sheet	☐Yes ☐No ☐NA	☐Yes ☐No ☐NA	☐Yes ☐No ☐NA	☐Yes ☐No ☐NA
▪ Qualitative information on the company's development	☐Yes ☐No ☐NA	☐Yes ☐No ☐NA	☐Yes ☐No ☐NA	☐Yes ☐No ☐NA
▪ Information on the market development	☐Yes ☐No ☐NA	☐Yes ☐No ☐NA	☐Yes ☐No ☐NA	☐Yes ☐No ☐NA
▪ Target-actual comparisons	☐Yes ☐No ☐NA	☐Yes ☐No ☐NA	☐Yes ☐No ☐NA	☐Yes ☐No ☐NA
How great were the differences in the target-actual comparisons?	very great ☐ ☐ ☐ ☐ no diff.	very great ☐ ☐ ☐ ☐ no diff.	very great ☐ ☐ ☐ ☐ no diff.	very great ☐ ☐ ☐ ☐ no diff.
Were the reports provided always on-time i.e. provided immediately after the end of the reporting period?	☐ ++ ☐ + ☐ O ☐ - ☐ --	☐ ++ ☐ + ☐ O ☐ - ☐ --	☐ ++ ☐ + ☐ O ☐ - ☐ --	☐ ++ ☐ + ☐ O ☐ - ☐ --

	Before the 1st financing by VC	**After the 1st financing by VC**	**After the 2nd financing by VC**	**After the 3rd financing by VC**
How sufficient was the information provided to the board and shareholders for effective monitoring??	☐ ++ ☐ + ☐ O ☐ - ☐ --	☐ ++ ☐ + ☐ O ☐ - ☐ --	☐ ++ ☐ + ☐ O ☐ - ☐ --	☐ ++ ☐ + ☐ O ☐ - ☐ --
How strong was the influence of the VCs on the company's way of reporting?		very strong ☐ ☐ ☐ ☐ no infl.	very strong ☐ ☐ ☐ ☐ no infl.	very strong ☐ ☐ ☐ ☐ no infl.
Was the corporate governance reviewed regularly by the board or the management of the company?	☐Yes ☐No ☐NA	☐Yes ☐No ☐NA	☐Yes ☐No ☐NA	☐Yes ☐No ☐NA
Was the corporate governance implemented in order to comply with corporate governance codes or requirements of stock exchanges?	☐Yes ☐No ☐NA	☐Yes ☐No ☐NA	☐Yes ☐No ☐NA	☐Yes ☐No ☐NA

What impact had the venture capitalist's influence on the professionalization of the corporate governance?	☐ ++ ☐ + ☐ O ☐ - ☐ --
What impact had the quality of corporate governance on your company's performance?	☐ ++ ☐ + ☐ O ☐ - ☐ --
What impact had the quality of corporate governance on your company's valuation?	☐ ++ ☐ + ☐ O ☐ - ☐ --

	Before the 1st financing by VC	**After the 1st financing by VC**	**After the 2nd financing by VC**	**After the 3rd financing by VC**
How competitive was the company relative to its direct and indirect competitors?	☐ ++ ☐ + ☐ O ☐ - ☐ --	☐ ++ ☐ + ☐ O ☐ - ☐ --	☐ ++ ☐ + ☐ O ☐ - ☐ --	☐ ++ ☐ + ☐ O ☐ - ☐ --
Was the company performing according to plan?	☐ ++ ☐ + ☐ O ☐ - ☐ --	☐ ++ ☐ + ☐ O ☐ - ☐ --	☐ ++ ☐ + ☐ O ☐ - ☐ --	☐ ++ ☐ + ☐ O ☐ - ☐ --
Did the owners (VC) plan a sale of the company? ▪ Seconday sale: sale to financial investor ▪ Trade sale: sale to strategic investor from related industr ▪ IPO: public offering	☐Secondary Sale ☐Trade Sale ☐IPO	☐Secondary Sale ☐Trade Sale ☐IPO	☐Secondary Sale ☐Trade Sale ☐IPO	☐Secondary Sale ☐Trade Sale ☐IPO
What was the average growth rate of the company? ▪ Growth in employees	____%	____%	____%	____%
▪ Growth in sales	____%	____%	____%	____%
▪ Growth in cash-flows	____%	____%	____%	____%
What was the average performance of the company? ▪ EBITDA-margin	____%	____%	____%	____%
▪ Net-profit-margin	____%	____%	____%	____%
▪ Return-on-Equity	____%	____%	____%	____%
▪ Return-on-Assets	____%	____%	____%	____%

	Between the 1st and the 2nd financing rounds by VC	Between the 2nd and the 3rd financing rounds by VC
How did the valuation of the investors change from one financing round to the next?	☐ ++ ☐ + ☐ O ☐ - ☐ --	☐ ++ ☐ + ☐ O ☐ - ☐ --
How did the multiples used for the company's valuation change between financing rounds? (in case of decrease add "-" e.g. "-10") ▪ Change of sales-multiple in percent	_____%	_____%
▪ Change of cash-flow-multiple in percent	_____%	_____%
▪ Change of EBITDA-multiple in percent	_____%	_____%
Is the product offer of the company of technological nature?	☐ ++ ☐ + ☐ O ☐ - ☐ --	☐ ++ ☐ + ☐ O ☐ - ☐ --
Is the product offer of the company innovative?	☐ ++ ☐ + ☐ O ☐ - ☐ --	☐ ++ ☐ + ☐ O ☐ - ☐ --
Is the business of the company highly specific?	☐ ++ ☐ + ☐ O ☐ - ☐ --	☐ ++ ☐ + ☐ O ☐ - ☐ --
How important are intangible assets for the company?	☐ ++ ☐ + ☐ O ☐ - ☐ --	☐ ++ ☐ + ☐ O ☐ - ☐ --
Does the top management team of the company possess: ▪ Start-up experience?	☐ ++ ☐ + ☐ O ☐ - ☐ --	☐ ++ ☐ + ☐ O ☐ - ☐ --
▪ Industry experience?	☐ ++ ☐ + ☐ O ☐ - ☐ --	☐ ++ ☐ + ☐ O ☐ - ☐ --
▪ Functional experience in finance, sales or marketing?	☐ ++ ☐ + ☐ O ☐ - ☐ --	☐ ++ ☐ + ☐ O ☐ - ☐ --
How dynamic is your market?	☐ ++ ☐ + ☐ O ☐ - ☐ --	☐ ++ ☐ + ☐ O ☐ - ☐ --
How attractive is your market?	☐ ++ ☐ + ☐ O ☐ - ☐ --	☐ ++ ☐ + ☐ O ☐ - ☐ --

Universität Hamburg

Maik Kleinschmidt
Prof. Dr. Alexander Bassen

UNIVERSITEIT GENT

Prof. Dr. Sophie Manigart
Prof. Dr. Lutgart Van den Berghe

The University of Nottingham

Prof. Dr. Mike Wright

Survey on Venture Capital and Corporate Governance

Thank you for taking your time to answer the questionnaire. We highly appreciate your support of our research project.

Please provide us with your e-mail address so that we can send you the report with the results in the first half of 2006.

Please feel free to comment the questionnaire or the topic of the study here:

Annex 1: Questionnaire of the survey

Variable	Name	Description	Scale	Values	Sources
EXPLANATORY VARIABLE					
Agency and business risk index	abind	Mean index of the indicators for agency risk: managerial ownership (dummy), age of portfolio company (interval), specific of the business (interval), importance of intangible assets (interval), degree of technology of product (interval); and for business risk: CEO is found of company (dummy), start-up experience of top management team (interval), functional experience of top management team (interval), number of products (dummy), degree of dynamics of industry (interval), attractiveness of market (interval)	ratio	0-1	Questionnaire, Database
CG quality index (self assessment)	cgqind	Mean index of efficiency of assessment of managers, selection of new managers, bonding of managers, compensation of managers, composition of board (monitoring and advice), work of board (monitoring and advice) and reporting discipline (all interval)	ratio	0-1	Questionnaire
CG quality index (criteria)	cgqinc	Mean index of all variables included in the sub-indexes of quality of selection and assessment of managers, of compensation of managers, of bonding of managers, of composition of board, of work of board and of reporting discipline	ratio	0-1	Questionnaire
CG advice index (self assessment)	cgaind	Mean index of efficiency of selection of new managers, composition of board (advice) and work of board (advice; all interval)	ratio	0-1	Questionnaire
Index of quality of selection of managers	mseind	Mean index of profile of preferred candidate (dummy) and sources of selection of managers (interval)	ratio	0-1	Questionnaire
Efficiency of composition of board: advice	bsoae	Efficiency assessed by respondend: "--" (1), "-" (2), "o" (3), "+" (4), "++" (5)	interval	1-5	Questionnaire
Index of quality of board composition	bsiind	Mean index of proportion of independent board members, board members with industry experience, executive experience, international experience, functional experience, startup experience, experience from listed companies, support by experts/consultants, chairman of board also CEO, proportion of non-executive board members (all dummy)	ratio	0-1	Questionnaire
Efficiency of work of board: advice	bwoae	Efficiency assessed by respondend: "--" (1), "-" (2), "o" (3), "+" (4), "++" (5)	interval	1-5	Questionnaire
Index of quality of work of board	bwoind	Mean index of number of board meetings, length of board meetings, proportion of time devoted to strategic and monitoring issues and documentation of board's responsibilities	ratio	0-1	Questionnaire
CG advice index (criteria)	cgacin	Mean index of index of quality of selection of managers, index of quality of board composition: qualification and proportion of (board) time devoted to strategic issues	ratio	0-1	Questionnaire
Planned IPO	csale	1 if IPO is planned	dummy	0/1	Questionnaire
CONTROL VARIABLES					
Development stage of portfolio company	pcfrde/cdev	Development Status of portfolio company: seed(1), start-up (2), expansion (3), bridge (4), MBO/MBI (5)	ordinal	1-5	Questionnaire, Database
Size of portfolio company	cempn	Number of employees: 1-9 (1), 10- 49 (2), 40-249 (3), >250 (4)	interval	1-4	Questionnaire
Region of portfolio company	landgr	Location of portfolio company: Germany/Austria/Switzerland (1), France/BeNeLux (2), Northern Europe (3), UK/Ireland (4), Eastern Europe (5), Southern Europe (6)	nominal	1-6	Database
Distance venture capitalist-portfolio company	lvcdist	Distance between the locations in km: 0-50 (1), 51-500 (2), >501 (3)	interval	1-3	Database

Annex 2: Variables related to hypotheses on reasons of venture capitalists

Variable	Name	Description	Scale	Values	Sources
RESPONSE VARIABLES - SELF ASSESSMENT					
CG quality index (self assessment)	cgqind	Mean index of efficiency of assessment of managers, selection of new managers, bonding of managers, compensation of managers, composition of board (monitoring and advice), work of board (monitoring and advice) and reporting discipline (all interval)	ratio	0-1	Questionnaire
CG monitoring index (self assessment)	cgmind	Mean index of efficiency of assessment of managers, composition of board (monitoring), work of board (monitoring) and reporting discipline (all interval)	ratio	0-1	Questionnaire
Efficiency of assessment of managers	masse	Efficiency assessed by respondend: "--" (1), "-" (2), "o" (3), "+" (4), "++" (5)	interval	1-5	Questionnaire
Efficiency of composition of board: monitoring	bsome	Efficiency assessed by respondend: "--" (1), "-" (2), "o" (3), "+" (4), "++" (5)	interval	1-5	Questionnaire
Efficiency of work of board: monitoring	bwome	Efficiency assessed by respondend: "--" (1), "-" (2), "o" (3), "+" (4), "++" (5)	interval	1-5	Questionnaire
Efficiency of reporting discipline	rmone	Efficiency assessed by respondend: "--" (1), "-" (2), "o" (3), "+" (4), "++" (5)	interval	1-5	Questionnaire
CG bonding index (self assessment)	cgbind	Mean index of efficiency of bonding of managers and compensation of managers (all interval)	ratio	0-1	Questionnaire
Efficiency of bonding of managers	mbone	Efficiency assessed by respondend: "--" (1), "-" (2), "o" (3), "+" (4), "++" (5)	interval	1-5	Questionnaire
Efficiency of compensation of managers	mcome	Efficiency assessed by respondend: "--" (1), "-" (2), "o" (3), "+" (4), "++" (5)	interval	1-5	Questionnaire
CG advice index (self assessment)	cgaind	Mean index of efficiency of selection of new managers, composition of board (advice) and work of board (advice; all interval)	ratio	0-1	Questionnaire
Efficiency of selection of new managers	msele	Efficiency assessed by respondend: "--" (1), "-" (2), "o" (3), "+" (4), "++" (5)	interval	1-5	Questionnaire
Efficiency of composition of board: advice	bsoae	Efficiency assessed by respondend: "--" (1), "-" (2), "o" (3), "+" (4), "++" (5)	interval	1-5	Questionnaire
Efficiency of work of board: advice	bwoae	Efficiency assessed by respondend: "--" (1), "-" (2), "o" (3), "+" (4), "++" (5)	interval	1-5	Questionnaire
Efficiency of assessment and selection of managers	maas	Mean index of efficiency of assessment and selection of managers (all nterval)	ratio	0-1	Questionnaire

Variable	Name	Description	Scale	Values	Sources
RESPONSE VARIABLES - CRITERIA					
CG quality index (criteria)	cgqinc	Mean index of all variables included in the sub-indexes of quality of selection and assessment of managers, of compensation of managers, of bonding of managers, of composition of board, of work of board and of reporting discipline	ratio	0-1	Questionnaire
CG monitoring index (criteria)	cgmcin	Mean index of assesment of managers, proportion of independent board members, index of quality of board except stratetic invovlement, index of quality of reporting discipline	ratio	0-1	Questionnaire
CG bonding index (criteria)	cgbcin	Mean index of index of quality of bonding of managers and index of quality of compensation of managers	ratio	0-1	Questionnaire
CG advice index (criteria)	cgacin	Mean index of index of quality of selection of managers, index of quality of board composition: qualification and proportion of (board) time devoted to strategic issues	ratio	0-1	Questionnaire

Variable	Name	Description	Scale	Values	Sources
RESPONSE VARIABLES - CRITERIA					
Conduct of assessment of managers	massn	Assessment of managers by board or shareholders at least once a year: no (0), yes (1)	dummy	0/1	Questionnaire
Replacements of managers per financing round	mrepn	Number of replacements of managers per financing round	ratio	>=0	Questionnaire
Index of quality of selection of managers	mseind	Mean index of profile of preferred candidate (dummy) and sources of selection of managers (interval)	ratio	0-1	Questionnaire
Profile of preferred candidate	mselpr	Selection of new managers on basis of profile of preferred candidate: no (0), yes (1)	dummy	0/1	Questionnaire
Sources for selection of managers	msels	Mean index of use of headhunter and VC's network	ratio	0-1	Questionnaire
Use of headhunter	mselhh	Use of headhunter for selection of new managers: no (0), yes (1)	dummy	0/1	Questionnaire
Use of VC's network	mselvc	Use of VC's network for selection of new managers: no (0), yes (1)	dummy	0/1	Questionnaire
Index of quality of bonding of managers	mboind	Mean index of managers with stock-options programmes with vesting period, non-compete clauses and managerial ownership	ratio	0-1	Questionnaire
Managers with stock options programmes with vesting period	mbonop	Use of stock options programmes with vesting period for managers: no (0), yes (1)	dummy	0/1	Questionnaire
Managers with non-compete clauses	mbonnc	Use of non-compete clauses for managers: 1/0	dummy	0/1	Questionnaire
Managerial ownership	mboow n	Managers with ownership in company: <1 % (0), >1 % (1)	dummy	0/1	Questionnaire
Index of quality of compensation of managers	mbvin	Mean index of managers with annual bonus and variable compensation linked to mid-/long-term development, importance of annual bonus versus variable compensation linked to mid-/long term development and level of compensation compared to industry	ratio	0-1	Questionnaire
Managers with annual bonus	mcoma b	Use of annual bonus for managers' compensation: no (0), yes (1)	dummy	0/1	Questionnaire
Managers with variable compensation linked to mid-/long-term development	mcomv e	Use of variable compensation linked to mid/long-term development: no (0), yes (1)	dummy	0/1	Questionnaire
Importance of annual bonus versus variable compensation linked to mid-/long-term development	mcomi m	Most important compensation part: fixed (0), equal (1), variable (1)	dummy	0/1	Questionnaire
Level of compensation compared to industry	mcomc o	Comparison of managers' compensation with potential compensation outside the firm: "--" (1), "-" (2), "o" (3), "+" (4), "++" (5)	interval	1-5	Questionnaire
Index of quality of board composition	bsiind	Mean index of proportion of independent board members, board members with industry experience, executive experience, international experience, functional experience, startup experience, experience from listed companies, support by expperts/consultants, chairman of board also CEO, proportion of non-executive board members (all dummy)	ratio	0-1	Questionnaire
Proportion of independent board members	bspin	Number of independent board members / number of board members: <50% (0), >=50% (1)	dummy	0/1	Questionnaire

Variable	Name	Description	Scale	Values	Sources
RESPONSE VARIABLES - CRITERIA (contd.)					
Index of quality of reporting discipline	rind	Mean index of number of reports of year, timeliness of reporting, provision of cashflow statement, profit-and-loss-account, balance sheet, target-actual comparison, qualitative information of company, information on market development and extent of target-actual differences	ratio	0-1	Questionnaire
Number of reports per year	rrn	Number of reports per year: <=10 (0), >10 (1)	dummy	0/1	Questionnaire
Timeliness of reporting	ront	Timeliness of reporting: "--" (1), "-" (2), "o" (3), "+" (4), "++" (5)	interval	1-5	Questionnaire
Completeness of reporting	rcompr	Mean index of provision of cashflow statement, profit-and-loss-account, balance sheet, target-actual comparison, qualitative information on company, information on market development,, extent of target-actual differences	ratio	0-1	Questionnaire
Provision of cashflow statement	rcfs	Provision of cashflow statement in report: no (0), yes (1)	dummy	0/1	Questionnaire
Provision of profit-and-loss-account	rpla	Provision of profit-and-loss-account in report: no (0), yes (1)	dummy	0/1	Questionnaire
Provision of balance sheet	rbs	Provision of balance sheet in report: no (0), yes (1)	dummy	0/1	Questionnaire
Provision of target-actual comparison	rtac	Provision of target-actual comparison in report: no (0), yes (1)	dummy	0/1	Questionnaire
Provision of qualitative information on company	rqco	Provision of qualitative information in report: no (0), yes (1)	dummy	0/1	Questionnaire
Provision of information on market development	rmda	Provision of information on market development in report: no (0), yes (1)	dummy	0/1	Questionnaire
Extent of target-actual differences	rdiff	Exactness of planning - etent of target actual comparison: "--" (1), "-" (2), "o" (3), "+" (4), "++" (5)	interval	1-5	Questionnaire
Variable	**Name**	**Description**	**Scale**	**Values**	**Sources**
EXPLANATORY VARIABLES					
Index of VC's influence on all CG elements	vciind	Mean index of VC's influence on assessment of managers, on selection of new managers, on bonding of managers, on compensation of managers on composition of board, on work of board, on reporting discipline (all interval)	ratio	0-1	Questionnaire
Index of VC's influence on CG elements with monitoring function	vcimon	Mean index of VC's influence on assessment of managers, on composition of board, on work of board, on reporting discipline (all interval)	ratio	0-1	Questionnaire
VC's influence on assessment of managers	mvci	Strength of influence: four answer possibilities from "no influence" (1) to "very strong" (4)	interval	1-4	Questionnaire
VC's influence on composition of board	bsovci	Strength of influence: four answer possibilities from "no influence" (1) to "very strong" (4)	interval	1-4	Questionnaire
VC's influence on work of board	bwovci	Strength of influence: four answer possibilities from "no influence" (1) to "very strong" (4)	interval	1-4	Questionnaire
VC's influence on reporting discipline	rvci	Strength of influence: four answer possibilities from "no influence" (1) to "very strong" (4)	interval	1-4	Questionnaire

Variable	Name	Description	Scale	Values	Sources
EXPLANATORY VARIABLES (contd.)					
Index of VC's influence on CG elements with bonding function	vcibon	Mean index of VC's influence on bonding of managers and on compensation of managers (all interval)	ratio	0-1	Questionnaire
VC's influence on bonding of managers	mbovci	Strength of influence: four answer possibilities from "no influence" (1) to "very strong" (4)	interval	1-4	Questionnaire
VC's influence on compensation of managers	mcovci	Strength of influence: four answer possibilities from "no influence" (1) to "very strong" (4)	interval	1-4	Questionnaire
Index of VC's influence on CG elements with advice function	vciadv	Mean index of VC's influence on selection of new managers, on composition of board and on work of board (all interval)	ratio	0-1	Questionnaire
VC's influence on selection of new managers	msevci	Strength of influence: four answer possibilities from "no influence" (1) to "very strong" (4)	interval	1-4	Questionnaire
VC's influence on composition of board	bsovci	Strength of influence: four answer possibilities from "no influence" (1) to "very strong" (4)	interval	1-4	Questionnaire
VC's influence on work of board	bwovci	Strength of influence: four answer possibilities from "no influence" (1) to "very strong" (4)	interval	1-4	Questionnaire
CONTROL VARIABLES					
Development stage of portfolio company	pcfrde/cdev	Development Status of portfolio company: seed(1), start-up (2), expansion (3), bridge (4), MBO/MBI (5)	ordinal	1-5	Questionnaire, Database
Size of portfolio company	cempn	Number of employees: 1-9 (1), 10- 49 (2), 40-249 (3), >250 (4)	interval	1-4	Questionnaire
Region of portfolio company	landgr	Location of portfolio company: Germany/Austria/Switzerland (1), France/BeNeLux (2), Northern Europe (3), UK/Ireland (4), Eastern Europe (5), Southern Europe (6)	nominal	1-6	Database
Distance venture capitalist-portfolio company	lvcdist	Distance between the locations in km: 0-50 (1), 51-500 (2), >501 (3)	interval	1-3	Database

Annex 3: Variables related to hypotheses about corporate governance quality

Variable	Name	Description	Scale	Values	Sources
RESPONSE VARIABLES - SELF ASSESSMENT					
CG quality index (self assessment)	cgqind	Mean index of efficiency of assessment of managers, selection of new managers, bonding of managers, compensation of managers, composition of board (monitoring and advice), work of board (monitoring and advice) and reporting discipline (all interval)	ratio	0-1	Questionnaire
CG monitoring index (self assessment)	cgmind	Mean index of efficiency of assessment of managers, composition of board (monitoring), work of board (monitoring) and reporting discipline (all interval)	ratio	0-1	Questionnaire
CG bonding index (self assessment)	cgbind	Mean index of efficiency of bonding of managers and compensation of managers (all interval)	ratio	0-1	Questionnaire
CG advice index (self assessment)	cgaind	Mean index of efficiency of selection of new managers, composition of board (advice) and work of board (advice; all interval)	ratio	0-1	Questionnaire
RESPONSE VARIABLES - CRITERIA					
CG quality index (criteria)	cgqinc	Mean index of all variables included in the sub-indexes of quality of selection and assessment of managers, of compensation of managers, of bonding of managers, of composition of board, of work of board and of reporting discipline	ratio	0-1	Questionnaire
CG monitoring index (criteria)	cgmcin	Mean index of assesment of managers, proportion of independent board members, index of quality of board except stratetic invovlement, index of quality of reporting discipline	ratio	0-1	Questionnaire
CG bonding index (criteria)	cgbcin	Mean index of index of quality of bonding of managers and index of quality of compensation of managers	ratio	0-1	Questionnaire
CG advice index (criteria)	cgacin	Mean index of index of quality of selection of managers, index of quality of board composition: qualification and proportion of (board) time devoted to strategic issues	ratio	0-1	Questionnaire
EXPLANATORY VARIABLES - ABILITIES					
Index of abilities	lvcabi	Mean index of control rights of lead-VC-F index and index of abilities of lead-VC-F and IM	ratio	0-1	Questionnaire/ Database
Control rights of lead-VC-F index	lvccri	Mean index of pwnership rights and board seat of lead-VC	ratio	0-1	Questionnaire
Ownership rights of lead-VC	lvcown	Ownership share of lead-VC in percent	ratio	0-100%	0
Board seat lead-VC	lvcbos	Representative from lead-VC on board: no (0), yes (1)	dummy	0/1	Questionnaire

Variable	Name	Description	Scale	Values	Sources
EXPLANATORY VARIABLES - ABILITIES (Contd.)					
Characteristics of lead-VC-F index	lvccin	Mean index of independent lead-VC-F, number of portfolio companies, invested capital, age, international activity index and reputation of lead VC-F	ratio	0-1	Database
Type of lead-VC-F	lvctyp	Type/affiliation of lead-VC firm: financial institution (1), governmental investor (2), corporate venture capitalist (3), independent venture capitalist (4), other (5)	nominal	1-5	Database
Independent lead-VC-F	lvcind	Affiliation of general parter of VC: non-independent general partner (0), independent general partner (1)	dummy	0/1	Database
Number of portfolio companies lead-VC-F	lvcpcs	Number of current portfolio companies: <20 (0), 20-99 (0,33), 100-499 (0,66), >=500 (1)	ratio	0-1	Database
Invested capital VC-F	lvccap	Lead-VC firm's current total invested capital in USD: <20 Mio. (0), 20-99,9 Mio. (0,33), 100-499,9 Mio. (0,66), >= 500 Mio. (1)	ratio	0-1	Database
Age of VC-F	lvcage	Lead-VC firm's current age in years: <= 5 years (1), 6-10 years (2), >10 years (3)	ordinal	1-3	Database
International activity of VC-F: region	lvcint	Lead-VC firm's current international investment activity by regions: regional investments (1), national investments (2), European investments (3), global investments (4)	ordinal	1-4	Database
Reputation of VC-F	lvcrep	Reputation of Lead-VC firm, analysed by means of number of active participation in important VC industry events (Super Investor, Super Return, EVCA conference) and number of news articles in important industry news services (AltaAssets, Private Equity Week) since 2004: low reputation (0), high reputation (1)	dummy	0/1	Database
Abilities of VC-IM index	aimind	Mean index of Experience of VC investment manager in VC industry, (portfolio company's) industry, internationlly, start-up, number of contacts per quarter and trustfullness of relationship	ratio	0-1	Questionnaire
Experience in VC industry VC-IM	imvcex	Substantial experience of the investment manager of the lead-VC in the venture capital industry (> 5 years): no (0), yes (1)	dummy	0/1	Questionnaire
Industry experience VC-IM	imidex	Substantial experience of the investment manager of the lead-VC in the industry of the portfolio company: no (0), yes (1)	dummy	0/1	Questionnaire
International experience VC-IM	imitex	Substantial international experience of the investment manager of the lead-VC: no (0), yes (1)	dummy	0/1	Questionnaire
Startup experience VC-IM	imsuex	Substantial start-up experience of the investment manager of the lead-VC: no (0), yes (1)	dummy	0/1	Questionnaire
Number of contacts per quarter VC-IM	immeet	Contact between the managers of the portfolio company and the investment manager of the lead-VC personally and by phone per quarter: 0 (0), 1-3 (0,33), 4-9 (0,66), >= 10 (1)	ratio	0-1	Questionnaire
Number of portfolio companies per employee of VC	imnpc	Average number of PCs per employee of VC	ratio	>=0	Database
Trustfullness of relationship VC-M	imtrus	Trustfulness of relationship between the managers of the portfolio company and the investment manager of the Lead-VC in the opinion of the respondent: "--" (1), "-" (2), "o" (3), "+" (4), "++" (5)	interval	1-5	Questionnaire

Variable	Name	Description	Scale	Values	Sources
CONTROL VARIABLES					
Development stage of portfolio company	pcfrde/cdev	Development Status of portfolio company: seed(1), start-up (2), expansion (3), bridge (4), MBO/MBI (5)	ordinal	1-5	Questionnaire, Database
Size of portfolio company	cempn	Number of employees: 1-9 (1), 10- 49 (2), 40-249 (3), >250 (4)	interval	1-4	Questionnaire
Region of portfolio company	landgr	Location of portfolio company: Germany/Austria/Switzerland (1), France/BeNeLux (2), Northern Europe (3), UK/Ireland (4), Eastern Europe (5), Southern Europe (6)	nominal	1-6	Database
Index of VC's influence on all CG elements	vciind	Mean index of VC's influence on assessment of managers, on selection of new managers, on bonding of managers, on compensation of managers on composition of board, on work of board, on reporting discipline (all interval)	interval	0-1	Questionnaire

Annex 4: Variables related to hypotheses about venture capitalist's abilities

Variable	Name	Description	Scale	Values	Sources
RESPONSE VARIABLES - FIRM VALUE					
Impact of CG quality on firm performance	cgper	Impact of good corporate governance on portfolio company's performance in the opinion of the respondent: "--" (1), "-" (2), "o" (3), "+" (4), "++" (5)	interval	1-5	Questionnaire
Competitiveness relative to direct and indirect competitors	ccomco	Competitiveness of the portfolio company compared to its competitors in the opinion of the respondent: "--" (1), "-" (2), "o" (3), "+" (4), "++" (5)	interval	1-5	Questionnaire
Performance according to plan	cperpl	Performance of the portfolio company according to the plan in the opinion of the respondent: "--" (1), "-" (2), "o" (3), "+" (4), "++" (5)	interval	1-5	Questionnaire
EBITDA-margin	cpereb	Average EBITDA/sales in percent	ratio	>=-100%	Questionnaire
Net-profit-margin	cpernp	Average net profit/sales in percent	ratio	>=-100%	Questionnaire
Return-on-equity	cperre	Average return/equity in percent	ratio	>=-100%	Questionnaire
Return-on-assets	cperra	Average return/assets in percent	ratio	>=-100%	Questionnaire
Growth in employees	cgrem	Average growth rate of number of employees in percent	ratio	>=-100%	Questionnaire
Growth in sales	cgrsa	Average growth rate of number of sales in percent	ratio	>=-100%	Questionnaire
Growth in cashflows	cgrcf	Average growth rate of number of cashflows in %	ratio	>=-100%	Questionnaire
Change of valuation between financing rounds	cchval	Change of valuation by investors between financing rounds: "--" (1), "-" (2), "o" (3), "+" (4), "++" (5)	interval	1-5	Questionnaire
Change of sales multiple	cchsal	Change of sales multiple used for valuation between financing rounds in percent	ratio	>=-100%	Questionnaire
Change of cashflow multiple	cchcf	Change of cashflow multiple used for valuation between financing rounds in percent	ratio	>=-100%	Questionnaire
Change of EBITDA multiple	ccheb	Change of EBITDA multiple used for valuation between financing rounds in percent	ratio	>=-100%	Questionnaire

EXPLANATORY VARIABLES - SELF ASSESSMENT					
CG quality index (self assessment)	cgqind	Mean index of efficiency of assessment of managers, selection of new managers, bonding of managers, compensation of managers, composition of board (monitoring and advice), work of board (monitoring and advice) and reporting discipline (all interval)	ratio	0-1	Questionnaire
EXPLANATORY VARIABLES - CRITERIA					
CG quality index (criteria)	cgqinc	Mean index of all variables included in the sub-indexes of quality of selection and assessment of managers, of compensation of managers, of bonding of managers, of composition of board, of work of board and of reporting discipline	ratio	0-1	Questionnaire
CONTROL VARIABLES					
Development stage of portfolio company	pcfrde/ cdev	Development Status of portfolio company: seed(1), start-up (2), expansion (3), bridge (4), MBO/MBI (5)	ordinal	1-5	Questionnaire, Database
Size of portfolio company	cempn	Number of employees: 1-9 (1), 10- 49 (2), 40-249 (3), >250 (4)	interval	1-4	Questionnaire
Region of portfolio company	landgr	Location of portfolio company: Germany/Austria/Switzerland (1), France/BeNeLux (2), Northern Europe (3), UK/Ireland (4), Eastern Europe (5), Southern Europe (6)	nominal	1-6	Database
Industry of portfolio company	pcindus t	Main industry of portfolio company: Hard-/Software (1), Medical/Health (2), Biotechnology (3), Communication (4), Other Business/Consumer Services (5), Industrial Goods/Energy (6), Semiconductors/Electomics (7), Other (10)	nominal	1-10	Database

Annex 5: Variables related to hypotheses about effects on firm value

Criteria	t=0 - before the 1st financing round				
	N	Min	Max	Mean	Std. Dev.
Agency and business risk index	138	44,6	89,3	68,3	9,9
CG quality index (self assessment)	139	18,8	93,8	59,4	14,5
CG quality index (criteria)	123	0,0	100,0	53,8	26,0
CG advice index (self assessment)	138	8,3	100,0	57,6	17,2
CG advice index (criteria)	125	0,0	100,0	43,9	31,4
Efficiency of selection of new managers	139	1,0	5,0	3,3	0,9
Index of quality of selection of managers	57	0,0	100,0	57,0	37,1
Efficiency of composition of board: advice	138	1,0	5,0	3,3	0,8
Index of quality of board composition	131	0,0	92,9	36,0	29,7
Efficiency of work of board: advice	138	1,0	5,0	3,3	1,0
Index of quality of work of board	135	0,0	100,0	37,7	26,4
Planned IPO	138	0,0	3,0	1,3	1,0

Criteria	t=1 - after the 1st financing round				
	N	Min	Max	Mean	Std. Dev.
Agency and business risk index	-	-	-	-	-
CG quality index (self assessment)	139	18,8	100,0	69,1	15,3
CG quality index (criteria)	135	0,0	100,0	72,1	25,2
CG advice index (self assessment)	138	0,0	100,0	66,3	18,1
CG advice index (criteria)	129	0,0	100,0	66,1	26,7
Efficiency of selection of new managers	139	1,0	5,0	3,5	0,9
Index of quality of selection of managers	78	0,0	100,0	71,8	31,0
Efficiency of composition of board: advice	138	1,0	5,0	3,7	0,9
Index of quality of board composition	135	0,0	97,5	59,0	24,3
Efficiency of work of board: advice	138	1,0	5,0	3,7	1,0
Index of quality of work of board	136	0,0	100,0	54,5	21,5
Planned IPO	138	0,0	3,0	1,5	1,1

Criteria	t=2 - after the 2nd financing round				
	N	Min	Max	Mean	Std. Dev.
Agency and business risk index	-	-	-	-	-
CG quality index (self assessment)	74	25,0	100,0	67,8	16,4
CG quality index (criteria)	73	0,0	100,0	75,6	25,2
CG advice index (self assessment)	73	8,3	91,7	65,6	18,7
CG advice index (criteria)	67	0,0	100,0	67,9	26,6
Efficiency of selection of new managers	74	1,0	5,0	3,7	0,9
Index of quality of selection of managers	41	0,0	100,0	75,0	28,0
Efficiency of composition of board: advice	73	1,0	5,0	3,6	1,0
Index of quality of board composition	70	0,0	97,5	58,5	26,1
Efficiency of work of board: advice	73	1,0	5,0	3,6	1,0
Index of quality of work of board	70	15,0	100,0	54,5	21,1
Planned IPO	73	0,0	3,0	1,4	1,1

Criteria	t=3 - after the 3rd financing round				
	N	Min	Max	Mean	Std. Dev.
Agency and business risk index	138	25,0	88,1	70,8	9,3
CG quality index (self assessment)	30	40,6	96,9	69,9	13,9
CG quality index (criteria)	28	20,0	100,0	77,8	21,8
CG advice index (self assessment)	30	25,0	100,0	68,3	17,6
CG advice index (criteria)	28	37,5	100,0	78,7	20,0
Efficiency of selection of new managers	30	2,0	5,0	3,7	0,8
Index of quality of selection of managers	18	0,0	100,0	81,9	25,4
Efficiency of composition of board: advice	30	2,0	5,0	3,7	0,9
Index of quality of board composition	29	0,0	97,5	60,0	26,8
Efficiency of work of board: advice	30	1,0	5,0	3,8	1,0
Index of quality of work of board	28	35,0	80,0	58,4	15,9
Planned IPO	30	0,0	3,0	1,4	1,1

Annex 6: Descriptive analysis of variables related to venture capitalists' reasons

Criteria	t=1 - after the 1st financing round				
	N	Min	Max	Mean	Std. Dev.
Index of abilities	134	6,5	100,0	61,1	19,0
Control rights of lead-VC-F index	137	0,0	100,0	61,5	28,0
Ownership rights of lead-VC	112	2,4	100,0	38,0	24,8
Board seat lead-VC	137	0,0	1,0	0,8	0,4
Characteristics of lead-VC-F index	139	2,8	100,0	53,2	28,0
Type of lead-VC-F	139	1,0	5,0	3,4	1,2
Independent lead-VC-F	138	0,0	1,0	0,7	0,5
Number of portfolio companies lead-VC-F	130	0,0	1.260,0	185,1	375,5
Invested capital VC-F	128	0,0	14.000,0	1.312,2	2.718,7
Age of VC-F	134	1,0	3,0	2,4	0,7
International activity of VC-F: region	139	1,0	4,0	3,2	1,0
Reputation of VC-F	139	0,0	1,0	0,3	0,4
Abilities of VC-IM index	136	0,0	100,0	69,0	24,2
Experience in VC industry VC-IM	134	0,0	1,0	0,8	0,4
Industry experience VC-IM	136	0,0	1,0	0,6	0,5
International experience VC-IM	129	0,0	1,0	0,7	0,5
Startup experience VC-IM	122	0,0	1,0	0,7	0,5
Number of contacts per quarter VC-IM	131	1,0	150,0	11,1	15,9
Number of contacts per quarter VC-IM	130	0,0	14,0	2,7	2,3
Trustfullness of relationship VC-M	137	1,0	5,0	4,4	0,9

Criteria	t=2 - after the 2nd financing round				
	N	Min	Max	Mean	Std. Dev.
Index of abilities	63	14,6	98,6	62,0	19,9
Control rights of lead-VC-F index	72	0,0	100,0	56,4	32,8
Ownership rights of lead-VC	51	0,0	100,0	33,7	20,8
Board seat lead-VC	72	0,0	1,0	0,8	0,4
Characteristics of lead-VC-F index	73	5,6	100,0	54,0	27,2
Type of lead-VC-F	73	1,0	4,0	3,5	1,1
Independent lead-VC-F	72	0,0	1,0	0,7	0,4
Number of portfolio companies lead-VC-F	68	0,0	1.260,0	176,2	325,2
Invested capital VC-F	67	0,0	14.000,0	1.181,7	2.831,4
Age of VC-F	69	1,0	3,0	2,4	0,7
International activity of VC-F: region	73	1,0	4,0	3,3	0,9
Reputation of VC-F	74	0,0	1,0	0,2	0,4
Abilities of VC-IM index	66	20,0	100,0	72,6	22,5
Experience in VC industry VC-IM	65	0,0	1,0	0,8	0,4
Industry experience VC-IM	66	0,0	1,0	0,6	0,5
International experience VC-IM	64	0,0	1,0	0,7	0,4
Startup experience VC-IM	64	0,0	1,0	0,7	0,5
Number of contacts per quarter VC-IM	63	0,0	90,0	11,8	14,0
Number of contacts per quarter VC-IM	68	-0,1	14,0	3,1	2,8
Trustfullness of relationship VC-M	66	2,0	5,0	4,4	0,8

Criteria	t=3 - after the 3rd financing round				
	N	Min	Max	Mean	Std. Dev.
Index of abilities	26	14,6	98,6	57,6	20,0
Control rights of lead-VC-F index	29	0,0	100,0	45,1	33,5
Ownership rights of lead-VC	21	0,0	100,0	29,4	21,0
Board seat lead-VC	29	0,0	1,0	0,7	0,5
Characteristics of lead-VC-F index	29	2,8	94,4	53,1	27,7
Type of lead-VC-F	28	1,0	4,0	3,6	1,0
Independent lead-VC-F	29	0,0	1,0	0,8	0,4
Number of portfolio companies lead-VC-F	27	0,0	735,0	122,1	213,6
Invested capital VC-F	27	0,0	14.000,0	778,4	2.657,6
Age of VC-F	27	1,0	3,0	2,4	0,6
International activity of VC-F: region	29	1,0	4,0	3,2	1,0
Reputation of VC-F	29	0,0	1,0	0,3	0,5
Abilities of VC-IM index	27	25,0	100,0	73,6	24,5
Experience in VC industry VC-IM	27	1,0	1,0	1,0	0,0
Industry experience VC-IM	27	0,0	1,0	0,5	0,5
International experience VC-IM	25	0,0	1,0	0,7	0,5
Startup experience VC-IM	26	0,0	1,0	0,8	0,4
Number of contacts per quarter VC-IM	26	2,0	40,0	9,4	8,8
Number of contacts per quarter VC-IM	27	0,0	9,5	3,1	2,8
Trustfullness of relationship VC-M	26	3,0	5,0	4,8	0,5

Annex 7: Descriptive analysis of variables related to venture capitalists' influence on corporate governance

Criteria	t=0 - before the 1st financing round				
	N	Min	Max	Mean	Std. Dev.
CG quality index (self-assessment)	139	18,8	93,8	59,4	14,5
CG quality index (criteria)	123	0,0	100,0	53,8	26,0
CG monitoring index (self-assessment)	138	12,5	100,0	57,9	16,3
CG monitoring index (criteria)	133	0,0	85,9	44,8	19,9
CG bonding index (self-assessment)	136	0,0	100,0	64,8	21,8
CG bonding index (criteria)	118	12,5	95,8	50,7	19,0
CG advice index (self-assessment)	138	8,3	100,0	57,6	17,2
CG advice index (criteria)	125	0,0	100,0	43,9	31,4
Efficiency of assessment and selection of managers	139	0,0	100,0	58,6	18,5
Efficiency of assessment of managers	139	1,0	5,0	3,4	0,9
Replacements of managers per financing round	83	0,0	3,0	0,3	0,7
Efficiency of selection of new managers	139	1,0	5,0	3,3	0,9
Index of quality of selection of managers	57	0,0	100,0	57,0	37,1
Efficiency of bonding of managers	137	1,0	5,0	3,8	1,1
Index of quality of bonding of managers	118	0,0	100,0	60,7	26,7
Efficiency of compensation of managers	136	1,0	5,0	3,4	1,1
Index of quality of compensation of managers	127	0,0	93,8	41,7	24,2
Level of compensation compared to industry	131	1,0	5,0	2,7	1,1
Index of quality of board composition	131	0,0	92,9	36,0	29,7
Efficiency of composition of board: monitoring	138	1,0	5,0	3,1	0,8
Proportion of independent board members	116	0,0	1,0	0,1	0,2
Efficiency of composition of board: advice	138	1,0	5,0	3,3	0,8
Industry experience of independent board members	123	0,0	8,0	1,0	1,5
Executive experience of independent board members	122	0,0	9,0	1,4	1,7
International experience of independent board members	97	0,0	5,0	1,0	1,3
Functional experience of independent board members	122	0,0	9,0	0,9	1,3
Startup experience of independent board members	114	0,0	4,0	0,7	1,0
Experience as managers or board member in listed companies of independent board members	124	0,0	1,0	0,3	0,5
Efficiency of work of board: monitoring	138	1,0	5,0	3,2	0,9
Efficiency of work of board: advice	138	1,0	5,0	3,3	1,0
Index of quality of work of board	135	0,0	100,0	37,7	26,4
Number of board meetings per year	136	0,0	25,0	4,8	4,2
Distribution of agenda and relevant information	115	2,0	5,0	4,0	1,0
Proportion of time devoted to strategic issues	132	0,0	100,0	25,5	23,9
Efficiency of reporting discipline	138	1,0	5,0	3,5	1,0
Index of quality of reporting discipline	127	6,5	100,0	60,8	22,9
Number of reports per year	130	0,0	16,0	3,5	4,5
Timeliness of reporting	128	1,0	5,0	3,4	1,2
Extent of target-actual differences	117	1,0	4,0	2,5	1,0
Number of board members	128	0,0	10,0	3,3	2,1
Proportion of time devoted to monitoring issues	132	0,0	85,0	17,0	16,6
Proportion of Time devoted to Operational Issues	132	0,0	100,0	36,9	29,2
One tier: proportion of non-executive board members	89	0,0	1,0	0,3	0,3
Conduct of assessment of managers	108	0,0	1,0	0,6	0,5
Importance of annual bonus versus variable compensation linked to mid-/long-term development	108	1,0	3,0	1,6	0,8
Managers with variable compensation linked to mid-/long-term development	111	0,0	1,0	0,2	0,4

Criteria	t=1 - after the 1st financing round				
	N	Min	Max	Mean	Std. Dev.
CG quality index (self-assessment)	30	40,6	96,9	69,9	13,9
CG quality index (criteria)	28	20,0	100,0	77,8	21,8
CG monitoring index (self-assessment)	138	12,5	100,0	68,8	15,0
CG monitoring index (criteria)	136	0,0	96,6	60,7	16,0
CG bonding index (self-assessment)	139	0,0	100,0	70,8	22,3
CG bonding index (criteria)	132	19,8	100,0	64,7	17,4
CG advice index (self-assessment)	138	0,0	100,0	66,3	18,1
CG advice index (criteria)	129	0,0	100,0	66,1	26,7
Efficiency of assessment and selection of managers	30	37,5	100,0	65,4	16,3
Efficiency of assessment of managers	30	2,0	5,0	3,6	0,8
Replacements of managers per financing round	18	0,0	2,0	0,7	0,8
Efficiency of selection of new managers	30	2,0	5,0	3,7	0,8
Index of quality of selection of managers	18	0,0	100,0	81,9	25,4
Efficiency of bonding of managers	30	2,0	5,0	3,9	0,9
Index of quality of bonding of managers	28	33,3	100,0	81,0	20,6
Efficiency of compensation of managers	30	2,0	5,0	3,6	1,0
Index of quality of compensation of managers	29	0,0	87,5	49,8	24,6
Level of compensation compared to industry	30	1,0	5,0	2,9	1,1
Index of quality of board composition	29	0,0	97,5	60,0	26,8
Efficiency of composition of board: monitoring	30	1,0	5,0	3,6	1,0
Proportion of independent board members	26	0,0	1,0	0,2	0,3
Efficiency of composition of board: advice	30	2,0	5,0	3,7	0,9
Industry experience of independent board members	24	0,0	8,0	2,3	1,8
Executive experience of independent board members	24	0,0	6,0	2,8	1,4
International experience of independent board members	24	0,0	7,0	2,6	1,7
Functional experience of independent board members	24	0,0	6,0	2,3	1,6
Startup experience of independent board members	23	0,0	5,0	1,7	1,5
Experience as managers or board member in listed companies of independent board members	25	0,0	1,0	0,8	0,4
Efficiency of work of board: monitoring	30	2,0	5,0	3,8	0,9
Efficiency of work of board: advice	30	1,0	5,0	3,8	1,0
Index of quality of work of board	28	35,0	80,0	58,4	15,9
Number of board meetings per year	29	3,0	40,0	8,6	6,7
Distribution of agenda and relevant information	27	3,0	5,0	4,6	0,6
Proportion of time devoted to strategic issues	28	5,0	70,0	35,5	16,1
Efficiency of reporting discipline	30	3,0	5,0	4,3	0,7
Index of quality of reporting discipline	29	52,8	100,0	81,1	10,5
Number of reports per year	29	1,0	16,0	7,3	4,5
Timeliness of reporting	29	2,0	5,0	4,1	0,9
Extent of target-actual differences	29	1,0	4,0	2,3	0,9
Number of board members	28	2,0	8,0	5,6	1,4
Proportion of time devoted to monitoring issues	28	0,0	90,0	25,9	19,0
Proportion of Time devoted to Operational Issues	28	5,0	80,0	37,5	21,0
One tier: proportion of non-executive board members	24	0,0	1,0	0,5	0,4
Conduct of assessment of managers	26	0,0	1,0	0,8	0,4
Importance of annual bonus versus variable compensation linked to mid-/long-term development	24	1,0	3,0	1,6	0,8
Managers with variable compensation linked to mid-/long-term development	27	0,0	1,0	0,3	0,4

Criteria	t=2 - after the 2nd financing round				
	Mean	Std. Dev.	N	Mean	Max
CG quality index (self-assessment)	59	14,5	139,0	18,8	100,0
CG quality index (criteria)	54	26,0	135,0	0,0	100,0
CG monitoring index (self-assessment)	73	37,5	100,0	69,6	14,9
CG monitoring index (criteria)	71	25,0	88,3	60,2	14,7
CG bonding index (self-assessment)	74	0,0	100,0	66,7	25,4
CG bonding index (criteria)	69	25,0	100,0	64,7	17,0
CG advice index (self-assessment)	73	8,3	91,7	65,6	18,7
CG advice index (criteria)	67	0,0	100,0	67,9	26,6
Efficiency of assessment and selection of managers	59	18,5	139,0	0,0	100,0
Efficiency of assessment of managers	3	0,9	139,0	1,0	5,0
Replacements of managers per financing round	0	0,7	100,0	0,0	5,0
Efficiency of selection of new managers	3	0,9	139,0	1,0	5,0
Index of quality of selection of managers	57	37,1	78,0	0,0	100,0
Efficiency of bonding of managers	4	1,1	139,0	1,0	5,0
Index of quality of bonding of managers	61	26,7	132,0	33,3	100,0
Efficiency of compensation of managers	3	1,1	139,0	1,0	5,0
Index of quality of compensation of managers	42	24,2	137,0	0,0	100,0
Level of compensation compared to industry	3	1,1	138,0	1,0	5,0
Index of quality of board composition	36	29,7	135,0	0,0	97,5
Efficiency of composition of board: monitoring	3	0,8	138,0	1,0	5,0
Proportion of independent board members	0	0,2	123,0	0,0	1,0
Efficiency of composition of board: advice	3	0,8	138,0	1,0	5,0
Industry experience of independent board members	1	1,5	123,0	0,0	8,0
Executive experience of independent board members	1	1,7	122,0	0,0	9,0
International experience of independent board members	1	1,3	99,0	0,0	7,0
Functional experience of independent board members	1	1,3	122,0	0,0	10,0
Startup experience of independent board members	1	1,0	121,0	0,0	10,0
Experience as managers or board member in listed companies of independent board members	0	0,5	124,0	0,0	1,0
Efficiency of work of board: monitoring	3	0,9	138,0	1,0	5,0
Efficiency of work of board: advice	3	1,0	138,0	1,0	5,0
Index of quality of work of board	38	26,4	136,0	0,0	100,0
Number of board meetings per year	5	4,2	136,0	0,0	25,0
Distribution of agenda and relevant information	4	1,0	128,0	2,0	5,0
Proportion of time devoted to strategic issues	26	23,9	132,0	0,0	80,0
Efficiency of reporting discipline	4	1,0	138,0	1,0	5,0
Index of quality of reporting discipline	61	22,9	134,0	30,6	100,0
Number of reports per year	4	4,5	129,0	0,0	20,0
Timeliness of reporting	3	1,2	133,0	1,0	5,0
Extent of target-actual differences	2	1,0	126,0	1,0	4,0
Number of board members	3	2,1	133,0	0,0	11,0
Proportion of time devoted to monitoring issues	17	16,6	132,0	0,0	70,0
Proportion of Time devoted to Operational Issues	37	29,2	132,0	0,0	100,0
One tier: proportion of non-executive board members	0	0,3	94,0	0,0	1,0
Conduct of assessment of managers	1	0,5	121,0	0,0	1,0
Importance of annual bonus versus variable compensation linked to mid-/long-term development	2	0,8	116,0	1,0	3,0
Managers with variable compensation linked to mid-/long-term development	0	0,4	129,0	0,0	1,0

Criteria	t=3 - after the 3rd financing round				
	N	Min	Max	Mean	Std. Dev.
CG quality index (self-assessment)	30	40,6	96,9	69,9	13,9
CG quality index (criteria)	28	20,0	100,0	77,8	21,8
CG monitoring index (self-assessment)	30	43,8	100,0	70,4	13,9
CG monitoring index (criteria)	29	32,2	87,8	63,8	14,1
CG bonding index (self-assessment)	30	25,0	100,0	69,6	19,9
CG bonding index (criteria)	28	33,3	93,8	64,9	16,9
CG advice index (self-assessment)	30	25,0	100,0	68,3	17,6
CG advice index (criteria)	28	37,5	100,0	78,7	20,0
Efficiency of assessment and selection of managers	30	37,5	100,0	65,4	16,3
Efficiency of assessment of managers	30	2,0	5,0	3,6	0,8
Replacements of managers per financing round	18	0,0	2,0	0,7	0,8
Efficiency of selection of new managers	30	2,0	5,0	3,7	0,8
Index of quality of selection of managers	18	0,0	100,0	81,9	25,4
Efficiency of bonding of managers	30	2,0	5,0	3,9	0,9
Index of quality of bonding of managers	28	33,3	100,0	81,0	20,6
Efficiency of compensation of managers	30	2,0	5,0	3,6	1,0
Index of quality of compensation of managers	29	0,0	87,5	49,8	24,6
Level of compensation compared to industry	30	1,0	5,0	2,9	1,1
Index of quality of board composition	29	0,0	97,5	60,0	26,8
Efficiency of composition of board: monitoring	30	1,0	5,0	3,6	1,0
Proportion of independent board members	26	0,0	1,0	0,2	0,3
Efficiency of composition of board: advice	30	2,0	5,0	3,7	0,9
Industry experience of independent board members	24	0,0	8,0	2,3	1,8
Executive experience of independent board members	24	0,0	6,0	2,8	1,4
International experience of independent board members	24	0,0	7,0	2,6	1,7
Functional experience of independent board members	24	0,0	6,0	2,3	1,6
Startup experience of independent board members	23	0,0	5,0	1,7	1,5
Experience as managers or board member in listed companies of independent board members	25	0,0	1,0	0,8	0,4
Efficiency of work of board: monitoring	30	2,0	5,0	3,8	0,9
Efficiency of work of board: advice	30	1,0	5,0	3,8	1,0
Index of quality of work of board	28	35,0	80,0	58,4	15,9
Number of board meetings per year	29	3,0	40,0	8,6	6,7
Distribution of agenda and relevant information	27	3,0	5,0	4,6	0,6
Proportion of time devoted to strategic issues	28	5,0	70,0	35,5	16,1
Efficiency of reporting discipline	30	3,0	5,0	4,3	0,7
Index of quality of reporting discipline	29	52,8	100,0	81,1	10,5
Number of reports per year	29	1,0	16,0	7,3	4,5
Timeliness of reporting	29	2,0	5,0	4,1	0,9
Extent of target-actual differences	29	1,0	4,0	2,3	0,9
Number of board members	28	2,0	8,0	5,6	1,4
Proportion of time devoted to monitoring issues	28	0,0	90,0	25,9	19,0
Proportion of Time devoted to Operational Issues	28	5,0	80,0	37,5	21,0
One tier: proportion of non-executive board members	24	0,0	1,0	0,5	0,4
Conduct of assessment of managers	26	0,0	1,0	0,8	0,4
Importance of annual bonus versus variable compensation linked to mid-/long-term development	24	1,0	3,0	1,6	0,8
Managers with variable compensation linked to mid-/long-term development	27	0,0	1,0	0,3	0,4

Annex 8: Descriptive analysis of variables related to the quality of corporate governance

Criteria	t=1 - after the 1st financing round				
	N	Min	Max	Mean	Std. Dev.
Index of abilities	134	6,5	100,0	61,1	19,0
Control rights of lead-VC-F index	137	0,0	100,0	61,5	28,0
Ownership rights of lead-VC	112	2,4	100,0	38,0	24,8
Board seat lead-VC	137	0,0	1,0	0,8	0,4
Characteristics of lead-VC-F index	139	2,8	100,0	53,2	28,0
Type of lead-VC-F	139	1,0	5,0	3,4	1,2
Independent lead-VC-F	138	0,0	1,0	0,7	0,5
Number of portfolio companies lead-VC-F	130	0,0	1.260,0	185,1	375,5
Invested capital VC-F	128	0,0	14.000,0	1.312,2	2.718,7
Age of VC-F	134	1,0	3,0	2,4	0,7
International activity of VC-F: region	139	1,0	4,0	3,2	1,0
Reputation of VC-F	139	0,0	1,0	0,3	0,4
Abilities of VC-IM index	136	0,0	100,0	69,0	24,2
Experience in VC industry VC-IM	134	0,0	1,0	0,8	0,4
Industry experience VC-IM	136	0,0	1,0	0,6	0,5
International experience VC-IM	129	0,0	1,0	0,7	0,5
Startup experience VC-IM	122	0,0	1,0	0,7	0,5
Number of contacts per quarter VC-IM	131	1,0	150,0	11,1	15,9
Number of contacts per quarter VC-IM	130	0,0	14,0	2,7	2,3
Trustfullness of relationship VC-M	137	1,0	5,0	4,4	0,9

Criteria	t=2 - after the 2nd financing round				
	N	Min	Max	Mean	Std. Dev.
Index of abilities	63	14,6	98,6	62,0	19,9
Control rights of lead-VC-F index	72	0,0	100,0	56,4	32,8
Ownership rights of lead-VC	51	0,0	100,0	33,7	20,8
Board seat lead-VC	72	0,0	1,0	0,8	0,4
Characteristics of lead-VC-F index	73	5,6	100,0	54,0	27,2
Type of lead-VC-F	73	1,0	4,0	3,5	1,1
Independent lead-VC-F	72	0,0	1,0	0,7	0,4
Number of portfolio companies lead-VC-F	68	0,0	1.260,0	176,2	325,2
Invested capital VC-F	67	0,0	14.000,0	1.181,7	2.831,4
Age of VC-F	69	1,0	3,0	2,4	0,7
International activity of VC-F: region	73	1,0	4,0	3,3	0,9
Reputation of VC-F	74	0,0	1,0	0,2	0,4
Abilities of VC-IM index	66	20,0	100,0	72,6	22,5
Experience in VC industry VC-IM	65	0,0	1,0	0,8	0,4
Industry experience VC-IM	66	0,0	1,0	0,6	0,5
International experience VC-IM	64	0,0	1,0	0,7	0,4
Startup experience VC-IM	64	0,0	1,0	0,7	0,5
Number of contacts per quarter VC-IM	63	0,0	90,0	11,8	14,0
Number of contacts per quarter VC-IM	68	-0,1	14,0	3,1	2,8
Trustfullness of relationship VC-M	66	2,0	5,0	4,4	0,8

Criteria	t=3 - after the 3rd financing round				
	N	Min	Max	Mean	Std. Dev.
Index of abilities	26	14,6	98,6	57,6	20,0
Control rights of lead-VC-F index	29	0,0	100,0	45,1	33,5
Ownership rights of lead-VC	21	0,0	100,0	29,4	21,0
Board seat lead-VC	29	0,0	1,0	0,7	0,5
Characteristics of lead-VC-F index	29	2,8	94,4	53,1	27,7
Type of lead-VC-F	28	1,0	4,0	3,6	1,0
Independent lead-VC-F	29	0,0	1,0	0,8	0,4
Number of portfolio companies lead-VC-F	27	0,0	735,0	122,1	213,6
Invested capital VC-F	27	0,0	14.000,0	778,4	2.657,6
Age of VC-F	27	1,0	3,0	2,4	0,6
International activity of VC-F: region	29	1,0	4,0	3,2	1,0
Reputation of VC-F	29	0,0	1,0	0,3	0,5
Abilities of VC-IM index	27	25,0	100,0	73,6	24,5
Experience in VC industry VC-IM	27	1,0	1,0	1,0	0,0
Industry experience VC-IM	27	0,0	1,0	0,5	0,5
International experience VC-IM	25	0,0	1,0	0,7	0,5
Startup experience VC-IM	26	0,0	1,0	0,8	0,4
Number of contacts per quarter VC-IM	26	2,0	40,0	9,4	8,8
Number of contacts per quarter VC-IM	27	0,0	9,5	3,1	2,8
Trustfullness of relationship VC-M	26	3,0	5,0	4,8	0,5

Annex 9: Descriptive analysis of variables related to the venture capitalists' abilities

Criteria	t=0 - before the 1st financing round				
	N	Min	Max	Mean	Std. Dev.
Competitiveness relative to direct and indirect competitors	127	1,0	5,0	3,5	1,0
Performance according to plan	125	1,0	5,0	3,2	1,2
EBITDA-margin	65	-25,0	40,0	7,6	11,5
Net-profit-margin	57	-25,0	75,0	4,9	11,9
Return-on-equity	52	-25,0	300,0	15,0	44,8
Return-on-assets	48	-25,0	100,0	8,3	18,0
Growth in employees	102	-30,0	500,0	27,3	64,2
Growth in sales	100	-10,0	2.000,0	41,7	201,1
Change of valuation between financing rounds	-	-	-	-	-
Change of sales multiple	-	-	-	-	-
Change of EBITDA multiple	-	-	-	-	-

Criteria	t=1 - after the 1st financing round				
	N	Min	Max	Mean	Std. Dev.
Competitiveness relative to direct and indirect competitors	131	1,0	5,0	3,9	0,8
Performance according to plan	128	1,0	5,0	3,3	1,2
EBITDA-margin	65	-50,0	50,0	7,4	17,3
Net-profit-margin	59	-25,0	75,0	4,6	13,6
Return-on-equity	52	-25,0	100,0	11,7	19,3
Return-on-assets	47	-25,0	100,0	10,3	18,3
Growth in employees	109	-50,0	2.000,0	94,5	266,3
Growth in sales	104	-40,0	1.000,0	46,6	116,6
Change of valuation between financing rounds	65	1,0	5,0	3,7	1,0
Change of sales multiple	27	-58,0	1.000,0	83,3	215,0
Change of EBITDA multiple	18	-25,0	200,0	19,9	53,9

Criteria	t=2 - after the 2nd financing round				
	N	Min	Max	Mean	Std. Dev.
Competitiveness relative to direct and indirect competitors	68	1,0	5,0	4,1	0,8
Performance according to plan	66	1,0	5,0	3,1	1,1
EBITDA-margin	26	-50,0	40,0	3,2	17,9
Net-profit-margin	25	-50,0	75,0	1,8	20,4
Return-on-equity	22	-25,0	100,0	7,1	23,9
Return-on-assets	20	-25,0	100,0	5,5	23,5
Growth in employees	51	-50,0	400,0	45,5	76,9
Growth in sales	49	0,0	1.000,0	88,1	184,8
Change of valuation between financing rounds	27	2,0	5,0	3,0	0,9
Change of sales multiple	9	-30,0	300,0	28,9	102,2
Change of EBITDA multiple	7	-30,0	0,0	-4,3	11,3

Criteria	t=3 - after the 3rd financing round				
	N	Min	Max	Mean	Std. Dev.
Competitiveness relative to direct and indirect competitors	28	1,0	4,0	3,9	0,8
Performance according to plan	25	1,0	5,0	3,1	1,2
EBITDA-margin	6	-50,0	20,0	-4,3	27,8
Net-profit-margin	6	-50,0	20,0	-5,3	27,2
Return-on-equity	5	-25,0	20,0	-4,6	20,0
Return-on-assets	4	-25,0	50,0	7,0	31,3
Growth in employees	18	-30,0	100,0	20,0	32,2
Growth in sales	18	0,0	100,0	43,9	47,6
Change of valuation between financing rounds	-	-	-	-	-
Change of sales multiple	-	-	-	-	-
Change of EBITDA multiple	-	-	-	-	-

Annex 10: Descriptive analysis of variables related to the portfolio companies' firm value

Literature

Achleitner, A.-K. (2002): Entrepreneurial Finance – Herausforderungen auch in Deutschland, in: BetriebsBerater, 57. Jg., 2002, pp. 142-150.

Achleitner, A.-K./Bassen, A. (2002): Controllingsysteme in jungen Wachstumsunternehmen – terra incognita, in: Betriebs-Berater, 57 Jg., 2002, pp. 1192-1198.

Achleitner, A.-K./Bassen, A. (2004): Venture-Capital-bezogenes Controlling: Wie unterscheiden sich die Aspekte der verschiedenen Ebenen?, in: C. Meyer/D. Pfaff: Finanz- und Rechnungswesen, Jahrbuch 2004, Zürich 2004.

Admati, A. R./Pfleiderer, P. (1994): Robust Financial Contracting and the Role of Venture Capitalists, in: Journal of Finance, vol. 49, 1994, pp. 371-402.

Adner, R./Helfat, C. E. (2003): Corporate Effects And Dynamic Managerial Capabilities, in: Strategic Management Journal, vol. 24, 2003, pp. 1011-1025.

Aggarwal, R. K. /Samwick, A. A. (1999): The Other Side Of The Trade-Off: The Impact of Risk on Executive Compensation, in: Journal of Political Economy, vol. 107, 1999, pp. 65-105.

Aghion, P./Bolton, P. (1992): An Incomplete Contracts Approach to Financial Contracting, in: Review of Economic Studies, vol. 59, pp. 473-494.

Alchian, A. A./Demsetz. H. (1973): The Property Rights Paradigm, in: Journal of Economic History, vol. 33, 1973, pp. 16-27.

Alchian, A./Woodward, S. (1988): The Firm is Dead; long live the Firm – A Review of Oliver E. Williamson's The Economic Institutions of Capitalism, in: Journal of Economic Literature, vol. 26, 1988, pp. 65-79.

Aldrighi, D. M. (2003): The Mechanisms of Corporate Governance in the United States: An Assessment, in: Revista Brasileira de Economia, vol. 57, 2003, pp. 469-514.

Alvarez, S. A./Busenitz, L. W. (2001): The entrepreneurship of resource-based theory, in: Journal of Management, vol. 27, 2001, pp. 755-775.

Amit, R./Brander, J./Zott, C. (1998): Why Do Venture Capital Firms Exist? Theory And Canadian Evidence, in: Journal of Business Venturing, vol. 13, 1998, pp. 441-466.

Amit, R./Glosten, L./Muller, E. (1990): Entrepreneurial Ability, Venture Investments, And Risk Sharing, in: Management Science, vol. 36, 1990, pp. 1232-1245.

Anderson, M. C./Banker, R. D./Ravindran, S. (2000): Executive Compensation in the Information Technology Industry, in: Management Science, vol. 46, 2000, pp. 530-547.

Andersson, S./Gunnarsson, K. (1999): Riskfinansiärerns roll is tyrelsearbetet, Thesis at Halmstadt University.

Aoki, M. (1999): Information and Governance in the Silicon Valley Model, Working Paper Stanford University, available at: http://ideas.repec.org/p/wop/stanec/99028.html, call date: 04.02.06.

Aragon-Correa, J. A./Sharma, S. (2003): A Contingent Resource-Based View Of Proactive Corporate Environmental Strategy, in: Academy of Management Review, vol. 28, 2003, pp. 71-88.

Arthurs, J. D./Busenitz, L. W. (2003): The Boundaries and Limitations of Agency Thoery and Stewardship Theory in the Venture Capitalist/Entrepreneur Relationship, in: Entrepreneurship Theory and Practice, vol. 28 , 2003, pp. 145-162.

Audretsch, D. B./Lehmann, E. (2002): Does The New Economy Need New Governance? Ownership, Knowledge And Performance, Centre for Economic Policy Research Discussion Paper No. 3626, available at: hhtp://www.cepr.org/pubs/dps/DP3626.asp, call date: 08.03.2005.

Bader, H. (1996): Private Equity als Anlagekategorie – Theorie, Praxis und Portfoliomanagement für institutionelle Investoren, Diss., Stuttgart 1996.

Baker, M./Gompers, P. A. (2003): The Determinants Of Board Structure At The Initial Public Offering, in: Journal of Law and Economics, vol. 46, 2003, pp. 569-598.

Bankman, J. (1994): The Structure Of Silicon Valley Start-Ups, in: UCLA Law Journal, vol. 41, 1994, pp. 1737-1768.

Barney, J. B. (1991): Firm Resources and Sustained Competitive Advantage. In: Journal of Management, vol. 17, pp. 99-120.

Barney, J. B./Busenitz, L. W./Fiet, J. O./Moesel, D. D. (1989): The Structure of Venture Capital Governance: An Organizational Economic Analysis of Relations Between Venture Capital Firms and New Ventures, in: Best Paper Proceedings of Academy of Management 1989, pp. 64-68.

Barney, J. B./Busenitz, L. W./Fiet, J. O./Moesel, D. D. (1994): The Relationship Between Venture Capitalists and Managers in New Firms: Determinants of Contractual Covenants, in: Managerial Finance, vol. 20, 1994, pp. 19-30.

Barney, J. B./Busenitz, L. W./Fiet, J. O./Moesel, D. D. (1996a): The Substitution of Bonding For Monitoring In Venture Capitalist Relations With High Technology Enterprises, in: Journal of High Technology Management Research, vol. 7, 1996, pp. 91-105.

Barney, J. B./Busenitz, L. W./Fiet, J. O./Moesel, D. D. (1996b): New Ventures Teams' Assessment Of Learning Assistance From Venture Capital Firms, in: Journal of Business Venturing, vol. 11, 1996, pp. 257-272.

Barney, J. B./Hansen, M. H. (1994): Trustworthiness As A Source Of Competitive Advantage, in: Strategic Management Journal, vol. 15, 1994, pp. 175-190.

Barney, J. B./Wright, M./Ketchen, D. (2001): The Resource-Based View of the Firm: Ten Years after 1991, in: Journal of Management, vol. 27, 2001, pp. 525-642.

Bascha, A./Walz, U. (2000): Hybride Finanzierungsinstrumente als Anreiz- und Kontrollmechanismen bei Venture Capital, in: FinanzBetrieb, 2. Jg., 2000, pp. 410-418.

Bascha, A./Walz, U. (2001): Convertible securities and optimal exit decisions in venture capital finance, in: Journal of Corporate Finance, vol. 8, 2001, pp. 285-306.

Bassen, A. (2002a): Institutionelle Investoren und Corporate Governance – Analyse der Einflussnahme unter besonderer Berücksichtigung börsennotierter Wachstumsunternehmen, Habil., Wiesbaden 2002.

Bassen, A. (2002b): Ausgestaltung der Corporate Governance bei Start-up-Unternehmen, in: Hommel, U./Knecht, T. C. (Ed.): Wertorientiertes Start-up-Management, München 2002, pp. 149-162.

Bassen, A./Kleinschmidt M./Prigge, S./Zöllner, C. (2006a): Deutscher Corporate Governance Kodex und Unternehmenserfolg, in: DBW, 66. Jg., 2006, pp. 375-401.

Bassen, A./Kleinschmidt M./Zöllner, C. (2004): Corporate Governance Quality Study 2004 – Analyse der Corporate Governance deutscher Unternehmen aus Investorensicht, FinanzBetrieb, 6. Jg. (2004), pp. 527-533.

Bassen, A./Kleinschmidt M./Zöllner, C. (2006b): Corporate Governance of German Growth Companies - Empirical Analysis of the Corporate Governance Quality and the Structure of Supervisory Boards of Companies listed on Tec-Dax, in: Journal of Corporate Ownership and Control, vol. 3, 2006, pp. 128-137.

Bauer, R./Günster, N./Otten, R. (2003): Empirical Evidence on Corporate Governance in Europe, Working Paper, available at: http://ssrn.com/abstract=444543; call date: 31.01.2006.

Baum, J. A. C./Silverman, B. S. (2004): Picking winners of building them? Alliance, intellectual and human capital as selection criteria in venture financing and performance of biotechnology startups. In: Journal of Business Venturing, vol. 19, 2004, pp. 411-436.

Baums, T./Möller, M. (2002): Vertragsgestaltung zwischen Start-up-Unternehmen und Investoren (Contracting), in: U. Hommel/T. Knecht: Wertorientiertes Start-Up Management, München 2002, pp. 396-412.

Baysinger, B./Hoskisson, R. E. (1990): The Composition of Board of Directors and Corporate Strategy, in: Academy of Management Review, vol. 15, 1990, pp. 72-87.

Beatty, R. P./Zajac, E. J. (1994): Managerial Incentives, Monitoring, and Risk Bearing: A Study of Executive Compensation, Ownership, and Board Structure in Initial Public Offerings, in: Administrative Science Quarterly, vol. 39, 1994, pp. 313-335.

Bebchuk, L./Cohen, A./Ferrell, A. (2004): What matters In Corporate Governance, Harvard – John M. Olin Center for Law, Economics, And Business, Working Paper No. 491, available at: http://papers.ssrn.com/abstract_id=593423, call date: 08.03.2005.

Bebchuk, L./Roe, M. J. (1999): A Theory of Path Dependence in Corporate Governance and Ownership, Working Paper, Columbia Law School Working Paper Series, available at: http://papers.ssrn.com/paper.taf?abstract_id=192414, call date: 27.10.2005.

Becht, M. (1999): European Corporate Governance: Trading off liquidity against control, in: European Economic Review, vol. 43, pp. 1071-1083.

Becht, M./Bolton, P./Röell, A. (2002): Corporate Governance and Control, ECGI Working Paper Series in Finance, Working paper No. 02/2002, available at: www.ssrn.com/abstract_id=343461, Call date: 22.10.2004.

Becker, G. (1964): Human Capital, Columbia University Press, New York 1964.

Beckman, C. M./Burton, M. D. (2004): Founding the Future: The Evolution of Top Management Teams from Founding to IPO, Working Paper, available at: http://web.mit.edu/iandeseminar/ Papers/Fall2005/BurtonBeckman2005.pdf, call date: 04.02.06.

Begley, T. M./Boyd, D. P. (1987): Psychological Characteristics associated with performance in entrepreneurial firms and small businesses, in: Journal of Business Venturing, vol. 2, 1987, pp. 79-93.

Beiner, S./Drobetz, W./Schmid, M. M./Zimmermann, H. (2004): An Integrated Framework of Corporate Governance and Firm Valuation – Evidence from Switzerland, ECGI Working Paper Series in Finance No. 34/2004, available at: http://ssrn.com/abstract=479322, call date: 28.02.2005.

Benston, G. J./Smith, C. W. Jr. (1976): A Transaction Cost Approach to the Theory of Financial Intermediaries, in: Journal of Finance, vol. 31, 1976, pp. 215-231.

Berg, A./Gottschalg, O. (2003): Understanding Value Generation in Buyouts, INSEAD Working Paper Series 2003/42/SM, Paris 2003.

Bergemann, D./Hege, U. (1998): Venture capital financing, moral hazard, and learning, in: Journal of Banking & Finance, vol. 22, 1998, pp. 703-735.

Berger, A. N./Udell, G. F. (1998): The economics of small business finance: The roles of private equity and debt markets in the financial growth cycle, in: Journal of Banking & Finance, vol. 22, 1998, pp. 617-673.

Berle, A. A./Means, G. C. (1932): The Modern Corporation And Private Property, MacMillan, New York 29132.

Berliner Iniativkreis (2000): German Code of Corporate Governance, Berlin 2000, available at: http://www.gccg.de/deu_German-Code-of-Corporate-Governance.pdf, call date: 23.09.2004.

Beuselinck, C./Deloof, M./Manigart, S. (2004): Venture Capital, Corporate Governance and Earnings Quality, Working Paper University of Gent, available at: http://www.feb.ugent.be/fac/research/WP/Papers/wp_04_221.pdf; call date: 31.01.2006.

Blac, B. S./Jang, H./Kim, W. (2003): Does Corporate Governance Predict Firms' Market Values? Evidence from Korea, Stanford Law School, Working Paper No. 237, available at: http://papers.ssrn.com/abstract=311275, call date: 07.03.2005.

Blaikie, N. W. H. (1991): A critique of triangulation in social research, in: Quality & Quantity, vol. 25, 1991, pp. 115-136.

Blair, N./Wallman, S. (2003): The Growing Intangibles Reporting Discrepancy, in: J. Hand/L. Baruch (Ed.): Intangible Assets: Values, Measures, and Risks, Oxford University Press, Oxford 2003, pp. 449-470.

Bloom, M. C./Milkovich, G. T. (1995): The Relationship Between Risk, Performance-Based Pay, And Organizational Performance, Paper presented at the Academy of Management Annual Meeting 1995, available at: http://www.nd.edu/~mbloom/amj_risk.pdf, call date: 31.01.06.

Boeker, W./Goodstein, J. (1991): Organizational Performance And Adaptation: Effects Of Environment And Performance On Changes In Board Composition, in: Academy of Management Journal, vol. 14, 1991, pp. 805-826.

Boeker, W./Wiltbank, R. (2005): New Venture Evolution and Managerial Capabilities, in: Organization Science, vol. 16, 2005, pp. 123-133.

Börsch-Supan, A./Köke, J. (2002): An Applied Econometricians' View of Empirical Corporate Governance Studies, in: German Economic Review, vol. 3, 2002, pp. 295-326.

Bortz, J./Döring, N. (1996): Forschungsmethoden und Evaluation, Berlin 1995.

Bourseli, A. K./Davidson, W. N. III/Abdulsalam, F. A. (2004): Role of Venture Capitalists in IPO Corporate Governance and Operating Performance, in: Quarterly Journal of Business & Economics, vol. 44, 2004, pp. 71-82.

Bowden, B. J. (1994): Bargaining, Size, And Return In Venture Capital Funds, in: Journal of Business Venturing, vol. 9, 1994, pp. 307-330.

Boyd, B. (1990): Corporate Linkages And Organizational Environment: A Test Of The Resource Dependence Model, in: Strategic Management Journal, vol. 11, 1990, pp. 419-430.

Boyd, B. (1994): Board Control And CEO Compensation, in: Strategic Management Journal, vol. 15, 1994, pp. 335-344.

Boyd, B. (1995): CEO Duality And Firm Performance: A Contingency Model, in: Strategic Management Journal, vol. 16, pp. 301-312.

Bradley, M./Jarrell, G. A./Kim, E. H. (1984): On the Existence of an Optimal Capital Structure: Theory and Evidence, in: Journal of Finance, vol. 39, 1984, pp. 857-878.

Brealey, R. A./Myers, S. C. (2000): Principles of Corporate Finance, Sixth Ed., Irwin McGraw-Hill, Boston 2000.

Brinkrolf, A. (2002): Managementunterstützung durch Venture-Capital-Gesellschaften, Eine Untersuchung des nichtfinanziellen Beitrags von Venture-Capital-Gesellschaften bei der Entwicklung ihrer Portfoliounternehmen, Diss., Wiesbaden 2002.

Brown, L. D./Caylor, M. L. (2004): Corporate Governance Study: The Correlation between Corporate Governance and Company Performance, available at: http://www.issproxy.com/pdf/Corporate%20Governance%20Study%201.04.pdf, call date: 01.02.06.

Brush, C. G./Vanderwerf, P. A. (1992): A Comparison Of Methods And Sources For Obtaining Estimates Of New Venture Performance, in: Journal of Business Venturing, vol. 7, 1992, pp. 157-170.

Budäus, D./Gerum, E./Zimmermann, G. (1988): Betriebswirtschaftslehre und Theorie der Verfügungsrechte, Hrsg., Wiesbaden 1988.

Busenitz, L. W./Fiet, J. O. (1996): The Effects of Early Stage Venture Capitalist Actions on Eventual Venture Disposition, in: Entrepreneurial and Small Business Finance, vol. 5, 1996, pp. 97-114.

Bushman, R. M./Smith, A. J. (2001): Financial accounting information and corporate governance, in: Journal of Accounting and Economics, vol. 32, 2001, pp. 237-333.

Bygrave, W. D. (1987): Syndicated Investments By Venture Capital Firms: A Network Perspective, in: Journal of Business Venturing, vol. 2, 1987, pp. 139-154.

Bygrave, W./Fast, N./Khoylian, R./Vincent, L./Yue, W. (1989): Early Rates Of Return Of 131 Venture Capital Funds Started 1978-1984, in: Journal of Business Venturing, vol. 4, 1989, pp. 93-105.

Cadbury Report (The Financial Aspects of Corporate Governance) in the version of 1 December 1992, available at: http://www.ecgi.org/codes/code.php?code_id=132, call date: 06.01.2006.

Callison, J. W. (2000): Venture Capital and Corporate Governance: Evolving the Limited Liability Company to Finance the Entrepreneurial Business, in: Journal of Corporate Law, vol. 25, 2000, pp. 97-124.

Carmines, E. G./Zeller, R. A. (1980): Reliability & Valididty Assessment, Thousand Oaks, London, New Dehli, 1980.

Carney, M. (2005): Corporate Governance and Competitive Advantage in Family-Controlled Firms, in: Entrepreneurship Theory and Practice, vol. 29, 2005, pp. 249-265.

Carpenter, M. A./Pollock, T. G./Leary, M. M. (2003): Testing A Model Of Reasoned Risk-Taking: Governance, The Experience Of Principals And Agents, And Global Strategy In High-Technology IPO Firms, in: Strategic Management Journal, vol. 24, 2003, pp. 803-820.

Carpenter, M. A./Westphal, J. D. (2001): The Strategic Context Of External Network Ties: Examining The Impact Of Director Appointments On Board Involvement In Strategic Decision Making, in: Academy of Management Journal, vol. 4, 2001, pp. 639-660.

Castanias, R. P./Helfat, C. E. (1991): Managerial Resources and Rent, in: Journal of Management, vol. 17, 1991), pp. 155-171.

Certo, S. T. (2003): Influencing Initial Public Offering Investors With Prestige: Signaling with Board Structures, in: Academy of Management Review, vol. 28, 2003, pp. 432-446.

Certo, S. T./Daily, C. M./Dalton, D. R. (2001): Signalling Firm Value Through Board Structure: An Investigation of Initial Public Offerings, in: Entrepreneurship: Theory and Practice, vol. 26, pp. 33-50.

Chan, Y.-S. (1983): On the Positive Role of Financial Intermediation in Allocation of Venture Capital in a Market with Imperfect Information, in: Journal of Finance, vol. 38, 1983, pp. 1543-1568.

Charan, R. (1998): Boards at Work: How Corporate Boards Create Competitive Advantage, Jossey-Bass, San Francisco 1998.

Chua, J. H./Woodward, R. S. (1993): Splitting The Firm Between The Entrepreneur And The Venture Capitalist With The Help Of Stock Options, in: Journal of Business Venturing, vol. 8, 1993, pp. 43-58.

Coase, R. H. (1937): The Nature of the Firm, in: Econometrica, New Series, vol. 4, 1937, pp. 386-405.

Coase, R. H. (1960): The Problem Of Social Cost, in: Journal of Law and Economics, vol. 3, 1960, pp. 1-44.

Coff, R. W. (1999): When Competitive Advantage Doesn't Lead to Performance: The Resource-Based View and Stakeholder Bargaining Power, in: Organization Science, vol. 10, 1999, pp. 119-133.

Coles, J. W./McWilliams, V. B./Sen, N. (2001): An examination of the relationship of governance mechanisms to performance, in: Journal of Management, vol. 27, 2001, pp. 23-50.

Collis, D. J. (1994): Research Note: How Valuable Are Organizational Capabilities?, in: Strategic Management Journal, vol. 15, 1994, pp. 143-152.

Combs, J. G./Ketchen, D. J. (1999): Explaining interfirm cooperation and performance: Towards a reconcipliation of predictions from the resource-based view and organizational economics, in: Strategic Management Journal, vol. 20, pp. 867-888

Conner, K. R. (1991): A Historical Comparison of Resource-Based Theory and Five Schools of Thought Within Industrial Organization Economics: Doe We Have a New Theory of the Firm?, in: Journal of Management, vol. 17, 1991, pp. 121-154.

Coopey, R. (2003): Corporate Governance, Management and British Venture Capital since 1945, in: R. Fitzgerald/A. Etsuo (Ed.): The Development of Corporate Governance in Japan and Britain, Ashgate 2003.

Core, J. E./Guay, W./Rusticus, T. (2004): Does weak governance cause weak stock returns? An examination of firm operating performance and analysts expectations, Working Paper, available at:

http://papers.ssrn.com/sol3/papers.cfm?abstract_id=533582, call date: 23.01.2006.

Core, J. E./Holthausen, R. W./Larcker, D. F. (1999): Corporate governance, chief executive officer compensation, and firm performance, in: Journal of Financial Economics, vol. 51, 1999, pp. 371-406.

Cumming, D. J./MacIntosh, J. G. (2002): Comparative Venture Capital Governance: Private Versus Labour Sponsored Venture Capital Funds, CESIFO Working Paper No. 853, available at: http://papers.ssrn.com/sol3/papers.cfm?abstract_id=382933, call date: 25.01.2006.

Cumming, D. J./MacIntosh, J. G. (2003): A cross-country comparison of full and partial venture capital exits, in: Journal of Banking & Finance, vol. 27, 2003, pp. 511-648.

Cyert, R. M./Kang, S.-H./Kumar, P. (2002): Corporate Governance, Takeovers, and Top-Management Compensation: Theory and Evidence, in: Management Science, vol. 48, 2002, pp. 453-469.

Daft, R. L. (1983): Learning the craft of organizational research, in: Academy of Management Review, vol. 8, 1983, pp. 539-546.

Dahlquist, M/Pinkowitz, L./Stulz, R. M./Williamson, R. (2002): Corporate Governance and the Home Bias, Georgetown University Working Paper, available at: http://faculty.msb.edu/lfp/hb102602.pdf, call date: 23.01.2006.

Daily, C. M./Dalton, D. R. (1992): The Relationship Between Governance Structure And Corporate Performance In Entrepreneurial Firms, in: Journal of Business Venturing, vol. 7, 1992, pp. 375-386.

Daily, C. M./Dalton, D. R./Canella, A. A. (2003): Corporate Governance: Decades of Dialogue and Data, in: Academy of Management Review, vol. 28, 2003, pp. 371-382.

Daily, C. M./McDougall, P. P./Covin, J. G./Dalton, D. R. (2002): Governance and Strategic Leadership in Entrepreneurial Firms, in: Journal of Management, vol. 28, 2002, pp. 387-412.

Dalton, D. R./Daily, C. M./Ellstand, A, Johnson, J. L. (1996): Meta-Analytic Reviews Of Board Composition, Leadership Structure, And Financial Performance, in: Strategic Management Journal. vol. 19, 1998, pp. 269-290.

Dalton, D. R./Daily, C. M./Johnson, J. L./Ellerstrand, A. E. (1999): Number of directors and financial performance: A meta analysis, in: Academy of Management Journal. vol. 42, 1999, pp. 674-686.

Deakins, D./O'Neill, E./Mileham, P. (2000): The role and influence of external directors in small entrepreneurial companies: some evidence on VC and non-VC appointed external directors, in: Venture Capital, vol. 2 (2000), pp. 111-127.

Demirag, I./Sudarsanam, S./Wright, M. (2000): Corporate Governance: Overview and Research Agenda, in: British Accounting Review, vol. 32, 1999, pp. 341-354.

Demsetz, H. (1967): Toward A Theory Of Property Rights, in: American Economic Review – Paper and Proceedings of the 79th Annual Meeting of the American Economic Association, vol. 57, 1967, pp. 347-359.

Denis, D. K. (2001): Twenty-five years of corporate governance research ... and counting, in: Review of Financial Economics, vol. 10, 2001, pp. 191-212.

Denis, D. K./McConell, J. J. (2003): International Corporate Governance, In Journal of Financial and Quantitative Analysis, vol. 28, 2003, pp. 1-36.

Dennis, W. J. Jr. (2003): Raising Response Rates in Mail Surveys of Small Business Owners: Results of an Experiment, in: Journal of Small Business Management, vol. 41, 2003, pp. 278-295.

Deutsch, Y./Ross, T. W. (2003): You Are Known by the Directors You Keep: Reputable Directors as a Signalling Mechanism for Young Firms, in: Management Science, vol. 49, 2003, pp. 1003-1017.

Deutsche Bank (2004): Beyond the Numbers – Corporate Governance in the UK, London 2004.

Dierickx, I./Cool, K. (1989): Asset Stock Accumulation And Sustainability Of Competitive Advantage, in: Management Science, vol. 35, 1989, pp. 1504-1513.

Dimov, D, P./Shepherd, D. A. (2005): Human capital theory and venture capital firms: exploring "home runs" and "strike outs", in: Journal of Business Venturing, vol. 20, 2005, pp. 1-21.

Dotzler, F. (2001): What Do Venture Capitalists Really Do, and Where Do They Learn to Do It?, in: The Journal of Private Equity, vol. 5, 2001, pp. 6-12.

Drobetz, W./Schillhofer, A./Zimmermann, H. (2003): Corporate Governance and Expected Return, ECGI Finance Working Paper No. 11/2003, available at: hhtp://www.ssrn.com/abstract_id=379102, call date: 05.05.2005.

Drukarzcyk, J./Schmidt, H. (1998): Lenders as a Force in Corporate Governance – Enabling Covenants and the Impact of Bankruptcy Law, in: Hopt, K. J./Kanda, H./Roe, M. J./Wymeersch, E./Prigge, S. (Ed.): Comparative Corporate Governance – The State of the Art and Emerging Research, Oxford 1998, pp. 759-786.

Duffner, S. (2003): Prinicipal–Agent Problems in Venture Capital Finance, WWZ/Department of Finance Working Paper No. 11/03, available at: http://www.wwz.unibas.ch/finance/publications/researchpapers/11-03%20PrincAgent.pdf, call date: 04.02.06.

ECGI (2005): Index of Codes, available at: http://www.ecgi.org/codes/all_codes.php, call date: 06.01.2006.

Ehrlich, S. B./De Noble, A. F./Moore, T./Weaver, R. R. (1994): After The Cash Arrives: A Comparative Study Of Venture Capital Investor Involvement In Entrepreneurial Firms, in: Journal of Business Venturing, vol. 9, 1994, pp. 67-82.

Eisele, F./Habermann, M./Oesterle, R. (2003): Die Beteiligungsauswahl durch Venture Capital-Gesellschaften: Entscheidungskriterien bei Projekten unterschiedlicher Reife, in: FinanzBetrieb, 5. Jg., 2003, pp. 403-413.

Eisenhardt, K. M. (1989a): Agency Theory: An Assessment and Review, in: Academy of Management Review, vol. 14, 1989, pp. 57-74.

Eisenhardt, K. M. (1989b): Marking Fast Strategic Decisions In High-Velocity Environments, in: Academy of Management Journal, vol. 32, pp. 543-576.

Eisenhardt, K. M./Winter, J. A. (2000): Dynamic Capabilities: What Are They?, in: Strategic Management Journal, vol. 21, 2000, pp. 1105-1121.

Elango, B./Fried, V. H./Hisrich, R. T./Polonchek, A. (1995): How Venture Capital Firms differ, in: Journal of Business Venturing, vol. 10, 1995, pp. 157-179.

Ellis, J. (2003): What's Wrong With Risk-Averse Venture Capitalists?; In: Fast Company, issue 72, July 2003, p. 54.

Engel, E./Gordon, E. A./Hayes, R. M. (2002): The Roles of Performance Measures and Monitoring in Annual Governance Decisions in Entrepreneurial Firms, in: Journal of Accounting Research, vol. 40. (2002), pp. 485-518.

EVCA (2004): Why and How to Invest in Private Equity, Special Paper, An EVCA Investor Relations Paper, Written by Alex Bance, Zaventem 2004.

EVCA (2005a): Employment Contribution of Private Equity and Venture Capital in Europe, Zaventem 2005, available at: http://www.evca.com/images/attachments/ tmpl_13_art_89_att_928.pdf, call date: 11.06.2005.

EVCA (2005b): EVCA Final Activity Figures for 2004, Zaventem 2005, available at: http://www.pwcmoneytree.com/exhibits/ EVCA_Final_Activity_2004_Release.pdf, call date: 11.06.2005.

EVCA (2005c): EVCA Corporate Governance Guidelines – Guidelines and good practice in the management of privately held companies in the private equity and venture capital industry, Zaventem 2005, available at: http://www.evca.com/pdf/ evca_corporate_governance_guidelines.pdf, call date: 12.06.2006.

EVCA (2006): EVCA Yearbook 2006 - Annual Survey 2005, Zaventem 2006.

Falconer, M./Reid, G. C./Terry, N. G. (1995): Post Investment Demand for Accounting Information by Venture Capitalists. In: Accounting and Business Research, vol. 25, 1999, pp. 186-196.

Fama, E. F. (1978): The Effects of a Firm's Investment and Financing Decision on the Welfare of ist Security Holders, in: American Economic Review, vol. 68, 1978, pp. 272-284.

Fama, E. F. (1980): Agency Problems and the Theory of the Firm, in: The Journal of Political Economy, vol. 88, 1999, pp. 288-307.

Fama, E. F. (1991): Efficient Capital Markets: II, in: Journal of Finance, vol. 46, 1991, pp. 1575-1617.

Fama, E. F. /Jensen, M. C. (1983): Separation of Ownership and Control, in: Journal of Law and Economics, vol. 26, 1983, pp. 301-325.

Feinendegen, S./Schmidt, D./Wahrenburg, M. (2003): Die Vertragsbeziehung zwischen Investoren und europäischen Venture Capital-Fonds: eine empirische Untersuchung und Klassifizierung unterschiedlicher Vertragsmuster, in: Zeitschrift für Betriebswirtschaft, 23. Jg., 2003, pp. 1167-1195.

Feldmann, H. (1995): Eine institutionalistische Revolution? : Zur dogmenhistorischen Bedeutung der modernen Institutionenökonomik, Berlin 1995.

Fenn, G./Liang, N./Prowse, S. (1997): The Private Equity Market, An Overview, in: Financial Markets, Institutions & Instruments, vol. 6, 1997, pp. 1-105.

Fielding, N./Schreier, M. (2001): Introduction: On the Compatibility between Qualitative and Quantitative Research Methods, in: Qualitative Social Research, vol. 2, 2001, available at: http://qualitative-research.net/fqs-end.htm, call date: 15.03.2006.

Fiet, J, O. (1991): Venture Capital Risk Assessment: An Empirical Test Comparing Business Angels And Venture Capital Firms, in: Academy of Management Proceedings 1991, 1991, pp. 73-77.

Fiet, J. O. (1995): Risk Avoidance Strategies In Venture Capital Market, in: Journal of Management Studies, vol. 32, 1995, pp. 551-574.

Fiet, J. O. (1998): Reliance Upon Informants In The Venture Capital Industry, in: Journal of Business Venturing, vol. 10, 1998, pp. 195-223.

Fiet, J. O./Hellriegel, D. (1995): Postcontractual Safeguards Against Venture Capital Risk, in: Entrepreneurship, Innovation, and Change, vol. 4, 1995, pp. 23-37.

Filatotchev, I./Chahine, S./Wright, M./Arberk, M. (2005): Founders' Characteristics, Venture Capital Syndication and Governance in Entrepreneurial IPOs, Working Paper King's College London, London 2005.

Finkelstein, S./D'Aveni, R. A. (1994): CEO duality as a double-edged sword: How boards of directors balance entrechment avoidance and units of command, in: Academy of Management Journal. vol. 37, 1994, pp. 1079-1108.

Fleischhauer, U./Hoyer, G. A. (2004): Studie: Private Equity als fester Bestandteil der Anlageportfolios europäischer Institutionen, in: FinanzBetrieb, 6. Jg., 2004, pp. 395-397.

Franke, N./Gruber, M./Henkel, J./Hoisl, K. (2004): Die Bewertung von Gründerteam durch Venture-Capital-Geber – Eine empirische Untersuchung, in: DBW, 64. Jg., 2004, pp. 651-669.

Franks, J./Mayer, C. (1990): Takeovers: Capital markets and corporate control: A study of France, Germany, and the UK, in: Policy: A European Forum, vol. 10, pp. 189-231.

Franks, J./Mayer, C. (1998): Bank Control, Takeovers, and Corporate Governance in Germany, in: Hopt, K. J./Kanda, H./Roe, M. J./Wymeersch, E./Prigge, pp. (Ed.): Comparative Corporate Governance – The State of the Art and Emerging Research, Oxford 1998, pp. 641-658.

Franks, J./Mayer, C./Renneboog, L. (2001): Who Disciplines Management in Poorly Performing Companies?, in: Journal of Financial Intermediation, vol. 10, 2001, pp. 209-248.

Fredrickson, J. W. (1984): The Comprehensiveness of Strategic Decision Processes: Extension, Observations, Future Directions, in: Academy of Management Journal, vol. 27, 1984, pp. 445-466.

Fredriksen, Ø./Klofsten, M. (1999): CEO Vs Board Typoologes In Venture Capital-Entrepreneur Relationships, Paper presented at the Babson Kauffman Entrepreneurship Research Conference 1999, available at: http://www.babson.edu/entrep/fer/papers99/XV/XV_A/XV_A%20Text.htm, call date: 27.06.05.

Fredriksen, Ø./Klofsten, M. (2001): Venture Capitalists' Governance Of Their Portfolio Companies, in: Journal of Enterprising Culture, vol. 9, 2001, pp. 201-209.

Fredriksen, Ø./Klofsten, M./Landström, H./Olofsson, C./Wahlbin, C. (1990): Entrepreneur-Venture Capitalist Relations: The Entrepreneurs' View, in: Frontiers of Entrepreneurship Research 1990, pp. 251-265, Wellsley 1990.

Freear, J./Sohl, J. E./Wetzel, Jr., W. E. (1994): Angels And Non-Angels: Are There Differences?, in: Journal of Business Venturing, vol. 9, 1994, pp. 109-123.

Fried, V. H./Bruton. G. D./Hisrich, R, D. (1998): Strategy And The Board Of Directors In Venture capital-backed Firms, in: Journal of Business Venturing, vol. 13, 1998, pp. 493-503.

Fried, V. H./Hisrich, R. D. (1994): Toward a Model of Venture Capital Investment Decision Making, in: Financial Management, vol. 23, 1994, pp. 28-37.

Furubotn, E. G./Pejovich, S. (1972): Property Rights and Economic Theory: A Survey of Recent Literature, in: Journal of Economic Literature, vol. 10, 1972, pp. 1137-1162.

Furubotn, E. G./Richter, R. (2000): Institutions and Economic Theory, Ann Arbor 2000.

Gabrielsson, J./Huse, M. (2002): The venture capitalist and the board of directors in SMEs: roles and processes, in: Venture Capital, vol. 4, 2002, pp. 125-146.

Gaida, M. (2002): How To Venture Capital: Finanzierung Von Start-Ups im Gefüge von Staat, Banken und Börsen. Eine vergleichende Untersuchung der deutschen und US-amerikanischen Unternehmensfinanzierung, Diss., Wiesbaden 2002.

Galbareth, J./Galvin, P. (2004): Which Resources Matter? A Fine-Grained Test Of The Resource-Based View Of The Firm, Academy of Management Proceedings 2004, Business Policy and Strategy Division, pp. L1-L6.

Galbraith, J. A. (1973): Designing Complex Organizations, Addison-Wesley Longman Publishing Co, Boston 1972.

German Corporate Governance Code (GCGC) as amended on May 21, 2003, available at:
http://www.ecgi.org/codes/code.php?code_id=43, call date: 06.01.2006.

Gerum, E./Wagner, H. (1998): Economics of Co-Determination in View of Corporate Governance, in: Hopt, K. J./Kanda, H./Roe, M. J./Wymeersch, E./Prigge, S. (Ed.): Comparative Corporate Governance – The State of the Art and Emerging Research, Oxford 1998, pp. 341-360.

Gibbs, P. A. (1993): Determinants of Corporate Restructuring: The Relative Importance of Corporate Governance, Takeover Threat, and Free Cashflow, in: Strategic Management Journal, vol. 14, 1993, pp. 51-68.

Gifford, S. (1997): Limited Attention And The Role Of The Venture Capitalist, in: Journal of Business Venturing, vol. 12, 1997, pp. 459-482.

Godfrey, P. C./Hill, C. W. L. (1995): The Problem Of Unobservables in Strategic Management Research, in: Strategic Management Journal, vol. 16, 1995, pp. 519-533.

Goergen, M./Manjou, M. C./Renneboog, L. (2004): Recent Developments in German Corporate Governance, ECGI Working Paper Series in Finance, Working paper No. 41/2004, available at:
http://www.ssrn.com/abstract_id=539383, call date: 22.10.2004.

Gompers, P. A. (1995): Optimal Investment, Monitoring, and the Staging of Venture Capital, in: Journal of Finance, vol. 50, 1995, pp. 1461-1489.

Gompers, P. A. (1998): Venture capital growing pains: Should the market diet?, in: Journal of Banking & Finance, vol. 22, 1998, pp. 1089-1104.

Gompers, P. A./Ishii, J. L./Metrick, A. (2003): Corporate Governance and Equity Prices, in: Quarterly Journal of Economics, vol. 118, 2003, pp. 107-155.

Gompers, P. A./Lerner, J. (1996): The Use Of Covenants: An Empirical Analysis of Venture Partnership Agreements, in: Journal of Law and Economics, vol. 39, 1996, pp. 463-499.

Gompers, P. A./Lerner, J. (1999): Am analysis of compensation in the U.S. venture capital partnership, in: Journal of Financial Economics, vol. 51, 1999, pp. 3-44.

Gompers, P. A./Lerner, J. (2001): The Venture Capital Revolution, in: Journal of Economic Perspectives, vol. 15, 2001, pp. 145-168.

Gompers, P./Lerner, J. (2001): The venture capital revolution, in: Journal of Economic Perspective, vol. 15, 2001, pp. 145-168.

Gompers, P./Lerner, J.(2002): The venture capital cycle Cambridge M.A. 2002.

Gorman, M./Sahlman, W. A. (1989): What do Venture Capitalists Do?, in: Journal of Business Venturing, vol. 4, 1989, pp. 231-248.

Grossman, S. J./Hart, O. D. (1983): An Analysis of the Prinicipal–Agent Problem, in: Econometrica, vol. 51, 1983, pp. 7-46.

Grundei, J./Talaulicar, T. (2003): Aufsichtsräte in jungen Technologieunternehmen: Ursachen und Implikationen von Überwachsungsdefiziten, in: FinanzBetrieb, vol. 5, 2003, pp. 190-202.

Grundsatzkomission Corporate Governance (2000): Corproate Governance-Grundsätze ('Code of Best Practice') für börsennotierte Gesellschaften, Frankfurt am Main 2000, available at: http://www.dai.de/internet/dai/dai-20.nsf/LookupDL/9F31DE0AC7378FFDC1256B29005EAA3B/$File/code0700d.pdf, call date: 23.09.2004.

Gugler, K. (2001): Takeovers and the market for corporate control, in: K. Gugler (Ed.): Corporate Governance and Economic Performance, Oxford University Press, Oxford 2001.

Gupta, A. K./Sapienza, H. J. (1992): Determinants Of Venture Capital Firms' Preferences Regarding The Industry Diversity And Geographic Scope of Their Investments, in: Journal of Business Venturing, vol. 7, 1992, pp. 347-362.

Gustafsson, A.-K. (1998): Vilken betydelse har externa riskfinansiärer för styrelsearbetet I SMEs?, Thesis at Halmstadt University.

Hall, R. (1992): The Strategic Analysis Of Intangible Resources, in: Strategic Management Journal, vol. 13, 1992, pp. 135-144.

Hall, R. (1993): A Framework Linking Intangible Resources And Capabilities To Sustainable Competitive Advantage, in: Strategic Management Journal, vol. 14, 1993, pp. 607-618.

Halloran J. M. (1985): Venture Capital And Public Offering Negotiations, 2nd edition (includes 1983 and 1984 supplements), New York/Washington 1985.

Hambrick, D. C. (1987): The Top Management Team: Key to Strategic Success, in: California Management Review, vol. 29, 1987, pp. 88-108.

Harrison, J, (1987): Strategic Use of Corporate Board Committees, in: California Management Review, vol. 29, pp. 109-125.

Hart, O. D. (1983): The Market Mechanism as an Incentive Scheme, in: The Bell Journal of Economics, vol. 14, 1983, pp. 366-382.

Hartmann-Wendels, T. (1987): Venture Capital aus finanzierungstheoretischer Sicht, in: Zeitschrift für betriebswirtschaflichte Forschung, 39. Jg. 1987, pp. 16-31.

Hartzell, J. C./Kallberg, J. G./Liu, C. H. (2004): The Role Of Corporate Governance In Initial Public Offerings: Evidence from Real Estate Investment Trusts, Working Paper, available at: http://papers.ssrn.com/sol3/abstract_id=342700, call date: 27.01.2006.

Hatherly, D./Innes, J./MacAndrew, J./Mitchell, F. (1994): An exploration of the MBO-financial relationship, in: Corporate Governance, vol. 2, 1994, pp. 20-29.

Hayn, M. (1998): Bewertung junger Unternehmen, Diss. Berlin 1998.

He L./Conyon M. J. (2004): CEO Compensation, Incentives. And Governance In New Enterprise Firms, in: Journal of Derivatives Accounting, vol. 1, 2004, pp. 47-60.

Healy, P. M./Wahlen, J. (1999): A review of the earnings management literature and its implications for standard setting, in: Accounting Horizons, vol. 13, 1999, pp. 365-383.

Heim, D. (2001): Private Equity-Fonds in der Portfoliotheorie aus Sicht deutscher Anleger, in: FinanzBetrieb, 3. Jg., 2001. S. 487-495.

Helfat, C. E./Peteraf, M. A. (2002): The Dynamic Resource-Based View: Capability Lifecycles, Tuck School of Business at Dartmouth Working Paper No. 03-08, available at: http://ssrn.com/abstract=386620, call date: 01.02.06.

Hellmann, T. (1998): The allocation of control rights in venture capital contracts, in: RAND Journal of Economics, vol. 29, 1998, pp. 57-76.

Hellmann, T. (2002): A theory of strategic venture investing, in: Journal of Financial Economics, vol. 64, 2002, pp. 285-314.

Hellmann, T./Lindsey, L/Puri, M. (2004): Building Relationships Early: Banks in Venture Capital, Discussion Paper Stanford University, available at: http://papers.ssrn.com/sol3/papers.cfm?abstract_id=474500, call date: 15.10.2005.

Hellmann, T./Puri, M. (2002): Venture Capital and the Professionlisation of Start-Up Firms: Empirical Evidence, in: Journal of Finance, vol. 57, 2002, pp. 169-197.

Hellwig, M. (1991): Banking, financial intermediation and corporate finance, in: A. Giovannini, A./Mayer, .: European financial integration, Cambridge 1991, pp. 35-72.

Hermalin, B. E./Weisbach, M. S. (2001): Boards of Directors as an Endogenously Determined Institution: A Survey of the Economic Literature, Working Paper, available at: http://islandia.law.yale.edu/ccl/papers/pan1.pdf; call date: 20.10.2004.

Hertig, G. (1998): Lenders as A Force in Corporate Governance – Criteria and Practical Examples for Switzerland, in: Hopt, K. J./Kanda, H./Roe, M. J./ Wymeersch, E./Prigge, S. (Ed.): Comparative Corporate Governance – The State of the Art and Emerging Research, Oxford 1998, pp. 809-835.

Higashide, H./Birley, S. (1998): Consequences of Conflicts in the Venture Capitalist-Entrepreneur Team Relationship in the United Kingdom, in: Frontiers of Entrepreneurship Research 1998, Wellesley 1998; available at: http://www.babson.edu/entrep/fer/XVI/XVIA/html/xvi-a.htm, call date: 14.03.05.

Higashide, H./Birley, S. (2002): The consequences of conflict between the venture capitalist and the entrepreneurial team in the United Kingdom from the perspective of the venture capitalist, in: Journal of Business Venturing, vol. 17, 2002, pp. 59-81.

Hill, C. W. L./Snell, S. A. (1988): External Control, Corporate Strategy, And Firm Performance In Research-Intensive Industries, in: Strategic Management Journal, vol. 9, 1988, pp. 577-590.

Hillman, A. J./Canella, A. A./Paetzold, R. L. (2000): The Resource Dependence Role Of Corporate Directors: Strategic Adaptation Of Board Composition In Response To Environmental Chance, in: Journal of Management Studies, vol. 37, 2000, pp. 235-255.

Hillman, A. J./Dalziel, T. (2003): Boards of Directors And Firm Performance: Integrating Agency And Resource Dependence Perspective, in: Academy of Management Review, vol. 28, 2003, pp. 383-396.

Himmelberg, C. P./Hubbard, R. G./Palia, D. (1999): Understanding the determinants of managerial ownership and the link between ownership and performance, in: Journal of Financial Economics, vol. 53, 1999, pp. 353-384.

Hochberg, Y. V. (2002): Venture Capital and Corporate Governance in the Newly Public Firm, Working Paper Stanford University Graduate School of Business, available at: http://www.stanford.edu/group/stvp/research/Hochberg.pdf, call date: 21.02.05.

Hoffmann, G. (2003): Corporate-Governance-Systeme und ihr Einfluss auf die Innovationsfinanzierung, Diss., Wiesbaden 2003.

Holderness, C. G./Sheehan, D. P. (1988): The Role Of Majority Shareholders In Publicly Held Corporations, in: Journal of Political Economics, vol. 20, 1988, pp. 317-346.

Holmström, B. (1979): Moral hazard and observability, in: Bell Journal of Economics, vol. 10, 1979, pp. 74-91.

Holström, B. (1999): Managerial Incentive Problems: A Dynamic Perspective, in: The Review of Economic Studies, vol. 66, 1999, pp. 169-182.

Hommel, U./Ritter, M./Wright, M. (2003): Verhalten der Beteiligungsfinanzierer nach dem "Downturn" – Ergebnisse einer empirischen Untersuchung, in: FinanzBetrieb, 5. Jg., 2003, pp. 323-333.

Hopt, K. J. (1998): The German Two-Tier Board: Experience, Theories, Reforms, in: Hopt, K. J./Kanda, H./Roe, M. J./Wymeersch, E./Prigge, S. (Ed.): Comparative Corporate Governance – The State of the Art and Emerging Research, Oxford 1998, pp. 227-258.

Hopt, K./Wymeersch, E. (1997): Comparative Corporate Governance: Essays and Materials, Hrsg., Berlin/New York 1997.

Hosmer, D. W./Lemeshow, S. (1989): Applied Logistic Regression – Whiley Series in Probability and Mathematical Statistics, New York 1989.

Hsu, D. H. (2004): What Do Entrepreneurs Pay for Venture Capital Affiliation, in: Journal of Finance, vol. 59, 2004, pp. 1805-1844.

Huber, T./Böhler, C. (2003): Externe Berichterstattung und Corporate Governance von Private Equity Funds – Anforderungen und Erwartungen der Schweizer Investoren, in: Der Schweizer Treuhänder, 8. Jg., 2003, pp. 1000-1006.

Hung, H. (1998): A typology of the theories of the roles of governing boards, in: Corporate Governance, vol. 6, 1998, pp. 101-111.

Huse, M. (2000): Boards of directors in SMEs: a review and research agenda, In. Entrepreneurship & Regional Development, vol. 12, 2000, pp. 271-290.

Huse, M. (2005): Corporate Governance: Understanding Important Contingencies, in: Corporate Ownership & Control, vol. 2, 2005, pp. 41-50.

Huse, M./Landström, H. (2002): Teaching Corporate Governance: Challenges For Research and Practice, Paper presented at EURAM conference Stockholm 2002, available at: http://www.ecsocman.edu.ru/images/pubs/2002/12/11/0000015723/ corp_gov_teaching.pdf, call date: 31.10.2005

Huson, M. R./Parrino, R./Starks, L. T. (2001): Internal Monitoring Mechanisms and CEO Turnover: A Long-Term Perspective, in: Journal of Finance, vol. 56, 2001, pp. 2265-2297.

Ingley, C. B./Van der Walt, N. T. (2001): The Strategic Board: the changing role of directors in developing and maintating corporate capability, in: Corporate Governance, vol. 9, 2001, pp. 174-185.

Ingley, C. B./Van der Walt, N. T. (2003): Do Board Processes Influence Director and Board Performance? Statutory and performance implications, in: Corporate Governance, vol. 13, 2005, pp. 632-653.

Jackson, S. E./Dutton, J. E. (1988): Discerning Threats and Opportunities, in: Administrative Science Quarterly, vol. 33, 1988, pp. 370-387.

Jain, B. A. (2001): Predictors of performance of venture capital-backed organizations, in: Journal of Business Research, vol. 52, 2001, pp. 223-233.

Janssen, J./Laatz, W. (2003): Statistische Datenanalyse mit SPSS für Windows, 4. Auflage, Berlin 2003.

Jeng, L. A./Wells, P. C. (2000): The determinants of venture capital funding: evidence across countries, in: Journal of Corporate Finance, vol. 6, 2000, pp. 241-289.

Jensen, M. C. (1986): Agency Costs of Free Cashflow, Corporate Finance, and Takeovers, American Economic Review, vol. 76, 1986, pp. 323-329.

Jensen, M. C. (1993): The Modern Industrial Revolution, Exit, and the Failure of Internal Control System, in: Journal of Finance, vol. 48, pp. 831-880.

Jensen, M. C./Meckling, W. H. (1976): Theory of the Firm: Managerial Behavior, Agency Costs And Ownership Structure, in: Journal of Financial Economics, vol. 3, 1976, pp. 305-360.

Jensen, M. C./Warner. J. B. (1988): The Distribution of Power Among Corporate Managers, Shareholders, And Directors, in: Journal of Financial Economics, vol. 20, 1988, pp. 3-24.

Jensen, M./Ruback, R. S. (1983): The market for corporate control: the scientific evidence, In. Journal of Financial Economics, vol. 11, 1983, pp. 5-50.

Joh, S. W. (2003): Corporate governance and firm profitability: evidence from Korea before the economic crisis, in: Journal of Financial Economics, vol. 68, 2003, pp. 287-322.

John, K./Lang, L. H. P./Netter, J. (1992): The Voluntary Restructuring of Large Firms in Response to Performance Decline, in: Journal of Finance, vol. 47, 1992, pp. 891-917.

Johnson, J. L./Daily, C. M./Ellstrand, A. E. (1996): Boards of Directors: A Review and Research Agenda, in: Journal of Management, vol. 22, 1996, pp. 409-438.

Johnson, R. A./Hoskisson, R. E./Hitt, M. A. (1993): Board of Director Involvement in Restructuring: The Effects of Board versus Managerial Control and Characteristics, in: Strategic Management Journal, vol. 14, Special Issue Summer 1993, pp. 33-50.

Johnson, R. B./Onwuegbuzie, A. J. (2004): Mixed Methods Research: A Research Paradigm Whose Time Has Come, In: Educational Researcher, Vol. 33, 2004, pp. 14-26.

Judge, W. Q./Miller, A. (1991): Antecedents And Outcomes Of Decision Speed In Different Environmental Contexts, in: Academy of Management Journal, vol. 34, 1991, 449-463.

Judge, W. Q./Zeithaml, C. P. (1992): Institutional And Strategic Choice Perspectives On Board Involvement In The Strategic Decision Process, in: Academy of Management Journal, vol. 35, 1992, pp. 766-794.

Kale, J. R./Noe, T. H./Ramirez, G. G. (1991): The Effect of Business Risk on Corporate Capital Structure : Theory and Evidence, in: Journal of Finance, vol. 46, 1991, pp. 1693-1715.

Kanniainen, V./Keuschnigg, C. (2003): The optimal portfolio of start-up firms in venture capital finance, in: Journal of Corporate Finance, vol. 9, 2003, pp. 521-534.

Kaplan, S. N./Reishus. D. (1990): Outside directorships and corporate performance, in: Journal of Financial Economics, vol. 27, 1990, pp. 389-410.

Kaplan, S. N./Strömberg, P. (2001): Venture Capitalists as Principals: Contracting, Screening, and Monitoring, in: American Economic Review, vol. 91, 2001, pp. 426-430.

Kaplan, S. N./Strömberg, P. (2003): Financial Contracting Theory Meets the Real World: An Empirical Analysis of Venture Capital Contracts, in: Review of Economic Studies (2003), vol. 70, pp. 281-315.

Kaplan, S. N./Strömberg, P. (2004): Characteristics, Contracts, and Actions: Evidence from Venture Capitalist Analyses, in: Journal of Finance vol. 59, 2004, pp. 2177-2209.

Kenney, M. (2000): Note on „Venture Capital", BRIE Working Paper142, E-conomy Project Working Paper 17, University of California, Berkeley, available at: http://e-conomy.berkeley.edu/publications/wp/wp142.pdf, call date: 01.08.2004.

Kiel, G. C./Nicholson, G. J. (2005): Evaluating Boards and Directors, in: Corporate Governance, vol. 13, 2005, pp. 613-631.

Kirzner, I. M. (1997): Entrepreneurial Discovery and the Competitive Market Process: An Austrian Approach, in: Journal of Economic Literature, vol. 35, 1997, pp. 60-85.

Klapper, L. F./Love, I. (2002): Corporate Governance, Investor Protection, and Performance in Emerging Countries, World Bank Policy Research Working Paper 2818, April 2002, available at: http://econ.worldbank.org; call date: 07.03.200.

Klein, B./Crawford, R. G./Alchian, A. A. (1978): Vertical Integration, Appropriable Rents, and the Competitive Contracting Process, in: The Journal of Law and Economics, vol. 26, 1978, pp. 297-326.

Klein, B./Leffler, K. (1981): The Role of Market Forces in Assuring Contractual Performance, in: Journal of Political Economy, vol. 89, 1981, pp. 615-641.

Knott, A. M./Bryce, D. J./Posen, H. E. (2003): On the Strategic Accumulation of Intangible Assets, in: Organization Science, vol. 14, 2003, pp. 192-207.

Kozer, M. (2002): Corporate Governance: Das Zusammenspiel von Internal Control und External Control, Diss., Aachen 2002.

Kraft, M. (1997): Der Ansatz der Logistischen Regression, in: Zeitschrift für Betriebswirtschaft, 67. Jg, pp. 636-641.

Kraft, V. (2001): Private Equity-Investitionen in Turnarounds und Restrukturierungen, Diss., Frankfurt am Main 2001.

Kroll, M./Wright, P./Toombs, L./Leavell, H. (1997): Forms of Control: A Critical Determinant of Acquisition Performance and CEO Rewards, in: Strategic Management Journal, vol. 18, 1997, pp. 85-96.

Krosnick, J. A./Fabrigar, L. R. (1997): Designing Rating Scales for Effective Measurement in Surveys, in: Lyberg, L./Biemer, P./Collins, M./Decker, L./ DeLeeuw, E./Dippo, C./Schwarz, N./Trewin, D. (Eds.): Survey Measurement and Process Quality. New York, 1997.

Kroszner, R. S./Strahan, P. E. (2001): Bankers on boards: monitoring, conflicts of interst and lender liability, in: Journal of Financial Economics, vol. 62, 2001, pp. 415-452.

Küting, K. (2000b): Möglichkeiten und Grenzen der Bilanzanalyse am neuen Markt (Teil II), in: Finanz Betrieb, 2. Jg., 2000, pp. 674-683.

La Porta, R./Lopez-de-Silanes, F./Shleifer, A./Vishny, R. W. (1998): Law and Finance, in: Journal of Political Economy, vol. 106, pp. 1113-1155.

La Porta, R./Lopez-de-Silanes, Fö./Shleifer, A./Vishny, R. (2000): Investor protection and corporate governance, in: Journal of Financial Economics, vol. 58, 2000, pp. 3-27.

Landström, H. (1993): Informal Risk Capital In Sweden And Some International Comparisons; In: Journal of Business Venturing, vol. 8, 1993, pp. 525-540.

Langberg, M. (2006): Why Enron wouldn't happen in the valley, in: San Jose Mercury News, 26.05.2006.

Lee, C./Lee, K./Pennings, J. M. (2001): Internal Capabilities, External Networks, And Performance: A Study on Technology-Based Ventures, in: Strategic Management Journal, vol. 22, 2001, pp. 615-640.

Leland, H. E./Pyle, D. H. (1977): Informational Asymmetries, Financial Structure, And Financial Intermediation, in: Journal of Finance, vol. 32, 1977, pp. 371-387.

Leleux, B./Surlemont, B. (2003): Public Versus Private Venture Capital: Seeding Or Crowding Out? A Pan-European Analysis, in: Journal of Business Venturing, Vol 18, 2003, pp. 81-104.

Lengström, D./Platin, J. (2000): Riskkapitalisters aktivitet i portföljbolagens styrelse, Thesis at Halmstadt University.

Lerner, J. (1994): The Syndication of Venture Capital Investments, in: Financial Management, vol. 23, 2994, pp. 16-27.

Lerner, J. (1995): Venture Capital and the Oversight of Private Firms, in: The Journal of Finance, Vo. 50, 1995, pp. 301-318.

Lerner, J. (1998): “Angel” financing and public policy: An overview, in: Journal of Banking & Finance, vol. 22, 1998, pp. 773-783.

Lerner, J. (1999): The government as venture capitalist: The long-run effects of the SBIR program, in: Journal of Business, vol. 72, 1999, pp. 285-318.

Lippert, R. L./Moore, W. T. (1995):Monitoring versus Bonding – shareholder rights and management compensation, In: Financial Management, Vol. 24, 1995, pp. 54-62.

Lippman S. A./Rumelt, R. P. (1982): Uncertain imitability: an analysis of interfirm differences in efficiency under competition, in: Bell Journal of Economics, vol. 13, 1982, pp. 418-438.

Lockett, A./Thompson, S. (2001): The Resource-Based View and Economics, in: Jopurnal of Management, vol. 27, pp. 723-754.

Long, T./Dulewicz, V./Gay, K. (2005): The Role of the Non-executive Director: findings of an empirical investigation into the differences between listed and unlisted UK boards, in: Corporate Governance, vol. 13, 2005, pp. 667-679.

Lynall, M. D./Golden, B. R./Hillman, A. J. (2003): Board Composition From Adolescence To Maturity: A Multitheoretic View, in: Academy of Management Review, vol. 28, pp. 416-431.

Macmillan, I. C./Khulow, D./Khoylian, R. (1988): Venture Capitalists' involvement in their investments: Extent and performance, in: Journal of Business Venturing, vol. 4, 1988, pp. 27-47.

Macmillan, I. C./Zeman, L./Subbanarasimha, P. N. (1987): Criteria Distinguishing Successful From Unsuccessful Ventures In The Venture Screening Process, in: Journal of Business Venturing, vol. 2, 1987, pp. 123-137.

Makadok, R. (2001): Towards A Synthesis Of The Resource-Based And Dynamic Capability Views of Rent Creation, in: Strategic Management Journal, vol. 22, 2001, pp. 387-401.

Manigart, S. (1994): The Founding Rate Of Venture Capital Firms In Three European Countries (1970-1990), in: Journal of Business Venturing, vol. 9, 1994, pp. 525-541.

Manigart, S. /Lockett, A./Meuleman, M./Wright, M./Landström, H./Bruining, H./Desbrières, P./Hommel, U. (2002): Why Do European Venture Capital Comapanies Syndicate?, ERIM Report Series Research in Management, ERS-2002-98-ORG, Erasmus Universiteit Rotterdam 2002.

Manigart, S./De Waele, K./Wright, M./Robbie, K./Dsbrières P./Sapienza, H. J./Beekman, A. (2002): Determinants of required return in venture capital investments: a five-country study, in: Journal of Business Venturing, vol. 17, 2002, pp. 291-312.

March, J. G./Simon, H. A. (1958): Organizations, John Wiley, New York 1958.

Markman, G. D./Balkin, D. B./Schjoedt, L. (2001): Governing the innovation process in entrepreneurial firms, in: Journal of High Technology Management Research, vol. 12, 2001, pp. 273-293.

Martens, M. L./Arcand, J. P./Walker, T. J. (2005): Institutional and Strategic Consequences of Founder-CEO Transition Decisions in IPO Firms, Paper presented at the Babson Kauffman Entrepreneurship Research Conference, Wellesley, MA, 2005.

Mathews, J. A. (2002): A resource-based view of Schumpeterian economic dynamics, in: Journal of Evolutionary Economic, vol. 12, 2002, pp. 39-54.

May, A. (1991): Zum Stand der empirischen Forschung über Informationsverarbeitung am Aktienmarkt – Ein Überblick, in: Zeitschrift für betriebswirtschaftliche Forschung, 43. Jg., 1991, pp. 313-359.

McConell, J. J./Servaes, H. (1990): Additional evidence on equity ownership and corporate value, in: Journal of Financial Economics, vol. 27, 1990, pp. 595-612.

McGee, J. E./Megginson, W. L. (1995): Cooperative Strategy And New Venture Performance: The Role Of Business Strategy And Management Experience, in: Strategic Management Journal, vol. 16, 1995, pp. 565-580.

McGuire, J. (2000): Corporate Governance and Growth Potential: an empirical analysis, in: Corporate Governance, vol. 8, 2000, pp. 32-42.

Melin, L./Nordqvist, M. (2002): The Role of Cultural and Institutional Processes in Shaping Corporate Governance Systems in Family Firms, Paper presented at the Academic Research Forum, FBN Annual World Conference, Helsinki 2002, available at:
http://cref.u-bordeaux4.fr/Nouveau%20Site/ARTICLES/
Melin%20et%20Nordqvist% 202002.pdf, call date: 31.10.2005.

Michalisin, M. D./Smith, R. D./Kline, D. M. (1997): N Search of Strategic Assets, in: International Journal of Organizational Analysis, vol. 5, 1997, pp. 360-387.

Miller, D./Shamsie, J. (1996): The Resource-Based View Of The Firm In Two Environments: The Hollywood Film Studios From 1936 to 1956, in: Academy of Management Journal, vol. 39, pp. 519-543.

Modigliani, F./Miller, M. H. (1958): The Cost Of Capital, Corporate Finance And The Theory Of Investment, in: American Economic review, vol. 48, 1958, pp. 261-297.

Morck, R./Shleifer, A./Vishny, R. W. (1988): Management Ownership And Market Valuation – An Empirical Analysis, in: Journal of Financial Economics, vol. 20, 1988, pp. 293-315.

Murphy, K. J. (2003): Stock-based pay in new economy firms, in: Journal of Accounting and Economics, vol. 34, 2003, pp. 129-147.

MxCulloch, C. E./Searle, S. R. (2000): Generalized, Linear, and Mixed Models, New York, 2000.

Nelson, R./Winter, S. (1982): An Evolutionary Theory of Economic Change, Cambridge 1982.

Neubauer, F. F./Lank, A. G. (1998): The Family Business – Its Governance for Sustainability, New York 1998.

Nicholson, G. J./Kiel, G. C. (2004): A Frameworkfor Diagnosing Board Effectiveness, in: Corporate Governance, vol. 12, 2004, pp. 442-460.

Norusis, M. J. (2006): SPSS 14.0 Advanced Statistical Procedures Companion. New York 2006.

OECD (2003): Survey of corporate governance developments in OECD countries, available at:
http://www.oecd.org/topic/
0,2686,en_2649_37439_1_1_1_1_37439,00.html, call date: 20.10.2004.

OECD Principles of Corporate Governance, version of 2004, available at:
http://www.ecgi.org/codes/code.php?code_id=87, call date. 06.10.2006.

Ooghe, H./Manigart, S./Fassin, Y. (1991): Growth Patterns Of The European Venture Capital Industry, in: Journal of Business Venturing, vol. 6, 1991 S. 381-404.

Peck, S. J./Ruigrok, W. (2000): Hiding behind the Flag? Prospects for Change in German Corporate Governance, in: European Management Journal, vol. 18, 2000, pp. 420-430.

Peteraf, M. A. (1993): The Cornerstones Of Competitive Advantage: A Resource-Based View, in: Strategic Management Journal, vol. 14, 179-191.

Peteraf, M. A./Bergen, M. E. (2003): Scanning Dynamic Competitive Landscapes: A Market-Based And Resource-Based Framework, in: Strategic Management Journal, vol. 24, 2003, pp. 1027-1041.

Pfeffer, J. (1972): Size and Composition of Corporate Boards of Directors: The Organization and its Environment, in: Administrative Science Quarterly, vol. 17, pp. 218-228.

Picot, A. (1982): Transaktionskosten in der Organisationstheorie: Stand der Diskussion und Aussagewert, in: Die Betriebswirtschaft, 42. Jg., 1982, pp. 267-284.

Polanyi, M. (1962): Personal Knowledge, Routledge and Paul Kegan, London 1962.

Pollok, T. G./Baker, T./Fund, B. R.: Who's Minding the Store? Venture Capitalist Styles And The Replacement of Founder-CEOs, Paper presented at the Babson Kauffman Entrepreneurship Research Conference, Wellesley, MA. 2005.

Potthoff, E./Trescher, K./Theisen, M. R. (2003): Das Aufsichtsratsmitglied – Ein Handbuch der Aufgaben, Rechten und Pflichten, Stuttgart 2003.

Powell, T. C. (1992): Organizational Alignment As Competitive Advantage, in: Stratefic Management Journal, vol. 13, 1992, pp. 119-134.

Prigge, S. (1998): A Survey of German Corporate Governance, in: Hopt, K. J./ Kanda, H./Roe, M. J./Wymeersch, E./Prigge, S. (Ed.): Comparative Corporate Governance – The State of the Art and Emerging Research, Oxford 1998, pp. 943-1044.

Rau-Bredow, H. (1992): Zur theoretischen Fundierung der Institutionenökonomie, Diss., München 1992.

Rechner, P. L./Dalton, D. R. (1990): CEO Duality And Organizational Performance: A Longitudinal Analysis, in: Strategic Management Journal, vol. 12, 1990, pp. 155-160.

Rediker, K. J./Seth, A. (1993): Boards Of Directors And Substitution Effects Of Alternative Governance Mechanisms, in: Strategic Management Journal, vol. 16, 1993, pp. 85-99.

Regierungskommission Corporate Governance (2001): Unternehmensführung – Unternehmenskontrolle – Modernisierung des Aktienrechts – Bericht der Regierungskommission „Corporate Governance, Berlin 2001, available at: http://www.jura.uni-duesseldorf.de/dozenten/noack/texte/cg/komplett.doc, call date: 23.09.04.

Regierungskommission Deutscher Corporate Governance Kodex (2002): Deutscher Corporate Governance Kodex vom 07. November 2002.

Richter, R./Furubotn, E. G. (2003): Neue Institutionenökonomik: eine Einführung und kritische Würdigung, Tübingen 2003.

Riekert, P. D. (2004): Venture Governance, Diss., Wiesbaden 2004.

Ringleb, H. M./Kremer, T./Lutter, M./v. Werder, A. (2003): Kommentar zum Deutschen Corporate Governance Kodex, München 2003.

Roberts, E. B. (1991): High Stakes for High-Tech Entrepreneurs: Understanding Venture Capital Decision Making, in: Sloan Management Review, vol. 32, 1991, pp. 9-20.

Robinson, R. B. Jr. (1987): Emerging Strategies In The Venture Capital Industry, in: Journal of Business Venturing, vol. 2, 1987, pp. 53-77.

Roe, M. J. (1998): German Co-Determination and German Securities Markets, in: Hopt, K. J./Kanda, H./Roe, M. J./Wymeersch, E./Prigge, pp. (Ed.): Comparative Corporate Governance – The State of the Art and Emerging Research, Oxford 1998, pp. 361-372.

Rosenstein, J. (1988): The Board And Strategy: Venture Capital And High Technology, in: Journal of Business Venturing, vol. 3, 1988, pp. 159-170.

Rosenstein, J./Bruno, A. V./Bygrave, W./Taylor, N. (1993): The CEO, Venture Capitalists, And The Board, in: Journal of Business Venturing, vol. 8, 1993, S: 99-113.

Rosenstein, S./Wyatt, J. G. (1990): Outside Directors, board independence, and shareholder wealth, in: Journal of Financial Economics, vol. 26, 1990, pp. 175-191.

Ross, S. A. (1973): The Economic Theory of Agency: The Principal's Problem, in: American Economic Review, vol. 63, 1973, pp. 134-139.

Ruhnka, J. C./Young, J. E. (1987): A Venture Capital Model Of The Development, in: Journal of Business Venturing, vol. 2, 1987, pp. 167-184.

Ruhnka, J. C./Young, J. E. (1991): Some Hypotheses About Risk in Venture Capital Investing, in: Journal of Business Venturing, vol. 6, 1991, pp. 115-133.

Ruppen, D. (2001): Corporate Governance bei Venture Capital-finanzierten Unternehmen, Diss., St. Gallen 2001.

Sahlman, W. A. (1990): The structure and governance of venture-capital organizations, in: Journal of Financial Economics, vol. 27, 1990, pp. 473-521.

Salop, J./Salop, S. (1976): Self-Selection and Turnover in the Labor Market, in: Quarterly Journal of Economics, vol. 90, 1976, pp. 619-628.

Sapienza, H. J. (1992): When Do Venture Capitalists Add Value, in: Journal of Business Venturing, vol. 7, 1992, pp. 9-27.

Sapienza, H. J./Gupta, A. K. (1994): Impact of Agency Risks and Task Uncertainty on Venture Capitalist-CEO Interaction, in: Academy of Management Journal, Vol 37, 1994, pp. 1618-1632.

Sapienza, H. J./Korsgaard M. A./Goulet, P. K./Hoogendam, J. P. (2000): Effects of agency risk and procedural justice on board processes in venture capital-backed firms, in: Entrepreneurship & Regional Development, vol. 12, 2000, pp. 331-351.

Sapienza, H. J./Manigart, S./Vermeir, W. (1996): Venture Capitalist Governance And Value Added in Four Countries, in: Journal of Business Venturing, vol. 11, 1996, pp. 439-469.

Sapienza, H. J./Timmons, J. A. (1989): The Roles of the Venture Capitalists in New Ventures: What Determines Their Importance?, in: Academy of Management Best Papers Proceedings, pp.74-78.

Schefczyk, M. (2000): Erfolgsstrategien deutscher Venture Capital-Gesellschaften, 2. Auflage, Stuttgart 2000.

Schenk, G. (2003): Standardisierung im Berichtswesen, in: A. K. Achleitner/A. Bassen: Controlling von jungen Unternehmen, Stuttgart 2003, pp. 397-421.

Schmidt, D./Wahrenburg, M. (2003): Contractual Relations between European VC-Funds and Investors: The Impact of Reputation and Bargaining Power on Contractual Design, CFS Working Paper No. 2003/15, Center for Financial Studies, Johann Wolfgang Goethe Universität Frankfurt am Main 2003.

Schmidt, R. H. (1985): Venture-Capital aus der Sicht der Finanzierungstheorie, in: Betriebswirtschaftliche Forschung und Praxis, 37. Jg. 1985, pp. 421-437.

Schmidt, R. H. (2001): Kontinuität und Wandel bei der Corporate Governance in Deutschland, in: Neuere Ansätze der Betriebswirtschaftslehre – in memoriam Karl Hax, Gruppe Handelsblatt, Düsseldorf 2001, pp. 61-87.

Schoppe, S. G./Waas von Czege, A. G./Münchow, M. M./ Stein, I./Zimmer, K. (1995): Moderne Theorie der Unternehmung, Wien 1995.

Shane, S. (2000): Prior Knowledge and the Discovery of Entrepreneurial Opportunities, in: Organizational Science, vol. 11, 2000, pp. 448-469.

Shane, S./Cable, D. (2002): Network Ties, Reputation, and the Financing of New Ventures, in: Management Science, vol. 48, 2002, pp. 364-381.

Shane, S./Venkataraman, S. (2000): The Promise of Entrepereneurship As A Field Of Research, in: Academy of Management Review, Vol. 25, pp. 217-226.

Shen, W. (2003): The Dynamics Of The CEO-Board Relationship: An Evolutionary Perspective, in: Academy of Management Review, vol. 28, 2003, pp. 466-476.

Shepherd, D. A./Zacharakis, A./Baron, R. A. (2003): VCs' decision processes: Evidence suggesting more experience may not always be better, in: Journal of Business Venturing, vol. 18, 2003, pp. 381-401.

Shleifer, A./Vishny, R. V. (1997): A Survey of Corporate Governance, in: Journal of Finance, vol. 52, 1997, pp. 737-783.

Shleifer, A./Vishny, R. W. (1986): Large Shareholders and Corporate Control, in: Journal of Political Economy, vol. 94, 1986, pp. 461-488.

Short, H./Keasy, K./Wright, M./Hull, A. (1999): Corporate governance: from accountability to enterprise, in: Accounting and Business Research, vol. 29, 1999, pp. 337-352.

Sirmon, D. G./Hitt, M. A. (2003): Managing Resources: Linking Unique Resources, Management, and Wealth Creation in Family Firms, in: Entrepreneurship Theory and Practice, vol. 27, 2003, pp. 339-358.

Sloan, R. G. (2001): Financial accounting and corporate governance: a discussion, in: Journal of Accounting and Economics, vol. 32, 2001, pp. 335-347.

Smith, A. (1776): An Inquiry into the Nature and Causes of the Wealth of Nations, zitiert nach der fünften Auflage (1789), available at: http://www.econlib.org/library/Smith/smWNtoc.html, call date: 02.08.2004.

Smith, C./Watts, R. L. (1992): The investment opportunity set and corporate financing, dividend and compensation policies, in: Journal of Financial Economics, vol. 32, 1992, pp. 263-292.

Smith, J. K./Smith, R. L. (2000): Entrepreneurial Finance, New York 2000.

Spreemann, K. (1990): Asymmetrische Information, in: Zeitschrift für Betriebswirtschaftslehre, 60. Jg. 1990, pp. 561-586

Stiglitz, J. E. (1974): On the Irrelevance of Corporate Finance Policy, in: American Economic Review, vol. 64, 1974, pp. 851-866.

Strieder, T. (2004): Erläuterungen zum Deutschen Corporate Governance Kodex, in: FinanzBetrieb, 6. Jg., 2004, pp. 13-27.

Stulz, R. M. (1987): Managerial Control Of Voting Rights – Financing Policies and the Market for Corporate Control, in: Journal of Financial Economics, vol. 20, 1988, pp. 25-54.

Sundaramurthy, C./Lewis, M. (2003): Control And Collaboration: Paradoxes Of Governance, in: Academy of Management Review, vol. 28, 2003, pp. 397-415.

Sweeting, R. C./Wong, C. F. (1997): A UK 'Hands-Off' Venture Capital Firm and the Handling of Post-Investment Investor-Investee Relationships, in: Journal of Management Studies, vol. 34, 1997, pp. 125-152,

Sykes, H. B. (1990): Corporate Venture Capital: Strategies For Success, in: Journal of Business Venturing, vol. 5 (1990), pp. 37-47.

Sykes, H. B. (1992): Incentive Compensation For Corporate Venture Personnel, in: Journal of Business Venturing, vol. 7, pp. 253-265.

Sykes, H. B./Block, Z. (1989): Corporate Venturing Obstacles: Sources And Solutions, in: Journal of Business Venturing, vol. 4, 1989, pp. 159-167.

Talaulicar, T./Grundei, J./v. Werder, A. (2001): Corporate Governance deutscher Start-ups: Ergebnisse einer empirischen Erhebung, in: Finanzbetrieb, 3. Jg., 2001, pp. 511-519.

Teece, D. J./Pisano, G./Shuen, A. (1997): Dynamic Capabilities and Strategic Management, in: Strategic Management Journal, vol. 18, 1997, pp. 509-533.

Temprorale, R./Ismann, B. (1999): Zulassungsvoraussetzungen und Folgepflichten im Rahmen des IPO konkretisiert am Neuen Markt, in: FinanzBetrieb, 1. Jg., 1999, pp. 263-265.

Theisen, R. M. (2003): Herausforderung Corporate Governance, in: Die Betriebswirtschaft, 63. Jg., 2003, pp. 441-464.

Tirole, J. (2001): Corporate Governance, in: Econometrica, vol. 69, 2001, pp. 1-35.

Tomer, J. F. (1987): Organizational Capital, Praeger, New York 1987.

Triantis, G. G. (2001): Financial Contract Design in the World of Venture Capital, in: University of Chicago Law Review, vol. 68, 2001, pp. 305-323.

Tykvova, T. (2004): Who Are the True Venture Capitalists in Germany? ZEW – Centre for European Economic Research Discussion Paper No. 04-16, available at: ftd://ftp.zew.de/pub/zew-docs/dp/dp0416.pdf; call date: 01.03.2005.

Ueda, M. (2004): Banks versus Venture Capital: Project Evaluation, Screening, and Expropriation, in: Journal of Finance vol. 59, 2004, pp. 601-621.

Van den Berghe, L. /Levrau, A. (2002): The Role of the Venture Capitalist as Monitor of the Company: a corporate governance perspective, in: Corporate Governance, vol. 10, 2002, pp. 124-135.

Van den Berghe, L./Levrau, A. (2004): Evaluating Boards of Directors: what constitutes a good corporate board, in: Corporate Governance, vol. 12, 2004, pp. 461-478.

Verbeke, G., and Molenberghs, G. (2000): Linear Mixed Models for Longitudial Data, New York 2000.

Von Osnabrugge, M. (1999): A Comparison of Business Angel And Venture Capitalist Investment Procedures: An Agency Theory-Based Analysis, in: Frontiers of Entrepreneurship Research 1999, Wellesley 1999; available at: http://www.babson.edu/entrep/fer/papers99/award%203/award3.html, call date: 14.03.05.

Walker, G./Weber, D. (1984): A Transaction Cost Approach to Make-or-Buy Decisions, in: Administrative Science Quarterly, vol. 29, 1984, pp. 373-391.

Wallman, M. H. (2005): A New Approach To Building Shareholder Value, in: The Corporate Board, 7-8/2005, pp. 1-6.

Walsh, J. P./Seward, J. K. (1990): On the Efficiency of Internal and External Corporate Control Mechanisms, in: Academy of Management Review, vol. 15, 1990, pp. 421-458.

Wang, S./Zhou, H. (2004): Staged financing in venture capital: moral hazard and risks, in: Journal of Corporate Finance, vol. 10, 2004, pp. 131-155.

Weber, C. (2002): Diversifikation versus Spezialisierung – Vorteilhaftigkeit von Portfoliostrategien bei Venture Capital Investments, Diss., Hamburg 2002.

Weil, Gotshal & Manges (2002): Comparative Study of Corporate Governance Codes Relevant to the European Union and its Member States, Final Report & Annexes I-III on behalf of the European Commission, Internal Market Directorate General, available at: http://www.ecgi.org/codes/code.php?code_id=25, call date: 06.01.06.

Weimer, J./Pape. J. C. (1999): A Taxonomy of Systems of Corporate Governance, in: Corporate Governance, vol. 7, 1999, pp. 152-166.

Welbourne, T. M./Cyr, L. A. (1999): The Human Resource Executive Effect in Initial Pubic Offering Firms, in: Academy of Management Journal, vol. 42, 1999, pp. 616-629.

Wernerfelt, B. (1984): A Resource-based View of the Firm, in: Strategic Management Journal, vol. 5, 1984, pp. 171-180.

Westphal, J. D. (1999): Collaboration In The Boardroom: Behavioral And Performance Consequences Of CEO-Board Social Ties, in: Academy of Management Journal, vol. 42, 1999, pp. 7-24.

Wetzel, W. E. Jr. (1987): The Informal Venture Capital Market: Aspects Of Scale And Market Efficiency, in: Journal of Business Venturing, vol. 2, 1987, pp. 299-313.

Whincop, M. J. (2000): Entrepreneurial Governance, Working Paper, available at: http://ssrn.com/abstract=254169, call date: 14.03.05.

Wilhelm, J. E. M. (1985): Arbitrage theory: introductory lectures on arbitrage-based financial asset pricing, Berlin 1985.

Williamson, O. E. (1975): Markets and hierarchies, analysis and antitrust implications, New York 1975.

Williamson, O. E. (1981): The Economics of Organization: The Transaction Cost Approach, in: American Journal of Sociology, vol. 87, 1981, pp. 548-577.

Williamson, O. E. (1985): The Economic Institutions of Capitalism– Firms, Markets, Relational Contracting, New York/London 1985.

Winter, S. G. (2003): Understanding Dynamic Capabilities, in: Strategic Management Journal, vol. 24, 2003, pp. 991-995.

Winters, T. E./Murfin, D. L. (1988): Venture Capital Investing For Corporate Development Objectives, in: Journal of Business Venturing, vol. 3, pp. 207-222.

Wiseman, R. M./Gomez-Mejia, L. R. (1998): A Behavioural Agency Model of Managerial Risk Taking, in: Academy of Management Review, vol. 23, 1998, pp. 133-153.

Witt, P. (2003): Corporate Governance-Systeme im Wettbewerb, Wiesbaden 2003.

Witt, P./Brachtendorf, G. (2002): Gründungsfinanzierung durch Großunternehmen, in: Die Betriebswirtschaft, vol. 62, pp. 681-692.

Worldbank (1999): Corporate Governance – A Framework for Implementation – Overview, available at: http://www.worldbank.org/html/fpd/privatesector/cg/docs/gcgfbooklet.pdf, call date: 02.08.2004.

Wright, M./Lockett, A. (2003): The Strutuce and Management of Alliances: Syndication in the Venture Capital Industry, in: Journal of Management Studies, vol. 40, 2003, pp. 2073-2102.

Wright, M./Robbie, K. (1998): Venture Capital And Private Equity: A Review And Synthesis, in: Journal of Business Finance and Accounting, vol. 25, 1998, pp. 521-569.

Wright, P./Ferris, S. P./Sarin, A./Awasti, V. (1996): Impact of Corporate Insider, Blockholder and Institutional Equity Ownership on Firm Risk Taking, in: Academy of Management Journal, vol. 29, 1996, pp. 441-463.

Yermack, D. (1996): Higher market valuation of companies with a small board of directors, in: Journal of Financial Economics, vol. 40, 1996, pp. 185-211.

Yerramilli, V. (2004): Joint control and redemption rights in venture capital contracts, ECGI Finance Working Paper No. 37/2004, available at: http://ssrn.com/abstract=481362, call date: 27.01.2006.

Zacharakis, A./Shepherd, D. A: (2005): A non-additive decision-aid for venture capitalists' investment decisions, in: European Journal of Operational Research, vol. 162, 2005, pp. 673-689.

Zahra, S. A. (1991): Predictors And Financial Outcomes Of Corporate Entrepreneurship: An Explanatory Study, in: Journal of Business Venturing, vol. 6, 1991, pp. 259-285.

Zahra, S. A./Neubaum, D. O./Huse, M. (2000): Entrepreneurship in Medium-Size Comapnies: Exploring the Effects of Ownership and Governance Systems, in: Journal of Management, vol. 26, 2000, pp. 947-976.

Zahra, S. A./Pearce/John A. II. (1989): Boards of Directors and Corporate Financial Performance: A Review and Integrative Model; In: Journal of Management, vol. 15, 1989, pp. 291-334.

Zemke, I. (1995): Die Unternehmensverfassung von Beteiligungskapital-Gesellschaften: Analyse des institutionellen Designs deutscher Venture Capital-Gesellschaften, Diss., Wiesbaden 1995.

Zider, B. (1998): How Venture Capital Works, in: Harvard Business Review, vol. 76, 1998, pp. 131-139.

MIX
Papier aus verantwortungsvollen Quellen
Paper from responsible sources
FSC® C105338

If you have any concerns about our products,
you can contact us on
ProductSafety@springernature.com

In case Publisher is established outside the EU,
the EU authorized representative is:
Springer Nature Customer Service Center GmbH
Europaplatz 3, 69115 Heidelberg, Germany

Printed by Libri Plureos GmbH
in Hamburg, Germany